TIDEWATER TRIUMPH

THE DEVELOPMENT AND
WORLDWIDE SUCCESS
OF THE CHESAPEAKE BAY
PILOT SCHOONER

TIDEWATER TRIUMPH

THE DEVELOPMENT AND WORLDWIDE SUCCESS OF THE CHESAPEAKE BAY PILOT SCHOONER

GEOFFREY M. FOOTNER

TIDEWATER PUBLISHERS • CENTREVILLE, MARYLAND

Tidewater Publishers
P.O. Box 456
Centreville, Maryland 21617

Footner, Geoffrey M. (Geoffrey Marsh), 1923-
        Tidewater triumph : the development and worldwide success of the
Chesapeake Bay pilot schooner / Geoffrey M. Footner. — 1st ed.
                p. : ill., maps, plans ;   cm.
        Includes bibliography references and index.

        1. Schooners - Chesapeake Bay Region (Md. and Va.) - History. 2. Pilot
boats - Chesapeake Bay Region (Md. and Va.) - History. 3. Naval architecture
- Chesapeake Bay Region (Md. and Va.) - History. 4. Schooners. 5. Pilot boats.
1. Title.
VM311.F7F66

ISBN 0-87033-511-1

FIRST EDITION 1998

Book Design by Caroline Rowntree
Printed by Thomson-Shore, Dexter, Michigan

CONTENTS

ACKNOWLEDGEMENTS

A few years back, while reading at Mystic Seaport, I came to know Dorothy Brewington. After sharing distinguished careers with Marion V. Brewington until his death, Mrs. Brewington continued to work at Mystic Seaport Museum. Years before, Marion Brewington wrote two highly praised books, *Chesapeake Bay Log Canoes and Bugeyes* and *Chesapeake Bay, A Pictorial History*, before leaving Maryland for curatorial positions in New England. Representing the Calvert Marine Museum, I received from Dorothy Brewington the couple's personal collection of paintings and artifacts as well as a collection of Mr. Brewington's research notes, all related to Chesapeake Bay.

Later, as I worked on this manuscript, I returned to Calvert Marine Museum to study the Brewington files. At first they seemed not to have any specific focus; but as my work progressed and as I became familiar with the contents of those file drawers, it occurred to me that Brewington had intended to write the story I tell here. There was no mistaking the direction his research was heading. He was collecting newspaper articles, drawings, photographs and other data for a book about the naval-architectual relationships of Chesapeake Bay pilot boats, Baltimore schooners and pungies. His work helped me; but more to the point it was a great encouragement to know that Brewington had intended to travel a parallel course.

Most authors of serious studies of the Chesapeake Bay region deal with social, economic, or political events and fail to probe life on the water–the Bay's sailors, ships, cargoes and trade routes, and the natural and economic factors that produced the short bright maritime history of the region. An exception was Howard I. Chapelle, who was fascinated by the "Baltimore clipper" and returned to the subject many times over his career. All writers of maritime history owe him a debt; among other things he provided us with vessel plans, the originals of which he retrieved from the files of England's National Maritime Museum, and to which we refer continually. His work is a point of departure, and from it we know what is there–not necessarily how to get there.

Many people guided me through the masses of data that afforded the raw material for this study. Original source material came from the National Archives, Maryland Historical Society, Maryland Hall of Records, Virginia State Library, Virginia Historical Society, and from the fine archives and library of the Mariners' Museum of Newport News.

The Peale Museum in Baltimore, Chesapeake Bay Maritime Museum, and the Calvert Marine Museum were very helpful. The Peabody Essex Museum, Essex Shipbuilding Museum, Independence Seaport Museum, and Mystic Seaport Museum provided me with photographs. The libraries of Johns Hopkins University, particularly the George Peabody Library, which contains many rare maritime publications, were most helpful.

Dr. Bill Dudley and the Naval Historical Center in Washington, D.C. were other great resources.

Great Britain's National Maritime Museum, the Public Records Office, and the Science Museum, spread around London, are not for the timid; but in time they contributed tremendously to my growing book. Krigsarkivet (military archives) in Stockholm, along with the Marinmuseum, Karlskrona, provided information on Swedish Navy schooners. I thank Svande Holmberg for sharing his research; Lena Animmer for translating his work and for many of the Swedish documents that contributed to the text; Beril Olofsson, photographer, Krigsarkivet, for selecting their best work; and, finally, Ylva Lindstrom, librarian of Marinmuseum, who guided me to the above institutions and people.

Photographs from Paris used in the book are proof enough of the aid given by Les Musées de la Marine, Les Amis des Musées, and from French Marine Archives at Vincennes. However, it was Monsieur Michel Merle d'Aubigné, president of Les Amis, who, in memory of a sailing cruise on Chesapeake Bay, unlocked the doors of the archives of France for me. My thanks as well to Madame Ulane Bonnel, a director of Les Amis. For what could eventually prove to be a great discovery, I thank Dr. Mario Marzari of Trieste for sharing his investigations at the Biblioteca di Trieste and the Arsenal of Venice, during which he may have found the only existing plan of the USS *Enterprize*, which is in the collection of the Biblioteca.

Jim Dilts gave me his research on the Baltimore & Ohio Railroad. Martin Seymour of Corston Village helped me in England–and will never see his nation's institutions in the same light again after dealing patiently with Her Majesty's bureaucracies. I thank Charles Shoemaker who generously turned over his research on Hampton pilot boats to me.

If I was able to overcome my handicaps in the science and art of naval architecture (and I hope I have), credit goes to Quentin Snediker, shipmaster, researcher and author of a fine book on our shared passion, Chesapeake Bay schooners. Captain Walter Simmons, naval architect and gentleman sailor of Chesapeake baycraft, did a sentence-by-sentence examination of the text and I thank him for it.

At the top of my list of boosters is Frederick C. Leiner, who read every word of a very confusing first draft and provided a critique as my energies failed. I am grateful to Dr. Arthur Middleton for encouragement that could originate only with him, for correcting a later draft. William M. P. Dunne, a friend now deceased, opened his files to me and gave fierce advice.

I acknowledge my debt to the shipwrights of Maryland and Virginia who provided me with a great story. Did it ever happen before in maritime history that such an obscure group of shipbuilders, most without formal training in their twin trades of architecture and construction, many who could sign only their mark on carpenter certificates, had such an impact on naval architecture worldwide? It is through such examples of art and craft and–yes–genius that the human race rises to fresh levels of accomplishment.

UNIDENTIFIED BALTIMORE SCHOONER IN A PAINTING
BY W. J. HUGGINS, THOUGHT TO BE A COPY OF A
CHINESE PAINTING. THE VESSEL IS POSSIBLY
GREYHOUND, BUILT IN FELLS POINT BY JAMES
BEACHAM IN 1826 AND EMPLOYED AS AN OPIUM
SCHOONER IN CHINA.
National Maritime Museum, London.

INTRODUCTION

It will surprise most readers to discover that the Baltimore clipper schooner originated as a pilot boat and that this pilot boat originated on Chesapeake Bay. While a subject included in this book is the Baltimore clipper, the reality is that the Baltimore clipper of the War of 1812, which is analyzed in print almost yearly by someone, was never called such a thing. William Price, Thomas Kemp and the other shipwrights of Fells Point called their famous privateers "schooners, pilot-boat built."

Where did these backwater shipwrights get their brilliant pilot-schooner design? From the Swedes or the shipbuilders of the Mediterranean, report some writers. From Bermuda, says Howard I. Chapelle. Many Americans and some Frenchmen, too, believe that this beautiful and influential schooner was a creation of the French. The truth is simpler. The design that spread around the world was born along the shores of the world's most famous and productive estuary—Chesapeake Bay.

Concluding that the sharp, fast pilot schooner of legend was first shaped in Virginia or Maryland owes more to inference than hard evidence—its proof is the flow of information from the earliest mention of grain and flour trade at Baltimore and the vessels that served that trade. Little information survives to describe the earliest of the Bay's pilot schooners—vessels owned by pilots, farmers, small merchants, and watermen. Their stories seldom made the pages of the newspapers, except occasionally after a tragic incident on the Bay. Normally, owners and builders advertised only larger schooners for sale. Government records, enrollments, licenses and a few statistics provide clues. Court records partially reveal events in individual lives. With the visual aid of a few old prints, models, drawings and photographs, some random facts and figures, plus a measure of dead reckoning, we have attempted to plot the course of the pilot schooner in these pages.

Looking back over 260 years of Chesapeake maritime history, it was a remarkable coincidence that the schooner appeared just when the region could benefit from it. Large, bulky ships were fine for tobacco, but as trade with the West Indies grew, the merchants of Maryland and their shipwrights concentrated more and more on the development of fore-and-aft-rigged vessels. The schooner was the favored vessel in

Maryland waters, the Bermuda sloop in Virginia.

The schooner rig—two masts then—can be traced back to Dutch and English vessels of the seventeenth century. Although the type has obscure origins in northern Europe, its greatest usefulness and perfection were achieved along the Atlantic coast of America and in the Caribbean during the nineteenth century. And, as we will discover, its greatest influence upon the world began in Chesapeake Bay during the 1730s.

Physical, political and economic conditions determine the most suitable vessels for a region's commerce. When a type evolves that adapts well to prevailing circumstances, shipowners and their communities prosper. In the development of suitable craft, nothing is more important than the natural limits imposed on a trade route. Is there deep water at the ports of loading and discharge? Are ports of call separated by the open sea? How much of the total voyage is in relatively sheltered waters? What is the distance between a port of loading and final destinations for cargoes carried? What is the usual weather? How favorable are the winds?

While Bermuda-type sloops gave good service on open water, the schooner proved the best rig for the more restricted channels of the upper two thirds of Chesapeake Bay–Maryland's water. Here the Bay has many rivers that feed into it and meander into the land as tidal estuaries of varying width. Narrow natural channels and shifting winds required sailing vessels of draft to make frequent adjustments of course. Sloops could do this, but their big mainsails called for effort and concentration on the part of crews of only a few sailors. The sails of schooners with similar short crew were easier to manage. These were schooner waters.

To grasp the importance of watercraft in Chesapeake maritime history, the Bay and its rivers and creeks must be viewed as a network of roadways. Whereas water is seen today as a barrier to road travel, prior to 1900 it was land travel that was slow and difficult. Access to navigable waterways gave life and wealth to the towns and farms of the Chesapeake's tidewater, and when the Bay developed into a great transportation thoroughfare the estuary and its vessels held the region together. Maneuverability and ease of sail-handling are the virtues of any successful craft in such natural conditions of twisting waterways and variable winds. This, plus a demand for speed, made a sharp-built schooner–that is, one with significant deadrise–the choice of Bay mariners. Maryland's principal early trade route, Fells Point to the West Indies, gave advantages to swift, maneuverable two-masted schooners, especially if cargoes were perishable.

Continuing war at sea in the eighteenth century also spurred the development of sharp, fast schooners. Vessel owners of the eighteenth and early nineteenth centuries had to run a gauntlet of political conditions. Were there pirates and privateers to evade? Was the nation at war? Did the wars of other nations hazard the safety of a voyage? Were there high risks or did the chances of interference with a voyage seem to be low? Merchants and shipowners considered the policies and laws of their own country–particularly when there were embargoes, trade restrictions or a war in progress.

The economics of a trade route are based on the types of cargo to be exchanged. Before the invention of climate-control equipment, a most important consideration in the world of shipping was the perishability of commodities. The West Indies plantations needed food, and most food products were then in danger of spoilage. Grain and flour stowed in confined spaces without ventilation before the invention of cleaning and drying machinery, and then carried into tropical climates, were perishable. Speed was necessary to avoid loss.

Always important were the physical characteristics of cargo. Was it dense or light and bulky? (While a pound of iron and a pound of feathers balance the scales, they do not occupy the same amount of space in the hold of a ship.) Space is a most important characteristic of any vessel, particularly as it relates to the need for speed. Normally, with vessels of similar length, the larger the cargo area the slower the vessel will be under sail. Down through ages of vessel development, sailing craft were subject to a dilemma of compromise–speed versus cargo capacity. For most merchant sailing vessels, design weighed in on the side of burden; speed was almost always a design consideration that received less emphasis.

On Chesapeake Bay, because of the characteristics of the principal cargoes, which were grain and flour; because of the dangers inherent in voyages to the West Indies; and because of the natural characteristics of the route, it became necessary for shippers to reverse the normal balance and favor vessels of speed and limited cargo space. Chesapeake merchants, mariners and shipwrights participated in a process of trial and change over many decades as their efforts concentrated on increasing the speed of their topsail schooners.

The Chesapeake region had a one-crop economy–tobacco–for a hundred years, and then came sudden change. Agricultural and economic diversification pivoted around the year 1730. Momentum to diversify agricultural production increased as Maryland and Virginia began to ship grain to southern Europe and the West Indies. The first lots at Baltimore Town on the Patapsco River were placed on sale that year. The schooner appeared in local waters. Merchants began to trade. Flour mills and iron works were constructed and prospered. A merchant fleet was built. In a more pronounced way than it would in Virginia, a new era began for Maryland in the 1730s.

As Maryland and Virginia changed from simple and rural one-crop colonies to more complex societies with towns, ports and a variety of products to trade, commerce on the Bay grew. Exports increased, as war among European powers created special opportunities for the region. The resulting unstable maritime conditions in the West Indies and on the North Atlantic in the eighteenth century produced a steady demand for food and other products of the tidewater country.

Maryland's first offshore merchant

marine grew quickly from one of insignificance before 1730 to a fleet of ships, snows, brigs, and sloops–and, most important, an increasing number of schooners. Between 1748 and 1750 approximately 30 sloops, 6 snows, 11 ships, 4 brigs, and 16 vessels with schooner rig were launched by Maryland shipwrights. Many of the sloops were small plantation craft.[1]

Maryland's first merchant fleet represented the several designs of American and European vessels of the period. But because of the continuing wars at sea and the nature of the West Indies trade, the schooner began a long period of development. The Caribbean trade remained extremely risky from 1730 until 1815, and this, along with Baltimore's comparative advantages in that trade, caused vessel design to improve through those 80-odd years.

The Chesapeake Bay pilot schooner may be said to have fully evolved before 1750.[2] The hull sat low in the water, and had sharp ends with raking stem and stern post. A straight keel that sloped downward significantly from bow to stern (i.e., had considerable drag) gave the design deeper draft in the stern. Consistently, in all the variations of the Chesapeake pilot-schooner model, beam was widest forward of amidships. The principal variable in different versions of the pilot-schooner model was size. As the functions of these schooners changed, lengths, widths and depths of hulls changed–generally, however, in proportion to each of the other dimensions.

Baltimore schooners, the large offshore vessels that developed after 1790, were of the same design as the original pilot boat and its early baycraft derivative.

The most significant characteristics of the design were the fairly shallow hull with significant deadrise–or the angle of rise above horizontal as the vessel's underbody rose outward from the keel, slack or easy turn of bilges, and a long fine run which afforded an easy flow of water from bow to stern. Cargo space was limited. These schooners had one flush deck, end to end, with only deckhouse tops and hatches protruding above it. Quarterdecks were eliminated, and bulwarks were dispensed with on many models of pilot schooner.

The masts of the pilot schooner raked sharply aft, and were a most distinguishing feature. Foremasts were set well forward to make a cargo hold accessible. With large sail area so far forward, the schooners had a tendency to drift off to leeward. Raking masts placed the center of effort farther aft and balanced the helm.

Though the origin of the Baltimore schooner, or Baltimore clipper, as it is so often called today, was with Chesapeake builders, the first foreign buyers of these vessels were French. This has given rise to considerable historical discussion of French influence on Baltimore schooner design. An examination of ship plans at France's Ministry of Defense facilities, Les Musées de la Marine, Service Historique de la Marine, and Archives Nationale, did not uncover any evidence that French

PILOT SCHOONER
PUNGY *WAVE*,
BUILT IN 1863. SHE
SANK IN 1957, SIX
YEARS SHORT OF A
CENTURY OLD.
Frank A. Moorshead Jr.
Collection.
The Mariners' Museum,
Newport News, VA.

naval vessels included schooners of pilot-boat design prior to 1801.

Maryland shipbuilders continued to refine the design of offshore topsail schooners up to the end of the eighteenth century. After 1792 Baltimore merchants began replacing them with larger schooners of pilot-boat construction. The size of these Baltimore schooners grew until they exceeded 300 tons burden. Included in this group were the great pilot-model schooners of the War of 1812: *Rossie, Comet, Monmouth, Chasseur,* and others by Thomas Kemp; *Maria, Dolphin* and *Sabine,* built by Fells Point's leading shipwright, William Price. Their mission was blockade-running and privateering.

Chesapeake Bay pilot schooners were usually more conservative in hull design and rig following the War of 1812. Covered with the glory of their victories in America's second war with Great Britain, the high profile of these very successful armed schooners dipped below the horizon of most mainstream maritime historians. However, because of their speed, prominence came again to Chesapeake schooners and brigs in the last decades of commercial sail when fast sailing vessels seemed to be one response to the growing reliability of steamships.

Along the course to extinction, many variations of Chesapeake pilot schooners sailed in specific trades. There were coastwise schooners, bay schooners, oyster schooners, opium schooners, slavers, clipper schooners and fruit schooners. There were revenue schooners, dispatch schooners and U.S. Navy schooners. And

there were British Royal Navy, French Navy and Royal Swedish Navy schooners of pilot-boat design. At the starting line of the modern sport of yacht racing in the United States was the Chesapeake Bay pilot schooner in the form of schooner yachts that rich men raced in the last half of the nineteenth century. The model became so popular and internationalized that few mariners beyond the shores of Chesapeake Bay knew where the design originated.

Pilot-boat schooners, or pilot schooners, built for use on Chesapeake Bay after 1840, and a hundred years after they first appeared, began to be called "pungy boats" by Chesapeake watermen. Many maritime historians thought this was a new vessel type, modeled after the big schooners of the War of 1812. It was not new. Colonial records reveal that a cargo version of the pilot boat similar to the pungy evolved several decades before the Revolutionary War; and from that influential Bay vessel a whole family of Chesapeake pilot schooners developed.

The "schooner, pilot-boat built" had a long and successful run. Joseph Brooks built the last Chesapeake Bay pilot schooner, a pungy boat, in 1885. Brooks had built *Amanda F. Lewis* in 1884. She hauled freight out of Coan River, a tributary of the Potomac, and was the last of her model in commercial service on the Bay. Her owner converted her to power in 1940.[3] *Wave*, a pungy converted to a yacht after decades of service as an oyster boat and Bay freighter, sank in 1957, six years short of her one hundredth year.[4]

Endnotes - Introduction

1. Commission Book 82, Maryland Hall of Records, Md HR 4012-1.

2. In this book, a class or model of schooner is called *Chesapeake Bay pilot schooners* and individual types are called by specific contemporary names. The baycraft versions are *schooner boats, pilot-boat schooners* or *pilot schooners,* and after 1850 *pungies* or *pilot schooners.* The large schooners that came into use as blockade runners and privateers between 1792 and 1815 are called *Baltimore schooners.* Contemporary shipwrights also called them "schooners, pilot-boat built." Offshore schooners built after 1815 will be referred to as *pilot schooners* if they are known to be of that model. All of the different types of pilot schooners take their design from the Annapolis and Hampton pilot boats which evolved on the Bay sometime after 1730.

   Today almost everybody refers to the armed schooner of the War of 1812 as a Baltimore clipper. Throughout this manuscript the large schooners of the era from 1793 to 1815, armed by the merchants of Baltimore, and reaching 350 tons burden, are called *Baltimore schooners.* The name *Baltimore clipper* was not in general use until after 1830. The differences in the two versions of Chesapeake pilot-schooner design will be developed in Chapter 7.

   The name Baltimore clipper received its greatest currency with the publication of Howard I. Chapelle's, *The Baltimore Clipper,* (Salem, Massachusetts: The Marine Research Society, 1930). The term clipper is used throughout Chapelle's book, but particularly note pages 61-62 and 142-45. He is credited with the dubious honor of revising history by popularizing the name clipper for the earlier models. In fact, he was not the first. If square-rigged ships, called clippers, had not existed in the last decades of commercial sail, contemporary names used by owners and shipwrights of Chesapeake Bay schooners–that is, pilot boat, pilot-boat-built schooner, or merely pilot schooner and Baltimore

   schooner–would not be so necessary to make clear.

3. *Amanda F. Lewis*, pungy boat, carpenter certificate signed by Joseph W. Brooks, 1884. Record Group 41, National Archives, Washington, D.C.; Robert H. Burgess, *Chesapeake Circle* (Cambridge, Maryland: Cornell Maritime Press, Inc., 1965), 197; M. V. Brewington, *Chesapeake Bay, A Pictorial Maritime History* (Cambridge, Maryland: Cornell Maritime Press, Inc., 1953), 89, 164; U.S. Coast Guard Documentation Number 106304, *List of Merchant Vessels of the United States* (LMV), 25th List (Washington, D.C.: U.S. Government Printing Office, 1893).

4. *Wave*, pungy boat, built Accomac County, 1863; sank, Zug Island Canal, Detroit, Michigan, 24 June 1957: U.S. Coast Guard official No. 26694; RG41, National Archives.

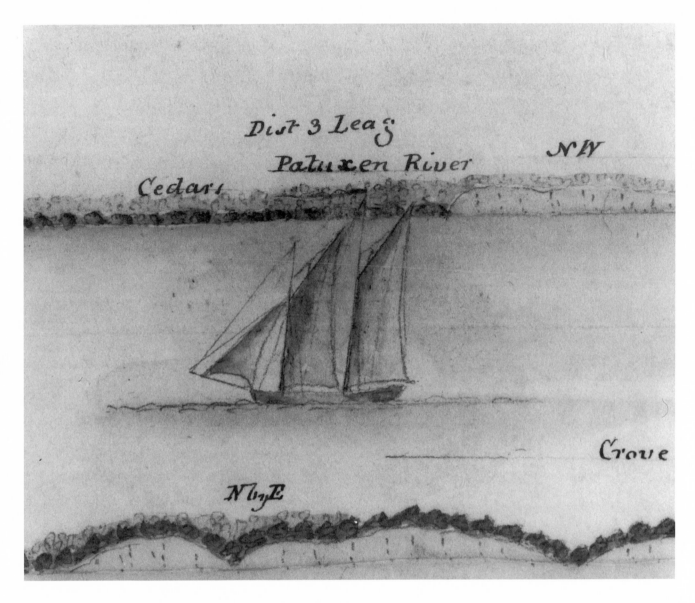

A CHESAPEAKE BAY PILOT SCHOONER SKETCHED
AS A DETAIL FOR JOHN HILLS' BRITISH ADMIRALTY
CHART, 1781.

William L. Clements Library Collection,
University of Michigan, Ann Arbor, MI.

THE FIRST PILOT SCHOONERS

One hundred years after Europeans arrived in Maryland in 1634, the only indigenous vessels seen on Chesapeake Bay were the occasional pilot boat or ferry. Commerce between Maryland and Virginia was negligible for a century. The virtual absence of trading activity between the two colonies or between regions within each colony, and an export trade limited to tobacco carried in British ships from self-sufficient plantations, meant that there was little need for baycraft prior to 1730.

Early Chesapeake Bay small craft consisted of open shallops and pinnaces, both types generally equipped with sails and oars. These boats of European origin shared many similar features. Small sloops built by slaves, and employed for excursions to Annapolis or Williamsburg, or to move tobacco and supplies from one plantation to another, became the first local craft adapted for short trading voyages and for passengers.

Maryland boatwrights must have incorporated characteristics of shallops, pinnaces and sloops into the design of the Bay's first pilot boats, vessels that delivered pilots to inbound English tobacco ships. Later, as Maryland's commerce and foreign trade became centralized at Baltimore and Fells Point, a commercial version of the pilot boat developed to haul grain and other products from the farms of the region to the new port at the mouth of the Patapsco. The approximate time, 1740, marks the beginning of a consistent movement of grain to Baltimore. Chesapeake Bay mariners, farmers and merchants began to acquire the pilot-model schooners, which they called schooner boats, or occasionally pilot boats. The generic use of the term has caused 250 years of confusion. These were two-masted schooners, often with gaff topsails for extra sailpower in light air.

While there are no pictures or descriptions of these early schooner boats, the fact is that the pilot schooner, often mentioned in dispatches and journals during the Revolutionary War, began to be used 40 years before at the beginning of the grain trade. Prior to the rebellion, the commercial adaptation of the pre-existing pilot boat rarely ventured beyond the limits of Chesapeake Bay. After the Revolutionary War, the bigger two-masted, pilot-boat schooners traded with the world.

Ships from Great Britain loaded tobacco at river landings throughout the colonial period. As grain trade with the

West Indies and southern Europe developed in the 1730s and 1740s, Maryland developed her merchant fleet, which, like the tobacco ships, continued to load cargo at river landings. With no central location for the receipt and warehousing of the colony's developing export trade, commerce remained fragmented. Indeed, prior to the rise of Baltimore and Norfolk, the entire Chesapeake was one big seaport for tobacco and grain ships.

A merchant of Chestertown, or a planter/merchant of Talbot County, purchasing grain to complete his cargo, would buy from his neighbors. Early Chestertown exports consisted of grain grown in Kent or Queen Anne's counties. Exports from Oxford, the port of entry for Talbot County, originated at landings along the Choptank, Miles and Wye Rivers. Surviving colonial Customs reports show that only Somerset County in Maryland and Accomac County in Virginia traded with each other. The commerce of the lower Eastern Shore, isolated from the rest of the Chesapeake region, developed its own directions after displaced Virginians settled Somerset County in the seventeenth century.

Henry Callister, former resident agent of Foster, Cunliffe & Co., of Liverpool, and in 1748 an independent merchant at Oxford, requested that a supplier in Great Britain send his shipments only in vessels destined for the Eastern Shore, not to any location on the Western Shore of Maryland except Annapolis, "as we have little commerce with them."[1] Callister's note testifies to the scarcity of shipping services on Chesapeake Bay in the 1740s.

The isolation of the counties from each other disappeared as baycraft began to operate between Baltimore and the rest of Maryland and Virginia. This unusual situation of a merchant marine developing with, and helping along, the integration of the region, produced a new craft specifically adapted for the carriage of grain, produce and passengers between Baltimore and rural Maryland and Virginia. It was natural for the Chesapeake Bay pilot boat to be adapted to the Bay's developing commerce.

Along with the Bay commerce came trade with a larger world. The increasingly complex nature of the region's Atlantic commerce was a result of demand for agricultural products, mostly to be shipped to the slave plantations of the West Indies. Increasingly, Caribbean colonies of the European nations depended upon food products from North America. In the beginning of the Caribbean trade, planters sold to New England trading vessels calling at Chesapeake Bay landings, but soon independent merchants and planter-merchants sold directly to the sugar plantations of the West Indies and built vessels to carry their exports.

Dr. Charles Carroll of Annapolis led a small band of independent merchants who transformed the colony. Carroll dealt exclusively in tobacco sales from the date he commenced trading until about 1731 when he initiated barter deals in other products.[2] His activities may be traced from 1715 until 1755, the year of his death, through his correspondence. While others may have been equally involved in Maryland's expanding trade, no evidence exists to challenge Dr. Carroll's position at the forefront of these developments. His letters reveal his interest in an iron industry in Maryland as early as 1722 when he purchased iron ore deposits on Benjamin Howard's land near the Patapsco River.[3] Dr. Carroll established the Baltimore Iron Works with the father of Charles Carroll of Carrollton, also Charles Carroll, and with Daniel Carroll, and two of Lord Baltimore's men, Daniel Dulany and Benjamin Tasker. This iron industry began around 1731, in those pivotal few years at the beginning of the 1730s.[4]

Carroll bought land in Baltimore County adjacent to the Patapsco River, and while he continued to maintain his residence at Annapolis, he used his plantation on the Patapsco as the center of a variety of commercial activities. The land from which he ran these activities bordered the Baltimore Iron Works property and the river, not far from the location where Gwynns Falls flows into the middle branch of the Patapsco River, approximately two miles from the Basin and the villages of Baltimore and Fells Point.[5]

Maryland's more famous Carroll family, distantly related to Dr. Carroll, acquired land at the head of the Patapsco River's northwest branch even before they joined Dr. Carroll in developing the Baltimore Iron Works. The proprietary government granted Charles Carroll and Daniel Carroll, with others, rights to develop the area around the northern rim

of the Basin and in 1730 lots were offered for 40 shillings per acre. The beginning of Baltimore consisted of 60 lots above the Basin, west of Jones Falls.[6]

Dr. Carroll's trade spread to different sections of Maryland and Virginia as he dispatched baycraft to complete a sale of iron or to acquire a cargo of flour. His activities inspired more commercial activity between other regions of Chesapeake Bay and the Patapsco settlements. In a typical sequence of transactions in the year 1742 he purchased flour from Jethro Brown at Northeast and arranged to barter salt for wheat with a man named Jackson at Susquehanna.[7] Captain Saterwhite, with Carroll's baycraft *Swallow*, picked up Jackson's and a Mr. Georges' wheat and delivered this grain to Brown's flour mill.[8] These transactions represented a break with the past, and an end to the isolation of places up and down the Bay.

Dr. Carroll purchased a bay sloop in Somerset County, capacity 40 hogsheads of tobacco, in 1743.[9] That same year he bartered rum for corn in Somerset County and bread and iron for salt with Edward Barns, merchant of Oxford.[10] Carroll informed Barns that Samuel Galloway had sugar, and he sold iron to Thomas Ringgold of Chestertown.[11] In 1754 he built a tobacco ship on the Patapsco and advertised that he had good strong decked vessels to bring tobacco from any part of the Bay.[12] Carroll's ties and communications with other merchants in Maryland were the first steps toward centralizing the colony's commerce. His initiatives in time eliminated Maryland's

dependence on tobacco exports and began the use of Chesapeake Bay as a highway of commerce.

Dr. Carroll died in 1755, but before his death he had succeeded in establishing markets for iron in Maryland, Virginia, and Great Britain. His fleet of Maryland baycraft and offshore vessels, including the schooners *Baltimore* and *Annapolis*, built on the Bay in the 1730s, led the way to the greater development of Maryland's merchant marine. His efforts to sell products overseas and to deliver them in Maryland ships made him a model for the merchants of Baltimore Town who followed; Baltimore's commercial development began to gain momentum just prior to Dr. Carroll's death.

Darby Lux, a sea captain, came ashore in 1743 and purchased two Baltimore lots to the west of the Basin.[13] He established a store and warehouse, and with Thomas Harrison, Bryan Philpot, and Nicholas Rogers formed the nucleus of an expanding group of merchants and shipowners. Along the marshy shore of the Basin, lot owners built the town's first houses, taverns and warehouses.

Out in the Basin, silt from Jones Falls made the water so shallow that no vessels could use it except small craft. About a thousand feet offshore, a narrow channel at the foot of Federal Hill connected the Basin with Fells Point, less than a mile downstream. Only in this channel did the depth of water reach eight feet. Ships waiting for cargoes anchored off Fells Point. There the water was deep enough for large ships.

Since there was deep water just downstream from Baltimore Town, this seems to question the wisdom of Baltimore's location on a shallow body of water. But it was the intention of the founders to develop a commercial center near the region's flour mills. The Carrolls' plan called for Maryland's first entrepôt to be the point of interchange for a fleet of

baycraft delivering grain to the Basin and, hence, up the hills by oxcart to mills on streams just beyond the village. Wharves and warehouses extending into the Basin would receive and store barrels of flour delivered back to the Basin from the mills. The planners selected the location as the first trails, later a road system, fanned out from the village to mills located on streams flowing into the north and middle branches of the Patapsco River.

Baltimore's location, between Gwynns and Jones Falls, the region's most important mill streams, eliminated the need for bridges or dangerous fording points. Fells Point, located east of the Patapsco's rushing streams, made it unsuitable as a transfer point for grain carried overland. Taking into consideration the conditions then, the growing flour industry just above the fall line determined the location of Baltimore Town. The rapid growth of the region provides proof that the developers were correct.

Baltimore would not become Maryland's hub of commerce until a transportation system developed. The gamble lay in the unknown response of the colony's farmers to the call for grain. Planted from Harford and Cecil counties in the northern Bay to the Eastern Shore and southern Maryland, grain required transportation to the Basin. Baltimore's grain dealers, anxious to encourage farmers to deliver to the Basin, provided a major incentive–the promise of cash payment. This innovation replaced an antiquated system at Oxford and Chestertown of paying farmers for their wheat and corn after a ship topped off a complete cargo. As vessels loaded at landings with no grain storage facilities, farmers were forced to wait weeks as a ship slowly accumulated a full cargo.

Farmers responded favorably, Baltimore prospered, and Chesapeake Bay became Maryland's highway to the world. Along with the commerce came the Bay's indigenous schooner. The very first image of this craft is seen in the far left corner of the painting of Spencer's Shipyard shown on the previous page. An unfamiliar eye sees a blur of three sails. Closer study reveals the raked masts, the distinctive three-sail plan of the pilot schooner, and very vaguely the low flush-deck profile unique to the model.

While the circumstances surrounding the development of a cargo-carrying model of the pilot boat are clear, and the particulars of Baltimore's development as a port for a fleet of baycraft are certain, little information exists to describe the Bay's early cargo schooners. It is clear that before the first wharves were built on Baltimore's basin in 1759, cargo-carrying models of the pilot schooner were busy on the Bay. But they remain elusive. The first "for sale" notice that describes one of these commercial craft specifically as a pilot boat appeared in 1776.[14] An English chart maker painted the first recognizable image of the type sometime during the Revolutionary War.

One of the first vessels owned by a Baltimore merchant was the sloop *Baltimore Town*, which Captain Darby Lux had built in Baltimore County in 1746.[15] In the years between 1746 and the start of the Seven Years War in 1758, Baltimore's offshore merchant fleet grew rapidly. This was an important development, representing a break with the past, when most ships loading on the Bay flew the king's flag or that of one of the New England colonies. Lux, Nicholas Rogers, Dr. Carroll and others gained control of an increasing percentage of Maryland's export trade in goods other than tobacco as the number of Maryland vessels trading beyond the Bay increased.

This fleet became an important contributor to Baltimore's rising prosperity. Sixteen ships sailed from the Annapolis Naval District, which included the Patapsco, during the last quarter of 1753, and eight of them were built in Maryland. These ships carried the following cargoes: beans (3), peas (2), lumber (3), wheat (7), barrel staves (8), iron (4), flour (7), corn (10) and tobacco (2).[16] Between January and June, 1754, of the 29 vessels clearing the district, 18 were Maryland-owned. Twelve of these Maryland vessels sailed for the West Indies, two for Lisbon and four for Virginia.[17]

This variety of commodities and the growing number of Maryland ships illustrates the increasing complexity of the local economy. The construction of wharves, warehouses, and special handling equipment at Fells Point inevitably followed.

In the third quarter of 1757, 14 of 31 ships clearing the Annapolis/Baltimore Port District to destinations beyond Maryland were Maryland-owned.[18] This percentage grew apace, and by 1776, when all tobacco trade with Britain ceased and New England vessel owners diverted their ships from Chesapeake Bay, Baltimore merchants captured control of the state's foreign trade.

This Baltimore fleet enabled the Patapsco River port of Fells Point to overwhelm Oxford, Chestertown and the other ports of Maryland by the beginning of the Revolutionary War. As a rising percentage of the colony's grain production was carried by baycraft into Baltimore for eventual export, less remained available at outports. As grain offerings diminished, vessel turnaround time dragged out at Annapolis, Chestertown and Oxford, causing ship owners to refuse charters that specified one of these outports. At Fells Point, chartered vessels earned dispatch bonuses for quick turnaround.

John Smith and William Buchanan constructed twin 1000-foot wharves in the Basin of Baltimore's inner harbor in 1759. Smith and Buchanan, accompanied by the Sterett and Spear families, had moved to Baltimore from Pennsylvania a few years earlier. No group contributed more to Baltimore's early mercantile success than these ex-Pennsylvania grain merchants.[19]

The two earth-filled piers located at Water Street reached the shallow channel that connected the Basin to deeper water at Fells Point. As the depth of water in the Basin did not exceed eight feet even at the end of Smith and Buchanan's wharves, they were built to receive incoming pilot-boat schooners loaded with grain or to handle flour for transshipment to Fells Point. Lighters, barges or flats transshipped flour and grain to larger ships anchored downstream. Wagons hauled the grain sold by the merchant-wharf owners to the flour mills north and west of Baltimore Town.

Charlestown, a small river port on the upper Bay, became an early casualty of growing commercial and shipping activity on the Patapsco River. As exports of grain, flour, iron, bread, and wood products increased at Fells Point, the small port on the Northeast River, faced with competition for grain and flour from both Philadelphia and Baltimore, shut down and several of the town's merchants and shipowners moved to Baltimore. This group included Mark Alexander, the Hollingsworth family, Abraham and Isaac van Bibber, and Benjamin Pearce, all of whom were to play important roles in Baltimore's and Fells Point's future.

William Spear built a third long wharf in the Basin in 1764. On an island at the end of his facility, Spear located ovens to bake ship's bread.[20] A strong market existed for this product in the West Indies. Eastern Shore ports could not supply bread, and Spear's new facility gave shipping further incentive to load at Fells Point.

With an expanding hinterland, new wharves and warehouses, and a growing list of available products, vessels loaded at Fells Point in greater numbers and with prompt turnaround time. Momentum for the consolidation of shipping activities at Fells Point increased as pilot schooners discharged products from all sections of Maryland and from Virginia. After discharging grain, Bay vessels took aboard imports such as rum, molasses and European manufactures consigned in other parts of Maryland and Virginia. Each passing year brought greater centralization of Maryland's trade, and with it

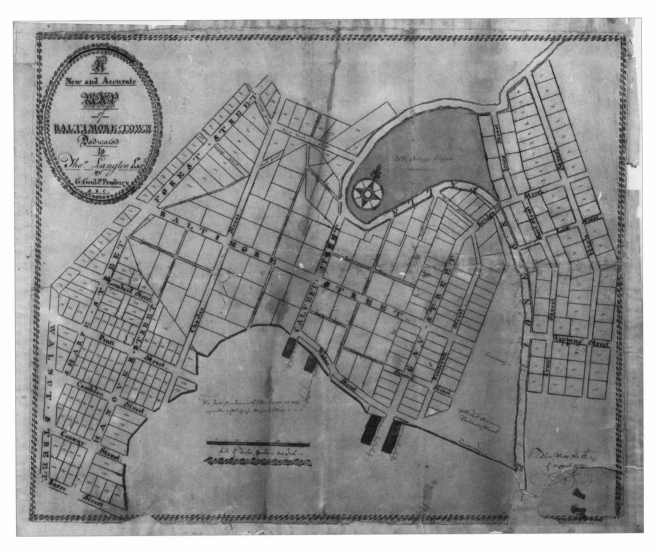

came a larger number of pilot schooners on Chesapeake Bay.

A road system leading in and out of Baltimore took decades to develop. A quicker solution came as farmers, foresters, mariners and shipwrights in Maryland and Virginia converted the rivers of the estuary and Chesapeake Bay into a grand highway of commerce. As Maryland's overseas trade expanded, Chestertown's port expanded too. Its

location 25 miles up the Chester River placed the village's merchants in a competitive position with Philadelphia grain exporters for the wheat and corn of Cecil and Kent counties. Farmers in this region of northern Maryland, located east of the Susquehanna River, could ship either overland to landings on Delaware Bay or to points on the Chesapeake.

Thomas and William Ringgold led a small group of merchants at the little village port after 1750. With the support of Philadelphia bankers, Ringgold vessels, built in Maryland, handled direct exports of grain, principally to Spain and Portugal. *Chester* had the capacity for several thousand bushels of grain. The larger *Friendship*, owned by the firm of Smyth and Sudler, loaded cargo for southern Europe.[21] However, as Philadelphia exporters continued to buy grain in Chestertown's hinterland and as Bay schooners diverted Kent, Queen Annes and Cecil county grain to Baltimore, port activity at Chestertown decreased.

Exports from Chestertown leveled off in the period of the Seven Years War (1758-63). As war with Britain approached, Chestertown merchants, James Piper for one, commenced operating grain schooners between Chestertown and Baltimore. This quick, safe voyage and prompt payment cut their risks. Cargoes were small but delays were minimized and repeat business assured. Piper moved into Baltimore along with the swelling tide of merchants as war began. Thomas Ringgold put his new *Lovely Polly*, a 250-ton ship, up for sale in September of 1776.[22] Soon after this, Chestertown ceased to trade foreign.

Oxford's most prosperous years preceded the diversification of agriculture when tobacco was the only export. Richard Bennett III, the region's richest planter-merchant, died in 1749 and Robert Morris, Oxford's leading factor, died in 1750. Foster, Cunliffe & Co. closed their Eastern Shore offices, including the one at Oxford, in 1754, and Gilbert & Co.

departed in 1756. As tobacco production on the Eastern shore declined, a growing number of vessels cleared the port with grain for southern Europe and the West Indies; but the new grain trade was not to survive. Faced with increased competition from Baltimore and Fells Point, Oxford's grain trade eventually evaporated.

New England ships, commencing voyages at northern ports, offered Eastern Shore planter-merchants cargo that consisted of products made in the northern colonies or imported from England. After calling at Oxford, where they traded their wares for grain, they continued their voyages to the West Indies. These Yankee vessels returned to their Northern ports directly, or following a run from the West Indies to Great Britain, completing a triangular voyage. A second trade route involved English vessels commencing voyages at London or from British outports such as Whitehaven, and sailing to the West Indies. On a second leg, they entered Oxford with British manufactures and rum, sugar and molasses from the islands. After these ships with their mixed cargo reached the Eastern Shore, they lay at anchor accumulating cargoes of tobacco for the return voyage to Great Britain.

These triangular trade patterns reduced Oxford's role to that of a passive receiver and supplier of goods. With few locally owned ships, control of voyages and their profits were in the hands of absentee shipowners. To illustrate the point, in 1762 there were 57 ships that cleared Oxford for destinations outside of

Maryland. Only three of them were owned locally.[23]

Finally with the colonies in rebellion, and faced with the growing economic and political power of her competitor on the Patapsco, the port of Oxford lost out completely when war with England commenced. After the opening of hostilities, neither British nor New England ships entered Chesapeake Bay, and without a local fleet the port of Oxford ceased to operate in foreign trade.

Jeremiah Banning, former sea captain and Oxford's Customs officer, lamenting the loss of the town's sea trade and the dominance of the Eastern Shore by the merchants of Baltimore, wrote in his journal:

"Choptank - who in days of yore out rivaled her proudest sisters in shipping, trade, and commerce, and to which Oxford, her eldest born, principally gave birth to, has now sunk into a second hand traffic and instead of at once boldly launching her wealth into the bosom of the ocean, little swift sailing argosies pour her golden grain, the maise, the thick jointed and the Orinoco, into the lap of an upstart sister."[24]

Annapolis, the colony's capitol, lost its political clout with the opening of the Revolutionary War. Baltimoreans filled much of the power vacuum as the town's merchants took up the cause of independence. The shift of economic and political power to Baltimore Town was a significant development during the rebellion.

Fortunately for the good of the new State of Maryland and its battle for politi-cal freedom, the goals of the high-flying merchant/politicians paralleled the goals of the colonies. As John Truslow Adams wrote, "It is a mistake to think of America of 1776-1783 as a nation of patriots pressing their services to gain their freedom."[25] It was good business to be patriotic.

Chesapeake Bay shipbuilding records are almost nonexistent for the period between 1776-1783. References to design are rare. This situation is further confused as the English and other Europeans often referred to the complete region of Chesapeake Bay as Virginia, ignoring the fact that Maryland was a separate colony. As distinct Chesapeake "schooner-boats" developed, records identify them frequently as "Virginia-built," and it was a common misconception to assume that the Virginia pilot boat, the small schooner used to deliver pilots to incoming ships, was the original model for all pilot boats and for commercial versions of the "schooners, pilot-boat built" which later evolved. Maryland pilots worked in Chesapeake waters at a very early date, too. Nevertheless, commercial pilot schooners, pungies, and the multitude of variations of the pilot-boat schooner around the world are often referred to as adaptations of the "Virginia" pilot boat when, in fact, they may have originated in Maryland.

Nevertheless, Virginia may have its claims. There are a number of possible Virginia places of origin for the flush-deck schooner, and one of them is Hampton Roads. The *Virginia Gazette* of 15 July 1737 contained an announcement of a

Quare as to [...]
Virginia Pilot boat – G.J. 1795 {*The Jib and Staysail only used in very fine*

lost "pilot boat with two masts, twenty-four foot keel, nine foot beam." An earlier issue of the journal offered for sale a "twenty-two foot keel boat, two-masted vessel, schooner fashioned."[26] These may have been small prototypes of the "schooner, pilot-boat built."

Virginia promulgated comprehensive pilot rules in 1755. As they included a scale of fixed rates, speed became an important consideration for competing pilot boats.[27] Vessels for pilots, as well as cargo-carrying schooners, seem to have become larger after the 1750s. It is possible that Virginia pilots did not switch to decked schooners until that time, and that those early Virginia schooner boats were the prototype for the Hampton pilot boat seen in paintings, circa 1795. No one can absolutely say where the pilot-schooner type originated. Pilots met incoming ships at many points on the Bay, and their vessels, as they developed, became similar over time. Skimpy records reveal that shipwrights were building pilot schooners at Baltimore, in the north-

A VIRGINIA PILOT BOAT PAINTED BY GEORGE TOBIN OF THE ROYAL NAVY IN 1794. SMALL PILOT BOATS LIKE THIS ONE WERE IN USE ON THE BAY BEFORE 1740. *Mystic Seaport Museum, Mystic, CT.*

ern Bay, in St. Marys County, on the Eastern Shore, in Mathews County, Virginia, and at Hampton at an early date.

A decked baycraft schooner existed in Maryland waters at least 30 years before the Revolution. John Hall of Anne Arundel County had *Molly*, a schooner, built in 1734.[28] In 1741, *Susannah* was registered in Kent County.[29] Then in quick order, *Samuel*,[30] *William*,[31] *Lark*,[32] *Ranger*[33] and *Cumberland*[34] appeared in Maryland registers. These schooners were all small, 15 tons or less, and most were built in Anne Arundel or Kent Counties. Their owners, facing each other across the Bay, placed these schooners into service as ferries and pilot boats. Much of the activity in 1740 still involved moving people across Chesapeake Bay, as they traveled to and from Annapolis and the Eastern Shore, or between the northern and southern colonies. Annapolis pilots guided ships into the Patapsco River and up to the northern Bay.

Asbury Sutton registered *Samuel*, a schooner measuring eight tons, in 1742. Sutton, a butcher, became a prominent Annapolis storekeeper. *Samuel*'s first master was Horatio Samuel Middleton, also of Annapolis. After working for Sutton for a year or so, Middleton became a shipowner, an innkeeper and an operator of ferry boats to the Eastern Shore. Members of his family became Chesapeake Bay pilots.[35] Middleton's Tavern is still located in Annapolis at the head of City Dock. A note on one of Middleton's ferries in a journal described her as a "neat sailing boat, twenty foot keel, rigged schooner fashion, *decked* [italics added] to her stern sheets and neatly painted green."[36] This newspaper item, while not very detailed, may describe a flush-deck pilot schooner.

The description of Middleton's schooner as single-decked in the *Maryland Gazette* does not prove that his schooner boats were of Chesapeake pilot-boat design. The note does confirm that small schooners placed in service on the Bay as ferries, pilot boats and local traders eliminated waists, quarterdecks and other structures and produced a schooner that was essentially of pilot-boat configuration.

ENDNOTES - CHAPTER ONE

1. Letter, Henry Callister to William Murray, 6 April 1748: Callister Papers, 1741-80. New York Public Library. Photostats in the Easton Public Library, Easton, Maryland, 4 vols.

2. Dr. Charles Carroll's correspondence, 1722-35, *Maryland Historical Magazine* Vols. 18-20, and MHS-MS 208, 208:1, Maryland Historical Society. *Maryland Historical Magazine* hereafter cited as MHM; Maryland Historical Society hereafter cited as MHS. Correspondence prior to about 1735 dealt exclusively with tobacco.

3. Dr. Carroll's accounts, MHM, Vol. 20, 66 and MHS-MS, 211.

4. Dr. Carroll's correspondence, MHM, Vol 20, 165. Editor notes that one volume is missing, for the years 1739-42. Also, MHS-MS 208, 208:1.

5. Letter, Charles Carroll, Barrister, to Robert Lloyd of Wye, 11 December 1755. MHM Vol. 31, 312-13.

6. Garrett Power, "Parceling Out Land in the Vicinity of Baltimore: 1632-1796, Part 1." *MHM*, Vol. 87, No. 4, Winter 1992, 460-62.

7. Letter, Dr. C.C. to Mr. Jackson, 16 September 1742; also, Letter, Dr. C.C. to Mr. Brown, 18 September 1742. MHM, Vol. 20, 165 & 183.

8. Letter, Dr. C.C. to Captain Saterwhite, 10 March 1742. MHM Vol. 20, 258-73.

9. Letter, Dr. C.C. to Robert Jenkins Henry, 12 January 1743. MHM, Vol. 20, 359-75.

10. Letter, Dr. C.C. to Michael Holland, 21 March 1743; also, Letter Dr. C.C. to Edward Barns, 8 August 1744. HMH Vol. 21, 243-60.

11. Letter, Dr. C.C. to Thomas Galloway, 15 September 1751. MHM Vol. 24, 246-84.

12. Letter, Dr. C.C. to John Hanbury & Co., London, 29 August 1754. MHM Vol. 27, 229.

13. J. Thomas Scharf, *History of Baltimore County and City.* (Philadelphia: Louis H. Everts, 1881), 56-57.

14. *Maryland Gazette,* 5 December 1776.

15. *Baltimore Town,* sloop, 36 tons, built Baltimore County, 1746; registered 9 May 1750, Commission Book 82, Maryland Hall of Records, MdHR-4012-1, hereafter cited as MdHR.

16. Prefederal Custom House Records, Naval Officer Records, Port of Annapolis, MdHR-1372-2.

17. Ibid.

18. Ibid.

19. Frank A. Cassell, *Merchant Congressman in the Young Republic–Samuel Smith of Maryland, 1752-1839.* (Madison, Wisconsin: University of Wisconsin Press, 1971), 4-5.

20. Paul G. E. Clemens, *The Atlantic Economy and Colonial Maryland's Eastern Shore* (Ithaca, New York: Cornell University Press, 1980), 4-5.

21. Ibid., 203.

22. *Maryland Gazette,* 16 September 1776.

23. Naval Officer Records, Port of Oxford, MdHR-1372-1.

24. Jeremiah Banning, *Log and Will of Jeremiah Banning, 1733-1798* (New York: Privately printed by W. F. Austin, 1932). No page numbers.

25. John Truslow Adams, *The Epic of America.* (Boston: Little, Brown & Co., 1933), 95.

26. *Virginia Gazette,* 20 January 1737 and 15 July 1737.

27. Arthur Pierce Middleton, *Tobacco Coast* (Newport News, Virginia: The Mariners' Museum, 1953), Appendix B, Schedule of Rates for Pilotage in Virginia 1755 and 1762.

28. *Molly,* schooner, Commision book 82, MdHR, 119.

29. *Susannah,* schooner, Ibid., 100.

30. *Samuel,* schooner, Ibid., 103.

31. *William,* schooner, Ibid., 111.

32. *Lark,* schooner, Ibid., 117.

33. *Ranger,* schooner, Ibid., 112.

34. *Cumberland,* schooner, Ibid., 131.

35. *Maryland Gazette,* 23 June 1747.

36. Ibid., 17 February 1747.

BERMUDA SLOOP
DEVONSHIRE,
PAINTED BY AN
ANONYMOUS
BERMUDIAN
ARTIST. CIRCA 1730.
Smithsonian
Institution,
Washington, D.C.

CHAPTER TWO

THE FIRST OFFSHORE SCHOONERS

Virginia, founded in 1607 by a mercantile company, did not generate profits for the Crown or for its investors until tobacco, protected by England's Navigation Acts, became the colony's principal source of revenue. Maryland, a proprietary colony, except for the years 1689-1715 when it was a royal colony, followed Virginia's general path of growth as a single-crop venture for its planters and investors.

Tobacco, packed in hogsheads, was loaded into typical large transatlantic cargo vessels, and this placed the trade in the control of English merchants and shipowners. The seasonal movement of this single cargo from Chesapeake Bay to Great Britain involved a fleet of ships forced to seek employment in other trades upon completion of each year's tobacco voyages. This situation discouraged colonial participation in the ownership of vessels engaged in carrying tobacco. Obviously then, few Maryland or Virginia planters owned merchant ships as long as tobacco was the only export.

But monopolist control eventually depressed tobacco prices and forced plantation owners to invest in slaves and additional land, an ongoing effort to increase earnings. The emphasis on higher production of tobacco with intensive use of slave labor inhibited investment in shipyards and other industries, and reduced the region's reservoir of skilled craftsmen. In addition, for the first hundred years, Maryland and Virginia produced very little else except timber products and a small quantity of iron. There was no manufacture of hardware, cloth, or naval stores for shipyards.

English Navigation Acts, commencing with Oliver Cromwell's Act of 1651, prohibited the employment of foreign-owned ships in colonial trade, and the sale of tobacco to third nations by planters.[1] For a number of years, England lacked the power to enforce these shipping laws on the colonies, and direct Virginia and Maryland tobacco sales to Holland, France and other European countries continued after the Restoration. Gradually, the Crown tightened its grip, and enforcement of the Navigation Acts virtually chained tobacco economies to England. The Navigation Acts of 1660, reinforcing previous orders, required all tobacco to move in British vessels. No tobacco could be shipped directly to a foreign nation.[2] England placed a system of customs duties and drawbacks into effect, and the result was total elimination of sales of tobacco by the planters to their former European customers.

The ability to enforce the acts during the hundred years after 1660 kept the price of tobacco at levels that usually produced marginal profits for growers, and this had severe effects on the development of the colonies of Maryland and Virginia. It took approximately 20 years following 1660 for major purchasers in Europe to accept the English system of transshipment, the effects of which produced an equally long depression in the Chesapeake region.[3] The emigration of small farmers out of the Virginia and Maryland tidewater to the west, the Carolinas, Pennsylvania and New York was another result. The loss of these stalwart yeomen left a scarcity of craftsmen and a reduction in the number of small farms in the tidewater country.

The exodus, combined with falling emigration from England, ultimately placed the colonies in the hands of large planters. Life in Maryland and Virginia altered drastically near the close of the seventeenth century as tobacco growers brought in huge numbers of African slaves in a move to lower tobacco production costs. The one-crop economies of Maryland and Virginia, supported by slave labor, were not unlike the economies of the sugar islands in the West Indies, and very different from the developing colonies north of Maryland. Slavery in Maryland and Virginia produced an oligarchy of plantation owners who reigned for almost a hundred years. After 1730 the failure of tobacco production in several

tidewater regions brought an increased diversification of agriculture. The growth of an iron industry, the production of forest products and naval stores, and a switch to grain from tobacco, produced deep cracks in the plantation economy.

The strength of a one-crop economy may be gauged by its ability to hold off diversification. Strong European demand for sugar, and access to plentiful supplies, propped up the earnings of West Indies sugar plantations. On the other hand, the declining profits of tidewater tobacco plantations due to British control of distribution provided incentive for change in Maryland and Virginia. Maryland Governor Calvert's pessimistic report to the Lord Proprietor in 1729, with respect to the Chesapeake's regional economy, lamented that, "In Virginia and Maryland, the case is much otherwise; tobacco, as our staple, is our all, and indeed, leaves no room for anything else."[4] In spite of this pessimism, change came to Maryland almost abruptly while Virginia's tobacco economy and the single-crop plantation system, intact in the middle of the eighteenth century, diversified more slowly over the next hundred years.

Lord Baltimore's colony consisted of a collection of manors and farms, with Annapolis, the seat of government and the center of society, and the port of Oxford in Talbot County on the Eastern Shore, the only towns in 1730. Baltimore was a plat of unsold lots, and Fells Point was a landing. Charlestown at the head of the Bay was nonexistent in 1730, and at that time Chestertown, Georgetown and

Whitehaven were small villages.

Other than heavy shipments of tobacco to Britain, the principal characteristic of Maryland's external trade between 1730 and 1750, the first decades of change, was its insignificance compared to the commerce of northern colonies. No banking system operated in the colony, and there existed only the barest outline of an infrastructure in the form of a thin layer of Maryland merchants financially dependent on Philadelphia bankers or British mercantile houses. Much of local trade remained with English and Scottish factors, operating stores on the Potomac and Patuxent Rivers, at Whitehaven in Somerset County, and at other locations on the Eastern and Western Shores. Commercial activity remained focused on purchasing tobacco for export and derivative trading.

Maryland ships began to appear with the beginnings of diversification of trade beyond the Bay early in the 1730s. Shipwrights built schooners, brigs and an occasional ship for trade with other British possessions and southern Europe. With this rather sudden beginning of an indigenous merchant-shipping fleet, carrying mostly grain, the schooner occupied an important position. Offshore schooners, trading principally to the West Indies, developed separately from the region's pilot-boat schooners, which were built to carry cargo within the limits of Chesapeake Bay. Two differently modeled schooners, then, docked at Baltimore and Fells Point until Maryland shipowners discarded the traditional topsail

schooners of the eighteenth century for an offshore version of the pilot-boat schooner in the first decade of the nineteenth century.

An unknown Somerset County shipwright built Maryland's first registered schooner, an otherwise anonymous vessel named *Sarah* in 1731.[5] That same year Patrick Creagh purchased a schooner named *Elizabeth* built in New England.[6] The registration of schooners in Maryland after 1733 continued at a fast pace. In the next ten years owners registered a total of 18 Maryland-built schooners at Annapolis, plus several others built in New England. Local shipwrights built a number of sloops and brigs during the same period. This investment in Maryland vessels gave added stimulus to the growth of the colony's external trade.

Maryland shipowners quickly recognized the advantages offered by vessels of schooner rig to the region's coastwise and West Indies commerce, and Maryland shipbuilders gave them vessels whose unique details were the result of an absence of ship-construction tradition. Innovations of design and construction were made in Chesapeake Bay shipyards that seem not to have been influenced by the conservatism of a preexisting ship-construction industry. Chesapeake shipbuilders readily experimented with new ideas in search of models suited to the physical, economic and political conditions evolving with the growth of export trade. Before the schooner, ships in Maryland had their capacities measured in hogsheads. After 1731, burden began to be measured by grain capacity.[7] The cargoes had changed; the measurement standards had changed; in the course of things vessel design was changing, too.

A major change in the nature and direction of a region's commerce in such a short interval of years is rare. Maryland shipwrights, pushed by their merchant clients, embraced the schooner model, and in response to a unique set of trading and political conditions developed the two-masted, fore-and-aft-rigged vessel into a beautiful, relatively fast, functional craft. With good local woods, good design components borrowed from other periods and places, adaptations for current conditions, and fresh ideas about physics and speed, Maryland's rural shipbuilders developed the fastest schooners on the West Indies route.

Dr. Charles Carroll of Annapolis entered the West Indies trade in 1731 when he collected a debt for an heir in sugar, rum and molasses.[8] His fleet would eventually include baycraft, sizable cargo ships, and two large Maryland-built schooners, *Annapolis*[9] and *Baltimore*.[10] Carroll and his partners in the Baltimore Iron Works built *Baltimore* in anticipation of iron shipments to London. John Casdorp, a shipwright of Annapolis, received the contract to build her on 10 September 1733.[11] The shipwright's contract specified a delivery date of 1 June 1734. Her register is dated October 8th of that year and states that she measured 60 tons burden, making her the largest schooner built in Maryland up to that time.

Baltimore's contract included general specifications, some details of her design, and her dimensions. Dr. Carroll specified a "scooner" with keel measuring 38', straight rabbet, beam of 17', and depth of hold 8 or 8-1/2'. The contract expressed in general terms a requirement that she should have "sufficient rake fore and aft." As the amount of rake is not specified, it is not possible to calculate her length overall.

The earliest ship plan of a Chesapeake craft is of *Mediator*, a sloop built about 1744, ten years after *Baltimore*. Her plan is reproduced below. *Baltimore*'s contract and *Mediator*'s plan provide the base for a comparison of Chesapeake Bay offshore schooners as they developed over the decades. Early Chesapeake craft were deep and wide compared to length. Bows were short, high and full. Heavy, short masts, bulky quarterdecks, and high bulwarks combined with the wide and deep hull, are features shared by *Baltimore* and *Mediator*. Their voyages probably took at least twice the sailing time as the next generation of vessels launched from Chesapeake shipyards.

Mediator's place of construction is not noted on the draft.[12] Her keel, with its varying thicknesses, suggests that she was Bermuda-built, and is proof enough that she was not built in Maryland. Since Virginia's plantation fleet consisted of Bermuda sloops and sloops built in Virginia by slaves taught by their counterparts in that island, it is not unusual for a Virginia-built sloop of this period to be similar to the Bermuda model.

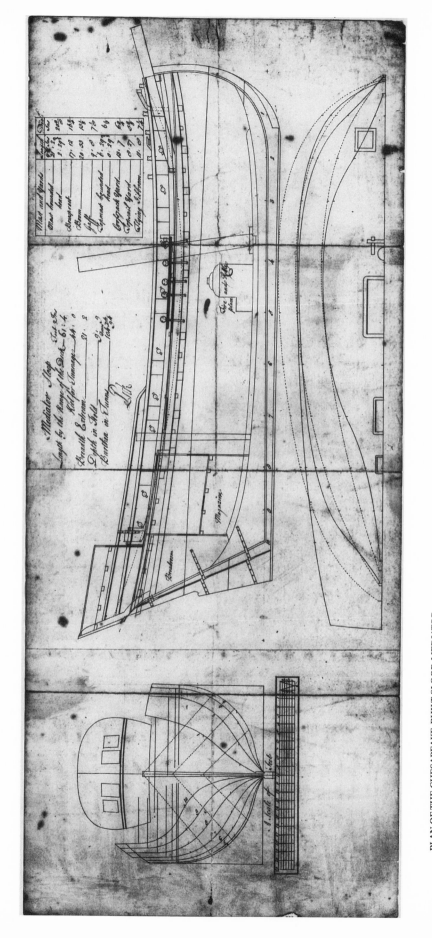

PLAN OF THE CHESAPEAKE-BUILT SLOOP *MEDIATOR*.

National Maritime Museum, London.

Mediator's lines are of a vessel some-what larger than *Baltimore*. She measured 61'4" x 21'2" x 9'9". Her keel length for tonnage measurement is given as 44 feet. The sloop's extremely wide beam, almost half her keel length, and her deep hold produce proportions not very different from *Baltimore*. It is reasonable to con-clude that, in spite of different rigs, ship-wrights in this period emphasized similar features, whether they were building vess-els in Maryland, Virginia, or Bermuda.

There are major components of *Mediator's* design that are repeated in the designs of later Chesapeake-built craft. Her keel drags somewhat and her stern-post rakes significantly. *Mediator's* builder gave her more than customary deadrise and her beam is widest forward of amid-ships. Her mast rakes, she has two or more jibs, and at least two square topsails, features found in post-Revolutionary off-shore schooners. This Virginia or Bermuda-built sloop has a low quarter-deck to afford more headroom in the after cabin.

Baltimore's contract called for a quar-terdeck and a two-and-one-half-foot waist amidships. The contract specified a flush deck fore and aft. According to Falconer's *Universal Dictionary of the Marine*, pub-lished in the eighteenth century, a deck, flush fore and aft, "implies a continued floor laid from stem to stern upon one line, without any stops or intervals."[13] To be able to reconstruct the actual deck con-figuration of *Baltimore* with this defini-tion, it is necessary to assume that Dr. Carroll's schooner had a waist amidships

created by a raised cabin top, and possibly a raised forecastle. The cabin top aft served as her quarterdeck. Entrance to the cabin was through a passageway leading from the waist amidships.

While an exact interpretation of the contract is impossible, Dr. Carroll's spec-ification of a schooner with a single deck, end to end, is of note. A single deck, end to end, was a feature of all Chesapeake schooners including pilot schooners. *Baltimore*, like other sailing vessels of the eighteenth century, had galleries and badges, customary details built into the sterns of vessels with quarterdecks.

Under the terms of the *Baltimore* con-tract, Casdorp used two-inch oak plank-ing in her construction and ceiled her inside with oak planks an inch and a half thick. He fastened her with locust treenails, and constructed her deck with two-inch pine planks. This was custom-ary, substantial, eighteenth-century con-struction.

While it is not possible to recreate *Baltimore's* spars, rig or sail plan, she, unlike *Mediator*, probably had no rake to her masts. This conclusion is drawn from the knowledge that 30 years later the Maryland schooners' masts shown in the Gray's Inn Creek painting on page 20 had no rake. *Baltimore's* sails included one or more jibs, gaff-rigged main and foresail, and probably gaff- or gunter-rigged top-sail or topsails.

A number of schooners were launched by Somerset County ship-wrights, beginning with *Sarah* in 1731. That county and Worcester County, carved out of it in 1742, launched more schooners than any other part of Maryland. Information on 15 such vessels built before 1748 survives. Records include *Mary and John*,[14] four tons burden, and *Peggy*,[15] ten tons, probably built for trading with Accomac County, and *Charming Esther*, registered but with no tonnage listed. The remaining 12 range from *Providence*[16] at 20 tons to *Industry*,[17] registered at 80 tons, measurements that suggest vessels burdensome enough to have been employed outside the limits of Chesapeake Bay.

That merchants of Somerset and Worcester counties owned most of Maryland's first schooners sheds light on that isolated part of the lower Eastern Shore. While Virginia shipping records from this early period have not survived, Maryland registers reveal that the lower Eastern Shore counties of the two colonies conducted active trade before 1700 in grain, meat and wood products.[18] Colonel Levin Gale owned the largest merchant fleet in Somerset County in 1734. His vessels included several brigs and at least two of the earliest schooners, *Sarah*[19] and *Bladen*.[20] The Gale family of Somerset traded in partnership with the Gales of Whitehaven, England, a powerful merchant group. As tobacco shipments ceased completely in Somerset County in 1730, it is likely that other commodities such as grain and meat were traded for decades before that year that began significant change, and in vessels built on the Chesapeake for trading commodities other than tobacco.

Maryland ships, sailing to New England, the Carolinas, and the West Indies, faced capture by the enemies of Great Britain through most of the eighteenth century, a time of almost continuous war at sea that sometimes spread into Chesapeake Bay. Maryland merchants favored the fast, nimble schooner as their best hope of survival. The West Indies trade required aggressive owners and clever masters. Levin Gale of Somerset led his region just as Dr. Charles Carroll provided leadership on the Western Shore. On the upper Eastern Shore, Thomas Marsh, planter and merchant of Queen Anne's County, and one of the first of that region to ship grain to the West Indies, became an early schooner owner. Colony records reveal that Thomas Marsh IV owned the schooner *Nancy*, 20 tons, registered in 1734 and built in Talbot County in 1733.[21] He purchased a second schooner, *Swallow*, 30 tons, built on the Wye River in 1734.[22] When Richard Bennett III, the richest planter in Talbot County, entered the West Indies trade his fleet included *Hopewell*, a schooner of 40 tons burden, built in Talbot County in 1736.[23] Bennett owned her jointly with John Bartlett. While trading in the Caribbean in 1742 *Hopewell*, captained by Samuel Martin, was captured by the Spanish and then retaken by HMS *Rose*.[24]

Virginia began to increase her external trade about 1730, too, but her merchant marine differed in composition as most Virginia vessels were offshore sloops. Norfolk, a transshipment port for North Carolina's tobacco, pork and other products, developed during the 1730s.[25] Virginia's tidewater plantations increased direct trade in grain with Bermuda and the West Indies at the same time. Virginia's fleet grew at the expense of New England traders who had dominated the trade of the lower Bay since the Dutch departed at the end of the seventeenth century.[26]

Although agricultural diversification in tidewater Virginia resulted in larger harvests of grain in the eighteenth century, there were fewer independent merchants than there were in Maryland. The entrenched planters of Virginia dominated a commercial and political structure that continued to keep a firm grip on the colony. Replacement of white indentured servants and free men with slave labor, and low prices for tobacco, forced many farmers to abandon tidewater Virginia. Their holdings were absorbed by the larger plantations. William Byrd, Robert Carter and other large planters controlled vast holdings and intermittent communities, and to a large extent they controlled the lives of the surviving small farmers, dependent on the big operators for supplies and to purchase their crops of tobacco. The large planters also absolutely controlled the lives of their slaves. Thirty thousand slaves served Virginia masters in 1730, a figure that represented 26 percent of the colony's population.[27]

Plantation vessels, many of them built by slaves who were sometimes trained by black Bermudian ship carpenters, carried much of Virginia's commerce.[28] As tobacco production fell in the tidewater region, Virginia's planters increased grain acreage in response to demand from Bermuda and the West Indies, and these cargoes were carried in Bermuda-model sloops. Tidewater Virginia's location on the wider lower Chesapeake Bay, nearer the open sea and the West Indies, with broad reaches, may have been better adapted to the sloop rig. As Maryland's shipwrights experimented with new ideas, Virginia's plantation carpenters routinely followed the models of their predecessors. Sloops continued to carry the commerce of the lower Bay. Much of Virginia's exported grain went to Bermuda in sloops built in that island, another reason for the significant presence of sloops in Virginia's portion of Chesapeake Bay. Between 3 September and 31 December 1737, 38 sloops entered or cleared Norfolk, and of this total 25 were registered in Bermuda.[29]

Swedish naval architect Fredrik Henrik af Chapman devoted extensive research to the vessels of the eighteenth century. His book of plans, which included the lines of a Bermuda sloop, was published in 1768.[30] His plan of the Bermuda model confirms that those sloops had significant influence on Bay sloops such as *Mediator*, and less direct influence on schooner models. Subtle characteristics of rigging and hull, and the use of materials common to Bermuda-built vessels, reappear in Chesapeake Bay craft. The Bermuda sloop's hull, with significant deadrise, combined with low freeboard, less superstructure and lighter spars than other contemporary craft, increased its speed and stability. Strong, light cedar found in abundance in Bermuda, and used for framing as well as planking, reduced vessel weight, and the common sail plan, with raked mast and square topsails, made Bermuda sloops good sailers with speed under fair conditions. Reduced weight above the waterline, light construction and raked masts reappear as important characteristics of Chesapeake Bay craft.

Wars with France, King George's War (1744-48) and the Seven Years War, ending in 1763, resulted in heavy losses to Bermuda's fleet, and Maryland and Virginia ships trading to the West Indies were frequently captured or lost in the 1740s and 1750s. Nothing influenced the evolving Chesapeake schooner to a greater degree than the continuing war at sea. Hulls became sharper at the expense of cargo space. Builders improved masts, rigging and sails. Topsails gave Chesapeake schooners greater speed in light air, and their sharp hulls and simple sail plans made them fast, maneuverable and capable of sailing close to the wind, features that allowed them to sail out of danger. But for all of these characteristics, by the end of the Seven Years' War the number of Maryland's schooners had been reduced by half while the fleets of Virginia and Bermuda were virtually destroyed.[31]

Chesapeake-built schooner design kept evolving, as observed in the vessels pictured in the painting of Gray's Inn Creek Shipyard. The overmantel painting, reproduced in Chapter 1, depicts typical

Chesapeake Bay vessels of about 1760. This was 25 years after John Casdorp launched *Baltimore*. Shown in the painting are big tobacco ships on the left side of the painting; a snow, a brig, and a Bermuda sloop in the center; then a sloop and two schooners on the right side of the panel.

The Maryland offshore schooners pictured on the right side are vessels for in coastwise trade and West Indies trade as well as carrying grain to southern Europe. They retain high freeboard and quarterdecks. Their sternposts are raked, and

TYPICAL MARYLAND TOPSAIL SCHOONER OF THE COLONIAL PERIOD. PORTION OF A 1788 PAINTING BY CHARLES WILLSON PEALE. *Maryland Historical Society, Baltimore.*

their bows, though convex, have somewhat raked stems and relatively sharp entrances. Schooner masts are still without rake and gaff topsails prevail. However, the two schooners, painted side by side, are different. The one to the left is fuller-bodied than the one on the right, which has a handsome profile because of a shallower curve of sheerline and a lower quarterdeck. It illustrates the changes as schooners became sharper and more graceful and lost the extreme curve of sheerline characteristic of earlier times. The model on the right represents advanced design circa 1760.

The sloop in the painting is rigged Bermuda-fashion with a pronounced rake to her mast, three jibs, and square topsails, much like *Mediator* of 20 years earlier. She retains the extreme sheer associated with early sloops and shows little change in design over the years.

With the start of the Revolutionary War, the Dutch island of St. Eustatius became the port of destination for many of Maryland's blockade runners. The Chesapeake fleet, still somewhat traditional in design and small in size, had difficulty outsailing the Royal Navy, and losses were high. Captain Jeremiah Yellott lost his Maryland-owned sloop *Rising Sun*, but he got himself to Statia, the popular name of the island, according to a report by Maryland's representative, Abraham van Bibber. Agent van Bibber wrote that Captain Yellott reported that his vessel with "every other vessel from Maryland and Virginia had been lost."[32]

Little is known of Jeremiah Yellott

prior to his arrival at Baltimore except that he was born in Yorkshire, England. After the loss of *Rising Sun* he returned to Maryland and became one of Baltimore's leading maritime figures. He is credited with the design of the topsail schooner *Antelope*, built by John Pearce of North Point in 1780. Owners of *Antelope* were John Sterett, Jesse Hollingsworth, Charles Ridgely and Yellott.[33] With *Antelope*, Yellott is believed to have incorporated several new features of design for larger schooners, including raked masts and square topsails.

Antelope made several voyages under Captain Yellott's command. She became Baltimore's most successful private armed schooner, and completed trading voyages to France and to Guadeloupe in the Leeward Islands. She measured 130 tons burden–large for that time, and apparently exceeded only by the schooner *Somerset*, 142 tons. *Antelope*'s keel measured 62' compared to 56' for *Somerset*. *Antelope*, with a longer keel and less capacity than *Somerset*, had increased deadrise, resulting in a sharper hull.[34] She mounted 14 guns and carried sweeps, but no plan of her hull or deck layout exists. Although Captain Yellott's schooner was the latest in offshore Chesapeake schooner design, she was not a pilot schooner. She was instead a cargo schooner of a type that would soon be replaced by the Baltimore schooner of the nineteenth century.

The Maryland Journal and Baltimore Advertizer, 1 August 1780, printed a letter written by a passenger after a voyage on

BALTIMORE ARMED
SCHOONER,
PAINTING BY
CHARLES BURTON,
CIRCA 1815.
*National Maritime
Museum, London.*

Antelope.[35] In the letter of 28 June 1780, the passenger wrote that *Antelope*, in company with *Felicity* (another schooner owned by the same consortium), *General Scott*, and a fleet of 42 French vessels, was attacked by the British in a two-hour engagement. He wrote that *Antelope* received "much damage, our sails are a perfect riddle." The schooner's mainmast and foretopsail yard were nearly shot away, plus damage to the "square sail boom, the steering [studding] sail boom, and the steering [studding] sail yard nearly shot away." The passenger's description reveals some details of *Antelope*'s sail plan.

Yellott rigged *Antelope* as a square-topsail schooner. She carried many of the sails that are associated with later Baltimore schooners. She was another link in the evolution of the Chesapeake schooner rig, as for the most part her sail plan was passed to the large pilot schooners built a few years later.

The Maryland Journal reported in its issue of 8 August 1780 the arrival of *Antelope* and *Felicity* from St. Eustatius in eight days, land to land, a very fast passage averaging approximately 150 miles per day.[36] *Antelope* and *Felicity* received registers at Baltimore on 14 August 1780, the first group issued at the Maryland Customs Office at Baltimore, following its separation from the Annapolis district.[37]

These first Baltimore registers consisted of 34 vessels, all of them with consortia of owners, spreading risk. Of the total 24 were schooners.[38] Sixteen of the total, or almost half, were built on the Eastern Shore, six in Somerset County. Eight were built in Virginia. John Pierce built *Antelope* and *Felicity* in Baltimore County. Several were built on the Western Shore, but only two were built at Fells Point. Fells Point did not become a shipbuilding center for another two decades, although George Wells built the Continental frigate *Virginia* and converted the ship *Sidney* into the state frigate *Defence* there during the Revolution.

This chapter, concerned with the offshore schooner fleet of the Maryland merchant service from the first registered vessels in 1731 through the Revolution, provides facts that correct the long-held posi-

tion that early Maryland schooners placed in the West Indies trade were of the same design as offshore pilot schooners. They were not. Certainly, Chesapeake Bay shipwrights improved their offshore schooners from the year *Baltimore* was built to the topsail schooners of 1788, as pictured on page 39. True, too, the topsail-schooner model included elements of pilot-schooner design. However, to illustrate the differences between the traditional schooners prior to 1792 and later Baltimore schooners, a photograph of a painting of an offshore pilot schooner is shown on the previous page, and can be compared with the 1788 schooner in the Charles Willson Peale painting. Even though the original Maryland schooner is much changed and improved, the differences in the two models are clear. With the pilot-schooner model, quarterdecks are gone. Freeboard is reduced. A flush deck, clean from end to end, reduces weight above the waterline. The tall rig has relatively light spars, and the sail plan is extreme. The bow is raked, and the bowsprit simple and unadorned. What is not seen, but contributes changes just as important, are less beam, less depth and a sharp graceful hull below the waterline, plus lighter construction throughout as compared with the topsail schooner.

ENDNOTES - CHAPTER TWO

1. Henry C. Hunter, *How England Got its Merchant Marine (1066-1776)* (New York: National Council of American Shipbuilders, 1935), 119-42.

2. Ibid.,143-201.

3. Thomas J. Wertenbaker, *The Planters of Colonial Virginia* (New York: Russell & Russell, 1959), 86-100.

4. Letter, Governor Benedict Leonard Calvert to the Lord Proprietor, London. Maryland Archives, Vol. xxv:602.

5. *Sarah*, schooner, Register #43, Commission Book 82 , Maryland Hall of Records, Colonial Papers, Md.HR 4012-1. Maryland Hall of Records hereafter cited as Md.HR.

6. *Elizabeth*, schooner, Register #25, MdHR 4012-1.

7. *Maryland Gazette*, dated 7 June 1753, 3 January 1754, and 16 September 1756.

8. Letter, Dr. Charles Carroll to John Sunson, 9 November 1731. *Maryland Historical Magazine,* Vol. 19:287. From Dr. Charles Carroll, Letter Books, Maryland Historical Society, MHS-MS 208, 208.1. Maryland Historical Society hereafter cited as MHS.

9. *Annapolis*, schooner, unknown date; no register found.

10. *Baltimore*, schooner, built 1734, Commission Book 82, Register #38. MdHR-4012-1.

11. *The American Neptune*, Vol. VI, 303-04. Carroll/Casdorp Contract reprinted from Carroll-Maccubbin Papers, MHS-MS-219.

12. *Mediator*, sloop, no register located.

13. William Falconer, *A Universal Dictionary of the Marine* (London: T. Cadell, 1780).

14. *Mary and John*, schooner, Register# 51, Commission Book 82, MdHr 4012-1.

15. *Peggy,* schooner, Register #114, Ibid.

16. *Providence*, schooner, Register #37, Ibid.

17. *Industry*, schooner, Register #125. Ibid.

18. Robert J. Brugger, *Maryland, A Middle Temperament* (Baltimore: Johns Hopkins University Press, 1988), 65.

19. *Sarah*, schooner, Register #78, Commission Book 82, MdHR 4012-1.

20. *Bladen*, schooner, Register #97, Ibid.

21. *Nancy*, schooner, Register #7. Ibid.

22. *Swallow*, schooner, Register #21, Ibid.

23. *Hopewell*, schooner, Register #46, Ibid.

24. *Rose*, Ibid, 97. HMS *Rose* was stationed off the North American coast during this period.

25. Thomas J. Wertenbaker, *Norfolk, Historic Southern Port* (Durham, North Carolina: Duke University Press, 1962), 30, 35. (Quoting colonial records of North Carolina, Vol. 1).

26. Ibid., 36. (Quoting *Virginia Magazine of History and Biography*, Vol. xxxvi:359).

27. Thomas J. Wertenbaker, *The Planters of Colonial Virginia* (Princeton, New Jersey: Princeton University Press, 1922), 131, quoting British Public Record Office: CO5-1322, Report of Governor Gooch.

28. Henry C. Wilkinson, *Bermuda in the Old Empire* (London-New York: Oxford University Press, 1950), 112.

29. David C. Klingman, *Colonial Virginia's Coastwise and Grain Trade* (New York: Arno Press, 1975), 99.

30. Fredrik Henrik af Chapman, *Architectura Navalis Mercatoria* (Stockholm, 1768).

31. Arthur Pierce Middleton, *Tobacco Coast* (Newport News, Virginia: The Mariners' Museum, 1953), 279. (Quoting Maryland Archives, vol. xxxi:145 & vol. xxxii: 23.)

32. Letter, Abraham van Bibber to William Patterson, 11 September 1778. MHS, Vertical File, MS1812.

33. *Antelope*, topsail schooner, *Baltimore Register*, 17 August 1780; *Somerset*, topsail schooner, *Baltimore Register*, 10 November 1780; MdHR 2042-2.

34. Ibid.

35. *Maryland Journal and Baltimore Advertizer*, 1 August 1780.

36. Ibid., 8 August 1780.

37. *Felicity*, topsail schooner, *Baltimore Register*, 17 August 1780. MdHR 2042-2.

38. *Baltimore Register,* MdHR 2042-2.

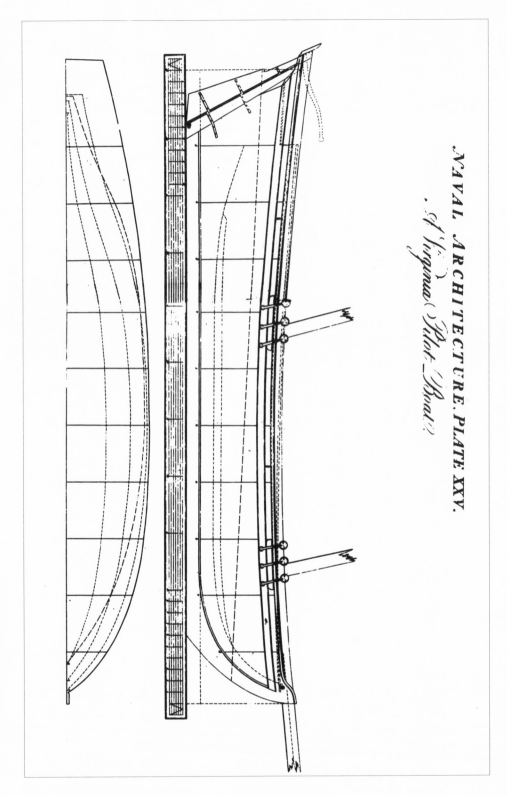

NAVAL ARCHITECTURE. PLATE XXV.

A Virginia Pilot Boat.

LINES OF A VIRGINIA PILOT BOAT, SHOWN IN
DAVID STEEL'S *NAVAL ARCHITECTURE*, 1805.

CHAPTER THREE

PILOT SCHOONERS
OF THE REVOLUTION

With the start of the War for Independence, Marylanders, confronted with the powerful presence of the Royal Navy, discovered quickly that their ships were unable to deal with Britain's sea power. Offshore schooners and sloops were regularly intercepted once outside Chesapeake Bay. Maryland's and Virginia's revolutionary leaders moved quickly to acquire pilot schooners to ease the desperate supply situation of the Confederation.

Most land battles of the War for Independence were fought in New York and New Jersey or in the southern colonies, and Chesapeake Bay was the communications link between the theaters of war. More than that, it was a region unoccupied by the British and an agricultural resource planted with grain and busy with milling. It was America's granary. Seldom mentioned in print before the war, the Bay's pilot-boat schooners shed their anonymous past as orders and dispatches frequently mentioned them after 1775.

Great Britain controlled the Atlantic Ocean from Canada to the West Indies. The Royal Navy could seal or occupy any Atlantic port at will–Boston, New York, Newport, Philadelphia, Charleston and Savannah were all occupied. At the mouth of Chesapeake Bay, Norfolk burned and the Royal Navy blocked the Capes. After Philadelphia fell, Baltimore became the principal Atlantic port not occupied during the conflict. Merchants, mariners, and shipbuilders moved into Baltimore from Pennsylvania, New York, Virginia and from other regions. Suddenly the village was a boom town.

The war subjected shipping on Chesapeake Bay to three types of harassment. The Royal Navy capped the mouth of the Bay from time to time and cruised inside attacking Maryland and Virginia vessels and shipyards. Rebel blockade runners slipping out of the Bay for France and the West Indies faced almost certain capture, particularly early in the war. Secondly, privateer vessels, many owned by New York loyalists, descended on the Bay to disrupt rebel communications and supply lines. They attacked and captured baycraft, principally those hauling grain and other food products. Loyalists sailed their prizes to New York and sold the grain to the British occupying army. Third, Chesapeake supply craft faced harassment and capture by Maryland and Virginia loyalists sailing small pilot schooners out of the creeks and small islands of the lower Eastern Shore.

These raiders, called pirates or picaroons by patriots, cruised the Bay without commissions, bent on profiting from the unstable conditions. Chesapeake Bay, while not a battleground, became such a dangerous body of water during the Revolution that Maryland and Virginia quickly organized state navies in an attempt to restore control.

Chesapeake Bay vessels were hard hit in the Caribbean as well. The Councils of Safety for Maryland and Virginia turned to the pilot-boat schooner to provide a solution to a desperate supply problem. On 24 April 1775, Richard Henry Lee of Virginia wrote to Landon Carter that "we propose sending a pilot boat immediately for gun powder and she can bring the Richmond quantity [of gun powder] if their cash is quickly collected."[1] Lee's letter concerning a pilot-boat schooner to be sent to St. Eustatius is the first record of the dispatch of baycraft on a voyage outside the Bay during the rebellion. It is the first mention of a pilot schooner in official dispatches. The "Richmond" reference above is to Richmond, Virginia.

Early in the conflict the Royal Navy sealed the entrance of the Patapsco River, blocking traffic in and out of Baltimore. Maryland's Council of Safety placed an embargo on trade. Shipping activity on Chesapeake Bay came to a halt with a few war-driven exceptions. George Woolsey, a merchant, informed an associate in Philadelphia that the only working vessels were those loading for the account of the Council.[2] The reference was to pilot schooners the Council chartered to carry flour to the West Indies. Maryland's Council of Safety also chartered John Middleton's and William Pitt's pilot boats to patrol the entrance of the Patapsco River to warn if the British formed to attack Baltimore.[3] Then they purchased the pilot schooner *Dolphin* and dispatched her to various locations on the Bay for cargo. In April, 1776, the Council sent *Dolphin* to Martinique with a cargo of flour.[4]

Abraham van Bibber of Baltimore was purchasing agent for Maryland and Virginia on the Dutch-owned island of St. Eustatius; Richard Harrison of Virginia represented the two states at the French colony of Martinique. The strategy called for Maryland and Virginia products to be shipped to warehouses on the islands, and with the earnings from these transactions Harrison and van Bibber purchased arms and gunpowder.

The Dutch were the free traders of the eighteenth century. Although neutral, the merchants of St. Eustatius traded in arms and war materials with the rebelling colonies, much to the chagrin of Great Britain. Surrounded by the island possessions of England, France, and Spain, the Dutch at Statia received Chesapeake Bay vessels delivering flour, grain and tobacco. From this free port, American farm products could be sold and transhipped throughout the region to friends and enemies alike, all desperate for foodstuffs to sustain island slave populations.

A typical wartime voyage was made by the pilot schooner *Chatham*. The Maryland Council chartered *Chatham* from her owners, William Lux and Daniel Bowley, for a voyage to St. Eustatius with a cargo of 100 barrels of flour in February of 1776.[5] Government records do not designate types of schooners, as all fore-and-aft vessels with two or more masts receive the generic name "schooner" in American and British naval and customs records. *Chatham* is described, however, as a pilot schooner in Maryland's Revolutionary War Orders of Council. In commercial service several years prior to the Revolution, *Chatham*'s activities support the position taken that pilot-boat schooners were in cargo service on the Bay many years prior to 1775.[6] *Chatham* was built in 1763, according to her enrollment.

Colonel Henry Hollingsworth, stationed at the head of the Elk River, the Bay's principal transshipment point between the north and south, expedited supplies and men in and out of shuttling baycraft. Samuel Purviance, Jr. informed the Council that "a pilot boat was sent to the Head of Elk for 36 barrels of powder and twelve chests of arms." This was about 10 March 1776.[7] To emphasize the importance of the pilot schooners, the Council noted on 1 May 1776 "the impracticability of square sail vessels escaping the bay; that small sharp rigged vessels would more probably meet with success."[8]

The Council purchased a second pilot-boat schooner named *Dolphin* for the Maryland Navy. Because of the duplication of names, records are difficult to separate. However, as part of Maryland's naval force, the exploits of the second

Dolphin and her sister, *Plater*, are covered in the state's Revolutionary War records. *Plater* became part of the Maryland Navy on 24 April 1777, the date that the Council appointed Benjamin King her commander. Captain Richard Coward's appointment as captain of *Dolphin* is dated 29 April 1777.[9] Once in service, Maryland's pilot schooners were seldom inactive. On 17 May 1777 the Council dispatched *Plater* to the York River with a cargo of medicine.[10] She sailed for Bladensburg in July to pick up a cargo of cordage.[11]

Dolphin, normally involved in non-military missions, participated in an incident unimportant to the war's outcome but one that received wide notice because Joshua Barney, Maryland's naval hero and one of the Continental Navy's most capable officers, played the leading role. The Council chartered *Dolphin* to the Continental Navy in January, 1778. Her orders directed her to the Continental frigate *Virginia*, Captain James Nicholson commanding, where she was assigned to tender and scout duties.[12] Nicholson made several attempts to get his new ship past British vessels lurking in the lower Bay and out to open water. Barney, one of *Virginia*'s officers, took command of *Dolphin*, and sailed her on a scouting cruise to the vicinity of Tangier Island. Young Barney had previous experience on a pilot-boat schooner six years before when he was a boy of 12.[13]

Enroute down the Bay, Barney hailed the sloop *Peggy*. Later, upon sighting a British warship, he came about and sped back up the Bay. Approaching *Peggy* once again, Barney tried to warn her and a hail of iron greeted *Dolphin.* He veered off, called his crew to quarters, and bore down again on the sloop. The capable Barney poured fire from the pilot schooner's swivel guns until he saw *Peggy's* master waving a white flag. As *Dolphin* came up on *Peggy's* lee, a ship's boat lashed to the sloop became visible. During the interval that took Barney down the Bay, a boarding party from the British sloop of war *Otter* had captured *Peggy.* Barney took his British prisoners aboard and sailed back up the Bay to warn Nicholson of the British presence.[14]

The military duties of Maryland's pilot-boat schooners included keeping the Eastern Shore picaroons in check. *Dolphin* and *Plater* conducted patrols to discover their activities and to capture the leaders–Marmaduke Mister, Joseph Wheland, Jr., and members of the Timmons family.[15] Between forays, they helped sustain the war effort. On a typical mission *Dolphin* and *Plater* sailed to Baltimore 22 May 1778, to load Captain Keesport's arms and deliver the cargo to Colonel Hollingsworth at Head of Elk.[16]

Maryland's war records do not include specific details of the State Navy's pilot-boat schooners. They had crews of about six men. They mounted swivel guns and were fitted with sweeps. Each carried the standard sail plan of the pilot-boat schooner: one large jib, a free-footed gaff foresail, a large boomed gaff mainsail, and a gaff topsail.[17] There is no record of their measurements. A rough idea of their capacity may be revealed by the different cargoes carried. *Dolphin* on a voyage to Hampton carried 62 barrels of flour and three barrels of beef.[18] On another occasion she delivered 40 horses.[19] On still another voyage, *Dolphin* delivered 70 barrels of herring to the Head of Elk.[20] Because their hulls were sharp and shallow, these vessels did not have large cargo holds.

Dolphin, with William Middleton in command, was in Continental service in March of 1781 with orders to transport troops under the command of the Marquis de Lafayette from the Head of Elk to Virginia.[21] General Lafayette and his men were reinforcements for the southern Continental army fighting Lord Cornwallis's advance. The Maryland Council of Safety received word on 9 April 1781 that the British had captured *Dolphin* in Virginia waters. Captain William Middleton became a prisoner and was taken to England. The British refused to exchange him.[22] *Plater* participated in the Battle of Yorktown in October of 1781, ferrying troops and supplies, including 15,543 pounds of beef loaded at William Paca's landing on the Eastern Shore.[23] She continued to serve in the Maryland Navy after Yorktown.

Victory at Yorktown was made possible by the French Navy's success in breaking the Royal Navy blockade of Chesapeake Bay. After the Bay was freed of British warships and Tory privateers, Eastern Shore picaroons, continuing to prey on Bay traffic, became *Plater's* principal mission. The pirates became so bold that they assumed that "precautions for their security is unnecessary."[24] In April 1782, *Plater* was ordered on a cruise the purpose of which was to "rid us of enemy vessels and depopulate Tangier Island."[25]

The Virginia Navy during the Revolutionary War had an experience different from Maryland's. Only rarely did *Dolphin* and *Plater* engage in military action, but in Virginia waters at the mouth of the Bay, where the Royal Navy and New York loyalist privateers were concentrated, naval action was not infrequent.

Commodore James Barron of Hampton, Virginia, along with his brothers, headed a flotilla of schooners and gunboats that included the pilot-boat schooners *Liberty* and *Patriot*. Other pilot schooners in Barron's little fleet were *Fly* and *Molly*, usually deployed as scout or lookout vessels. *Molly*, burden only 12 tons, on at least one occasion sailed to St. Eustatius in company with the pilot-boat schooner *Betsey*.[26]

Liberty, Commodore James Barron's flagship, is described as a pilot-boat schooner of 60 tons burden, but her measurements are not known. The commissioners purchased her for Virginia's State Navy in December, 1775, and she served throughout the war. *Liberty* engaged enemy forces at least 20 times. She captured the sloop *Dorothy*, owned by the loyalist family of John Goodrich,[27] and her most important exploits were the capture of the British transport *Oxford* and the schooner *Fortunatus*.

Liberty (James Barron), sailing in company with *Patriot* (Richard Barron), captured *Oxford* with 200 troops on board. This event took place 21 June 1776.[28] The most brilliant victory for these schooners involved *Liberty* against *Fortunatus*, a British naval tender of 120 tons armed with ten six pounders and manned by a crew of 50. Captain James Barron, along with other members of his family and a dozen volunteers, captured *Fortunatus* after decimating her crew with bags of musket balls shot from *Liberty*'s swivel guns. That engagement took place in the spring of 1779.[29]

As the war dragged on the activities of Joseph Wheland, Jr., one of the picaroon leaders of the Eastern Shore, were particularly effective disrupting supply lines in the southern part of the Bay. A joint operation of *Liberty*, *Patriot*, *Dolphin* and *Plater* sortied down the Bay in September of 1780. Off Tangier Island, *Liberty* and *Patriot* captured five picaroon craft and then joined with Captain William Middleton in *Dolphin* and Captain Gilbert Middleton in *Plater* in an attempt to corner Wheland, reported to be at the helm of "a small pilot boat with a white bottom."[30]

Joe Wheland escaped and continued to harass rebel vessels. He captured the Philadelphia-owned pilot schooner *Greyhound* in Hooper Straits on 6 July 1782 and gained a cargo of salt, produce, and meat as well as the vessel. *Greyhound*, built in Maryland in April, 1779, could stow 85 hogshead of tobacco. An unusually large pilot schooner for this early period, she sailed in the West Indies trade prior to her sale at auction in Philadelphia in June of 1780.[31]

Between 1776 and 1783, Maryland and Virginia news journals contained many reports of vessels lost to picaroon, loyalist and Royal Navy activity on the Bay and beyond. Contemporary information suggests that more than half of the Maryland and Virginia merchant marine was lost at sea in captures and other mischances, and that several hundred baycraft were seized by Eastern Shore picaroons, privateers and British warships. There was soon some respite from the Royal Navy, however. Following the passage of a vast British armada the length of the Bay to Elk Landing on its expedition to take Philadelphia in August 1777, the Royal Navy left the Chesapeake to New York privateers and local pirates.

Among the loyalist privateers on patrol just outside the Capes were the Goodriches, operating a small fleet of armed sloops and schooners out of Bermuda. Bridger Goodrich's privateer [*Andrew*] *Hammond*, a large Bermuda sloop, took a number of prizes that included some Bermuda-owned vessels hauling grain to that island so dependent on such vessels for its bread. Angry Bermudians ran the family out of their safe haven to occupied New York, from which base they continued to prey upon rebel commerce in the Chesapeake. Bridger Goodrich's fleet included a large pilot schooner mounting 22 guns and with a crew of 100 men.[32]

It is through Abraham van Bibber's correspondence that we know of Captain John Sinclair's Continental privateer. His pilot-boat schooner *Nicolson*, 30 tons,

arrived at St. Eustatius in the spring of 1777 and discharged a cargo that included 13 casks of indigo. On his return voyage, Sinclair captured a British schooner bound for Newfoundland with a cargo of rum. Later, he took *Nicolson* into the Virginia Navy.[33] But except for isolated instances such as Captain Sinclair's prize, pilot schooners were rarely identified as privateers in the records. Called schooner boats, Maryland's *Enterprize* and *Rebecca and Sally* were pilot schooners that may be identified as privateers. *Enterprize* took several enemy craft and may have served for a period in the Continental Navy.[34] Usually these baycraft were too small to be effective against large merchant ships at sea. Frequently mentioned as privateers in popular histories of the Revolution in the tidewater country are Chesapeake "clipper" schooners. They did not exist. Maryland and Virginia ships, brigs, and traditional topsail schooners such as *Antelope* carried privateering commissions, and small pilot schooners such as *Nicolson* and *Enterprize* had brief fame as privateers, but there were no clippers.

The specifications of pilot schooners in register records after the Revolution reveal a relatively standardized craft. Using a sample of 51 schooners built on Chesapeake Bay and enrolled at Baltimore between 1781 and 1790, the length on deck of this group averaged 45' 6"; average beam was 14' 6"; and depth was on average an even five feet. Only four of 51 vessels measured longer on deck than 50' and only two measured less than 40'. Forty-one of the 51 schooners measured between 4' 5" and 5' 5" in depth of hold. On an average, length overall was about three times width and about nine times depth.[35]

When post-Revolution pilot schooners from the Bay are compared to those built in the years between 1841 and 1850, the similarity is startling. A sample, consisting of 19 pilot schooners from the middle of the nineteenth century, contemporarily called pungies, averaged 48.39' in length, 16.66' width, and had average depth of hold at 5'. The proportions of these schooners built 50 or 60 years after the post-Revolution pilot schooners are length 9.305 times depth and length 2.904 times beam. Very gradually, the Bay pilot schooner of the nineteenth century was given increased beam for greater cargo capacity. And the later Bay schooners were built with less draft to better navigate silting rivers. Pungies built during the last period of construction of the pilot-boat schooner, 1871 to 1885, averaged 2.99 times beam in length and 10.46 times depth in length. Length of these last pungies was approximately 59', width 19.7', and depth of hold an average of 5.64'. The sample used included 78 documented pungies built between 1871 and 1885.[36] Length measurements quoted here and elsewhere are length on deck. It seems conservative to conclude that the Chesapeake Bay pilot schooner that originated during the eighteenth century had by 1785 reached its final form, after which the model remained relatively unchanged for the next hundred years, although vessels became somewhat larger.

Judge Thomas Jones of Walnut Grove on the Patapsco River left a remarkable record of vessel arrivals between 1789 and his death in 1812.[37] His tabulation supposedly includes Baltimore arrivals of all vessels in overseas trade, plus every baycraft that called at the port for a period of 22 years. The Judge's record-keeping is incredible, and it is probably incomplete. Assuming that whatever errors introduced into the figures are constant, the totals produce a graph that illustrates the increase in the number of baycraft, mostly pilot schooners, that came to Baltimore's Basin during the period of the port's greatest commercial expansion. These baycraft hauled produce and building materials in support of the city's growing population, and they continued to haul wheat for the flour mills and grain and other products for transfer to ships and warehouses in the port.

The voyages of Baltimore-bound baycraft originated on every river that flowed to Chesapeake Bay. Hundreds of coves where pilot schooners could nudge against the land served as landings. Every waterfront farm had one. At most locations there was insufficient cargo to top off even a small schooner. Low yields of individual farms made it necessary for baycraft to call at several landings for a full cargo. Accumulation and storage of grain was impossible; it would have required a warehouse at every turn of a river. And it was unnecessary; the schooners accumulated and moved the grain. These small-farm and fast-transit conditions kept baycraft in service until

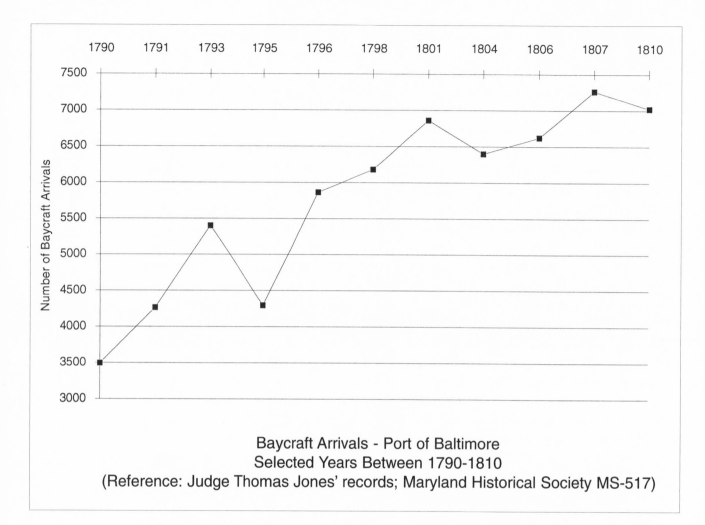

Baycraft Arrivals - Port of Baltimore
Selected Years Between 1790-1810
(Reference: Judge Thomas Jones' records; Maryland Historical Society MS-517)

replaced by motor vessels and trucks in the twentieth century. Steamboat lines did not usually compete with the Bay's sailing craft until after the Civil War. They restricted their stops to population centers or to widely separated wharves. Their specialty was packaged freight and passengers.

Captain Jeremiah Yellott dispatched one of his baycraft to the Choptank River to load grain in December 1794. To obtain a full cargo of 1700 bushels, Yellott's schooner loaded at John Goldsborough's landing, then Richard Trippe's, and finished at William Dawson's farm.[38] This was typical of the Bay's grain trade. Limited yields and hundreds of shallow landings, combined with a quick voyage to Baltimore, preserved this trade for the Bay's schooners. And the trade in turn preserved the vessels. Shipwrights, once locked into a design by unchanging conditions and cargoes, become bound by tradition. This is shipbuilding conservatism, and is overcome only when significant changes occur: political, economic or technical, such as the invention of the small gasoline engine.

Bay traffic increased significantly after the Revolutionary War as Baltimore developed into a major seaport. Judge Jones' vessel-arrival statistics show that arrivals of baycraft doubled between 1789 and 1800. Most Maryland farms delivered their products to mills above Baltimore's fall line or for export. A portion of Virginia's grain found its way by boat to the Patapsco River, too, and a good percentage of that state's imports arriving at Baltimore were transshipped by baycraft to river ports in Virginia's tidewater.

Who were the owners of these pilot-boat schooners enrolled in Maryland? In addition to Bay watermen and mariners, pilot schooners were owned by farmers, most of whom had access to a landing. A merchant from Baltimore would own one or more to transport grain to Baltimore's warehouses. Other merchants carried their wares to rural buyers via baycraft. Gentlemen owned them for transport to political and social affairs. Pilot schooners were owned by the thousands all over Maryland and Virginia in the later eighteenth century and through the nineteenth. They were the sailmobiles of a waterborne population. Records of owners are available in Federal Custom House enrollments after 1789.[39] A few are listed below. They reveal much–and, truth to tell, leave even more to the imagination:

Thomas Rouse built the pilot-boat schooner *Ann* at Fells Point in 1797. She was owned by Ann McCubbin of Anne Arundel County. McCubbin was listed master, too. She also owned a vessel of 22 tons named *Betsey*.

Margaret German, who identified herself as a Baltimore merchant, owned *Barbara*, built in Sussex County, Delaware, date unspecified. James Carroll, Esq., owned *Barker*, built in 1791.

William Pitt, perhaps the same mariner who worked with the Maryland State Navy during the Revolution, owned a schooner named *Delight*. He also owned the schooner *Nancy*, 32 tons. Captain Pitt was a Fells Point pilot.

Lawrence Lazarre of Baltimore owned the pilot-boat schooner *Eliz and Ann*. Built at St. Michaels in 1793, this vessel's description on her enrollment stated that she had a square stern and a mermaid figurehead.

Henry Yearley of Baltimore shared ownership of *Experiment* with Ben Yearley of Kent County. John Stump, formerly of Harford County, and in 1794 a Baltimore merchant, owned *Fairplay*, a schooner built on the Choptank River in 1793.

William Johns of Baltimore owned and skippered *Friends*, one of the rare Bay pilot-boat schooners built in Baltimore during this period.

Thomas Giles and William Rutter, watermen of Somerset County, sold *Tryale*, built in 1795, 24 tons, to Michael Dillon of Baltimore County for $370.00. Charles Ridgely of Hampton had a pilot schooner he christened *Henry* built on the Choptank River.

Edward Ireland, Baltimore merchant, owned the pilot-boat schooner *Hope*.

Built in Dorchester County, she measured 44' x 13'6" x 5', her beam a foot less than most pilot schooners of her length. She had a square stern, no galleries, no badges and no figurehead. As noted previously, these were items associated with schooners of the seventeenth century. A gallery was a platform or balcony around the quarters or stern of a sailing vessel. Badges consisted of carvings around stern windows. Flush-deck pilot boat schooners never had quarterdecks, galleries or badges.

Little John was built on Broad Creek near St. Michaels in Talbot County, the location of Richard and Perry Spencer's shipbuilding facilities. Her owner, William Hall, lived in Harford County.

Eliphalit Gittings, a prominent Baltimorean, owned *Maria*, built in St. Marys County in 1797. Thomas Cator owned *Mary*, built in Dorchester County, where the Cator family owned estates.

Milford was built on Gwynn Island, Virginia, in 1797. Her owner, Robert Berry, stated in the enrollment papers that he lived in the "city" of Baltimore. Baltimore was incorporated by an act of the legislature in 1796, effective 1797.

James Philips of Harford County paid Henry J. Philips $1.00 for the schooner *Nancy* in 1799. Harford, cut out of Baltimore County, became a separate county in 1774. In the early days of flour milling, the farmers of Harford County moved their grain to mills in a fleet of pilot-boat schooners to the Basin at Baltimore Town. But after 1800, fewer baycraft were enrolled at Havre de Grace

as roads improved. Not much water traffic originated from Cecil County to Baltimore after the war, so it is assumed that much of the grain harvest of that county returned to its normal route by wagon to Delaware Bay for the account of Philadelphia merchants.

The city of Philadelphia, its hinterland pinched between the sea and the Susquehanna River, worried about the growing commercial power of Baltimore. As the latter increased its trading region with a road system that penetrated Pennsylvania west of the Susquehanna, Philadelphia business interests drew up plans for a road from a boat landing at Peachbottom, just above the Maryland line on the Susquehanna River, to a landing on Christiana Creek, Delaware Bay. The planners hoped that the road, when built, would be used to divert grain from Baltimore.[40] The road was not constructed at that time, and the Susquehanna River, a natural barrier, kept Pennsylvania's rich farmlands within reach of the merchants and teamsters of the Port of Baltimore into the twentieth century.

Thomas Todd, gentleman, owned a pilot schooner named *North Point*. Built with a sharp hull, she had a round stern, an unusual feature for a Bay schooner. Jonathan Davenport, a silversmith, owned a schooner called *Peggy*. Abraham Neild, a farmer, owned *Planter's Friend*.

President, owned by Captain Peter Gold and Moses Myers, a merchant of Norfolk, was operated in a packet service between Baltimore and Norfolk. Moreau de St. Méry, an emigré from San Domingo, wrote about his trip from Norfolk to Baltimore on *President*, 15 May 1794. Moreau described the packet as a schooner, an excellent sailer, well-built and with attractive cabins. The voyage became miserable in hot weather and no wind in the beginning, then a storm forced her to seek shelter behind Drum Point inside the mouth of the Patuxent River. Moreau wrote: "The schooner being loaded beyond measure, belied its reputation as a good sailer." He noted that waves came over the bow, normal behavior for pilot schooners with their low freeboard and sharp entry. This one, "loaded beyond measure," would have been dangerous in a storm.[41]

George Reese enrolled his *Susannah* at Baltimore in 1791, a new vessel. He described her as sharp-built, 49 tons, with measurements of 57' x 15'4" x 6'4", larger than most Chesapeake pilot schooners. Captain Reese, who lived in Fells Point, was a Baltimore pilot.[42] Since pilots stayed with their schooners, waiting for ships, many of the baycraft built specifically for this work were larger than the schooners carrying cargo on the Bay. This is confirmed by Hampton Roads enrollments of 1815, which list several boats built for pilots that were about the size of *Susannah*.

With *Two Brothers* the carpenter certificate of Gabriel Miller, boatwright, describes her as a pilot boat. David Stodder, the builder of the frigate *Constellation*, launched a vessel he called *Punch*, 2 November 1799. She measured 54'2" x 38' x 14'10" x 5'. Stodder built her

for his own account, and on her carpenter certificate he describes her as a pilot-boat schooner.[43]

During the period between the end of hostilities in 1783 and the ratification of the Constitution in 1789, each state had its own import tariff. To enforce hers, Virginia commissioned *Liberty*, which survived the war, and a new *Patriot*, as state revenue cutters. Specifications of these two craft are unknown, although the new *Patriot* was somewhat larger than the old *Liberty*. William Price of Hampton, engaged to perform maintenance work on the revenue cutters, supplied new spars for *Liberty* in June of 1787. Her masts measured 49' and 51'. Price also supplied the boom for the mainsail, which measured 36'.

Price invoiced the state for a 52' mast for *Patriot* on 12 July 1786, and for the same vessel he billed out a 56' mast 27 July 1787. And he made a 40'6" boom for *Patriot*. Below are the measurements of the spars made by William Price:

LIBERTY	PATRIOT
Mainmast - 51'	Mainmast - 56'
Foremast - 49'	Foremast - 52' or 54'
Mainboom - 36'	Mainboom - 40' 6"
Jibboom - none	Jibboom - 18'
Gaff - "	Gaff - 15' 6"
Topmast - "	Topmast - 14'

Price also repaired a "topsail yard" of 18', but he did not specify to which schooner it belonged. Price's invoices give us the information that *Patriot* and *Liberty* carried sail plans which included a lug foresail, mainsail, a large jib, one or more flying jibs, and a square topsail or topsails. The Virginia state records concerning revenue cutters end with their sale to private owners in 1789. [44]

Alexander Hamilton, the nation's first Secretary of the Treasury, ordered construction of two pilot schooners, *Active* and *Virginia*, for service as revenue cutters on Chesapeake Bay. These first Federal revenue vessels, placed into service in 1791, were also the first of many pilot schooners in the Treasury's new Revenue Cutter service. Congress appropriated money for the cutters in 1790. A sense of urgency existed as the new nation depended on import tariffs for most of its revenue, and widespread smuggling to avoid the payment of duties was reported by all customs districts. The Treasury's plan called for nine cutters, one to be stationed at each coastal state.

President George Washington paid close attention to the selection of captains for the cutters. He chose Richard Taylor, a hero of the Virginia Navy, to command the cutter *Virginia*, under construction at Hampton. Captain Taylor, after some hesitation (he had been wounded during the war) accepted Washington's commission. The President notified Hamilton of it, passing along Taylor's comment that "swiftness of sailing being especially required, the thought that the pilot boat construction would be best for that account, though very inconvenient in the point of accommodations." [45]

George Washington gave notice that his first choice for master of *Active* would be Captain Joshua Barney. Barney, proud to a point of arrogance, evidently did not respond to Washington's inquiries, as the President noted in a letter to Hamilton, that "Captain Barney was not in Baltimore when I passed through, nor could I learn with certainty whether he wished to receive the appointment or not." [46]

David Stodder built *Active*. There are no drawings of these early cutters, but it is thought that *Active* and *Virginia* had about the same dimensions. Hamilton described *Virginia* in a letter to the Collector of Customs at Boston: "The cutter building at Hampton is of the following dimensions - 40 feet, keel, straight rabbet, 17 feet beam and 6-1/2 feet hold, measuring forty seven tons." [47] *Virginia*, sold out of the Federal Revenue Service in 1797, was enrolled at the Port of New York. The certificate describes her as a square-stern schooner, built in Hampton, and with dimensions of 52'6" x 17'6" x 6'6", measuring 54-93/95 tons. [48] Her builder is unknown.

Captain David Porter, Sr., master of *Active* for several years, purchased her from the Treasury Department. Porter made some repairs and put her up for sale again in July 1798. A notice in a news journal described *Active* as being able to sail against a strong tide and still outsail "the high flying Hampton pilot boats." [49]

As the United States entered the last decade of the eighteenth century, the new nation developed a strong maritime presence. Along the Atlantic coast, pilot schooners were to be found at other ports. Where pilots competed, fast pilot boats were placed into service.

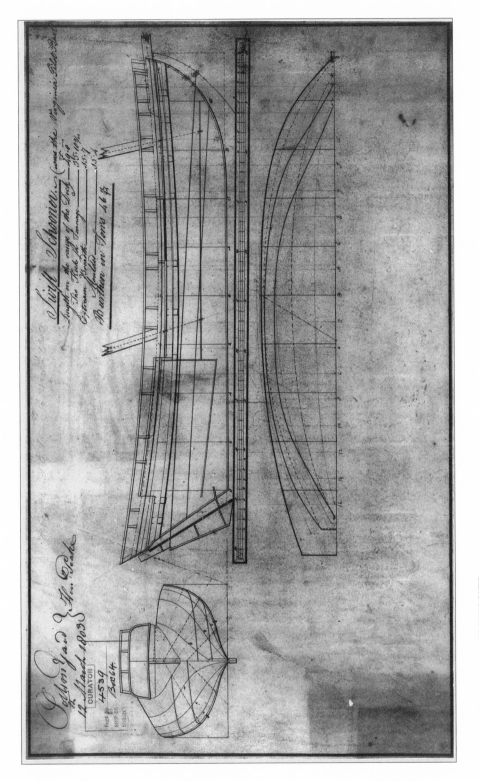

PLAN OF CHESAPEAKE PILOT SCHOONER

SWIFT, PURCHASED BY THE ROYAL NAVY IN 1794.

National Maritime Museum, London.

Schooners, pilot-boat built, dominated commercial traffic on Chesapeake Bay, and there is evidence of their use in coastwise trade, on Delaware Bay, in New York harbor, and along the Carolina coast.

There are no plans or drawings of pilot schooners built prior to 1794. British Admiralty records state that the Chesapeake Bay pilot schooner *Swift* was purchased that year. She served the British government for several years carrying dispatches. Her lines were taken off at the Royal Navy's Portsmouth dockyard in 1803 and she was broken up soon after.[50] These drawings are dated 12 March 1803, and are signed by Henry Peake. He calls her "Swift-Schooner (Was the Virginia Pilot Boat)" and gives measurements of 49' length overall and 15'7" beam; her depth is not given.

Swift's lines are generally similar to Chesapeake-built pilot schooners, but there are details of the plan which suggest that the schooner's drafts were altered. Like *Mediator*, built before 1744, this plan of *Swift* shows increased deadwood to the forefoot outside of the rabbet. Her transom, rudder post and tiller are unlike those seen in other drawings of Chesapeake pilot schooners.

Swift was to be the model for a class of dispatch schooners built in Bermuda and England between 1804 and 1808. This was the reason for taking off her lines, but Admiralty records suggest that this plan was changed significantly before a final design was accepted for the Royal Navy's first pilot schooners.

Swift as drawn measured 46 tons burden. She had greater than normal beam and a shorter run than the typical Chesapeake vessel. She was similar to Peter Gold's packet *President*, built in 1793 with measurements of 50' x 17' x 6'. *Swift's* original Virginia owner probably built her for packet service.

Swift as drawn had raked stem and sternpost, and a straight keel with considerable drag. As with all schooners of pilot-boat model, her greatest beam was forward of amidships, producing a relatively full convex entrance. Her full, wide hull was bulkier than most pilot schooners. *Swift* had significant deadrise or rise of floor, but with a greater fullness aft and slacker bilges than normal for the model. These features provided space for a large cabin abaft the mainmast. If she was a packet boat, this was a concession to passenger comfort. A more typical pilot schooner, with less fullness to the hull, would have a finer, longer run than *Swift*.

Swift had one flush deck, low freeboard and a rather large trunk-cabin top abaft the mainmast which provided her with a quarterdeck area. A smaller hatch covering protruded above the deck between the masts. She had pronounced sheer. As drawn, her rudder post does not pass through the middle transom as is normal in Chesapeake-built craft. Rather, her tiller seems to pass through the upper transom to the helmsman on deck.

Swift's single flush deck, clear of gear except hatch covers, and her rails along with low freeboard, are typical characteristics of pilot-boat design, features to reduce weight, and place a large percentage of the hull, as well as cargo, below the waterline. Pilot-boat schooners had a relatively shallow hull and were somewhat beamy, the combination of beam and weight below the waterline providing stability to support lofty masts and a large sail area. *Swift*'s drawing does not include her spar measurements or her sail plan.

A second set of drawings of a pilot-boat schooner appeared in David Steel's *Naval Architecture* in 1805.[51] The drawings are shown at the beginning of this chapter and below. Steel's Virginia Pilot Boat, as the drawing has become known, has purer, more characteristic lines of the type. Her straight keel and her three-part transom are of Chesapeake Bay design, and her rudder post passes through the transom. Additionally, her entrance is

convex with her maximum beam forward of amidships. The Steel pilot schooner falls into the same class as *Patriot* II of the Virginia Revenue Service or the Federal Revenue Cutter *Virginia*. Her extreme beam, 15.3', is less than *Swift*'s even though she is seven feet longer on deck. This feature, combined with a sharper hull, particularly aft of amidships, produces a long fine run, a key element of pilot-boat design.

Steel's schooner drawing and the Admiralty draft of *Swift*, appearing almost at the same time, are the first published plans of the Chesapeake pilot-boat schooner, the cargo-carrying version of the pilot boat and forerunner of the pungy of the nineteenth century.

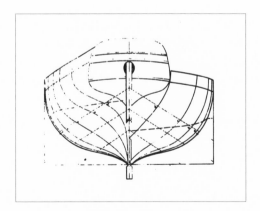

LINES OF A VIRGINIA PILOT BOAT, SHOWN IN DAVID STEEL'S *NAVAL ARCHITECTURE*, 1805.

ENDNOTES - CHAPTER THREE

1. Letter, Richard Henry Lee to Landon Carter, 24 April 1775; *Naval Documents of the American Revolution,* William Bell Clark, William James Morgan, and William S. Dudley, eds. (Washington D.C.: U.S. Government Printing Office, 1964), Vol 1-217. This reference is hereafter cited as NDAR.

2. Letter, George Woolsey to John Pringle of Philadelphia, 14 December 1775. NDAR, 2-1273.

3. Maryland Archives, Vol. xi, 103-04.

4. *Maryland Gazette,* 22 January 1776; Maryland Archives, Vol. xi, 98, 270, 300, 316.

5. NDAR, 3-1054, 1089, 1138.

6. *Maryland Gazette,* 30 December 1773 and 11 August 1774. Also, Maryland Hall of Records, MdHR 1372.

7. Letter, Samuel Purviance, Jr., to Maryland Council of Safety, Approximate date, 10 March 1776. Maryland Archives, Vol. xi, 219.

8. Minutes of Maryland Council of Safety, 1 May 1776. Maryland Archives, Vol. vii, 397.

9. Maryland Archives, Vol. xxi, 226, 232.

10. Maryland Archives, Vol. xxi, 259.

11. Ibid. 321.

12. Ibid. 508, 534, 535.

13. *Biographical Memoir of the Late Commodore Joshua Barney,* Edited by Mary Barney (Boston: Grey and Bowen, 1832), 26.

14. Hulbert Footner, *Sailor of Fortune, The Life and Adventures of Commodore Barney, USN* (New York: Harper & Brothers, 1940), 47-48.

15. Maryland Archives, Vols. xliii, 242 and xiv, 258.

16. Maryland Historical Society, Vertical File, MS 1814, 21 May 1778.

17. Maryland Archives, Vol. xliii, 160, 195, 276; Vol. xlv, 537.

18. Maryland Archives, Vol. xliii, 100.

19. Ibid., 349.

20. Ibid., 527.

21. Ibid., Vol. xlv, 347.

22. Ibid., Vol. xlv, 385, 451, 634, 651-52; Vol. xlvii, 222. Also Jack Kaminkow, *Mariners of the American Revolution* (Baltimore: Magna Carta Book Co., 1967).

23. Maryland Archives, Vol. xlviii, 515, 535, 579.

24. Ibid., 388.

25. Ibid., 130.

26. Robert Armistead Stewart, *The History of Virginia's Navy of the Revolution* (Richmond: By the author, 1933), 29. Stewart quotes Abraham van Bibber's correspondence.

27. Ibid., 6-7, 10-11. The Goodrich family included John Goodrich and several sons: John, Jr., William, Barlett, Bridger and Edward. Patriots at the start of the war, then caught with contraband, the family switched to Lord Dunmore's side. As masters of several vessels of his fleet, they brought havoc to Bay shipping during 1775 and 1776. John, Sr., Barlett and Bridger were captured and jailed but all escaped to join Britain's loyalist forces in New York and Bermuda.

28. Ibid., 11.

29. Ibid., 70-71.

30. Maryland Archives, Vol. xlv, 202.

31. *Maryland Journal and Baltimore Advertizer,* 6 June 1780 and 16 July 1782.

32. Stewart, 54-55; also, Henry C. Wilkinson, *Bermuda in the Old Empire* (London: Oxford University Press, 1950), 377, 390, 396-397. Run out of Bermuda because they seized other Bermuda ships, and forced to leave New York with America's victory, the family migrated to London, finally settling in Bristol. Later, Bridger and Edward Goodrich returned to Bermuda where they continued privateering activities as opportunities were presented. After 1800, they both owned respected merchant houses on the island. Both will be heard of again as they became naval agents for the Admiralty and contractors for Royal Navy ships.

33. C. O. Lanciano, Jr., *Captain John Sinclair of Virginia* (Gloucester, Virginia: Lands End Book, 1973), 66-67.

34. *Enterprize,* pilot schooner; Revolutionary War Vessel Bonds, National Archives; Marshall Booker, *Privateering from the Bay; Chesapeake Bay in the American Revolution,* Edited by Ernest McNeill Eller (Centerville, Maryland: Tidewater Publishers, 1981), 41n, 269-272. This schooner may have served in the Continental Navy before she was a Maryland privateer.

35. Ibid.

36. The author has identified from commercial and official sources approximately 700 pilot schooners-pungies. This group of baycraft is used to calculate statistical tables and charts in this book.

37. Judge Jones Records, Maryland Historical Society, MHS-MS-517.

38. Thomas A. Harrison, *Annals of Talbot County,* Industrial, Vol.vi, 19-21. Maryland Historical Society, MHS-MS 432.

39. Baltimore Enrollments, RG41 National Archives, hereafter cited as NA.

40. Transactions of the American Philosophical Society, Philadelphia, 1789, Vol. 1, 357.

41. Moreau de St. Méry, *American Journey, 1793-1798.* Translated and edited by Kenneth and Anna M. Roberts (Garden City, New York: Doubleday & Co., Inc., 1947), 71-73.

42. Baltimore Enrollments, RG41, NA.

43. *Two Brothers,* built by Gabriel Miller, boatwright; *Punch,* pilot schooner, built by David Stodder; carpenter certificate information from Granofsky Collection, Maryland Historical Society, MHS-MS 2383.

44. Invoices of William Price, 1784-89. Virginia Archives, Entry 300, Box 1133.

45. Letter, George Washington to Alexander Hamilton, 8 November 1790. *The Papers of Alexander Hamilton,* Edited by Harold C. Syrett (New York: Columbia University Press, 1967), Vol. vii, September 1790-January 1791, 143-44.

46. Letter, G.W. to A.H., 20 September 1790, Syrett, Vol. vii, 62.

47. A.H. to Benjamin Lincoln, Collector of Customs, Boston, 21 January 1791. Syrett, Vol vii, 446-47.

48. New York Enrollment #206, 11 July 1798. From Florence Kern, *Richard Taylor's U. S. Revenue Cutter Virginia* (Washington, D.C.: Alised Enterprises, 1977).

49. *Federal Gazette and Baltimore Daily Advertizer,* 9 July 1798.

50. J. J. Colledge, *Ships of the Royal Navy* (Annapolis: Naval Institute Press, 1987), 336.

51. David Steel, *Naval Architecture* (London: Published by the author, 1805), Vol. 2, Plate No. XXV.

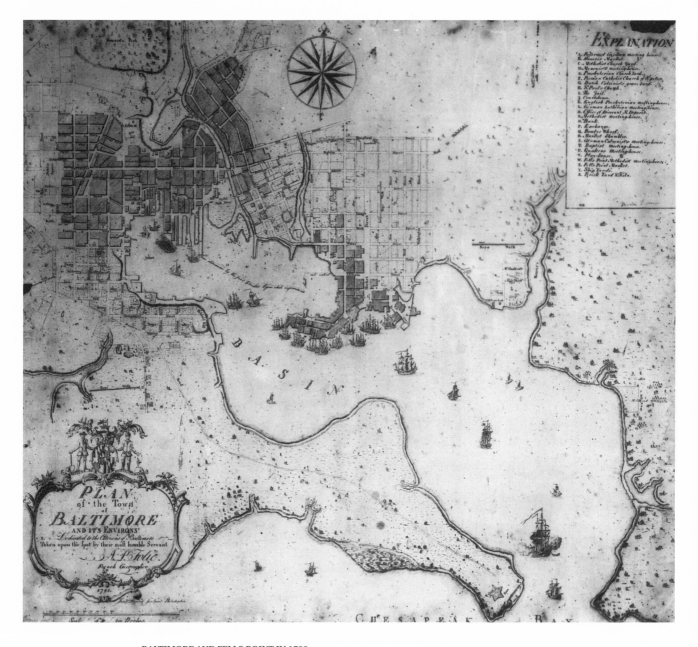

BALTIMORE AND FELLS POINT IN 1792

ARE SHOWN IN THIS WELL-KNOWN MAP BY A.R. FOLIO.

Maryland Historical Society, Baltimore.

CHAPTER FOUR

BALTIMORE SCHOONERS, PILOT-BOAT BUILT

Captain Jeremiah Yellott came ashore in 1781 for a career as merchant and shipowner which he anchored by marriage to his new partner's sister, Mary Hollingsworth.[1] He would become a leader of Baltimore's shipping community as America struggled through its formative years. Yellott's investments included 14 vessels and 44 voyages during the last years of the Revolution. In most of his ventures he shared ownership of vessels with Jesse Hollingsworth and John Sterett.[2] His brother-in-law Hollingsworth served as the Confederation's naval agent. The Steretts were important Baltimore merchants. Yellott, as United States Navy agent beginning in 1798, purchased the converted merchant ships USS *Baltimore* and USS *Montezuma* for the new navy and supervised the construction of USS *Patapsco*, USS *Maryland*, USS *Experiment* and USS *Enterprize*.

The Revolutionary War ended on Chesapeake Bay in the summer of 1783. As with the end of all wars, pent-up demand for goods produced an increase in commercial activity. Captain Yellott returned to sea, taking command of the schooner *Antelope*, a survivor of many wartime voyages. With a cargo of tobacco,

he sailed for Amsterdam to open a European market for this important product of Tidewater farms.[3] Bypassing England, and selling tobacco directly to customers on the continent produced an important change in Maryland's and Virginia's peacetime commerce. As the newly independent North American states would soon discover, developing new markets became the challenge as the United States struggled out of the bonds of colonialism over the next three decades.

Baltimore, after absorbing Fells Point in 1773, virtually dominated Maryland trade. Only remotely situated Somerset and Worcester Counties in Maryland, joining with Virginia's Eastern Shore counties, exported goods directly rather than through Baltimore or Norfolk. This remote area also traded with Philadelphia in locally-owned schooners and sloops operating outside the Bay on this short sea route.

Across the Bay, along Virginia's rivers—the Potomac, Rappahannock, York, James, and Elizabeth—planter-merchants operated their own vessels in foreign trade or loaded and discharged British ships at plantation landings as they had before independence. Virginia's overseas trade remained decentralized among several small ports and many river landings.

That hero of Maryland's Navy, Captain William Middleton, freed from British prison, returned to Chesapeake Bay. His pilot schooner *Sarah* cleared Baltimore on 29 January 1785 for the York River.[4] The Middletons, so much a part of the story of the pilot-boat schooner as it carried cargo and outsailed the Royal Navy in the eighteenth century, fade into history as local craft returned to their amorphous Bay trade after independence. As before the war, newspapers and official documents seldom mentioned the Bay's schooner fleet. The high profits of a risky wartime voyage or the delivery of gunpowder for Washington's army, feats that made them indispensable in wartime and newsworthy, were now old news.

As European markets opened up to America, Captain Yellott and his associates invested in new vessels, the ship-rigged *Iris* and *Pearce*, and the brigs *Commerce*, *Sally* and a new *Antelope*. Yellott also owned the sloop *Mohawk* and the schooners *Anna Maria* and *Camden*. He placed fore-and-aft-rigged vessels in the West Indies trade to St. Kitts, St. Croix, Havana and to the French islands. His schooners, though vastly improved, were still of traditional design. Relative safety at sea during the ten years following the signing of a peace treaty made speed a secondary requirement and made cargo space more important.[5]

United States ships lost access to the British West Indies when Navigation Laws, now directed against American ships, limited trade with England's colonies to British-owned vessels. The new republic was thus denied many of its traditional markets. However, Dutch islands were free ports and Spanish, Danish and Swedish possessions were accessible. And although Spain had colonial navigation laws similar to Britain's, she could not enforce them. France permitted American vessels up to 60 tons burden into her island ports. Whether or not French regulations could be enforced was a moot point as American vessels dominated shipping between United States ports and the French West Indies. Of a total of 101,417 tons of shipping entering U.S. ports from French islands in 1790, only 3,925 tons represented vessels flying the French flag.[6]

Baltimore's principal exports to the sugar islands continued to be flour, grain, bread, and other food items. Imports of food became all the more vital to island populations as increased sugar acreage left room for little else. Improvements in milling equipment, which reduced moisture content in Baltimore's flour, plus the short run between the Chesapeake and the Caribbean with bigger schooners and brigs, allowed the city's merchants to retain their comparative advantage. Though fast schooners reduced the chance of spoilage, good tightly ceiled vessels with normal speed proved satisfactory for this trade in times of peace.

By selling to French, Spanish, Dutch and other island importers, Baltimore merchants established a strong West

Indies trade despite the absence of trade with England's islands. American products reached British possessions in British ships legally, and also went through Dutch free ports or in American bottoms able to evade the Royal Navy. Sometimes British island governors declared their ports open to American shipping when there was danger of food shortages.

Virginia's foreign trade continued to be handled through British and French commercial agents buying and selling to planter-merchants. With trade fragmented as ships loaded and discharged at many locations, the old system perpetuated itself. A large portion of Virginia's foreign trade continued to be handled in vessels not owned by Virginians.

Norfolk's port activity during a five-month period between 2 March and 31 July, 1789, illustrates the point. During that interval a total of 35 British ships were recorded entering the port. The places of origin included the following British possessions: Jamaica-14, Antiqua-10, Barbados-3, Grenada-7, and St. Vincent-1.[7] During a six-week period between 1 March and 14 April, 1789, 25 Virginia-owned vessels entered Norfolk from ports outside Chesapeake Bay. Of the total, nine arrived from Philadelphia, four from New York and two from North Carolina. Only ten Virginia vessels completed foreign voyages during the period, and just six completed voyages to the West Indies. None of the ten vessels engaged in foreign trade were schooners. Four of them were sloops.[8]

Perhaps figures from these short periods do not produce a completely accurate picture of Norfolk's postwar foreign trade; they do illustrate the composition of Virginia's trade following the war. A dearth of independent merchants kept Virginia's merchant fleet small. Local shipowners preferred to send big sloops offshore, but pilot-boat schooners were used widely on the southern portion of the Bay. Eventually in the nineteenth century, foreign trade at Onancock on the Eastern Shore, Urbana on the Rappahannock River, and at small ports on the Potomac and York Rivers dried up, and the Hampton Roads ports of Newport News, Norfolk, and Portsmouth continued to compete with each other for Virginia's export and import trade until the creation of the Virginia Port Authority in 1978.

Charles Lee was Customs officer for the South Potomac District of the State of Virginia in 1785. Exports and imports entered several locations on the river, but Alexandria developed into the Potomac's principal port after the Revolution. Exports included tobacco, grain, some flour and forestry products. Alexandria's most important imports consisted of sugar, rum and European manufactures. After 1785, trade began to taper off until by 1787 no vessels in foreign trade docked at Alexandria. Virginia's customs procedures were more complex than Maryland's, making vessel owners subject to frequent penalties. To avoid these problems, ships bypassed the Virginia port for Georgetown, Maryland. Charles Lee called the situation "the fall of Alexandria."[9] The port's trade revived after

1789 when the U.S. Treasury Department established a national Customs service with uniform procedures.

At the close of America's first decade of independence, pilot schooners dominated marine traffic within the limits of Chesapeake Bay. The type was then fairly standardized in design and size. Baltimore merchants in 1790, happy with their traditional topsail schooners, brigs and ships, had no interest in using pilot schooners in offshore trades. As a matter of fact, enrollments and registers confirm that, prior to 1791, only the baycraft model of pilot schooner was built.

Hostilities between Great Britain and France resumed in 1793 after a decade of peace following the American Revolution. War among the Europeans offered lucrative opportunities for Baltimore's merchants, and there was soon a large increase in the Chesapeake region's overseas trade. The United States, by declaring its neutrality, placed its merchants in a position to collect vast profits by carrying non-military cargoes of the belligerent nations in vessels flying the American flag. In the view of the American government this activity was legal, but vessel losses mounted as the French and British acted against American ships carrying cargo formerly handled by their ships.

In the fall of 1793, the British government ordered all vessels carrying products of a French colony seized. They considered this action legal. Because neutral vessels had not carried the colonial produce of France in peaceful times, they determined that trade by neutrals should not be allowed during periods of war. President Washington disagreed and imposed an embargo on British imports to the United States. Great Britain backed off and commercial relations between the two nations stabilized with signing of the Jay Treaty in 1795.

To frame the facade of neutrality, American ship owners maintained the neutral status of their ships by carrying West Indies produce into American ports where the import cargo, once entered through Customs, became goods of American origin. Goods re-exported to a European port, principally sugar and coffee, then entered Europe as goods of a neutral nation. Additionally, colonial produce, imported into the United States under Customs bond, once on board an American carrier qualified exporters for refunds of duties under Customs drawback procedures.

Ships sailing directly from the West Indies to Europe faced high risk of capture by the Royal Navy or French privateers. Prices of sugar and other West Indies produce were very high in Europe, so the cost of transshipping via a neutral American port amounted to only a small percentage of the inflated price. The resulting opportunistic trade created tremendous profits for American shipowners, and Baltimore's merchants became rich after just a few such adventures.

The diplomatic premise for United States neutrality was "free ships make free goods." On a collision course with American diplomatic dogma was the

British Rule of 1756. The British position was that a neutral nation could not profit from wartime trade not previously conducted in times of peace. With the Jay Treaty, the two trading nations ignored rigid positions to accommodate current realities. Great Britain was conciliatory as her merchant fleet was fully employed and America, the world's number-two shipping nation and a big consumer of British goods, could do more harm as an ally of France.

The American insistence that her merchants had participated in trade between French colonies and American ports prior to 1793 made the clause on trade in the Jay Treaty unacceptable to the United States, and this section was never ratified. The clause specifically denied American vessels the right to carry molasses, sugar, coffee, cocoa and cotton from the United States to any port in the world. Rejected by the Senate, the controversial section of the treaty was not enforced in 1795, but became an issue in subsequent years when it was convenient for the British to enforce it.

British acquiescence to American neutral trade produced a large increase in the number of American ships involved in commerce with Britain and Europe. The trade with Europe in sugar, coffee and other produce of the West Indies exceeded 100,000 tons in 1796. America's trade with Great Britain and its colonies, including India and the West Indies, increased threefold.

While the benefits of the Jay Treaty were immediately positive for American merchants, the British policy of accommodation by non-enforcement left British-American trade policy in limbo, accounting for the on-again, off-again commercial war between Great Britain and the United States which culminated in the War of 1812.

On the other hand, the Jay Treaty was met with hostility by the French revolutionary government in Paris. To the French, the treaty placed America in a favorable position with Great Britain, yet provided means to starve out France and her empire if and when the British decided to enforce their Rule of 1756 by denying Americans the right to participate in neutral trade. Tensions continued to mount and American vessels, particularly those at sea in the West Indies, became subject to increasing seizures by the French Navy and privateers.

The effects of the Jay Treaty may be traced through the activities of the John Smith family firm of merchants. The firm's principals, Samuel and John Smith, Jr. applied themselves to making money in the 1790s, taking advantage of chaotic conditions brought on by insurrection in the French colonies and a new attack by Great Britain on France, already weakened by her revolution of 1789 and the rebellion of slaves in Haiti in 1792. Baltimore before 1792 was still a relatively small port city, but her overseas commerce was active and growing, and her merchants had unlimited access to grain, flour, bread and other food products upon which the West Indies planters and their slaves depended. Nevertheless, it was a hazardous enterprise to trade south. Not only would Samuel Smith's vessels need to avoid capture by the Royal Navy and British privateers, they would need to avoid capture by the disorganized naval forces of France, bitter over the Jay Treaty and prepared to seize American ships even as those ships supplied their own people. There were also privateers swarming around the French islands, and Smith's vessels had to avoid them to reach port. And there were pirate vessels with no allegiance lying in wait for fat merchant ships.

The adventures, as Smith called these trading voyages, may be traced through the correspondence of the firm as its managers, coolly in most instances, and always with a strategy, profited immensely during the years leading up to the start of America's Quasi War with France in 1798. The Smith ship *Louis*, John Deale, master, departed Fells Point for Port de Paix on Hispaniola in July 1794 with a cargo of flour and other grain and food products. To guide Captain Deale on the commercial aspects of disposing of his cargo, which was unsold, John Donnell, a participating merchant in the adventure, sailed on *Louis* as supercargo. As they sailed out of the harbor, Sam Smith was arranging insurance to cover risks of the voyage. In a letter to his agent he carefully pointed out that the outbound cargo was unsold, and therefore, as its owners were American, it would not be subject to British confiscation. The cargo that Donnell would purchase, coffee, would be paid for in specie (cash) and thus imme-

diately become American cargo not legally subject to an Admiralty Prize Court. He pushed to limit the premium to five percent of the value of the ship and cargo but had to settle for ten.

As the information recorded here is derived from Smith's outbound correspondence, a reader does not always know the complete story of a voyage, but the correspondence reveals that *Louis* reached Port de Paix and sold her cargo without mishap. In the meantime, the firm received word that their brig *Peggy* was captured by a Bermuda-owned three-masted schooner named *Enterprize*, owned by Bridger Goodrich, the loyalist from Virginia who had settled in Bermuda after his family left New York at the end of the Revolution.

Peggy was taken into Bermuda, and we read Sam Smith raging in his correspondence about the illegality of the action and the hopeless position the firm found itself in because of the corrupt judges on colonial prize courts. Smith was particularly agitated because he learned that Goodrich had five privateers positioned off the Florida Keys to intercept his ship *Louis*, which would be navigating those waters on her northbound voyage with a valuable cargo of coffee bought from Britain's enemy.

Smith moved quickly to control the situation. *Laura*, the firm's new pilot schooner, was made ready to sail. Captain Aldrick, her master, loaded a cargo of flour, beef and pork in her small hold. The captain's orders were to sail first to Bermuda and deliver Smith's instructions to his attorney concerning the disposition of *Peggy*'s case. At the completion of that mission, *Laura* was to sail to Port de Paix as quickly as possible to warn Captain Deale of *Louis* that Goodrich's privateers were waiting for him off Florida. When *Laura* completed these missions, Captain Aldrick was to sell his cargo at Port de Paix, load coffee and return to Fells Point.

Aldrick arrived and found Deale still loading a cargo of coffee aboard *Louis*. Forewarned, Captain Deale planned a new course to bring his ship through the Bahamas, safe from Bridger Goodrich but a dangerous route for a ship loaded with almost 500,000 pounds of coffee. Perhaps predictably, the ship ran aground in the Bahamas and lost her rudder. To save her, 60,000 pounds of coffee went over the side and lightened the vessel. Deale got water under her keel, made repairs and continued his voyage to Fells Point where he arrived about 1 March 1795. Smith bragged to a correspondent that profits for the voyage were $50,000, comparable to millions today. To complete the diplomatic manipulation to make the coffee an American product, it was discharged from *Louis*, entered through Customs at Baltimore, then reloaded on the ship *Carlisle* and sent on to Bremen. Smith did not have to pay American duties as they were refunded when *Carlisle* landed her cargo at her European destination.

It is not easy to piece together all the adventures that befell *Peggy* and her crew and cargo. She was captured twice by privateers before being captured by Bermudians. In the first instance she was taken before an Admiralty Court at Jamaica. Released from Jamaica, his cargo libelled, Captain Bryan sold the flour at St. Eustatius for cash. Sailing along the south coast of Hispaniola, *Peggy* was boarded by French privateers who forced her into a small cove where she hit a reef and lost her rudder. The pirates robbed her of everything they could move (she had no cargo) and left her. Captain Bryan was able to repair the damage and sail into a safe French port where he purchased a return cargo of coffee with the specie he had hidden from the thieves. With his coffee cargo on board, Captain Bryan, sick with fever, got underway but was hit by the main boom and fell overboard. The crew rescued him but he died. Mr. Storey, the mate, took command. Before they reached America, the brig was captured by Goodrich's *Enterprize* and taken into Bermuda where *Laura* had found her. Her cargo was libelled once again, and she was released, Mr. Storey reaching Fells Point about the same time as *Louis*.

Since Smith does not mention *Laura* again, it is assumed that the pilot schooner slipped through Goodrich's web and sailed back to Fells Point. When he returned, Captain Aldrick would have been well rewarded for his success as Sam Smith had promised him a salary of $50 a month and five percent of the gross receipts of his adventure.[10]

The Smiths enriched themselves despite the hazards of these voyages, although the adventures became increasingly difficult to conduct successfully with slower brigs and ships. *Laura*'s voyage proved a point: fast pilot schooners with smaller cargos were harder to catch and they could complete more voyages over a given period of time.

Revolution and the new war between France and Britain produced chaotic maritime conditions which made pilot schooners suddenly popular in the West Indies. Even before most Baltimore shipowners recognized the possibilities of offshore pilot schooners, maritime interests in the French islands saw the suitability of these schooners as blockade runners and privateers to counter the might of the Royal Navy. In the 1790s Baltimore shipowners had not reached the same level of desperation as the French, or even of the rebelling American colonists 20 years earlier. It is not surprising that most of the first offshore pilot schooners built were purchased by Frenchmen.

The pilot schooner model became familiar to French West Indians during the Revolutionary War. The acquisition of *Patriot* following the Battle of Yorktown, and her subsequent packet service at Cap François, Haiti, after 1783, was a contributing factor. Sales of pilot schooners after 1792 increased noticeably. Included was the sale of the William Price-built *Infant Patriot* to Pierre Santel of San Domingo, "together with her masts and spars as she now lays in the Port of Baltimore." *Infant Patriot* measured 40'3" along her keel, had a beam of 16', and depth of hold was 6' 5".[11] These measurements are very close to those of the Revenue cutter *Virginia*, built at Hampton in 1791, as well as to the

Virginia cutter *Patriot II* built several years earlier at Hampton, the Price yard's first location.

French agents in Baltimore made heavy purchases of Chesapeake Bay pilot-boat schooners in 1792. Many of these were baycraft: *Ann*, 33 tons;[12] *Experiment*, 44 tons;[13] *Greyhound*, 39 tons;[14] *Venus*, 36 tons;[15] and *Polly*, 39 tons[16] to identify a few. The French purchases reflected the growing unrest in the island colony we now know as Haiti and in other French West Indies possessions. Slave uprisings against French colonists, a minority among a population of black and mulatto slaves and laborers, had begun a year before hostilities between France and Britain started in 1793. By May of 1792 Port au Prince was in possession of the "mulatto" population. Whites controlled the towns of Cap François, Aux Cayes and Jérémie, and slaves controlled the countryside. This insurrection of Haiti's slave population, over 500,000 strong, with passive support by the revolutionary government of France, would send many of the 40,000 white French colonists fleeing to Jamaica and the United States.

Paul Bentalou, a merchant of French descent who had settled in Baltimore during the American Revolution, was appointed Naval Agent for the Republic of France. While his duties included husbanding French naval vessels and merchant ships, he also participated in the acquisition and outfitting of Chesapeake-built vessels for French privateers. Bentalou purchased the Maryland schooner *Industry*, built in Somerset

County in 1791.[17] After registering her on 2 July 1793, and outfitting her, Bentalou sent her to Charleston, South Carolina, under a French flag. With the southern city her new port, and renamed *l'Industrie*, she captured about a dozen British ships and sent them to Charleston between 1793 and 1795. In Charleston a prize court had been set up by the French Consul. Baltimore registers list several other Maryland ships purchased by Bentalou. James Cavan of Alexandria purchased several pilot schooners and other Maryland vessels, and then sold them to foreign interests during the same years. One such purchase was the pilot schooner *Maryland*, built by William Price in 1795.[18] Flying the French flag and with letters of marque granted by French Consuls, these Bay-built schooners formed an effective privateer force that operated out of American ports until the Federal government closed down their activities in 1795.[19]

Though it was France's need for privateering vessels that produced the original demand for large pilot schooners, there is no evidence that the French contributed to their design. Chesapeake Bay shipbuilders worked out models for the larger schooners, applying the proven proportions of the preexisting baycraft to produce the offshore version. The offshore pilot schooner's larger size resulted in a slightly different model, but the design remained true to the baycraft from which it was derived. One explanation for the development of these large pilot schooners includes the theory, unsup-

ported by any records, that these first Baltimore schooners represented the continuing evolution of traditional Maryland schooners, vessels of a type introduced to Chesapeake Bay in 1731 from New England. This thesis is incorrect.

A real problem for many maritime historians, particularly those who are naval architects, is that they do not understand the semantics of the time and the place. Builders of pilot boats of Hampton and Annapolis, builders of other schooner-rigged baycraft, and finally even the shipwrights who built the large offshore vessels identified as Baltimore schooners, were producing different versions of the original Chesapeake Bay pilot-boat model. These shipwrights all called the vessels they produced pilot boats. To them the only difference between the original baycraft pilot-boat schooner and the offshore Baltimore schooner was size.

While traditional topsail schooners changed significantly from Dr. Carroll's *Baltimore* in 1734 to Jeremiah Yellott's *Antelope* in 1780, the low-profile, shallow-hull, lightly-constructed pilot schooners, free of quarterdecks and topside weight, were always a unique model to their builders.

French demand, not French naval-architectural input, created the famous Baltimore schooner. A good example is *Flying Fish*, built in Somerset County, Maryland, in 1792. Her dimensions, 61' x 19'6" x 6'11", and especially the shallow depth of her hull, suggest that she was pilot-boat built. Referred to here as *Flying*

Fish I, (there were several schooners of this name) she received her Savannah register in December 1793, and was sold to French owners.[20] She was soon captured by the Royal Navy and then recaptured by the French in 1795. Renamed *Poisson Volant,* she enjoyed great success as a privateer, capturing a number of American merchant ships. The British retook her in 1797 and placed her in the Royal Navy. She was one of the earliest Chesapeake Bay pilot schooners taken into British service.[21]

A second schooner named *Flying Fish*, built in 1801, had dimensions of 73' x 22' x 9'.[22] Although she was built about eight years after the schooner we have identified as the first *Flying Fish*, this schooner's depth suggests that her model was closer in design to the traditional topsail schooners. *Flying Fish* II, also renamed *Poisson Volant* when commissioned by the French Navy, was captured by the Royal Navy in 1803, along with the French Navy schooner *La Supérieure*, a Baltimore schooner built in Talbot County in 1800.[23]

The seagoing version of the pilot schooner seems to have been built on the Bay everywhere at once. *Kitty*, built at Joppa, was sold at Cap François in 1792.[24] *Mary*, (78' x 21' x 7'8"), a sharp schooner built on the Nanticoke River in 1792 and measuring 111 tons burden, was transferred to a foreign buyer in 1793.[25] Good *Intent*, 81 tons, was built in 1792, and transferred in 1793.[26] *Little John*, built in Dorchester County in 1793, 106 tons, possibly was *Le Petit Jean*, a French privateer operating out of Charleston.[27] Lewis de Rochbrune, one of the first Eastern Shore shipbuilders to relocate at Fells Point, built *Hawke* in 1794 for John Carrere, a Baltimore merchant. This was the year that William Price built *Infant Patriot.*[28]

Naval architects speculating on the origins of the Baltimore schooner have forwarded the theory that the builders of Baltimore schooners were influenced by French vessels, specifically the lugger of Brittany. As most Marylanders and Virginians came to the American colonies from Great Britain or somewhere on the continent, it was natural that early shipbuilders incorporated influences from Europe in their vessels–except, of course, for the Chesapeake log canoe, a gift of native Americans to the white settlers.

Discussion of influences on ship design is mostly a speculative exercise conducted by naval architects. The development of a new design certainly entails the re-handling of preexisting design components. It is the emphasis that shipwrights place on specific aspects of design that determines the success of a new model built for a specific function–and in fact determines whether what results is really a "new" vessel. While a shipbuilder or shipwright may not be conscious of tradition, his ability to deal with the current needs of his clients will be influenced by tradition as he models a new vessel. Phasing out the traditional full-bodied schooners and adapting the speedier existing baycraft to offshore trades was a rare and noble accomplishment by the shipbuilders of the Bay, and it made the fortunes of Baltimore merchants as conditions in the West Indies deteriorated.

Although the French refugees at Baltimore in the 1790s had maritime traditions of their own, they embraced the swift pilot schooner of Chesapeake Bay as their best bet for what Baltimore's Smiths liked to call adventures. In June 1794, a Baltimore merchant of French descent, Lewis Pascault, placed the following advertisement in a Baltimore paper:

"A new vessel, burden 136 tons *of pilot boat construction* (italics added), built at Baltimore and launched the latter part of last month. She is built with live oak and cedar, nailed and finished in the French manner, being calculated for extra ordinary sailing." [29]

The builder of this schooner is unknown, although only four or five shipyards existed in Fells Point at that date. There is the possibility that one of the French immigrant shipwrights worked on this schooner, as the notice mentioned the schooner's finish in the French manner. This refers to carvings and other trimmings, characteristic of French-built craft but not usually required of Chesapeake Bay shipwrights. Moreau de St. Méry, in 1793, described American vessels as "strongly built, and the practice of keeping the upper works low adds greatly to their strength." He noted in his diary that American ships were good sailers but badly fitted-out. [30] That the schooner was described as "of pilot boat construction" virtually documents her

Chesapeake Bay design and origin.

A contemporary described Fells Point "as a part of Baltimore, but for all intents and purposes a separate town." Robert Weld, Jr., visiting the area in 1795, wrote that the Point included about 700 houses and "is the residence for seafaring people and for the junior partners [of the mercantile houses of Baltimore] who are stationed there to handle shipping." [31] It was during this last decade of the eighteenth century that shipwrights from Harford County in Maryland to Mathews County in Virginia moved to Fells Point.

David Stodder launched the schooner *Voluptus* at Fells Point in the fall of 1793. Her dimensions were 71' x 20'6" x 10' depth of hold. [32] Her last measurement, depth of 10 feet, provides the clue to her model, a schooner of the *Baltimore-Antelope* design. William Price built the schooner *Atlas* that same fall, and she measured 67'1" x 18'6" x 7'9", her hold more than two feet less deep than Stodder's *Voluptus*. [33] Price had built a schooner of pilot-boat model. Although this simple formula is not a foolproof method of identifying pilot schooners, it will be noted that at precisely the time that the construction of offshore pilot schooners commenced, the depth of new vessels dropped to conform with the ratios of length, breadth and depth associated with pilot-schooner design.

Shipwright Stodder built the schooner *Active* for Jeremiah Yellott in August of 1794. She measured 170 tons burden and her dimensions were 84' x 22'7" x 10'2". [34] *Active*'s depth makes identification of her model risky, but she was probably a pilot schooner. Richard Spencer of Talbot County built *Adventure* for Captain Yellott's account in 1795. Spencer's schooner, surely of the pilot-boat model, had dimensions of 94' x 24'3" x 10'3", and exceeded 200 tons burden.[35] The French captured *Adventure* off Guadeloupe the following year.[36] There is a painting of the Baltimore schooner *Adventure* reproduced in Melvin Jackson's book *Privateers in Charleston, 1793-1796,* although he dates the painting from 1793.[37] George Tobin's painting of a large Baltimore schooner at Hampton Roads in

1794 was not Yellott's *Adventure*, but one of the other large new schooners built in 1793-94. Such a large schooner of pilot-boat model would surely have attracted Tobin's attention.

Isaac Armistead relocated his shipyard to Fells Point about 1795. An early builder of Baltimore schooners, Armistead launched *Wolfe* for Robert Oliver. She was a sharp schooner of 143 tons burden and had measurements of 84'7" x 23' x 9'6".[38] He built *Friends Adventure* for David Stewart, *Happy Return* for Philip Rogers, and *Prosperity* for William Ringgold of Chester in Kent County.[39] This

UNIDENTIFIED
BALTIMORE
SCHOONER
ACCOMPANIED BY A
PILOT BOAT, 1794.
WATERCOLOR BY
GEORGE TOBIN.
National Maritime
Museum, London.

group of pilot schooners measured between 50 and 60 tons burden. *Happy Return* was condemned as a prize by the French in 1796.[40]

William Price launched a schooner named *St. Patrick* in the spring of 1796 at Fells Point.[41] He gave her a full and deep hull, but she was a flush-deck pilot schooner. He also built a very large pilot schooner called *Grace Ann* at Fells Point in 1796.[42] Her carpenter certificate is lost, and no builder is listed on her register. However, Robert Oliver noted on her Custom House register that John Gay "is the only owner," and in his letterbook he wrote to Gay about this schooner he had contracted with Price to build. She measured 220 tons burden, with a length of 93'6" and depth of just 10'8". *Grace Ann*'s size was greater than Thomas Kemp's *Rossie*, built in 1807, a renowned vessel of the War of 1812. It seems that by 1796 the Baltimore schooner had reached full size. Oliver wrote that *Grace Ann* was one of the most beautiful schooners ever built. She was built of live oak from stem to stern and cost almost $16,000. Gay was Oliver's agent on Martinique, and after a few voyages between Fells Point and that island the new schooner was sold to foreign buyers and lost at sea.

Privateers increased their attacks on American merchant vessels in 1796 after the Federal government moved to discourage the sale of ships to the French and shut down French privateer activity out of Charleston and other southern ports. Figures for captures by the French between 1797 and 1813 have been compiled, and the grand total of American ships is 1,434, according to Ulane Bonnel, writing about France's *guerre de course* tactics. She states that of this total, 692 passed through the courts with favorable decisions for the captors. This high total included vessels taken in all theaters. Madame Bonnel names the home ports of the prizes in most instances. Although Baltimore maintained a leading position in the neutral trade, the port's losses were less than ten percent of the 1,434 American vessels taken. This figure allows for significant margin of error because of incomplete data.[43]

The largest number of American losses to French privateers occurred between 1797 and 1800, a total of 834 vessels taken in just under four years. In this period, Madame Bonnel lists losses by Baltimore merchants at 38 vessels, or about four and a half percent of the total. Over the complete period of her study, 1797-1813, she lists only 82 losses for Baltimore shipowners. The Maryland captures included several baycraft pilot schooners, as well as brigs and ships on transatlantic trade routes.[44]

The conclusion that may be drawn from these inexact statistics is that Baltimore merchants, among the largest participants in the dangerous wartime shipping of the time, incurred relatively low losses, testimony to the skills of Chesapeake shipwrights in providing fast, nimble schooners, and of Chesapeake mariners in sailing them.

During this period of turmoil in the West Indies, the United States had not yet built its first navy ship. The loss of American ships and crews to the Barbary nations of North Africa stirred Congress in 1794 to appropriate funds to build six frigates. Work on the frigates slowed when problems in the Mediterranean subsided. But when France increased the level of belligerency in the Atlantic and the

Caribbean, the construction program was reactivated for three of the frigates in 1796. The construction of USS *Constellation* proceeded under the supervision of Captain Thomas Truxtun and shipwright David Stodder at Fells Point. The navy commissioned *Constellation* in the summer of 1798 as open but undeclared warfare commenced between France and the United States.

Fletcher Pratt, author of *The Navy, A History*, wrote that the designer of the first American frigates, Joshua Humphreys, modeled them on the lines of the pilot schooner. While one may agree that Humphreys did incorporate features commonly found in pilot-schooner design into his frigates, it may be more accurate to state that the Philadelphia builder-designer applied to his frigate design some basic hull characteristics of fast fore-and-aft-rigged vessels that had evolved in the Chesapeake during the previous 50 years.

No plans or models of the earliest large Chesapeake Bay pilot schooners have come to light, but carpenter certificates and registers with their record of owners provide useful information, as previously cited. There is evidence that drawings of the USS *Scourge*, formerly HMS *Transfer*, are the oldest Baltimore schooner lines on record. Sold out of the Royal Navy in 1802 to Count Golena of Malta, *Transfer* was captured in March of 1804 by USS *Siren*, Lieutenant Charles Stewart commanding. British records relate the schooner to the French privateer *Quatre Freres*, captured 21 November

1797. If this information is correct, USS *Scourge* was built in 1796 or earlier, at least four years prior to *Superior*, whose lines are reproduced in Chapter 5.

The plan, identified only as "*Transfer*, a fast vessel," has nothing else on its face. On the original, a curator informs that there is the following note on the reverse side: "for Captain Charles Stewart, Commanding United States Frigate *Constitution* off Boston, Massachusetts." Stewart was commander of USS *Siren* in 1804. This identifies the plan as the same discussed and redrawn by Howard Chapelle in *The Search for Speed Under Sail*. Chapelle did not make the connection between *Transfer* and USS *Scourge*.

J.J. Colledge identifies *Transfer* as a Royal Navy ship sold in Malta in 1802, which fits, and then describes her as a sloop of war, formerly the French privateer *Quatre Freres*, captured in November 1797. Jacques Vichot, compiler of a directory of French naval vessels, lists several craft by that name, including a corsair (privateer) of 1796-97 with no further description. There is no question that *Quatre Freres/Transfer/Scourge* is an early pilot-boat schooner built on Chesapeake Bay. Comparing her to the plan of *Superior* in the next chapter, their hull shapes are similar, particularly deadrise, long curving stems, and drag to the keel which gives both schooners a rather shallow forefoot.[45]

Shipbuilder William Price advertised a new pilot-boat schooner of 94-1/2 tons for sale in June 1798. He described his new schooner as built of the best sea-

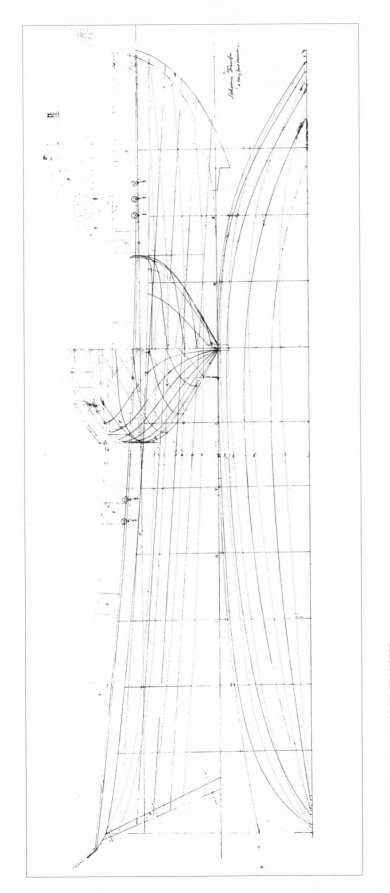

PLAN OF USS SCOURGE, EX-TRANSFER,

EX-QUATRE FRERES.

Lenthall Collection, The Franklin Institute, Philadelphia, PA.

soned white oak, supposedly remarkably fast, and completely finished. The fact that she remained unsold and that Price offered liberal credit to the buyers is worthy of note. The small-capacity pilot schooners were still looking for acceptance in 1798. Price, building on speculation, offered liberal terms to attract hesitant buyers.[46] Another possibility is that there was diminished demand for schooners at the beginning of America's undeclared war with France.

The switch from traditional eighteenth-century schooners, brigs and ships to pilot schooners on the Baltimore-to-West Indies trade route developed gradually. By 1800, in spite of high ship losses, the pilot-boat schooners still had not taken over the West Indies trade. Further, at the turn of the century, most Baltimore-owned schooners measured less than 100 tons burden. As long as merchants could afford rising insurance costs, many kept their older and larger brigs and ships.

Even as America's naval problems with France grew, the Royal Navy and British privateers continued to capture American ships. Estimates place losses to the Royal Navy and British privateers at approximately 90 Baltimore-owned merchant vessels in 1798.[47] Among the British privateers were the familiar Edward and Bridger Goodrich, whose vessels included *Enterprize*, already mentioned, and a schooner called *Experiment*.

Congress passed legislation in July of 1798 to authorize arming American merchant vessels. Under the act American captains could obtain letter-of-marque commissions permitting them to attack French vessels. While many Baltimore vessels carried these commissions and were armed, few actually became aggressive privateers during the Quasi War with France. Owners, more concerned with protecting their vessels against French privateers and preserving a profitable voyage, did not encourage masters to take French vessels as prizes. In the first nine months of these commissions, 61 Baltimore vessels received them, and there is no record that any of them brought in any French prizes. Of all the armed American merchant ships, only five captured French ships in that period.[49]

According to Federal vessel registers, the number of large pilot schooners built on Chesapeake Bay increased as the war began. Captain Yellott added *Cabot* (174 tons), *America* (139 tons), *Camden* (153 tons) and *Arb* (97 tons) to his fleet. *Arb* was built in Talbot County.[50] *Cabot*, built in April, 1799, completed a voyage from St. Thomas to Baltimore in ten days.[51] Thomas Tenant placed the schooners *Veteran* (112 tons), *Brutus* (114 tons), *Mexico* (67 tons) and *Spy* (90 tons) on the Baltimore-West Indies trade route in 1798.[52] He advertised a pilot schooner of about 80 tons for sale in 1799.[53] John Chalmers & Sons, ship chandlers, advertised two pilot schooners for sale at the beginning of 1799.[54] David Stodder, having completed *Constellation*, offered two pilot-boat-built schooners for sale at midyear in 1799.[55] Sales, as indicated by the number of newspaper offers, still lagged.

John Steele and Thomas Lambdin organized a new Baltimore shipyard in 1796. Steele, an early Fells Point builder, owned property on Pitt Street, just west of the Price yard. Steele and Lambdin delivered the flush-deck schooner *Ann*, a vessel of 156 tons, on 4 December 1798, to merchant John Hollins. Hollins obtained a letter-of-marque commission for *Ann* and dispatched her to the West Indies.[56] Steele and Lambdin built another pilot schooner of 75 tons on speculation the following year.[57]

Of the total of 65 Maryland schooners that received letter-of-marque commissions, the place of construction was noted for 43. Fells Point yards built just seven. Talbot and Dorchester County builders on the Eastern Shore built 15, and Maryland owners purchased the same number in Virginia. This breakdown illustrates once again that, at the turn of the century, Baltimore merchants continued to obtain most of their schooners from places other than Fells Point.[58]

Burden, expressed in tons on Federal registers, is known for 52 of the 65 schooners commissioned. More than half measured less than 100 tons. Twenty measured between 100 and 140 tons and only four could be classified as large schooners: *Ann* previously mentioned, *Charlotte* (176 tons) and *Exchange* (182 tons), both built near St. Michaels, and *Buckskin* (162 tons) built at Fells Point.[59]

William Price built *Buckskin* on speculation in 1798. Price called her "pilot-boat built" in his advertisement. He added that she was pierced for 16 guns and she would be sold complete with sails and rigging.[60] John Smith, Jr. purchased *Buckskin* and registered her 5 September 1798 at the Baltimore Custom House. She measured 83'3" x 22'6" x 9'10".[61] She was lost at sea in September 1800.[62] From that date, Baltimore schooners were more frequently sighted on the West Indies trade route. Guarding the route were America's first naval squadrons, which in 1800 included USS *Experiment* and USS *Enterprize*, the first Baltimore schooners built for the United States Navy.

ENDNOTES - CHAPTER FOUR

1. John Bosley Yellott, Jr., "Jeremiah Yellott-Revolutionary War Privateersman and Baltimore Philanthropist," *Maryland Historical Magazine,* Vol. 86-2, 179.

2. Todd Cooper, *Trial and Triumph, the Impact of the Revolutionary War on Baltimore Merchants;* Ernest M. Eller, Editor, *Chesapeake Bay in the American Revolution,* (Centreville, Maryland: Tidewater Publishers, 1981), 307.

3. Prefederal Customs Records, Baltimore Entrances and Clearances, 1783-89, Maryland Historical Society, MHS-MS-2301. Maryland Historical Society is hereafter cited as MHS.

4. Ibid.

5. Ibid.

6. A.T. Mahan, *Sea Power in its Relations to the War of 1812* (London: Sampson Low, Marston & Co. Ltd., 1905), Vol. 1, 83. Mahan quotes from American State Papers, Vol. x, 47.

7. Virginia Archives, Virginia State Library: Entry 302, Box 1151. This reference hereafter cited as VA.

8. Ibid.

9. VA, Entry 301, Boxes 1147, 1149.

10. Excerpted from Samuel and John Smith, Jr.'s company correspondence to various agents, customers, captains, etc. between 1 July 1794 and 20 March 1795; Book 111, MHS MS 1152. *Laura,* pilot schooner, Baltimore register #8, 10 January 1795, built by Charles Pearce, North Point, Maryland, measuring 59'11" x 17'2" x 6'11"; 62 tons burden. The Smiths purchased a second pilot schooner later that year: *Molly,* Baltimore register #122, 7 July, 1795; built by Thomas Kemp of St. Michaels, Maryland. Larger than *Laura,* she measured 62'4" x 18'5" x 7'5"; 73.5 tons.

11. William Calvert Steuart, "Notes on the Baltimore Clippers," *Maryland Historical Magazine,* Vol. 47, December 1952, 356. Steuart quotes an original bill of sale, copy in possession of the author.

12. *Ann,* pilot-boat schooner; Baltimore register #78, 1792, built in Maryland; transferred foreign at Port au Prince, 26 December 1792. RG36-41, National Archives. This reference hereafter cited as NA.

13. *Experiment,* pilot-boat schooner; Baltimore register #64, 1792: owner, Lewis Pascault; built Choptank, 1788, transferred to Charleston. RG36-41, NA.

14. *Greyhound,* pilot-boat schooner; Baltimore register #41, 1792; built East River, Virginia, 1792; sold to Port au Prince, 1792. RG36-41 NA.

15. *Venus,* pilot-boat schooner, Baltimore register #38, 1792; transferred at Hispaniola, July 1793, RG36-41, NA.

16. *Polly,* pilot-boat schooner; Baltimore register #30, 1792; owner, Claudius Bosse; built Choptank, 1784; sold at Aux Cayes, 1792. RG36-41, NA.

17. Paul Bentalou's Journal, MHS-MS125.

18. *Industry,* schooner, Baltimore register #71, 2 July 1793. *Maryland,* pilot schooner, Baltimore register #213, 14 November 1795; built by William Price at Fells Point; measuring 62' X 17'3" x 7'1/2". RG36/41, NA.

19. Melvin H. Jackson, *Privateers in Charleston,* 1793-1796.(Washington, D.C.: Smithsonian Institution, 1969), Appendix 2, 127-52.

20. *Flying Fish,* pilot boat schooner; Baltimore register # 84, August, 1793. RG36-41, NA.

21. J.J. Colledge, *Ships of the Royal Navy* (Annapolis: Naval Institute Press, 1987), 138.

22. *Flying Fish,* schooner; Baltimore register #2, 1802. RG36-41, NA.

23. Colledge, 138.

24. *Kitty,* pilot-boat schooner, Baltimore register #5, 1792; built at Joppa; transferred to Cap François, 1792. RG36-41, NA.

25. *Mary,* pilot-boat schooner, Baltimore register #39, 1792; built on Nanticoke River, 1792; transferred to foreign owners, 1793. RG36-41, NA.

26. *Good Intent,* pilot-boat schooner, 81 tons; Baltimore register #69, 1792; notation on register: transferred to foreign owners, March 1793. RG36-41, NA.

27. *Little John,* schooner, Baltimore register #2, 1794; built in Dorchester County, 1793. RG36-41, NA. Jackson, 138-39.

28. *Hawke,* pilot-boat schooner, Baltimore register #169, 1794. RG36-41, NA.

29. *Maryland Journal and Baltimore Universal Daily Advertizer,* 17 June 1794.

30. Moreau de St. Méry, *American Journey,* 1793-1798, Translated and edited by Kenneth and Anna M. Roberts (Garden City, New York: Doubleday & Company, Inc., 1947), 4.

31. *Baltimore Herald,* 25 March 1894, quoting Robert Weld, Jr., *Travels Through the United States in 1795.* MHS-MS, 1946.

32. *Voluptus,* schooner, Baltimore register #119, 1793. Certificates of Registry, 1789-1811. Bureau of Customs, RG36-41, NA.

33. *Atlas,* pilot-boat schooner, Baltimore register #195, 1794. RG36-41, NA.

34. *Active,* schooner, Baltimore register #124, 1794. RG36-41, NA.

35. *Adventure,* pilot-boat schooner, Baltimore register #107, 1795. RG36-41, NA.

36. Abstracts of Registers, 1798-1810. RG36-41, NA.

37. Jackson, 86.

38. *Wolfe,* pilot-boat schooner, Baltimore register #134, 1794. RG36-41, NA.

39. Registers #121, 216, & 225, 1794. RG36-41, NA.

40. Abstracts of Registers, 1798-1810. RG36-41, NA.

41. *St. Patrick,* Baltimore schooner, Register #74, 1796. RG36-41 NA.

42. *Grace Ann,* Baltimore schooner, Register #218, 1796. RG36-41 NA, and Robert Oliver's Letterbook 1795-1796, MHS 626.1.

43. Ulane Bonnel, *La France, Les Etats-Unis et la Guerre de Course,* 1797-1815 (Paris: Nouvelles Editions Latines, 1961), 319-407.

44. Ibid.

45. Howard I. Chapelle, *The Search for Speed Under Sail,* 1700-1855 (New York: W.W. Norton & Co., Bonanza Edition), 227-29; Journal of Midshipman F. Cornelius de Krafft, dated 18 March 1804. *Naval Documents Related to the United States Wars with the Barbary Powers,* edited by Dudley W. Knox (Washington, D.C.: U.S. Government Printing Office, 1941), volume III, 502-03. Also, Colledge, 353; Colledge gives *Transfer's* measurements as 80' x 23.5"; no depth of hold; also, Jacques Vichot, *Repertoire des Navires de Guerre Francais* (Paris: Edite par L'Association des Amis des

Museés de la Marine, 1967), 112.

46. *Federal Gazette and Baltimore Advertizer,* 5 June 1798.

47. Jerome R. Garitee, *The Republic's Private Navy* (Middletown, Connecticut: Wesleyan University Press for Mystic Seaport, Inc., 1977), 25.

48. Henry C. Wilkinson, *Bermuda from Sail to Steam, A History of the Island from 1784 to 1901* (London: Oxford University Press, 1973), Vol. 1, 79-81.

49. *Naval Documents Related to the Quasi War Between the United States and France,* Edited by Dudley W. Clark (Washington, D.C.: U.S. Government Printing Office, 1938), Vol. December 1800-January 1801, 364, 439. This reference hereafter cited as QW.

50. Abstract of Registers, 1798-1810, RG36-41, NA and QW, Vol. December 1800-January 1801, 376-438.

51. *Baltimore American and Daily Advertizer,* 18 May 1799.

52. QW, Vol. December 1800-December 1801, 376-436.

53. *Federal Gazette ,* 28 January 1799.

54. *Federal Gazette,* 1 January 1799.

55. *The Baltimore American,* 29 July 1799.

56. *Ann,* pilot-boat schooner, Baltimore carpenter certificate, and Baltimore register #207, 1798. RG36-41, NA.

57. *The Baltimore American,* 6 November 1799.

58. QW, December 1800-December 1801, 376-436.

59. Ibid.

60. *Federal Gazette,* 10 July 1798.
    Buckskin, pilot-boat schooner, Baltimore register #148, 1798. RG36-41, NA.

62. Ibid., pencil notation.

USS *ENTERPRIZE*, SHOWN FOLLOWING REBUILDING AT
THE VENICE ARSENAL IN 1805. THIS ETCHING BY JEAN
JEROME BAUGEAN SHOWS *ENTERPRIZE*'S RESHAPED
STERN.

Charles H. Taylor Collection.

Naval Historical Center, Washington, DC.

THE NAVY'S PILOT SCHOONERS

The United States Navy was separated from the Department of War in April of 1798. President Adams selected Benjamin Stoddert of Georgetown, Maryland, to be the first Secretary of the Navy. The undeclared Quasi War with France, fought in the Caribbean, challenged the French Navy and France's West Indies privateers who were plundering American ships. Stoddert's fleet consisted of three frigates, *United States, Constitution,* and *Constellation,* some converted merchant ships, and citizen-financed frigates and sloops of war. Included in the last group were USS *Maryland,* built by William Price, and USS *Patapsco,* built by Lewis de Rochbrune, both of Fells Point.

The U.S. Navy's first officers were a mixed bag of merchant seaman, old officers of the Continental Navy, and some young adventurers. Stoddert ordered his small fleet to patrol the sea lanes and guard the American merchant fleet in the West Indies.

French privateers preferred to attack in narrow passages where merchantmen had limited maneuverability. Their small boats and barges dashed out from island lairs and swarmed on helpless ships, schooners and brigs laboring through dangerous passages. The navy could patrol the normal sea lanes and convoy American vessels, and on occasion capture a French craft, but for the most part the larger ships of America's first naval squadrons proved to be ineffective against the small, fast schooners and shallow-draft barges and boats employed by the French.

The capture of the French privateer schooner *Le Croyable* by USS *Delaware* (Captain Stephen Decatur, Sr.) off the coast of New Jersey was the new navy's first prize. The schooner, believed to be a Chesapeake Bay pilot schooner, was taken into the U.S. Navy as USS *Retaliation.* With Lieutenant William Bainbridge her commander, she set sail 15 October 1798 to join the American fleet in the Caribbean. But, once there, Bainbridge got his schooner under the guns of the French frigates *Volontaire* and *l'Insurgente* and was forced to surrender.[1] USS *Retaliation* was the only American naval vessel lost to the French. Captain Bainbridge became a forceful opponent of Baltimore schooners inside the navy, a position that had significant consequences for the service in subsequent years.

During the first days of spring 1799,

Secretary Stoddert, at the suggestion of President Adams, wrote to his Fells Point Naval Agent, Captain Jeremiah Yellott, informing him that Congress had authorized the construction of six small vessels, as "only fast vessels could be effective against the French." Stoddert, with an informality inlaid with trust, instructed Yellott to have such a fast vessel built at Fells Point "as there is no person on the Continent better able to direct the construction of these kind of vessels, I beg the favor of you to have one built and fitted out as early as possible."[2]

Yellott or his superintendent, Captain William L. Richardson, supervised every phase of the construction of USS *Experiment*, the U.S. Navy's first Baltimore schooner. For a hull of pilot-boat construction, he appointed William Price to be the constructor.[3] Price proceeded to build a schooner generally based on the lines of the commercial versions he had been building since 1794, but probably with less rake to her stem and stern to give her stronger ends. No drawings or specifications for *Experiment* survive.

William Price received $3,787.71 for *Experiment* 's hull and copper work.[4] Her standing rigging, masts, yards, booms and gaffs were the work of the Fells Point firm of Dixson Brown. William Jacobs, the Point's leading sailmaker, made her sails.[5] The method of construction was to build the hull at Price's yard behind his Pitt Street house (now Fell Street). Once launched, the hull was towed a few hundred yards to Captain Yellott's wharf,

which fronted on Fell Street (now Thames Street).[6] Here Captain Richardson, formerly master of Yellott's schooner *Arb*, supervised subcontractors.[7] Joseph Biays crafted the joiner work and William Smith manufactured her rope. Thirty tons of pig iron ballast went into her bilges.[8]

About five weeks after ordering the construction of *Experiment*, Secretary Stoddert wrote to Captain Yellott and requested him to build a second pilot schooner as quickly as possible and "with respect to both I rely entirely on your judgement and experience."[9]

With William Price's shipyard busy building the sloop of war USS *Maryland*,[10] along with USS *Experiment*'s hull, Captain Yellott gave the order for the hull of the second pilot schooner to an Eastern Shore shipwright. This schooner Secretary Stoddert named *Enterprize* .[11]

The builder of USS *Enterprize*'s hull remains a question after almost two centuries. Although Captain Yellott's financial reports include a payment of $3,489.02 to Henry Spencer for *Enterprize*'s "builder's bill," the builder's name remains a mystery.[12] There is no record of a shipwright by that name in Maryland in 1799. The Spencer family had yards on the Chester River in Kent County and in the St. Michaels' region of Talbot County. At the time of *Enterprize*'s construction, both Richard and Perry Spencer were building pilot schooners, and the State of Maryland had honored both with the titles of State Shipwright. A third brother, Henry Spencer, a member of the crew of the Continental frigate *Virginia*, never

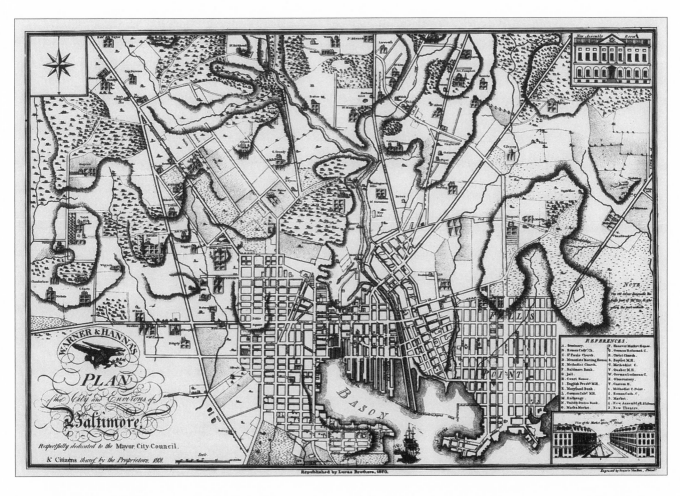

BALTIMORE AND
FELLS POINT.
WARNER AND
HANNA MAP, 1801.
Peabody Library,
Baltimore, MD.

returned to Talbot County following the Revolution, according to family records.[13]

There are possible explanations to the name in Yellott's accounts and for the use of the words "builder's bill." The term "builder's bill" implies that Henry Spencer was receiving payment in behalf of someone else. Another explanation is that the Federal government's accountant mistakenly substituted Henry for Perry, or possibly for Hugh Spencer, a shipwright working in Kent County. The basis for crediting Richard Spencer as *Enterprize*'s builder was his prior relationship with Captain Yellott, which included the building of the large pilot schooner *Adventure* in 1795.

The evidence in Yellott's accounts that tends to confirm that *Enterprize* was built outside of Baltimore are Dixson Brown's invoices. The Baltimore sparmaker billed Yellott $139.56 for the schooner's masts and spars plus $289.76 for stage hire and labor. As the masts for the schooner would be stepped during the construction of her hull, the extra invoice for stage hire and labor covered the cost of moving the riggers between Baltimore and the Eastern Shore.[14] Following the launching of *Enterprize*'s hull, Captain Yellott brought her to his dock at Fells Point to be completed under the supervision of Captain Richardson.[15]

Robert Smith, Secretary of the Navy in Thomas Jefferson's administration, making preparations to award the construction contract for the navy pilot schooner *Vixen* to William Price in 1803, contacted John Stricker, then Naval Agent at Baltimore, and asked him to obtain *Enterprize*'s dimensions from Captain Yellott, as "he wanted the new schooner built to her exact model." These are the figures supplied:

84' on the gun deck

60' length of keel

22'6" beam, moulded

23' out to outside of her bends

9'6" depth of hold[16]

USS *Experiment* and USS *Enterprize* might be assumed to be alike, but this may not be true. Following her sale to private owners, *Experiment* was registered at the Baltimore Custom House, 23 November 1801. The register includes the following measurements:

Her length..............................82'

Her breadth...........................23' 6"

Her depth............................. 9' 1"

She measures........................152 tons

and 53/95 parts of a ton[17]

Captain Yellott had *Experiment* ready for sea near the end of October, 1799.[18] Obtaining commitments from young officers to serve on the Baltimore schooners proved to be difficult and frustrating to Stoddert and Yellott. Several declined to serve. Finally, after agreeing to changes in the schooners' guns and quarters, Stoddert signed John Shaw as commander of *Enterprize* and William Maley for *Experiment*.[19]

Captain Yellott fought hard against the increased weight of more guns and protested that heavy timbers to protect crews quarters would hurt the sailing qualities of the schooners. Their ability to sail fast and close to the wind depended on keeping down weight above the waterline. To his pleas to keep the schooners free of the major changes demanded by Maley and Shaw, Stoddert responded that the Naval Agent's reasons were sound and that the young officers failed to estimate justly the opportunity to distinguish themselves. In support of Yellott, the Secretary wrote that "I did not mean to intimate a wish that any material alteration be made in *Enterprize*."[20]

Remarkably, 195 years after she was built, drafts of USS *Enterprize* seem to have turned up in Italy. This discovery was not a stroke of good fortune but rather a piece of detective work by Commander Michael L. Bosworth, USN. Bosworth, a naval architect assigned to the Office of the Chief of Naval Operations, made inquiries to the Venice Arsenal where *Enterprize* had a major overhaul in 1805. At the time he was preparing a student proposal to build a replica of the schooner in Baltimore.[21]

Bosworth's inquiry, which he sent in

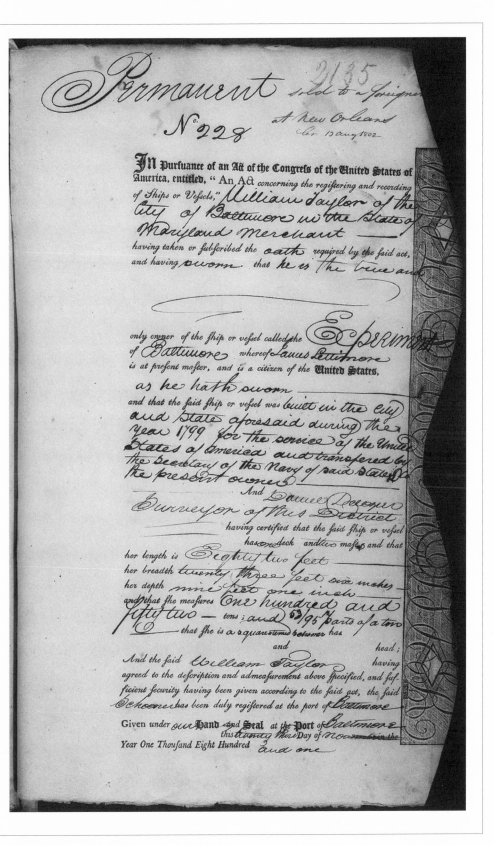

Permanent sold to a foreigner

2135

No. 228   at New Orleans
                          Cer. 13 Aug 1802

IN Pursuance of an Act of the Congress of the United States of America, entitled, "An Act concerning the registering and recording of Ships or Vessels," *William Taylor of the City of Baltimore in the State of Maryland Merchant* having taken or subscribed the *oath* required by the said act, and having *sworn* that *he is the true and*

only owner of the ship or vessel called the *EXPERIMENT* of *Baltimore* whereof *James Lettimore* is at present master, and is a citizen of the United States, *as he hath sworn* and that the said ship or vessel was *built in the City and State aforesaid during the year 1799 for the service of the United States of America and transfered by the Secretary of the Navy of said States to the present owner* And *Daniel Delozier Surveyor of this District* having certified that the said ship or vessel *has one deck and two masts* and that her length is *Eighty two feet* her breadth *twenty three feet six inches* her depth *nine feet one inch* and that she measures *One hundred and fifty two* — tons; and *52/95* parts of a ton — that she is a *square sterned schooner* has

and   head;

And the said *William Taylor* having agreed to the description and admeasurement above specified, and sufficient security having been given according to the said act, the said *Schooner* has been duly registered at the port of *Baltimore* Given under *our* Hand and Seal at the Port of *Baltimore* this *twenty third* Day of *November* in the Year One Thousand Eight Hundred *and one*

BALTIMORE CUSTOM HOUSE REGISTER OF USS *EXPERIMENT*, 1801. *National Archives, Washington, DC.*

1993, was unanswered for almost a year. Finally his letter passed into the right hands, for in August 1994 he received a response from Mario Marzari, biographer of engineer Andrea Salvini, naval architect of the Arsenal of Venice during the period that *Enterprize* was there. With the letter, Dr. Marzari enclosed a copy of his book and two drafts, one of which he believes records the lines and details of USS *Enterprize* after she was repaired under engineer Salvini's supervision.[22]

The Venice Arsenal plans do not include the schooner's name, but several experts have examined them and believe that Plan B, so identified by Marzari, may be the navy schooner after she was rebuilt. Dr. Marzari believes that Plan A was drawn by Salvini for his own purposes and does not necessarily reflect *Enterprize*'s lines or specifications. Marzari writes further that no information exists in the Venice Arsenal records to indicate that schooners of *Enterprize*'s design were familiar to Salvini before she arrived in late 1804. Confirmation of this find will not be possible until a search is made through the engineer's papers.

If it can be proved that Plan B is a draft of *Enterprize*, this would solve a unique mystery of naval history: just how different were *Experiment* and *Enterprize* from other Baltimore schooners. Their design is assumed to be the result of a collaboration between Yellott and the builder of *Experiment*, William Price. Were the navy schooners much like *Superior* and *Nautilus*, vessels built for merchant owners, or had Yellott, Price and the Spencers of St. Michaels designed schooners specifically for naval service?

Comparing the Venice draft of *Enterprize* with *Superior*, the answer, as suggested by Salvini's drawing, is that they were quite different. The Yellott-Price design, as illustrated by Plan B, was a relatively conservative pilot schooner. This may have been the result of the criticism Captain Yellott and William Price were receiving from Captains Thomas Truxtun and John Rodgers concerning the sharp design of USS *Maryland*, a citizen-financed sloop of war which Price was building next to the hull of *Experiment*. Or the conservatism of what may be *Enterprize*'s lines may simply reflect an awareness by these clever men that navy ships and naval officers had a different set of requirements than merchants.[23]

Salvini's drawing illustrates the principal differences between the naval and merchant interpretations of the Baltimore schooner. Drawing B shows a schooner with more balanced deckline and sheer that rises at the ends for greater buoyancy. In addition, her stem and sternpost have less rake, and there is less drag to her keel than *Superior* and later armed Baltimore schooners — but perhaps more drag than USS *Vixen*, a vessel supposedly modeled after *Enterprize* a few years later. The entrance shown is quite short. If rebuilt as this plan indicates, *Enterprize* was a far more solid gun platform than the commercial schooners, though not so bulky as to become a slow sailer. She still shows significant deadrise and one flush deck. And since the length, width and depth

proportions of the pilot schooner were adhered to, much of her hull volume remained below the waterline, which would give her the sailing characteristics of a pilot schooner.

Variances from the commercial version of the pilot schooner are confirmed by comparing the lines of *Enterprize* with *Superior*'s plan below and *Nonpareil*'s half model in the next chapter. The more stable Yellott-Price design reflects the knowledge that, as navy ships, *Experiment* and *Enterprize* would be expected to stand and fight, and not run, as would merchant schooners and privateers if an opponent turned out to be an armed vessel.

Thomas Robinson Jr., *Enterprize*'s commander during the period of the schooner's rebuild at Venice, mentioned

in his correspondence with the Secretary of the Navy that her keel was not lengthened. Robinson reported that he had replaced the schooner's rotten stern post and had taken the square tuck out of her transom. If her measurement on deck was correctly taken from her post, these changes aft would not have altered her length on deck, unless the rake of the sternpost was increased.[25]

Robinson wrote to the Secretary of the Navy that it was necessary to replace *Enterprize*'s bow and stern. He wrote that he was concerned to preserve her model below the waterline and mused how he wished to have permission to give her a few feet more keel. But there is nothing in his correspondence or anywhere else to suggest that *Enterprize*'s keel was length-

USS *ENTERPRIZE*, DRAWING BY ANTOINE ROUX, 1806. THIS DRAWING CLEARLY SHOWS *ENTERPRIZE*'S REBUILT BOW AND STERN.
Musée de la Marine, Paris.

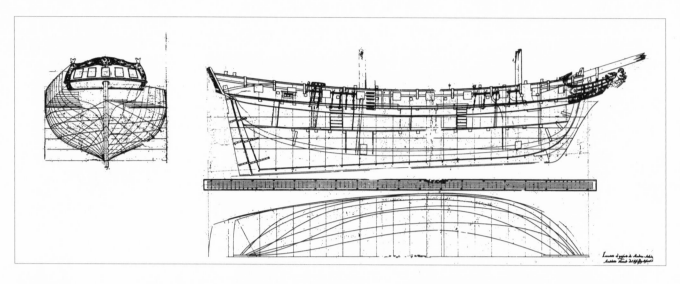

PLAN OF USS
ENTERPRIZE,
THOUGHT TO HAVE
BEEN DRAWN BY
ENGINEER ANDREA
SALVINI (PLAN A).
Courtesy of Mario
Marzari, Trieste,
Italy.

ened in Venice. However, by increasing the rake of *Enterprize*'s stem and stern-post, the arsenal's rebuild would have increased her length on deck without increasing her straight-rabbet keel length as originally built. These alterations as shown on Plan B, however, would change the location of her midsection, an adjustment which is indicated on the keel with two -O- marks, about six feet apart. This accounts for several additional feet in length on deck, bringing her overall deck measurement closer to the amount calculated by James Owner in 1808.

What Robinson and Salvini may have done was to replace her blunt bow, created by a tightly curved stem, with a longer and more raking stem which increased the fineness of her entrance and therefore, by this means, lengthened the schooner on deck. The new bow is visible in Roux's drawing which, by shadowing, he shows as somewhat concave. Likewise, the Salvini-Robinson transom is fully visible in the Baugean drawing.

The draft of *Superior*, a Baltimore schooner built in Talbot County the year after *Experiment* and *Enterprize* were built, is in the collection of England's National Maritime Museum. Her carpenter certificate and her original register, both dated 1800, are lost. On 7 January 1801, the Baltimore Custom House issued Temporary Register No. 7 to Robert Charles Boislandry and Felix Imbert of Philadelphia.[26] Notations on this register state that *Superior* was sold to foreigners while anchored at the French island of St. Barthélemy. Her new owner was the French Navy.[27] Renamed *La Supérieure*, she served in France's navy until 1803, when captured by the Royal Navy off San Domingo with *Poisson Volant*, ex-*Flying Fish* of Baltimore. As HMS *Superiere*, the Baltimore schooner was one of the earlier offshore pilot schooners to serve in the Royal Navy.[28] The Admiralty took off her lines, and the original plans are reproduced on page 92.

Superior's measurements are not on

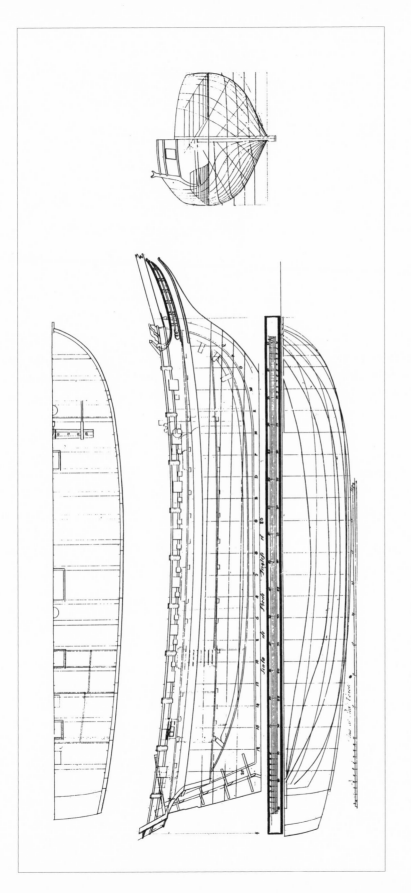

PLAN OF USS *ENTERPRIZE* AFTER REBUILDING,

THOUGHT TO HAVE BEEN DRAWN BY ENGINEER

ANDREA SALVINI (PLAN B)

Courtesy of Mario Marzari, Trieste, Italy.

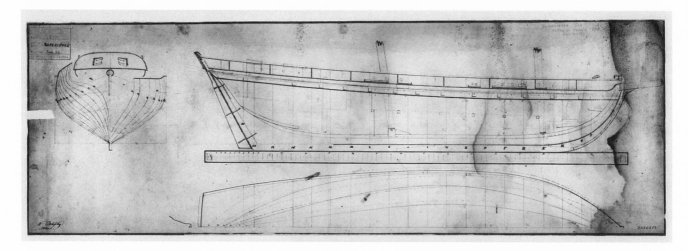

the British plan but her temporary Baltimore register lists them as 87'6" x 23'6" x 9'6" and tons burden of 172-48/95. A British Royal Navy directory gives her measurements as 86.5' x 23.5'.[29] Her plan shows a pilot schooner with a great amount of rake to her stem and sternpost. The combination of the extreme rake of the bow with excessive drag to her keel and an exceptional amount of deadrise provided *Superior* with a long fine run and the speed and agility of a racehorse. Her rather sharp hull would have a tendency to be crank in a blow, but her stability was improved by a conservative length/depth ratio of 9.1:1 and a length/breadth ratio of 3.7:1.

The drawing reveals that *Superior* was built with some tumblehome, placing her guns inboard and reducing somewhat the effect of their weight on the schooner's stability. Still, she was probably wet and difficult to handle, which would be one reason why the Royal Navy changed her rig from schooner to brig. *Superior*'s hull is much more gracefully

conceived than the Salvini *Enterprize* drawing called Plan B. With less deadrise, less drag to her keel and deep sheer rising to a broader bow, the possible *Enterprize* drawing B gives the navy schooner a bulkier profile. Both schooners would outsail other ships of the period, but *Superior* was probably faster, while *Enterprize*, would have been the better vessel at sea.

The numerous successes of the Baltimore schooners USS *Experiment* and USS *Enterprize* in 1800 and 1801 against French privateers demonstrated to the merchants of Baltimore and to the shipwrights of Fells Point and St. Michaels that their creation could outrun, or hit and run, anything afloat.

Lieutenant William Maley on his tour of duty as commander of *Experiment* captured at least 14 French vessels.[30] Lieutenant Charles Stewart, who replaced Maley, captured *Diana*, 14 guns, after cleverly separating her from an escort. Stewart also took *Deux Amis* and recaptured several American merchant vessels.

Enterprize, under Lieutenant John Shaw, took several French ships, including *La Flambeaux*, 12 guns and 110 men, and recaptured eleven American ships during a cruise that lasted eight months.[31]

Shaw, in a letter to a friend, wrote that he "took a total of thirteen sail of vessels, 300 French prisoners, and killed or wounded sixty-one."[32] Andrew Sterett replaced Shaw and captured the French vessel *L'Amour de la Patrie*.[33] The Baltimore pilot schooners had proven their value as naval vessels, despite the doubts of young officers and some veterans, and their success prepared the way for their wider use in the next decade as the nation moved toward the War of 1812.

Thomas Jefferson defeated the more hawkish Federalist party in the presidential election of 1800. The new president adopted a less-belligerent stance and reduced the navy's role on the high seas. He retained America's frigates on active or inactive status, but ordered all other small naval vessels, including USS *Experiment*, sold out of the service. The single exception was *Enterprize*, a lucky ship.

The navy scheduled an auction for *Experiment* in the autumn of 1801. Joshua Fox, Naval Constructor at Norfolk, was assigned to have her surveyed. A surveyor's report to the Secretary of the Navy concluded that the schooner's condition made her "not worth repairing."[34] As a second survey did not agree with the one ordered by Fox, Secretary Robert Smith ordered a third, made under his supervision. This survey confirmed the sound condition of *Experiment* and included the statement that the schooner would not require "one dollar's worth of repairs" to fit her for sea. Smith commented that as the administration will require a vessel of her size there is considerable uneasiness "from an apprehension that there was not due vigilance on our part."[35] *Experiment* was purchased by William Taylor in 1801, who sold her to foreigners. After her sale she disappeared from the records.[36]

Lieutenant Andrew Sterett assumed command of *Enterprize* in January, 1801. After a period of refitting, the schooner returned to action in the Caribbean. First, however, Sterett used his authority, normal for navy commanders in the period, and ordered changes in his schooner's spars. *Enterprize*, hauled alongside the frigate *President*, Captain Thomas Truxtun, commanding, had her masts removed and shortened.[37] Sterett's ideas may not have worked as the schooner received new masts at Fells Point that spring.[38] Alterations to *Enterprize*'s hull and rig continued through the years of her service. Eventually, re-rigged as a brig, she survived the War of 1812, during which the U.S. Navy lost several brigs, and confirmed her reputation for luck.

The already risky conditions at sea after 1800 became more hazardous with new attacks on American merchant ships by the corsairs of the Barbary Coast of North Africa. As the wars with France and other European powers dragged on, the Royal Navy stepped up activity off the French, Spanish and Portuguese coasts against United States shipping. Some observers believed that the renewed attacks by the North African nations had the support of the British government. The American government ordered a naval squadron to patrol the sea lanes off Gibraltar. A refitted USS *Enterprize* joined the fleet in the Mediterranean. Captain Alexander Murray wrote Navy Secretary Robert Smith that "if we are to continue this warfare nothing can be more eligible to cope with any force they [Barbary nations] fit out against us, than a number of such schooners as the *Enterprize*."[39]

The pirates used small craft, some the size of large rowboats, to attack merchant ships. The American consul at Tunis pointed out that a war against pirates could not be successfully prosecuted by frigates, and that vessels like *Enterprize* proved to be particularly handy for attack in coastal waters. "The pirates have no vessels able to fight our schooner," he reported.[40]

Responding to this advice, Smith initiated plans to rebuild that portion of the Navy eliminated the year before. A fine Baltimore-type schooner of unusually large dimensions was brought to his attention. In spite of an unfavorable report on the schooner by Captain William Bainbridge, Secretary Smith ordered Naval Agent John Stricker to purchase her from Thomas Tenant. Captain Bainbridge, in his report to the Secretary, stated that this vessel, named *Nautilus*, was so sharp that she had insufficient space for either crew or provisions, that the installation of bulwarks would hurt her sailing qualities, and that her extreme rake weakened her at the ends.[41]

Secretary Smith selected Lieutenant Richard Somers to take command of *Nautilus*. According to her register, she measured 184-40/95 tons burden and was built in Talbot County on Maryland's Eastern Shore. Tenant registered her as a new vessel at the Baltimore Custom House 25 September 1801. The register lists her dimensions as 87'6" x 25'8" x 9'10".[42] Her length-to-depth ratio is almost exactly 9:1 and length to beam, 3.41:1. The length of her keel is unknown. With greater beam and depth than *Superior*, she was probably more stable and a better sailer, particularly in a blow.

Keel lengths appear only on carpenter certificates and are not the actual length but an arbitrary formula with which to calculate carpenter's tonnage. Waterline lengths are usually unknown unless a plan is available. Ratios of length/depth and length/width are used in this text to illustrate variations in models as the Baltimore schooner developed, and to demonstrate how builders controlled stability. The builders of large schooners, pilot-boat built, clearly maintained a fairly constant length/depth ratio which, in turn, was related to the need to control stability by limiting weight above the waterline, then varying breadth with the degree of deadrise built into each schooner. It was a near-perfect balance of these characteristics that created the performance and the almost legendary success and beauty of Baltimore schooners.

In a letter to his brother, Lieutenant Somers described *Nautilus*'s bottom as like a wedge; that she would not stand

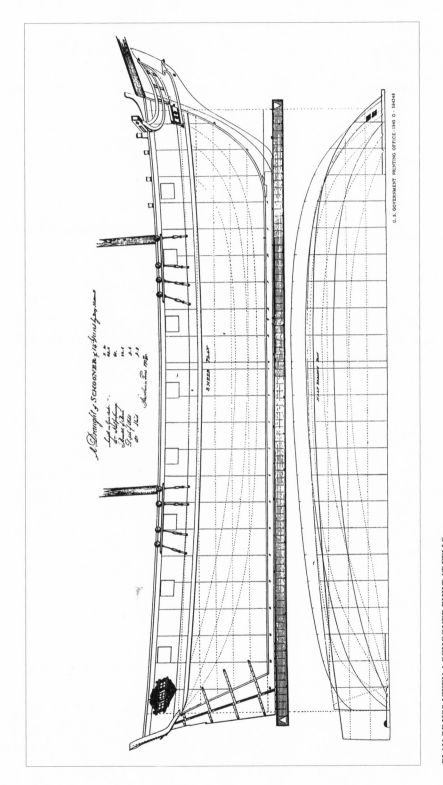

PLAN OF USS *VIXEN*, A SCHOONER BUILT AT FELLS
POINT BY WILLIAM PRICE IN 1803. FROM *BARBARY
WARS, PERSONNEL AND SHIP DATA, 1801-1807.*
U.S. *Government Printing Office, Washington, DC.*

without ballast; that her bow was so sharp that she could not keep it above water in any sea. He wrote, "the man that sold her says he will be damn'd if anything that ever floated can beat her sailing."[43] Enroute down the Bay, Somers reported that she passed everything while beating to windward, "specially a ship, a brig and one of the fast sailing pilot boats of Baltimore."[44] Nautilus crossed the Atlantic to Gibraltar in 28 days.[45]

Lieutenant Somers' report on his crossing to Secretary Smith stated that Nautilus sailed fast, easy and was tight and strong. To his brother he wrote that his Baltimore schooner arrived with no paint, rigging bleached, and a suit of sails half worn. "This thing would wear the devil out in a short time if he was anywhere forward of the mainmast." These comments, and a 28-day crossing, indicate heavy weather during much of the passage.[46] They are also a rare summary of the characteristics and sailing qualities of offshore Chesapeake Bay pilot schooners.

USS Nautilus, rigged as a brig, was captured by the Royal Navy in 1812. She served the English for several years, but her plan has not been located in Admiralty records at the National Maritime Museum.

Navy Secretary Smith decided to add another Baltimore schooner to the Mediterranean squadron. He wanted her built on the model of Enterprize and he asked Captain Bainbridge, stationed in Philadelphia, to have a drawing made according to dimensions which he passed along. Before Secretary Smith arranged with Bainbridge for a new draft, Smith asked Naval Agent Stricker to contact Jeremiah Yellott to procure Enterprize's plans. There is nothing in the record to indicate that Captain Yellott was able to produce Enterprize's draft. Upon receipt of a drawing from Philadelphia, Smith awarded the contract for the schooner to William Price. The navy named her USS Vixen.

Captain Bainbridge, superintendent for Vixen's construction, ordered Benjamin Hutton, Jr. of Philadelphia to prepare the vessel's plans. Hutton prepared the drafts under the eye of an officer who had lost a pilot schooner to the French and who had recommended against the purchase of the Baltimore schooner Nautilus. Hutton's plan, similar in many aspects to his brig Siren, but also not unlike Salvini's Plan B, had stout ends with limited rake, and little drag to her keel. Price received permission to substitute cedar for oak in her upper works, probably an attempt on his part to lessen weight above the waterline.[48]

Price launched Vixen 25 June 1803, and had her ready for commissioning the third of August. Lieutenant John Smith, her captain, reported that her voyage from Baltimore to Hampton Roads required 48 hours.[49] Her passage from the Roads to Gibraltar took 34 days, six days longer than that of Nautilus. She ended an undistinguished career when captured by the Royal Navy frigate Southhampton on 22 November 1812. It may be unfair to compare Vixen to other U. S. Navy pilot schooners since she was converted to a brig in 1804, just a year after she was delivered.

The navy's brigs and the Baltimore schooners USS *Enterprize*, USS *Nautilus* and other small vessels performed their Mediterranean missions successfully. The premature sale of the effective *Experiment*, a major embarrassment to the young navy and Robert Smith, and the ineffectiveness of her replacement, *Vixen*, did not dishonor the record. In neither the Quasi War nor the action against the Barbary nations had the American government declared war. In the Caribbean, USS *Experiment* and USS *Enterprize* performed well against an enemy slipping through narrow cuts between islands in small craft. In the Mediterranean they proved equally valuable in tight spaces alongshore and in encounters with small pirate vessels. The speed and agility of the Baltimore schooners served them well in both conflicts.

Nevertheless, some naval officers were uncomfortable with the extreme design of pilot schooners. The anti-schooner clique, which included Captain Bainbridge and the navy constructor, Joshua Fox, prevailed and schooners were eliminated from the fleet between 1804 and 1812. However, it was the U.S. Navy's experiences with *Experiment, Enterprize,* and *Nautilus* that indicated their value as privateers in the War of 1812.

Along the waterfront at Baltimore the success of the Navy's schooners in the Quasi War had immediate results. As tur-moil at sea continued on the Atlantic and down in the West Indies, the Baltimore schooner's usefulness became clear. After 1801, shipyards were established to build them, and the number of large schooners of pilot-boat construction increased dramatically.

Thomas Kemp opened his shipyard in Baltimore in 1805 at a location on a cove near the intersection of Aliceanna and Washington Streets in Fells Point.[50] At this location Kemp built the most famous of the armed Baltimore schooners. William Parsons moved his yard from Federal Hill to Fells Point in 1803. Joseph Caverly, David Watson and William Flannigain established Fells Point yards. David Stodder, builder of *Constellation*, and an early Baltimore builder of pilot schooners, died at Fells Point in 1804. At the time of Kemp's arrival from Talbot County, William Price was Fells Point's leading shipwright. History awarded Thomas Kemp greater fame.

In the years preceding the War of 1812, and particularly after 1806, the merchants of Baltimore added many large pilot schooners to their fleets. When the United States declared war on Great Britain in 1812, about 130 of these Baltimore schooners sailed out of Chesapeake Bay. Some of them roved as privateers attacking British shipping, others slipped through the Royal Navy's blockade with cargoes for France, for the islands of the West Indies, and for other destinations.

ENDNOTES - CHAPTER FIVE

1. Operational History, USS *Retaliation*, ex-*Le Croyable*, 1798-99; source data compiled by W.M.P. Dunne.

2. Letter, Secretary of the Navy Benjamin Stoddert to Naval Agent Jeremiah Yellott, Baltimore, 25 March 1799. *Naval Documents Related to the Quasi-War Between the United States and France,* Edited by Dudley W. Clark (Washington, D.C.: U.S. Government Printing Office, 1938), November 1798-March 1799, 514. This reference hereafter cited as QW.

3. *Documents Accompanying A Message From the President of the United States Containing Detailed Accounts of Expenditure of Public Monies by Naval Agents from 1st January 1797 to 31st December 1801*(Washington, D.C.: William Dunne, 1803), 228-31.

4. Ibid.

5. Ibid.

6. Ibid.

7. Ibid.; also, John Bosley Yellott, Jr., "Jeremiah Yellott - Revolutionary War Privateersman and Baltimore Philanthropist," *Maryland Historical Magazine,* Vol. 86, No. 2, Summer 1991, 180, 188, N28.

8. *Documents Accompanying*, 228-31.

9. Letter, Stoddert to Yellott, 30 April 1799. QW, Vol. April 1799-July 1799, 113.

10. *Federal Gazette,* 4 June 1799.

11. Letter, Stoddert to Yellott, 5 September 1799. QW, August 1799-December 1799, 161.

12. *Documents Accompanying*, 231-33.

13. Land Records, Talbot County, Maryland: 21-376-1783; 24-29, March, 1790 and *Descendants of James Spencer, Jr.* (St. Michaels, Maryland, Spencer Hall: Privately printed, 1892).

14. *Documents Accompanying*, 231-33.

15. Ibid.

16. Letter, Secretary of the Navy Robert Smith to Captain William Bainbridge, 21 March 1803; Letter, Secretary of the Navy Smith to John Stricker, Naval Agent, Baltimore, 26 March 1803. *Naval Documents Related to the United States Wars with Barbary Powers* (Washington, D.C.: U.S. Government Printing Office, 1939).

17. *Experiment*, Baltimore schooner; Baltimore register #228, 23 November 1801. RG 36-41, National Archives, hereafter cited as NA.

18. Letter, Stoddert to Lieutenant William Maley, 25 October 1799. QW, Vol. August 1799-December 1799, 320.

19. Letters, Stoddert to Yellott, 26 July; 26 September; 30 September; 1 October; 19 October; 25 October 1799; Letter, Captain Alexander Murray to Jeremiah Yellott, 20 May 1799. QW, April-July 1799 and August-December 1799.

20. Letters, Stoddert to Yellott, 1 October; 11 October; November 18, 1799. QW, August-December 1799.

21. Commander Bosworth's discovery of the *Enterprize* plans for a student project became a proposal to the United States Navy from Historic Fells Point Foundation, Inc. to build a replica of USS *Enterprize* at Fells Point in honor of the U.S. Navy's 200th birthday, 30 April 1998. The proposal was withdrawn when the Navy revealed that it had no plans to celebrate its bicentennial.

22. Letter, Mario Marzari to Michael Bosworth, Commander, USN, dated 9 August 1994.

23. Frederick C. Leiner, "The Baltimore Merchants Warships: *Maryland* and *Patapsco* in the Quasi-War with France," *Maryland Historical Magazine,* Vol. 88, No. 3, Fall, 1993; 268-70.

24. Joshua Fox Papers, Document 800: 2; Box 16: James Owner, foreman carpenter, Washington Navy Yard admeasured *Enterprize* 29 July 1808. Peabody Essex Museum, Salem, Massachusetts.

25. Thomas Robinson, Jr., to Secretary of the Navy, 18 February 1805. Naval Documents, BP 5.358-359.

26. *Superior*, Baltimore schooner; Baltimore temporary register #7, 7 January 1801, Baltimore, RG36, NA.

27. Jacques Vichot, *Repertoire des Navires de Guerre Français* (Paris: Edite per l'Association des Amis des Museés de la Marine, 1967), 132.

28. J.J. Colledge, *Ships of the Royal Navy* (Annapolis:

Vol. III, 376, 378. This reference hereafter cited as BP.

Naval Institute Press, 1987), 235.

29. Ibid.

30. Letter, Lieutenant William Maley to Stoddert, 27 August 1800, QW, June-November 1800, 293-99.

31. QW, December 1800-December 1801, 311-12.

32. Letter, Lieutenant John Shaw to an unnamed friend, 12 December 1800. QW, December 1800-December 1801, 28.

33. QW, December 1800-December 1801, 311-12.

34. Letter, Secretary of the Navy Robert Smith to William Pennock, Naval Agent, Norfolk, 31 August 1801. QW, December 1800-December 1801, 278.

35. Letter, Secretary of the Navy Smith to Pennock, 12 November 1801. QW, Ibid., 302.

36. Baltimore register #228, 1801, pencil notation.

37. Excerpts from the log of USS *President* (Captain Thomas Truxton), 16-25 January 1801. QW, December 1800-December 1801, 94.

38. Acting Secretary of the Navy Samuel Smith to Captain Truxton, 1 May 1801. Operational History, USS *Enterprize*, W.M.P. Dunne.

39. Letter, Captain Alexander Murray (*Constellation*) to Secretary of the Navy Smith, 5 July 1802. BP, Vol. II, 193.

40. Letter, William Eaton, U.S. Consul, Tunis, to Summert & Brown, Philadelphia, 9 July 1802. BP, Vol. II, 196.

41. Letter, Secretary of the Navy Smith to Naval Agent Stricker, Baltimore, 28 April 1803. BP, Vol. II, 394.

42. *Nautilus*, Baltimore schooner, Baltimore register #184, 1801. RG36/41, NA.

43. Letter, Lieutenant Richard Somers to his brother, 13 May 1803. BP, Vol. II, 404.

44. Letter, Lieutenant Richard Somers to Secretary of the Navy Smith, 28 June 1803. BP, Vol. II, 464.

45. Letter, Somers to Secretary of the Navy Smith, 31 July 1803. BP, Vol. II, 502.

46. Letter, Somers to William Jones Keen, 11 September 1803. BP, Vol. III, 27-28.

47. Letter, Secretary of the Navy Smith to Captain Bainbridge, 21 March 1803., BP Vol. II, 376. Smith gave Bainbridge the following dimensions: 84' x 60' keel x 22'5" (23' outside bends) x 9'6" depth of hold.

48. Letter, Secretary of the Navy Smith to Naval Agent Stricker, Baltimore, 1 April 1803. BP, Vol. II, 387.

49. Letter, Lieutenant John Smith to Secretary of the Navy Smith, 11 August 1803. BP, Vol. II, 509.

50. Kemp Papers, Microfilm, MS 2335, Maryland Historical Society, Baltimore Land Records, No. 172, 726, 6 July 1805, Maryland Hall of Records, Annapolis.

BALTIMORE
CARPENTER
CERTIFICATE
FOR THE ARMED
SCHOONER *SABINE*.

National Archives.

District of Baltimore

I William Price Master Carpenter in the City of Baltimore & State of Maryland do Certify, that the Pilot boat built Schooner Named the *Sabine*. Was built by me or under my direction at the City of Baltimore during the months of Sept. October & November 1812. for my Self and Sold to Mr Jamey Williams and John Gooden. of Baltimore County & State of Maryland. that the Said Schr. is Round tucked has one flush deck two masts; is Eighty two feet ten Inches length of Keel straight Rabbet, Twenty Six feet ten Inches breadth of Beam and twelve feet Six Inches depth of Hold and is two Hundred Ninety two $\frac{57}{95}$ Tons Carpenters measurement as Witness My hand this 9th day of December 1812.

William Price

CHAPTER SIX

BALTIMORE
SCHOONERS, 1807-1815

Thomas Kemp built a schooner called *Rossie* at Fells Point in 1807. She, like other Baltimore schooners launched in the years preceding the War of 1812, was a blockade runner built in response to the British Orders of Council and Napoleon's retaliatory blockade. Relations with the British government disintegrated that year as impressment of American sailors and vessel searches by the Royal Navy increased. The *Chesapeake-Leopard* affair, also in 1807, brought the two nations close to hostilities, and thereafter Baltimore merchants' groups recognized the possibility of war.[1] At best, they expected impressment of sailors and general harassment of America's neutral cargo fleet to increase.

William Price, who started building pilot schooners at Fells Point 13 years prior to 1807, launched several beautiful Baltimore schooners in the years between the incident involving USS *Chesapeake* and the opening of hostilities in 1812. One was *Nonpareil*, a fast pilot schooner and blockade runner.[2] Her owner was Thomas Tenant, who had experienced heavy losses in the Quasi War and now gambled his commercial survival on what he hoped would be the ability of the Baltimore schooner to sail away from blockade ships and any other enemies.

Price's carpenter certificate recorded *Nonpareil*'s dimensions as 64' keel x 23'6" x 9'10". On her register, dated 10 November 1807, the Baltimore Customs surveyor recorded her dimensions as 91' length on deck, 24' extreme beam and 9'11" depth. *Rossie*, registered by her first owner, Isaac McKim, during the same period, measured 97'6" x 23'6" x 10'.[4] Kemp's carpenter certificate stated that *Rossie*'s keel measured 70' for tonnage. Although her length exceeded that of *Nonpareil* by six and one half feet, the width and depth of the two schooners were close. However, *Rossie*'s proportionately shallower depth and narrower breadth was inconsistant with Price's pilot schooner and with usual pilot-schooner design .

Variations in the ratios of dimensions of pilot schooners among the shipwrights raises questions whether or not there were rules of proportion for a Baltimore schooner. Did understood ratios exist between length and depth and between length and breadth, or for that matter between width and depth? By checking a number of schooners built between 1800 and 1814, the greatest similarities exist in the ratios of overall length to depth. These ratios would carry over to the waterline length, which is not usually known, and to the length-to-depth ratio of keels and holds. Federal ship registers, fairly complete after 1789, specify length overall, extreme beam, and depth of the hold. The Congressional method of measuring length was the straight-line distance from the fore part of the stem to the after part of the sternpost at the level of the deck. In this manner the effect of deck sheer was eliminated. Breadth was the dimension of the broadest point of the hull above the wales. Depth was measured from the keelson to the underside of the deck planks at the midsection.[5]

Did Price and Kemp work with rules? No one has an answer, but certainly the pilot-schooner design, an outgrowth of the work of the Bay's boatbuilders over 50 years before 1800, had a fairly specific set of rules by 1807. The fact that Kemp strayed so far from what seems to have been a norm in the design of *Rossie* is puzzling.

The plans of captured Baltimore schooners drafted by the British Admiralty confirm some variation to the sharpness of hulls–that is, differences in the angle of the rise of the floor or bottom above the horizontal. Variations in the breadths of hulls were recorded, too. Both breadth and deadrise have strong implications for stability. Towering spars and other weight above the waterline, raising the schooner's center of gravity, were critical to stability. It was important to keep the rig light and concentrate

weight down low in the hull. The master would compensate for a pilot schooner's instability up to a point with ballast and cargo, and underway with sail selection and suitable trim. The builders of these vessels would give them initial stability, however, by adhering to a generally accepted relationship between breadth and deadrise. Copies of Chesapeake pilot schooners built beyond the Bay frequently failed to adopt the relatively conservative deadrise of the originals, in relation to hulls that were also conservatively wider than the copies.

Length and depth are important speed-related factors. With low freeboard, a single flush deck, and light spars and standing rigging, Baltimore schooners, with sails in correct trim, were easily able to evade capture on the open sea. But the captain and crew of a Baltimore schooner had to be extremely skilled shiphandlers and judges of sail trim. If chased by a Royal Navy ship, a Baltimore schooner depended on her most important sailing characteristic: the ability to sail fast close to the wind. Of the total of approximately 55 Baltimore schooners that embarked on one or more privateer cruises during the War of 1812, only about ten failed to return to their owners. Of the ten lost, just three were taken on the high seas; the others were run ashore or caught in a calm. A greater number of Baltimore schooners, receiving letter-of-marque trading commissions, became blockade runners. Many of these were captured by the Royal Navy, as a cargo vessel approaching her port is in a vulnerable position, with diminishing opportunities to maneuver.[6]

William Price did not describe *Nonpareil* as a schooner of pilot-boat construction on his carpenter certificate, as he did most of the schooners he built between 1807 and 1814. He called *Dolphin*, built in 1809, pilot-boat built.[7] She was a successful privateer until her capture in the Rappahannock River along with Baltimore schooners *Arab, Lynx* and *Racer* in April 1813.[8] The loss of four of these vessels was the result of their inability to defend themselves in confined waters with crews untrained for battle.

Other Baltimore schooners that William Price called "of pilot boat construction" included *Herald* (1807), *Luna* (1809), and his great letter-of-marque schooners of 1812, *Von Hollen, Revenge, Price* and *Sabine*.[9] John Price, William Price's son[10] described many of his schooners as pilot-boat built. His letter-of-marque schooners included *Tom, Phaeton* and *Cashier*[11] and all were pilot-boat built. John Price built the brig *Eclipse* in 1811 and a sloop named *Elizabeth* in 1815, both described as "pilot boat built" on carpenter certificates.[12] This is of note as it relates the term pilot boat specifically to the hull of the vessel and not to her rig.

The Prices, by calling their Baltimore schooners "pilot boats," linked the model to the Revolutionary War pilot schooners and to the commercial baycraft of the eighteenth century, and even farther back to the original pilot boats of Hampton and Annapolis. This description was not just a quirk of the Price family. Thomas Kemp described *Hebe* (1807) and *Breeze* (1807) as pilot boats.[13] *Globe*, built in Virginia in 1809 by Hunley and Gayle, is described as a pilot boat.[14] James Cordery built *Lynx* at Fells Point in 1812, and described her as pilot-boat built.[15] French refugee shipwrights with yards at Fells Point, when building a French lugger, called it a lugger; but when Bernard Salenave or Andrew Denoanda built Baltimore schooners they called them pilot boats on their carpenter certificates.[16]

Whatever was John Price's intent with his descriptions, it is nevertheless true that the traditional pilot-boat schooner's spar and sail plan was normally part of the total design as first documented on William Price's Hampton invoices to the State of Virginia for *Liberty* and *Patriot* in 1787-88. This basic schooner sail plan was never altered significantly as long as pilot schooners were built on Chesapeake Bay. Baltimore schooners *Nonpareil* and *Rossie*, revenue cutters, pilot boats, Baltimore clippers, yachts such as *America*, and all Chesapeake baycraft from the "schooner boat" of the eighteenth century to the last pungy boats of 1885, carried a large forestaysail, an overlapping gaff-rigged foresail, and a gaff-rigged and boomed mainsail. To these three basic sails all styles of topsails, jibs, steering sails and bonnets were added depending on the employment of the vessel.

Following the blockades of 1807 and the American embargos, Baltimore merchants introduced pilot schooners to

North Atlantic trade routes. With rising commodity prices, even with limited cargo capacity, Baltimore schooners could turn a profit for an owner on these long voyages, and they had a better chance of giving the Royal Navy the slip. Some of them did not give the Royal Navy the slip.

HMS *Diana* captured *Nonpareil* on her first voyage to Bordeaux.[17] In an adventurous attempt to run the British blockade, Thomas Tenant appointed Benjamin Quimbey, age 23, master of his beautiful schooner. The crew totaled eleven.[18] The ill-fated voyage began in November 1807, when Tenant dispatched her to Havana with a cargo of flour. At that Spanish port, Quimbey sold his cargo of Baltimore superfine flour and loaded a full cargo consisting of white and brown sugar and green coffee.[19] *Nonpareil*, operating under the rules of neutral vessels in colonial trade, returned to Baltimore to enter the cargo through Customs, a necessary ploy to re-define the origin of the cargo. By 1807, procedures had been simplified, making it unnecessary to off-load and reload the cargo before departing for France. All formalities for documentation of the transatlantic leg of *Nonpareil*'s voyage could be done in a day. To avoid legal difficulties, papers, including the Havana bills of lading, were removed from the vessel on arrival at Baltimore.[20] A new bill of lading covering the carriage of the cargo from Baltimore to Bordeaux was substituted. A consular invoice legalized by the French consul at Baltimore was prepared for Captain Quimbey along

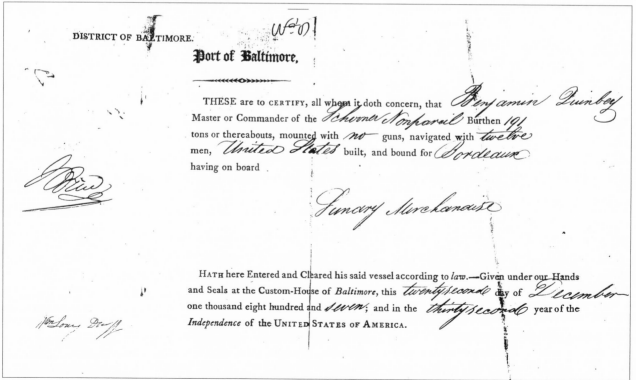

with other documents covering a voyage that had, on paper, originated at Baltimore. Provided with new documents covering a cargo of sugar and coffee, and new clearence documents for a voyage to Bordeaux, *Nonpareil* sailed from Baltimore 22 December 1807.

On the fourth day of February 1808, 44 days out of Baltimore, the Royal Navy's *Diana* captured *Nonpareil* within sight of Cordouan Lighthouse on the French coast. The Baltimore schooner offered no resistance when boarded by men from *Diana*'s tender. A prize crew consisting of Royal Marines directed Captain Quimbey to sail *Nonpareil* to the English port of Plymouth.[21]

Nonpareil's shipping documents included Tenant's instructions to John A. Morton, his agent in Paris, to "land the cargo at Bordeaux, arrange for the sale of the sugar and coffee, and acquire a full cargo of brandy for the return voyage." This and other shipping documents became part of the Admiralty Prize Court record at Plymouth.[22] The court ruled that Tenant's schooner was a prize and ordered vessel and cargo sold. The value of the schooner is unknown; the value before resale of the cargo as shown on Tenant's invoice was $21,375.12.[23]

The Royal Navy acquired *Nonpareil* and she served under the British flag until 1812.[24] A half model of her hull is in the collection of the National Maritime Museum at Greenwich. Apparently, the Admiralty took off her lines and made a half model for study by the Royal Naval College. The lines have since been lost.

FRENCH CONSULAR MANIFEST FOR *NONPAREIL*. *Admiralty Prize Court Records, London.*

Although the half model pictured is not a builder's model, it is probably a reliable record of *Nonpareil*'s hull as built since it was produced by a carver working from the schooner's plans taken off for the Admiralty. A builder's model would illustrate William Price's conception of the vessel before construction, and could be different from the schooner as built. *Nonpareil*'s half model is a rare and valuable tool for study, which is the reason the Royal Naval College had it carved. So while not a single set of Price-built pilot schooner plans exist today, it is a stroke of good fortune that has provided this contemporary half model of the shipwright's work.

Thomas Tenant's *Nonpareil* had to be fast, and at the same time have sufficient cargo space to make an adventure to France profitable. Profits were determined by the supply of colonial produce in France. Tenant took no chances in selecting sugar and coffee,[25] both scarce in Europe. Her return cargo, brandy, had a voyage occurred, was the nectar of America's merchant class.[26] Had Tenant gotten his brandy to the American market, he would have enriched himself significantly. As it was, his adventure ended with an insurance claim.

Nonpareil's cargo consisted of 310 boxes of sugar and 30 hogsheads, 20 barrels and 65 bags of coffee.[27] Since neither the weight or the cubic measurement of the cargo is known, it is assumed that this small cargo reflected the limits of *Nonpareil*'s capacity. Cargo was stowed wherever there was space, including the aft cabin reserved for captain and officers.

The crew had no specific area and hung their hammocks with the cargo and stores.

The principal cargo area was between the masts, with some stowed forward of the foremast. As the half model shows, the floor of the schooner amidships rises sharply from the keel to the waterline, leaving a very small space for freight. At the waterline forward of the mainmast, one can observe *Nonpareil*'s limited amount of freeboard. Bearing in mind that the gun ports are above her one flush deck, freeboard, the height of the topsides between the waterline and the deck, was probably less than 25 percent of the submerged portion of her hull.

Focusing on *Nonpareil*'s waterline, and ignoring the keel line, it will be observed that, even with her lack of depth forward, her bow was designed higher than her stern as she floated on her waterline. Price built this bow somewhat convex in shape at the waterline, but fairly full at the deck for buoyancy, increasing *Nonpareil*'s seaworthiness.

HALF MODEL OF
NONPAREIL, MADE
BY ORDER OF THE
ADMIRALITY FOR
STUDY BY THE
ROYAL NAVAL
COLLEGE.
National Maritime
Museum, London.

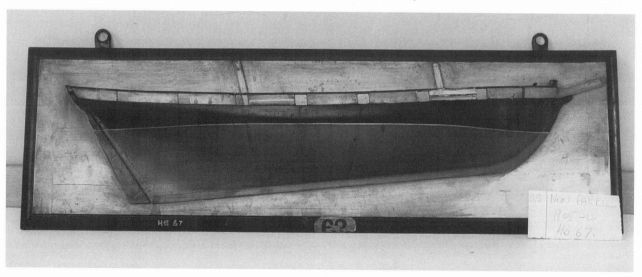

Concentrating on the section of *Nonpareil*'s hull abaft her mainmast, three important characteristics can be seen. They are, first, the deep drag of her keel, which is accentuated by the sweeping sheer of her deckline. This drag allowed these schooners to turn smartly and at the same time controlled leeway. Second, a tapering hull with hollow quarters produced a long fine run with minimum water resistance. The third notable characteristic is the extreme rake of the sternpost. Her total rake fore and aft, approximately 27', exceeds one third of her keel length. Raked ends, combined with a prominent amount of deadrise, reduced the volume of her submerged hull, a large percentage of her total mass. With ballast, the submerged hull provided *Nonpareil* with the stability to stand reasonably upright under the Baltimore schooner's characteristic large spread of sail. Adding to her stability was her 24' beam offsetting her angle of deadrise.

The United States Congress declared war on Great Britain on 18 June 1812, approximately 48 hours after the British government in London agreed to suspend the 1807 Orders of Council, the principal cause of the conflict. The Treaty of Ghent, which brought the war to a close, was signed 24 December 1814, six months after America's peace mission had arrived to negotiate an end to the hostilities.

The British Orders of Council which had increased the tempo of American war fever were issued in the spring of 1807. The British instituted a blockade banning neutral vessels from trade with European countries, including France. Napoleon responded with a blockade of neutral ships entering Great Britain's ports.

In America, the war fever was not universal. Any enthusiasm that existed in New England for a fight with Great Britain was related to sectional expansionism. American forces, mostly militia, failed in attempts to move into Canada. A proposed invasion in the fall of 1812 had to be postponed. Thomas Parker, Colonel of the 12th Infantry, summed up the situation to his superiors in October: supplies were inadequate, and there existed an "almost total want of discipline in the regular troops, and therefore, a successful issue could hardly be expected."[28] Maryland's Colonel William H. Winder reported from his camp, 2 December 1812, that "the last eight or ten days have shattered the regiment." Then he requested permission to go home for the winter.[29] Winder's uncle was Maryland's governor.

The Canadian invasion plan, resurrected in the spring of 1813 and attempted in a long campaign through the summer and fall, failed again. Winder, now a General, inexplicably became a British prisoner during a skirmish in which the British troops were put to rout.[30] Later, successful engagements conducted by America's freshwater navy commanders Oliver Hazard Perry and Thomas Macdonough held off British counterattacks. A general impasse developed in the northern theater. The naval engagements on the Great Lakes produced the United States Navy's first fleet victories.

British troops landed at Benedict on

the Patuxent River in Maryland, 20 August 1814, and marched on Washington. The nation's capital was burned as its defenders, under the command of General Winder, back from a Canadian prison, and now Commander of the Maryland and Virginia Military District, fled in an embarrassing rout. Only old Joshua Barney's sailors stood their ground until overwhelmed.

Next was the Battle of Baltimore, a decisive American victory, but remembered as a cautious British withdrawal before the main forces joined battle. General Samuel Smith, merchant, soldier and politician, pushed General Winder aside and took command of a well-planned defense of which Fort McHenry was the keystone. The death of General Ross, the British commander, a timid Royal Navy command, and a blocked channel off Fort McHenry, persuaded the British to leave Chesapeake Bay. Credit General Smith, General John Stricker and most of all Captain John Rodgers, USN, who organized 1,000 sailors into an effective artillery force.

This, then, outlines the campaigns of that most unusual of our wars. By 1812, Great Britain had waged war for the better part of two decades. Her navy was formidable, consisting of approximately 190 ships of the line (battleships of 74 guns), plus about 250 frigates (30 to 50 guns). This immense fleet was controlled by a powerful corps of senior officers who had developed policies and goals for the Royal Navy over the course of a generation, mostly independent of and sometimes in opposition to the best interests of Great Britain. Many of its officers became rich from enemy prizes. Ruthless captains controlled their ships by the lash, and crews were gathered by impressment rather than recruitment. The fleet's mission was to control the seas from the Mediterranean to the Baltic, and from Canada to South America. Many of the Royal Navy's great ships suffered rotting hulls and rigging due to poor maintenance and bad logistics. In spite of these problems, the size and firepower of the fleet allowed the Royal Navy to rule the waves. President James Madison's fleet consisted of a minuscule navy of several frigates in various states of readiness, a handful of brigs of questionable value, and two sloops of war, *Hornet* and *Wasp*.

After playing a significant role in the Quasi War and the Barbary Wars, the United States Navy entered the War of 1812 with no Baltimore schooners on its roster. While early individual victories by American frigates seemed important for public morale, these successes had little effect on the outcome of the war.[31] A confrontation with the Royal Navy by an American naval force was suicidal, and as the war progressed Britain's navy was able to bottle up most American naval movements.

British merchant vessels, trafficking in the Atlantic from Newfoundland in the north to the Windward Islands in the south, proved to be the vulnerable part of British maritime might. However, American frigates proved not to be the suitable vessels to attack convoys and

single ships, and U.S. Navy brigs were vulnerable to most Royal Navy cruisers. Aware of the value of pilot schooners in situations like this, the merchants of Baltimore sent their Baltimore armed schooners forth to attack the British where it hurt, to capture the ships and rich cargos of the Empire's merchant fleet.

The Baltimore armed schooners *Rossie*[32] and *Nonsuch*[33] quickly received letters-of-marque, and stood down the Bay only days after war was declared. Fells Point's nest of shipyards, frantically busy, rushed to complete new Baltimore schooners at their fitting docks, building time about 90 days from keel laying to delivery. Fells Point yards, together with the shipwrights of St. Michaels, built a naval force to fight the War of 1812 in its own way.

As *Rossie* worked her way down

Chesapeake Bay, her skipper, Joshua Barney, prematurely aged by the sea and old wounds, surely must have allowed his thoughts to drift back to the pilot schooner *Dolphin* and his engagement with the sloop *Peggy* 34 years before.[34] Barney took *Rossie* out just once but he enjoyed a successful cruise, capturing a score of British vessels.[35] On first wartime cruises, each of the Kemp-built privateers had the good fortune to be commanded by extremely able masters. *Rolla*'s master was James Dooley and Captain Thomas Boyle, Maryland's most famous privateer master, was aboard *Comet* from 1812 until

the spring of 1814 when he assumed command of the Baltimore armed schooner *Chasseur*.

Thomas Kemp laid *Comet*'s keel during the late winter of 1810 and he signed her carpenter certificate May 4 for Captain Thorndike Chase.[36] Captain Chase put her up for sale immediately. In a notice placed in the *Federal Gazette*, he described his schooner as protected by 26-ounce copper sheathing. He listed *Comet*'s capacity as 1,200 barrels of flour. Chase also informed buyers that she was pierced for 18 guns.[37] She did not sell, as Captain Chase registered her one year

RIGGED MODEL OF BALTIMORE SCHOONER *COMET*; THE VESSEL WAS BUILT IN 1809 BY THE THOMAS KEMP SHIPYARD AT FELLS POINT; THE MODEL WAS BUILT CIRCA 1810 BY KEMP SHIPYARD CRAFTSMEN.
*James Knowles
Collection, Baltimore.*

later.[38] When war was declared, *Comet*, still owned by Thorndike Chase, with other investors, and carrying letter-of-marque commission #4, dated 29 June 1812, followed *Rossie* and *Nonsuch* out of Chesapeake Bay.[39] Thomas Boyle was in command on her quarterdeck. Boyle's fame seems focused on his exploits with *Chasseur*, but his skilled seamanship and great success on four privateer cruises aboard *Comet* were the foundation of his unmatched record as a privateer captain. Along the way, Captain Boyle entered the U.S. Navy as a sailing master when *Comet* became a navy guard vessel on the Bay following his third cruise.[40]

Comet measured just slightly more than half the burden of *Chasseur*, 187 to 356 tons. The little schooner, which Kemp described as built "privateer fashion," had dimensions of 90'6" x 23'3" x 10'; her length of keel for tonnage was 68'. He built her with cargo hatches and gun ports. This, plus her wartime running rigging which placed lines, blocks and cleats on the outside of her bulwarks, may be the source of Kemp's term "privateer fashion." These features are seen in the photograph of the model, fashioned in the Kemp yard and still owned by a member of the Kemp family.

The exploits of his armed schooners made Thomas Kemp Chesapeake Bay's most famous shipwright. Baltimore's leading merchants bought his "privateer fashioned" armed schooners and his letter-of-marque traders. *Grecian*, of the latter category, was captured by the British and taken into the Royal Navy.[41] *Grampus*

became USS *Spitfire*.[42] His *Kemp*[43] and *Patapsco* successfully completed wartime trading voyages and privateer cruises. *Chasseur*[44] skippered by Captain Boyle, who took command 24 July 1814 for the first of his two cruises, became the "pride of Baltimore." Her last cruise commenced 23 December 1814 from New York, one day before the American negotiators agreed to the terms for a peace treaty. For this cruise Boyle converted *Chasseur's* rig from schooner to brig. On 27 February 1815, he captured HMS *St. Lawrence*, ex-Baltimore schooner *Atlas*, in a fierce engagement which commenced 26 February 1815.[45] *Atlas* was built in St. Michaels in 1808.[46]

Thomas Kemp built *Patapsco* during the summer of 1812 following the declaration of war. *Patapsco's* consortium of owners for her first voyage consisted of Andrew Clopper (3/8) and Henry Fulford, his partner, (1/8), Amos A. Williams (1/4) and Levi Hollingsworth (1/4).[47] The last mentioned was a member of a family of merchants that had moved to Baltimore from Elkton prior to the American Revolution, during which Jesse Hollingsworth financed a number of shipping adventures with Jeremiah Yellott. Levi became one of the top investors in Baltimore's wartime fleet. In a letter written in 1812 by the Baltimore branch of the Hollingsworth family to the firm of Levi Hollingsworth and Son of Philadelphia, the writer used the term "clipper" while referring to Baltimore schooners. The Baltimore Hollingsworths wrote that "six clippers are fitting out at the [Fells] Point, all of them will be ready for sea, probably in ten days."[48]

At this period, the word "clipper" was not used by shipwrights, masters or owners of these distinctive vessels. Their familiars called them pilot schooners, pilot-boat schooners, or schooners, pilot-boat built, and occasionally Baltimore schooners. The name Baltimore clipper did not enter common usage until after 1830. Chesapeake-built ships had no descriptive name prior to *Ann McKim*, a famous China trader that combined the Baltimore hull form with the spars and sail plan of a full-rigged ship. She was built in 1833 and described as a clipper by the *Baltimore Sun* in 1835.

Andrew Clopper's consortium placed *Patapsco* in service as a letter-of-marque trader, and in this capacity she completed voyages to France and to the West Indies. She served briefly in the United States Navy in 1813 as a scout vessel on lower Chesapeake Bay. In the latter part of the war, she cruised the Atlantic as a privateer. *Patapsco* performed well and her owners profited from their investment. She survived the war and her owners sold her to foreign buyers as her limited cargo space made her uneconomic to operate after the war.[49]

An account of *Patapsco's* construction and outfitting costs, as well as cost of the cargo for her first voyage were found among a miscellaneous batch of documents in the manuscripts of the Maryland Historical Society.[50] This document, in which each item of cost is listed, is not only a complete account of expenses, it is a record of each craftsman who participated in the building of this Baltimore schooner. The list of services performed becomes a guide to the progress of her construction as well as to the items of equipment purchased as Clopper, her husbanding agent, prepared her for sea. The breakdown of costs of each service performed and their relationship to total cost can be clearly analyzed, a unique record.

Thomas Kemp, her builder, received $26.00 per ton, carpenter's measure (215-56/95 tons) or a total of $5,605.32 for her hull with copper sheathing applied and her masts stepped. Kemp's invoice consisted of only 28 percent of the total cost of the pilot schooner. (See Appendix A for the complete breakdown of *Patapsco's* costs of construction.)

Patapsco's registered dimensions were 101'6" x 25' x 11'5." Her carpenter measurements were 74'3" keel length x 24'2" x 11'5."[51] Her burden in tons was 259-83/95. With less beam proportionately than earlier models, a slightly deeper hold balanced this adjustment. With rising floors and rather slack bilges carried to the waterline, and bulwarks and guns, *Patapsco* would be quite tender even riding low in the water full of cargo and armament. Her design made her uncatchable in fair weather, but dangerous to handle in heavy weather. Surviving ship logs contain frequent entries of decks awash, and more poignantly of men lost as green water swept down the flush decks of these schooners or came over the low bulwarks at high angles of heel.[52]

Drafts of the Baltimore schooners in the Ship Plan Section of the National Maritime Museum, Greenwich, England, are of those vessels captured by the Royal Navy. As *Patapsco* survived the war, there are no such drawings. Somewhat similar to *Patapsco* in size was Kemp's *Grecian*, delivered in March of 1812 to Isaac McKim. As in the case of several Baltimore trading schooners, the British captured her inside Chesapeake Bay.[53]

Baltimore schooners owned by Isaac McKim included *Valona*, built in 1806, *Rossie*, in 1807, *Grecian*, built in 1812, *Rossie* II, built by Kemp and Gardner in 1815, *Yellot*, a pilot schooner built in 1823, and, of course, the Baltimore clipper ship *Ann McKim*. His career reveals a deep commitment to the Chesapeake Bay pilot schooner model as it evolved over the first decades of the nineteenth century, and as adaptations in design continued after the close of the War of 1812.

Isaac McKim supposedly did not participate in privateering activities. HMS *Jaseur*'s capture of *Grecian* in February of 1814 would have been an extreme financial setback to any individual owner. Built during the winter of 1812, she probably completed her first voyage before Congress declared war in June. McKim obtained letter-of-marque commission #944 in December 1813 for *Grecian* and, although she carried cannon for protection, her adventures were commercial in 23 months at sea during which she completed several profitable voyages.[54]

Kemp's carpenter certificate for *Grecian* is lost, but he is listed as builder on her register dated 2 March 1812. Her measurements, by the Baltimore surveyor, are given as 99'6" x 24'2" x 10'7". When measured by the Admiralty at Portsmouth in 1816, the following dimensions were recorded: 95'1" x 23'10" x 10'5". The differences reflect variances in admeasurement practices of the two countries. Admeasuring could be fairly subjective during this period, making it difficult to draw a conclusion from the two sets of figures. In the interest of consistency, U.S. Customs measurements will be used in this text when available.

A naval architect-historian, studying *Grecian*'s plan, exclaimed, "the first radical concept to strike me is the remarkable amount of drag to the keel. Secondly, the bow shape precedes Herreshoff's *Gloriana* and Tom McManus's *James S. Steele* by more than 60 years. It eliminates deadwood forward, and the steeply angled sternpost cuts it considerably aft. [*Grecian* has] less deadrise than I would have expected. I would expect [her] to go to windward like a bitch, and with the accentuated drag, turn on a dime. With the deadrise, [she] would be a complete failure as a gun platform in stormy weather."[55]

Kemp incorporated unusual features of a pilot schooner into *Grecian*'s design. Her gun ports are unique and the reason for their shape is unknown. They may have been designed to reduce weight. Here again, Kemp's innovations were not explained in contemporary journals or in his papers. *Grecian*'s long curving stem, and her less convex, shallow bow, not unlike *Transfer* and *Superior*, illustrate a

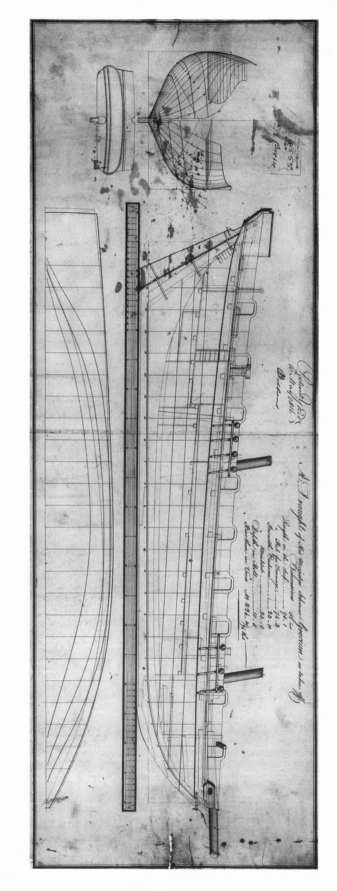

PLAN OF HMS *GRECIAN*, EX-BALTIMORE SCHOONER

GRECIAN, BUILT BY THOMAS KEMP

AT FELLS POINT IN 1812.

National Maritime Museum, London.

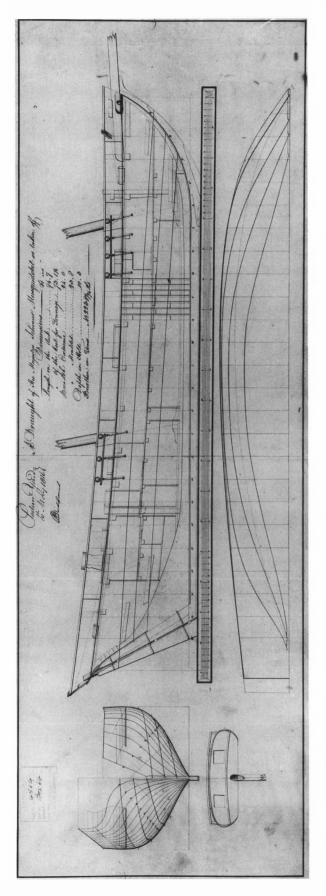

PLAN OF HMS *MUSQUIDOBIT*, EX- BALTIMORE
SCHOONER *LYNX*, BUILT BY JAMES CORDERY
AT FELLS POINT IN 1812.
National Maritime Museum, London.

Schooner Patapsco of Baltimore Richard Moon Com.ᵗ entering the Bay of Naples.

more extreme design for the pilot schooner which was repeated in the work of the shipbuilders of St. Michaels, where Thomas Kemp built ships before he came to Fells Point. Her bowsprit had little steeve–that is, the angle from the line of her deck sheer. And although her stern and transom are beautifully proportioned, it is her underbody that shows Kemp's brilliance as a modeler of these schooners. Here McKim's schooner has a sharper, longer entrance, quite different from the short, broad and convex bows of many other pilot schooners. She measured 229 tons burden.

The Admiralty took off the lines of HMS *Musquidobit*, ex-Baltimore schooner *Lynx*, at Portsmouth the same day as *Grecian*. She is an interesting pilot schooner to compare with Kemp's *Grecian*. James Cordery, like Kemp originally from the Eastern Shore, signed *Lynx*'s carpenter certificate on 12 June 1812. He described her as a pilot-boat-built schooner. For register, her burden was 225 tons, very close to that of *Grecian*. Her principal dimensions were 97' x 24'4" x 10'8".[56] Differences from *Grecian* included a more sweeping sheer. *Lynx* also had greater deadrise than *Grecian*, as floors rise in a sharper angle to the horizontal to a point just below her waterline. Cordery built *Lynx* with a deeper forefoot, giving her a somewhat shorter entrance and a fuller bow than Kemp's schooner. *Lynx*, a letter-of-marque trader, was captured with the three other Baltimore schooners in the Rappahannock River, April 1813. She served Britain's Royal Navy for five years.

Kemp described *Patapsco* in the builder's certificate as built "privateer fashion." She did not have *Grecian*'s odd-shaped gun ports; her deck, with less sheer, was designed to make it easier to bring her guns to bear on a potential target. Schooners such as *Patapsco*, when enbarked on privateer cruises, carried crews that exceeded 100 men with gear and supplies for several months at sea. This required them to be fitted-out differently compared with the blockade runners.

It is not known from Andrew Clopper's accounts or from Kemp's records what woods were used in *Patapsco*'s hull. While builders normally used oak for keel and frames, Kemp once advertised the sale of a pilot-boat schooner that he constructed with cedar frames. He used locust in his hulls for trim and for trunnels.[57] By 1812 live oak from the Carolinas and Georgia had become too expensive for Baltimore schooners, usually quickly fabricated for war and not for long peaceful periods of service. Mulberry was widely used, as well as chestnut, for special purposes such as stems and stern posts. Builders of smaller pilot schooners used white oak throughout the hull, fastening planking with locust trunnels, and often using pine for decks.

A painting of *Patapsco* is in the collection of the Maryland Historical Society. Executed by an unknown Italian artist, it shows the pilot schooner entering the Bay of Naples. Captain Richard Moon commissioned it prior to her sale after the end of the war. Moon entered the schooner at Baltimore 11 November 1815, stating that his last foreign port was Naples.[58]

The painting shows us a handsome pilot schooner, built as a privateer with no deck sheer. What the artist missed, a common problem for painters of these vessels, is the special bird-in-flight look of a pilot schooner with her cloud of sail attached to a small body–a combination that brings to mind a fish hawk or a sea eagle.

Patapsco had a basic pilot-schooner rig consisting of large jib or forestaysail attached to the bowsprit and to the head of the foremast; an overlapping lug foresail with a gaff at the head and free-footed without boom; and a mainsail with gaff and boom. These three sails constitute the center of her sail plan, the power base of the sailing rig of all Chesapeake Bay pilot schooners.

A Baltimore schooner normally carried a flying jib forward of the forestaysail attached to a sliding jibboom, as shown in the painting. These jibs and jibbooms were for light weather and would be taken in quickly in heavy wind and sea. Visible at the base of *Patapsco*'s foremast, resting on her rail, is her course or squaresail boom. Its sail is furled on a yard and secured above the deck. *Patapsco* carries two topmasts for square topsails. Above the fore and main topsails are the topgallant and royal sails.

Additional sails not shown in the painting, but normally carried, are studding sails, a ringtail, and bonnets, all normally part of a Baltimore schooner's sail inventory. The studding sails are light sails set as extensions to squaresails. A ringtail is an extension of the mainsail attached to the boom and the gaff abaft the leech. A bonnet is an extension attached to the foot of a sail. The sails shown on *Patapsco* are representative of the sail plan normally used by letter-of-marque traders or privateers. Pilot schooners, before the war and after, often had fore-and-aft topsails, sometimes referred to as gaff topsails.

A master of a Baltimore schooner had to be skilled in sail-handling. He also needed to be a figure of authority, as the survival of these tender craft depended upon a crew's skill and discipline. Sail changes were required frequently on each watch. The fore-and-aft lower sails had to be continually reefed and unreefed in response to the wind and its direction. Jibs and jibbooms had to be taken in and secured quickly, often while green water washed over the working crew. Baltimore schooners varied greatly in their success, and although there is little doubt that some were better built than others, in the end the great ones, traders or privateers, had superior seamen as officers and crews.

As *Patapsco* made ready for sea, Andrew Clopper secured a cargo which consisted of the following:

Sugar: 59 hogsheads—99,184 lbs.

Coffee: 850 bags———120,746 lbs.[59]

Cotton: 55 bales———13,859 lbs.

Logs: 3 tons————6,720 lbs.

The cost of *Patapsco*'s cargo was $37,754.92. A portion was procured on credit and covered by debentures, leaving an amount of $21,975.45 chargeable against the owners prior to sailing. As the cost of building and outfitting the schooner totaled $19,815.56, this brought the amount due from the owners at departure time to $41,791.01. However, only $27,870.60 was paid in before sailing; $3,072.86 was due in November 1812 and $10,847.55 in January 1813. The debentures totaled $15,779.47, and were due at various future dates, some in 1813, others unspecified. The cost to build, outfit, and make *Patapsco* ready for sea, with her cargo, totaled $57,570.48.[60]

The net weight of her cargo totaled approximately 107 long tons. As tare weight cannot be determined, the cargo's gross weight is unknown. Presumably, with her freight on board, cargo space was fully utilized. As logs were her only deadweight cargo, the less dense cotton, coffee and sugar filled her hold before she reached her marks. The amount that Captain Mortimer obtained for his cargo in France is not known.

Patapsco slipped out of Chesapeake Bay for Nantes, France, on 17 September

SURPRIZE CAPTURING THE STAR JAN.ʸ 27 1815.

1812. She returned to the Bay 28 March 1813. During a storm, Captain Mortimer evaded the British fleet and sailed his schooner under full canvas into the Bay, reaching Smith Point at the mouth of the Potomac River at 1800 hours the same day.[61]

The British captured or destroyed approximately 32 Baltimore schooners on trading voyages during the war. Bad weather accounted for eight, either lost at sea or grounding and breaking up.[62] High profits of a successful adventure made risks worthwhile. Risk could be ignored as a gamble, or could be spread by selling shares. Isaac McKim, (*Grecian, Valona*), Thomas Lewis, owner of *Leo*, and George Stiles, (*Nonsuch, Climax, Siro, Moro*) took no partners. All their vessels were trading schooners, except for Stiles's *Nonsuch*, so their willingness to take the whole risk seems incredible. During the war, insur-

THE BALTIMORE ARMED SCHOONER *SURPRIZE* CAPTURES THE BRITISH SHIP *STAR* IN THIS PAINTING BY GEORGE ROPES. *Peabody Essex Museum, Salem, MA.*

ance could be purchased at a rate of 50 percent of the value of a schooner and her cargo, approximately the loss ratio. McKim lost *Grecian*, Captain Stiles lost *Climax* and *Siro*. Both men survived these losses so profits produced by their other vessels had to be great.

In the spring of 1813, the British blockade of the Bay made it increasingly difficult for Baltimore's fleet to slip in and out. The merchant community petitioned the government to induct four Baltimore schooners into the U.S. Navy. The navy assigned *Patapsco*, *Comet* and *Revenge*, a Price-built schooner, as lookouts on the Bay and *Wasp* became a dispatch vessel. USS *Patapsco* proved to be ineffective on her mission and subject to official rebuke after a mutiny cost Captain Mortimer his command.

An unfortunate incident, probably the principal reason for the induction of *Patapsco* and the other Baltimore schooners into navy service, was the capture of the four Baltimore schooners in the Rappahannock River. While this event proved the vulnerability of these vessels in restricted waters, it did not alter the navy's decision to use them inside the Bay as guard vessels and lookouts.

In November of 1813, *Patapsco*, out of the navy and refurbished, prepared for a voyage that would take her first to Havana and then to France. She received letter-of-marque commission #918.[63] Clopper and Fulford, still her part-owners, added new members to the consortium. Henry Holden became agent for the voyage; George P. Stevenson and a new master,

Matthew Kelly, completed the joint venture.[64] Captain Kelly loaded 1,100 barrels of flour and 48 barrels of navy bread. The cargo was for the owners' account, and Kelly's orders were to sell it in Havana and to obtain a cargo of white sugar for the French market.[65]

Patapsco completed this triangular voyage successfully at New York in the late spring of 1814, for there is information that she cleared that port 12 June 1814 on her first privateer cruise.[66] She took several prizes and returned safely, her last action in the war. The following year *Patapsco* was sold to Joseph Harrick and Henry Creighton of Beaufort,[67] who sold her to foreigners in the spring of 1816.[68]

When Congress declared war, the U.S. Navy had no Baltimore schooners in its fleet, having refitted *Enterprize, Nautilus*, and *Vixen* as brigs. But shortly afterwards the service purchased George Stiles' privateer *Nonsuch* and a new schooner, *Carolina*, built by James Marsh in Charleston in 1812.[69] The navy also took into the service several Revenue Cutters, all schooners, at least two of which, *Surveyor* and *James Madison*, were built at Baltimore. The *Madison* took a British brig early in the war, and then was captured by the Royal Navy off Savannah.[70]

The U.S. Navy was acquiring schooners and brigs in late 1814 to form two squadrons to supplement the activity of privateers. Work on *Lynx* at the Washington Navy Yard was completed. Andrew Clopper sold *Grampus* to the navy and the service renamed her *Spitfire*.[71] These and other small vessels were part of a fleet commanded by Captains David Porter and Oliver Hazard Perry which was forming as war ended.

The return of Baltimore's fleet spread over the winter months of 1815 as word of a peace treaty slowly reached ships at sea. No official tally of the losses suffered by the British merchant fleet was kept. Several estimates place the total British losses between 1,300 and 1,600 ships. Journalists and historians have worked with various sets of unofficial records endeavoring to estimate the accomplishments of Baltimore schooners during the War of 1812. Approximately 127 commissioned vessels sailed out of the Port of Baltimore during the war. A generally accepted estimate is that Baltimore privateers took approximately 550 British ships. This figure becomes a rather startling percentage of the total number of prizes of the war when letter-of-marque traders, which made up more than half of Baltimore's fleet, are subtracted from the total, leaving approximately 55 Baltimore privateers. As America's private armed fleet exceeded 500 vessels, Maryland's privateer schooners, about 12 percent of the total commissioned, captured or sunk more than 40 percent of the British merchant ships lost!

Of the total Baltimore-owned commissioned schooners, Fells Point shipwrights are known to have built about 75, and Talbot County builders are thought to have launched 36. Six Baltimore schooners were built in Dorchester County and four in Queen Anne's County. Somerset County, once Maryland's leading producer of ships, built two letter-of-marque traders; two were built in Virginia, and St. Mary's and Ann Arundel Counties each accounted for one. The large number built in Talbot County is particularly notable as several local shipwrights, including Thomas Kemp, left the area for Fells Point before the war.[72]

After the war, the Baltimore fleet came home to the welcome of families and cheers from the city's crowds. In the first months of 1815, as fast as the large pilot schooners docked at Fells Point, owners sold them out of their fleets. The limited cargo space of the sharp wartime model could not turn a profit on peacetime trading voyages. However, the end of the long period of war did not bring an end to the Chesapeake Bay pilot schooner. Form following function, local builders adjusted to new conditions and built schooners to suit them. And much of the maritime world, excited by the success of these vessels, developed their own versions that sailed the seas from Scandinavia to China over the next decades.

ENDNOTES - CHAPTER SIX

1. USS *Chesapeake*/HMS *Leopard* affair, 22 June 1807. See A.T. Mahan, *Sea Power in its Relations to the War of 1812*.(London: Sampson Low, Marston & Co., Ltd., 1905), Vol 1, 155-70.

2. *Nonpareil*, Baltimore schooner; carpenter certificate, signed by William Price, 7 November 1807. RG36-41, National Archives, hereafter cited as NA.

3. *Nonpareil*, Register #210, 10 November 1807. RG36-41 NA.

4. *Rossie*, Register #151, 26 November 1812. Records of the Bureau of Marine Inspection and Navigation, RG36-41, NA. Also, Kemp's Papers, Maryland Historical Society, hereafter cited as MHS, MS 2335; Kemp supplies the following additional information about *Rossie*: Foremast located 18'9" from inside of stem to center of mast; mainmast position was 35'6" from center of mast to center of foremast; from center of main to taffrail rail was 41'6"; bowsprit was 20'0", outbound; main boom 62' long and 12.5' in diameter; transom 17' at the bend.

5. Joshua Montefiore, *Commercial Dictionary, containing the Present State of Mercantile Law, Practice and Custom* (Philadelphia: James Humphreys, 1804), 58-59; quoting Act of Congress, passed 4 August 1790, Secton 44.

6. John Philips Cranwell and William Bowers, *Men of Marque* (New York: W. W. Norton & Co., 1940), Appendix A, 401.

7. *Dolphin*, Baltimore schooner; carpenter certificate, signed by William Price, 16 February 1809. RG41 NA.

8. Cranwell, 106-10.

9. Carpenter certificates, signed by William Price: *Herald*, 14 March 1807; *Luna*, April, 1809; *Von Hollen*, 13 April 1812, *Revenge*, 24 September 1812; *Price*, 27 March 1812; *Sabine*, 7 January 1813. RG36-41 NA.

10. William Price, Last Will and Testament, 2 July 1828. Baltimore County Register of Wills, 1831, 80-82, Maryland Hall of Records.

11. Carpenter certificates, signed by John Price: *Tom*, 1 August 1812; *Phaeton*, April, 1812; *Cashier*, 29 December 1812. RG36-41 NA.

12. Carpenter certificates, signed by John Price: *Eclipse*,

27 June 1811; *Elizabeth*, 19 June 1815. RG41 NA.

13. Carpenter certificates, signed by Thomas Kemp: *Hebe*, 22 September 1807; *Breeze*, 24 October 1807. RG41 NA.

14. *Globe*, Baltimore schooner, carpenter certificate signed Hunley and Gayle, 12 September 1809. RG41 NA.

15. *Lynx*, Baltimore schooner, carpenter certificate signed by James Cordery, 20 June 1812, RG41 NA.

16. Carpenter certificates, signed by Bernard Salenave, *Expedition*, 18 October 1812; signed by Andrew Denoanda, *Bellona*, 24 October 1812, RG36 NA; Lugger *Cora*, Registered, 22 September 1813, builder, Andrew Descande. RG41 NA.

17. Captain Benjamin Quimbey's Deposition; Paragraph 3; Admiralty Prize Court Case: HCA 32-1608, Public Records Office, London.

18. Ibid. Ship documents: U.S. Customs Clearance Documents, Certified by French Consul, Baltimore.

19. Ibid. Deposition, paragraph 7.

20. Ibid. Bill of lading, consular invoice and manifest.

21. Ibid. Deposition, paragraph 3.

22. Ibid. Thomas Tenant's voyage instructions.

23. Ibid. Tenant's cargo invoice.

24. J.J. Colledge, *Ships of the Royal Navy* (Annapolis: Naval Institute Press, 1987), Volume 1, 243-44.

25. *Nonpareil*'s cargo invoice and bill of lading, HCA 32-1608, Public Records Office, London.

26. Ibid. Tenant's instructions to John Morton, Paris agent.

27. *Nonpareil*'s bill of lading, HCA-32-1608, Public Records Office, London.

28. Letter, Thomas Parker to General Alexander Smyth, 22 October 1812, Report 130, Letter 11; 13th Congress, 2nd Session: On the Manner in Which the War Was Conducted, 21 February 1814.

29. Ibid. Letter, William H. Winder to General Smyth, 2 December 1812. Letter 52.

30. Ibid. Letter, General Dearborn to Secretary of War, 6 June 1813. Report 127. 445.

31. U.S. frigates, individual victories, 1812: USS *Constitution* vs HMS *Guerriere*, 19 August, USS *United States* vs HMS *Macedonian*, 25 October, USS *Constitution* vs HMS *Java*, 29 December.

32. *Rossie*, Baltimore schooner, carpenter certificate,

signed by Thomas Kemp, 8 September 1807. RG41 NA.

33. *Nonsuch*, Baltimore schooner, carpenter certificate, signed by William Parsons, 30 June 1809. RG41 NA.

34. Mary Barney, Editor, *Biographical Memoir of the Late Commodore Joshua Barney* (Boston: Grey and Bowen, 1832), 64-65.

35. Cranwell, 63-71.

36. Baltimore schooner *Comet*; built by Thomas Kemp at Fells Point and sold to Thorndike Chase; Baltimore carpenter certificate dated 4 May 1810; RG36-41, NA. Also Kemp Papers, MHS MS 2335, microfilm Roll 3. Kemp wrote that *Comet* was originally ordered by Captain William Furlong. His notes provide the following additional information: carpenter measure 68' x 23' x 10' and 160-60/95 tons. The price: $22 per ton or $3,621.89.

37. *Federal Gazette*, 26 May 1810.

38. *Comet*, Baltimore register #18, 1811 and #141 & 142, 1812. RG36-41, NA.

39. Jerome R. Garitee, *The Republic's Private Navy* (Midddletown, Connecticut: Wesleyan University Press for Mystic Seaport Museum, 1977), 251.

40. Cranwell, 125-51.

41. *Grecian*, Baltimore schooner, Baltimore register #26, 2 March 1812; includes information that Thomas Kemp was builder. RG41 NA. Also, Kemp Papers, MHS MS 2335. Kemp provides her carpenter measure: 71' x 23'6" x 10'8" and 187.25 tons. Her cost was $23 per ton or $4,306.75.

42. *Grampus*, Baltimore schooner, carpenter certificate signed by Thomas Kemp; no date, 1812. RG41 NA.

43. Kemp, Baltimore schooner, Baltimore register # 66, 14 July 1812. RG41 NA.

44. *Chasseur*, Baltimore schooner, carpenter certificate signed by Thomas Kemp, 1 January 1813. RG41 NA.

45. "Log of the *Chasseur*," 26-27 February 1815. Maryland Historical Magazine, Vol. 1: 218. Also, Colledge, 302.

46. Baltimore schooner *Atlas*; built in Talbot County, Maryland in 1808 for Thomas Tenant; sold to Philadelphians in 1810; captured by Royal Navy, June 1813; and commissioned as HMS *St. Lawrence*, Captain James Gordon, commanding.

47. "Cost of the Schooner *Patapsco* and her Cargo"

48. Garitee, 115 and 58n, 306. Quoting letter T. and S. Hollingsworth to Levi Hollingsworth and Son, Philadelphia, 21 June 1812. Historical Society of Pennsylvania.

49. Cranwell, 336-45; also, *Patapsco*, Baltimore register #361, 21 December 1815. RG41, NA.

50. MHS, MS, 1931.

51. *Patapsco*, Baltimore schooner, carpenter certificate signed by Thomas Kemp, dated 8 September 1812. RG41 NA.

52. "Log of the Harpy," 22 April 1814. MHS, MS 2321, microfilm of original.

53. Cranwell, 186.

54. Garitee, 36, 95.

55. Letter, W.M.P. Dunne to author, dated 13 April 1993.

56. *Lynx*, Baltimore register #67, 14 July, 1812, RG41 NA.

57. *Federal Gazette*, 20 March 1806.

58. Baltimore Entrances #288, 11 November 1815, *Patapsco* from Naples; Captain R. Moon. MHS, MS 2301, microfilm from originals at RG41 NA.

59. Garitee, 178, Andrew Clopper purchased 850 bags of coffee for $22,213.91; cargo from the prize *Braganza*.

60. MHS, MS 1931.

61. Cranwell, 105: quoting Captain William J. Stafford's (*Dolphin*) journal.

62. Cranwell, Appendix A, 401.

63. Garitee, 254, Appendix A.

64. William M. Marine, *The British Invasion of Maryland, 1812-1815* (Hatboro, Pennsylvania: Tradition Press, 1965), 19-20, quoting letter, Henry Fulford to unknown person, 21 November 1813.

65. Ibid.

66. Cranwell, 336.

67. *Patapsco*, Baltimore register #361, 21 December 1815. RG41 NA.

68. Ibid.

69. Pratt, 418

70. H. R. Kaplan and James F. Hunt, *This is the Coast Guard* (Cambridge, Maryland: Cornell Maritime Press, Inc., 1972), 6.

71. Pratt, 42.

72. Baltimore registers, 1805-15, RG36/41 NA.

MHS, undated manuscript MHS, MS 1931.

HERMAPHRODITE BRIG *KITE*, BUILT BY
HUNT AND WAGGNER AT FELLS POINT IN 1847.
PAINTING BY JAMES GUY EVANS.
Peabody Essex Museum, Salem, MA.

CHAPTER SEVEN

A CLIPPER
BY ASSOCIATION

After centuries of exploration and conquest, warriors laid down their arms and naval fleets rotted in the decades following the Treaty of Ghent. Power and wealth began to grow from within rather than from military expeditions or the exploits of fleets. Steam-powered machinery, replacing nature's forces of wind and water, multiplied human productivity and entrepreneurial wealth beyond the dreams of the old explorers and freebooters. The United States and the Western World began to experience the impact of the Industrial Revolution.

In 1814, the year the British concentrated land and sea forces in Chesapeake Bay, a grim Baltimore watched its commerce dwindle to nothing. After the peace treaty was signed the region was stunned by an awareness that neutral trade with the West Indies did not revive. Britain and other European powers quickly reinstituted old nationalistic navigation laws that barred U.S. vessels from their colonial ports.

America's second war with Great Britain was a footnote to Europe's great conflicts; but for the United States it marked a radical change of direction. The original states, spread along the Atlantic seaboard, viewed with apprehension the settlement and development of land to the west and the growth of new manufacturing centers. Foreign trade and American shipping would soon no longer occupy leading positions in America's increasingly diversified economic structure. Shipowners lost ground to industrialists and to powerful merchant-distributors who carried America west with their enterprise.

Around Chesapeake Bay, the old fighters for independence soon died and the newly rich merchant-warriors of Baltimore converted their war profits into comfortable estates in the hills and valleys of the country north of Baltimore. Like veterans of all hard-fought battles, they seemed never quite adjusted to the many changes that arrived after the war. Baltimore's merchant families seemed to lose their aggressive entrepreneurial drive, but they continued to exercise a disproportionate amount of political and economic influence over Baltimore and Maryland affairs.

Formally organized commodity exchanges and financial institutions began to replace the informality of business contracts sealed by handshakes and personal letters of exchange. Foreign

commerce, of decreasing importance to the nation's total economic activity, became centered in New York where specialists in international banking and commodity trading maintained fluid markets and where most American importers established their businesses.

As Baltimore and other regional ports handled a decreasing portion of the nation's foreign commerce, Maryland and Virginia were freed of their dependence on an export economy that had shaped their destinies since early colonial times. While baycraft continued to handle the movement of grain for milling and export, Baltimore and the other cities along the fall lines of the region became large consumers of the products of farms and forests in rural Maryland and Virginia. The rich and mostly untouched catch of the rivers and the Bay was now an important source of food for urban populations. And although roads were built and steamboat wharves soon dotted the charts of every river of the estuary, these systems supplemented rather than diminished the number of pilot schooners on Chesapeake Bay.

Baltimore's wharves became the terminals for more and more vessels owned in other ports of America or by foreign interests. Much of Maryland's export trade, formerly carried directly overseas in Maryland ships, shifted to several coastal services which carried a significant portion of it into New York for transshipment abroad. A large percentage of the nation's imports, particularly packaged goods, entered the country through the port of New York.

Baltimore's flour and grain trade was strong in the postwar years as many islands of the Caribbean remained dependent on shipments from the port throughout the nineteenth century. New routes to South America developed to bring coffee, fertilizer, ores and metals to the region's consumers and industries. But over time the city lost the mercantile excitement of its first adventurous century as it became a smoky factory town. Its importance as an industrial center and a regional distribution hub eclipsed its role as a port for the next 150 years.

Baltimore's postwar reality came into focus in the large and small disasters of the economic crash of 1818. The depression set off by America's first financial crunch curtailed the dreams and plans of Baltimore's commercial interests. The crash revealed a city whose economic structure rested on weak foundations, a community of traders and seafarers ill-equipped to profit from the new business of a new era.

At the end of the War of 1812 Baltimore shipowners found themselves with a fleet of privateer-type schooners limited in cargo space and of only peripheral value on America's postwar trade routes. The high risks of former times, which produced the specialized craft of Chesapeake Bay, were replaced by peace and greater compliance with international law or international understandings enforced by European navies. With its wartime fleet obsolete, the great schooners disappeared from Chesapeake Bay to sail on routes where the instability or illegality of a trading opportunity required the speed and sailing qualities of these vessels of war.

Some armed Baltimore schooners found employment after 1815 in the clandestine operations of pirates and slavers. Foreign countries offered letter-of-marque commissions to Baltimore captains–some to fight for liberty in new navies of revolution against Spain in the Caribbean and South America, and others to operate under official sanction, making privateering cruises no different from those conducted by pirates. Some of these schooners remained under Baltimore ownership, while others, sold to foreign owners, continued to sail under the command of Baltimore masters.

The flour industry was still Baltimore's economic advantage. The region's millers aggressively embraced innovative machinery that produced the best flour, and strong demand remained in international markets. In 1820, a year that Baltimore struggled with its first depression, flour inspections, a good measure of shipments, totalled 582,000 barrels, up almost 200,000 since 1815. The expanding flour industry with new markets in South America and Europe kept a large fleet of baycraft schooners employed hauling grain. This expansion helped to stabilize the area's depressed shipbuilding industry during the postwar years.[1]

The Federal census of 1820 placed Baltimore's population at 62,739. In the next ten years the city added 17,882 people, including a growing number of immigrants from Europe. Jean Baptiste Marestier arrived in Baltimore during the winter of 1820. The French government sent the marine engineer and naval architect to report on the technological sophistication of America's steamboats. Marestier went beyond his primary mission, and after preparing the portion of his report on Chesapeake Bay steamboats he visited Fells Point's shipyards and wharves where he measured and made drawings of several pilot schooners. The Frenchman returned to Paris, where his work was published, providing historians and naval architects with a study of pilot schooners, including pilot boats, baycraft, coastwise schooners and Baltimore schooners.[2] His drawings included two schooners under construction at Fells Point during the first and second quarters of 1820.[3]

Marestier made his calculations under difficult circumstances as he was, in reality, an industrial spy climbing over ships in the water or on ways. He had the opportunity to board the Baltimore armed schooner *Mammoth*, (schooner No. 1) and record her measurements. Even so, his calculation of her length, 114.94', differs from her registered length, 112', by almost three feet.[4] This could occur from the mere physical difficulty of measuring or because his units of measure were either metric or the French foot, which is approximately 7 percent greater than an American foot.

One of the vessels Marestier described and drew was a pilot schooner he labeled No. 12. She was one of the two schooners under construction at the time of his visit,[5] and according to his calculations she measured 72' on deck. An example of a coastwise cargo craft of the nineteenth century, schooner No. 12 shows a decreased amount of deadrise and a more prominent turn of bilges in her lines, producing a fuller hull for increased cargo capacity.

Schooner No. 12's lines were graceful. Pronounced rake to her stem and stern post, noticeable drag to her keel, and graceful curve of sheer, gave her the classic pilot-schooner profile. Her entrance was convex and her after lines were distinguished by fuller waterlines. Reproduced below are Marestier's drawings of schooner No. 12, along with her measurements as the Frenchman calculated or estimated them.

PRINCIPAL DIMENSIONS[6] OF
MARESTIER SCHOONER NO. 12

LENGTH . . . . .21.85 meters (71.68 feet)
BEAM . . . . .6.40 meters (20.99 feet)
DEPTH AT BOW . . . . .2.57meters (8.43 feet)
DEPTH AT
MIDSECTION . . . . .2.50 meters (8.20 feet)
DEPTH AT STERN . . . . . .3.20 meters (10.50 feet)
OVERHANG OF BOW . . . .4.57 meters (14.99 feet)
DISTANCE MIDSECTION IS
FORWARD OF CENTER . .1.52 meters (4.99 feet)
RAKE OF STERNPOST . . .2.17 meters (7.12 feet)

Reuben Ross established a packet service between Baltimore and

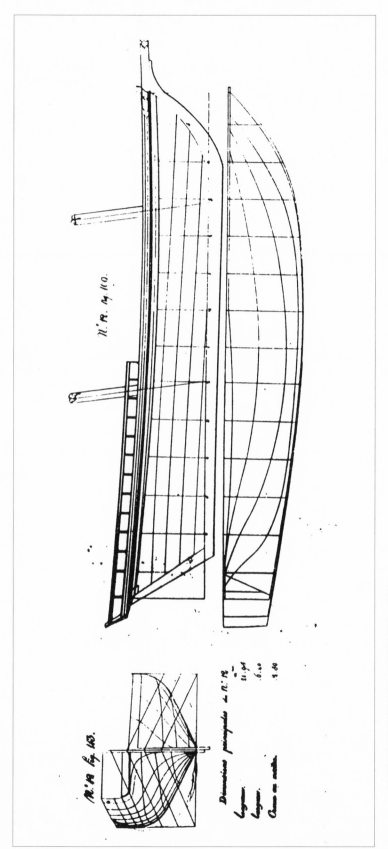

PLAN OF SCHOONER NO. 12 BY JEAN BAPTISTE
MARESTIER, PUBLISHED IN HIS STUDY OF
AMERICAN VESSELS, 1824.

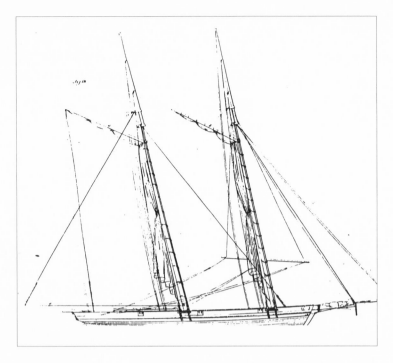

schooners rigged with boomless foresails overlapping the mainmast as illustrated by figure #116, this page.[9]

Marestier measured and drafted another Baltimore schooner under construction during his visit, which he labeled No. 6. She was one of the larger schooners built at Fells Point in 1820.[10] William Price built *Theban* in May and June of that year, and James Beacham built two large schooners that year–*Clio*, finished at the end of 1820, and *Lightning*, built in the spring. The latter more closely matched the time of Marestier's visit and the dimensions of his schooner No. 6. *Lightning*'s measurements were: 91' x 22'4" x 9'8". Price's *Theban* measured 91'x 22'9" x 10'3".[11] Marestier's drawing of No. 6 could be either of the two, although neither *Lightning* nor *Theban* had the same breadth as No. 6. If Marestier's schooner No. 6 was *Theban*, it would be the only drawing of a William Price pilot schooner in existence.

Alexandria in 1817, one of the first scheduled packet services in the U.S. These vessels sailed every Saturday for a number of years and included small schooners such as one called *Virginia Ross*.[7] Robert Robinson built *Virginia Ross* during the winter of 1820 at Fells Point. Her carpenter certificate, dated 30 June 1820, states her keel length for tonnage at 47'. Ross registered her on the same date and the surveyor recorded dimensions of 67'6" x 20'6" x 7'10", describing a schooner not unlike Marestier's No. 12, although the dimensions of No. 12 are slightly larger.[8]

Marestier's drawings included three fully-rigged schooners. One of these, figure #115, has a gunter or gaff topsail on her maintopmast, and square topsails on her foretopmast. What is unusual about this drawing is that he drew the foresail with a boom. Every other painting or drawing of a Chesapeake Bay pilot schooner made prior to 1850 shows these

PRINCIPAL DIMENSIONS
OF SCHOONER NO. 6[12]

LENGTH	.28.28 meters (92.78 feet)
BEAM	.7.32 meters (24.00 feet)
DEPTH OF BOW	.3.37 meters (11.06 feet)
DEPTH OF MIDSECTION	.3.05 meters (10.00 feet)
DEPTH OF STERN	.4.04 meters (13.25 feet)
OVERHANG OF BOW	.6.10 meters (20.01 feet)
DISTANCE MIDSECTION IS	
FORWARD OF CENTER . . .	.1.64 meters (5.38 feet)
RAKE OF STERNPOST	.2.97 meters (9.74 feet)
LENGTH OF MAINMAST .	.22.00 meters (2.18 feet)
LENGTH OF FOREMAST .	.21.30 meters (69.88 feet)

Other than in details, the schooners observed by Marestier were similar to pre-

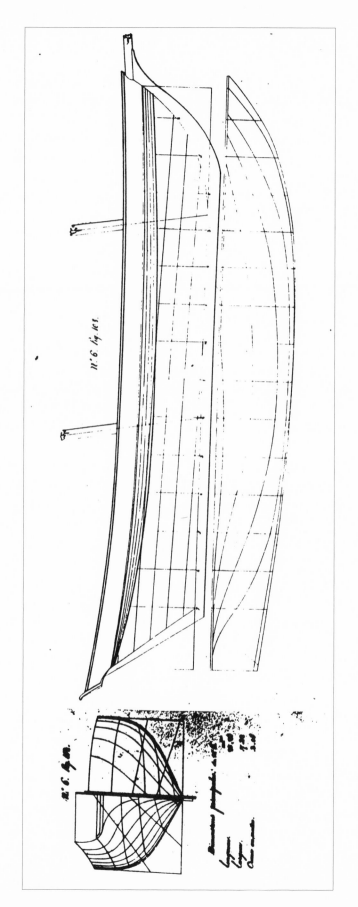

PLAN OF SCHOONER NO. 6 BY JEAN BAPTISTE
MARESTIER, PUBLISHED IN HIS STUDY OF
AMERICAN VESSELS, 1824.

war pilot schooners. Baltimore's foreign trade was in disarray in 1820 and local merchants had no clear picture of the future. Although the shipbuilders who had created the great Baltimore schooners were still in place, they, like Baltimore's merchants, were marking time during the transition from one economic era to another.

Isaac McKim of the powerful McKim family purchased three new Baltimore schooners in 1815 and 1816. Thomas Kemp and George Gardner built *Rossie* II for McKim in 1815.[13] McKim's new pilot schooner was just slightly larger than his first *Rossie* of 1807, according to her register. Kemp continued to use the description "privateer built," even though Baltimore's war had ended six months before she was launched. During this same period McKim purchased two post-war Baltimore schooners, *Tropic* and *Plattsburgh*,[14] also built by Kemp and Gardner. George Gardner, Thomas Kemp's partner during his last years in Baltimore, opened his own yard at the east end of Fells Point when Kemp returned to his farm in Talbot County.

The McKim family were among those mercantile powers adjusting to profound changes in Maryland's economy which had brought bankruptcy to many of the city's most prominent merchants between 1815 and 1819. A significant reality was that with peace the lucrative neutral trade had vanished. In addition, Baltimore's trade with the West Indies did not revive immediately. And perhaps most significantly the city's merchants did

not have a wide selection of exports to offer overseas buyers. Maryland tobacco was exported in limited amounts. Flour exports were large to the West Indies, but taste preferences and risk of spoilage on long voyages restricted its sale to many other areas. As milling equipment improved, flour exports to South America increased, with Brazil becoming a leading market where flour was exchanged for coffee. Finally, the region was still sparsely populated in 1820, and this kept demands for imports low.

The McKims entered the flour milling business soon after the Revolutionary War, and they adopted the newest steam machinery for this industry and several others. With demand high for cotton textiles, including cotton duck for sails, the McKims opened the Baltimore Steam Works Factory during the War of 1812. Additionally, there was a growing demand for copper, and new factories to process ore and to produce copper products and sheet were established around Baltimore during and following the war. Isaac McKim entered these trades.[15] Later the family purchased the Gunpowder Copper Works and developed an array of joint ventures with other trading and industrial groups.

Needing more than just flour to exchange for the raw materials of industry, such as copper ore and semi-refined ingots, almost all of which were available in the newly-independent nations of South America, McKim tried several approaches. He could use specie if he had it, although products and commodities were the preferred exchange. McKim found markets for flour but not necessarily for the products of Baltimore's mills. Richmond flour had greater acceptance in some countries than Baltimore's superfine. Eventually, McKim developed an ingenious plan which began with the purchase of Turkish opium for resale to other traders, mostly Baltimore merchants, then used the proceeds to buy copper and other products.

There is no record of McKim's employment of *Rossie* II and *Tropic,* but an incident that was covered by a local journal revealed much about *Plattsburgh's* maiden voyage. She departed from Fells Point 16 November 1816, with a cargo consisting of approximately 60 tons of coffee and $40,000 in specie. The captain's instructions were to sail to Smyrna, Turkey, sell the cargo and use the proceeds to buy opium. This plan was revealed when, once in international waters, the crew mutinied and sailed McKim's ship to Europe.[16]

Plattsburgh was sold in 1817 after the legal problems surrounding the mutiny were settled, but not before the aborted voyage revealed Isaac McKim's plan for broadening his narrow export base. There exists no record of any McKim ships sailing in the China trade, although *Ann McKim* sailed to China after she was sold to Howland and Aspinwall. However, there is circumstantial evidence that McKim resold opium acquired in Turkey to other Baltimore and Philadelphia merchants doing business in China. It is thought that McKim used the profits of these opium sales to buy copper, mostly

in Chile. As this multinational business grew, the McKim family established a base in South America at Valparaiso, the port where McKim's ships as well as those of his associates commenced or completed many voyages.[17]

This trade expanded over the years as McKim and others traded for copper along the Pacific coast of South America from Chile to Mexico. As far as is known all opium was sent to China while copper cargoes are believed to have been split between China and Baltimore. The fact that a number of Baltimore-owned vessels originated China voyages at Valparaiso was no coincidence. The Chinese were interested in a short list of Western products. Included were shipbuilding supplies, cotton manufactures, copper, Turkish opium, and tobacco, all of which McKim could deliver out of his stores in Chile. The only Chinese-export products he did not have direct access to were sealskins and ginseng.

George Gardner built *Yellot* for Isaac McKim in 1823. He called her a schooner, pilot-boat built, and on the carpenter certificate he recorded her length of keel, straight rabbet, as 70'3". She was just 141 tons, carpenter's measure. *Yellot* measured 179 tons burden and had registered dimensions of 93' x 22' x 9'8". Her keel was longer compared to earlier pilot schooners, and this, along with shorter ends, increased her cargo area. Her depth of hold was less in relation to her other dimensions, but her hull was probably fuller than the hulls of the wartime schooners. *Yellot* was an example of the pilot schooner in transition.[18]

In the more than ten years that Isaac McKim owned *Yellot* he dispatched her on many voyages to Mediterranean ports, to Chile, to other locations along the west coast of South America, to Philadelphia, and occasionally to Fells Point. There is enough information in Baltimore's old Maritime Exchange arrival and clearance records to understand *Yellot*'s mission within the larger scope of McKim's operations.[19]

This modified pilot schooner, sailing transatlantic and around Cape Horn both ways several times in ten years, delivered opium and other products to Valparaiso and returned to the United States with specie and copper. Sometimes *Yellot* sailed, with intermediate stops, directly for the Mediterranean if another vessel was available at Valparaiso to carry copper and specie to Fells Point.

Yellot must have been an exciting and attractive schooner with a small cargo area, low profile and great cloud of white cotton sails [McKim claimed that Chesapeake Bay schooners gained one mile per hour with cotton sails, as compared to linen sails of Russian or Holland duck].[20] Her speed attracted attention, and *Niles' Register* published the following record of one of her voyages:

Departed Valparaiso	*June 8, 1825*
Rounded Cape Horn	*June 26 . .18 days*
Off Rio de la Plata	*July 7 . . .11 days*
Looked into Pernambuco	*July 17 . .10 days*
Crossed the line	*July 20 . .3 days*
Off Cape Henry	*August 6 .17 days*
	. . .59 days total[21]

This rare record of an intercontinental voyage by a Chesapeake Bay pilot schooner allows comparison to the records of later ships on the same run. McKim's ship-rigged *Ann McKim*, one of America's most admired vessels, completed the voyage in 59 days ten years later.[22] *Ann McKim* had a run of 42 days from Cape Horn to the Chesapeake; *Yellot* did the distance in 41 days. The following year *Ann McKim* made a Valparaiso-to-Baltimore voyage in 53 days, a record that may never have been broken by any of the clipper ships of mid-century or by any other sailing vessel. Because of *Ann McKim*'s great beauty and limited amount of cargo space, some maritime historians have speculated that she was built on a whim or as a toy for McKim. This is incorrect. Isaac McKim was a hard-nosed businessman who built this vessel to cover the long distance between Chesapeake Bay and the Pacific coast of South America with flour, still perishable on long voyages over the equator.[23]

The Perkins Brothers, Thomas H. and James, Thomas H. Perkins, Jr., Samuel Cabot and John P. Cushing, all of Boston, purchased the schooner *Greyhound*, new from her builder James Beacham, in 1826, and operated her as an opium carrier in the China trade. The Perkins firm became the principal American opium traders after Cushing was appointed American consul at Whampoa.[24] While consul, Cushing set up an American opium-receiving ship at the Whampoa anchorage in the Pearl River estuary and broadened the scope of the firm's distribution system

Greyhound to Canton China. 1827.
Josiah Sturgis Esq. Commander

with schooners like *Greyhound*. She was 82' overall and was employed as a feeder vessel between the warehouse ship and the northern ports of China. Called sharp by her builder, she was smaller than *Yellot*, but had similar proportions.[25]

The schooners under discussion were purchased for their speed and did not greatly differ from prewar pilot schooners. In Far East mercantile circles, fast Chesapeake Bay schooners and brigs were called opium clippers, as were similar vessels built in India and in Great Britain. Therefore, *Greyhound*, built in

1826, and *Dart*, built for the trade in 1844, both schooners, were clippers by association and not by design.

William and George Gardner built the schooner *Dart* for the opium distribution network of Augustine Heard & Company in China. *Dart* was built at the same time as the Baltimore brig *Frolic*, also a Heard of Boston opium carrier, and discussed in the next chapter. No carpenter's certificate could be located so the Gardner brothers' description of their schooner is unknown. Her register measurements of 85'7" x 21' x 9'2" suggest that she was

BALTIMORE SCHOONER *GREYHOUND*, BUILT AT FELLS POINT IN 1826, IS SHOWN IN A PAINTING BY A CHINESE ARTIST. *From the Collection of the Museum of Arts and Sciences, Daytona Beach, FL. Gift of Kenneth W. Dow.*

THE COASTAL PILOT
SCHOONER *YOUNG
BRUTUS* IS SHOWN
IN THIS PAINTING
BY FREDERIC ROUX.
*Courtesy of Childs
Gallery, Boston.*

sharp-built and similar to *Greyhound*, built almost two decades earlier.[26]

Talbot County's shipbuilding industry, which peaked with the demand for Baltimore schooners during the War of 1812, flattened the forests for miles around St. Michaels. Some Talbot County shipwrights retired due to inactivity, and younger ones moved across the Choptank River to be near the virgin forests on its south shore, as the center of shipbuilding on the Eastern Shore shifted to Dorchester County. Among dozens of shipwrights building there was the Richardson family in and around Church

Creek. George and Isaac Davis, sons of John Davis, who built pilot schooners in Talbot County, located yards on Taylors Island. Dorchester County shipwrights, led by the Richardsons, built West Indies traders, coastal schooners and brigs for tramp trading, and vessels for the growing number of packet services that called at ports from New England to New Orleans.

Noah Richardson began building schooners before the War of 1812, and among them were four Baltimore armed schooners named *Brutus*, *High Flyer*, *Macedonian* and *Spartan*. The small privateer *High Flyer* became one of the best-known Maryland vessels of the War of 1812, and when captured became one of Admiral Cockburn's squadron which devastated Chesapeake Bay in 1814. She was recaptured and sold to Bostonians at war's end. Richardson's *Brutus* (there is a painting of her in Chapter 6) was purchased by Massachusetts owners and commissioned there for at least one privateering cruise in 1814.

The family dynasty that Noah Richardson founded included nine sons and came to an end with James B. (Jim) Richardson, Chesapeake Bay's famous builder, who died in 1991. Between Noah and Jim there were many Richardsons building wooden vessels on the Bay. Among their contemporaries, Thomas Kemp, William Price, and Noah Richardson stood above the rest. Although building pilot schooners required a close adherence to the proportions and characteristics of the type, these three artisans made small adjustments that moved their models to higher levels as the needs of their clients changed.

Noah Richardson built *Young Brutus* at Church Creek in 1818. She was not a large schooner, as her length on deck was just 86' or one foot longer than *High Flyer*, built in 1811. Carpenter measurements of the two schooners on their certificates were similar–53' x 20' x 8.5'–as were register measurements and burden. In the image here, the original of which is a watercolor painted by Frederic Roux, several Richardson innovations can be observed. First, the schooner, pilot-boat-built, has the more conservative rig of a coastal schooner, stout short spars with topmasts rigged for gaff sails, similar to the schooner pictured in the Marestier drawings. Of greater importance is the schooner's bow with a short, straighter stem and a sharp concave entrance, a significant change from the rounder, fuller convex bow of earlier pilot schooners. This change was repeated in later clipper brigs and schooners.[27]

Although Richardson described *Young Brutus* on her certificate as sharp, she probably had greater fullness below the waterline than the armed schooners of 1812. As the Fells Point shipbuilders continued in 1818 to build schooners nearly the same as before the war, perhaps it was Noah Richardson who led his contemporaries into the next stage of the Bay pilot-schooner design. *Young Brutus* was sold to foreign owners, which could explain how Roux happened to paint her. It is possible, too, that she was a slaver.

Levin and Standby Richardson built the sharp schooner *Mork* in 1824.[28] *Niles' Register* took note of her remarkable voyage to Haiti the following year, as "she reached Cape Henry (Haiti) in eight days from Baltimore and six from the Capes of the Chesapeake; and only nineteen days were occupied in her late passage to and from Haiti."[29]

It is not unreasonable to conclude that *Yellot, Greyhound, Mork, Dart* and even *Young Brutus*, as well as the schooners documented by Marestier, possessed pilot-schooner speed. This was what their owners wanted and this was the dominating characteristic of the

design. It is also true that in Baltimore's postwar foreign trade offshore schooners began to play a reduced role by 1830. Pilot schooners now shared Chesapeake Bay trade and the nearby coastal trade to and from ports in the Carolinas and north to New York with schooners of greater burden. Pilot schooners like *Mork* were sailed to and from the Caribbean in great numbers.

An example of the Baltimore schooners of the 1830s is *Mary and Francis,* built in Fells Point in 1832 with a striking clipper bow, a long graceful bowsprit and a jibboom pointing skyward at a sharp angle with the horizon. A painting of *Mary and Francis,* by an unidentified artist, is in the collection of Mystic Seaport Museum, and it shows us the flush-deck schooner that superseded the sharp pilot schooner.[30] Her dimensions were 92'9" x 22'5" x 8'2". As shown by the lines of *Isabella,* these schooners of the 1830s, with shallower holds and less deadrise, but with longer keels and shorter ends, had greater fullness of hull and greater cargo capacity.

The stability of a vessel like *Mary and Francis* was further increased by her more conservative rig. Her forestaysail was

smaller in area, as were her foresail and mainsail, and on shorter masts, compared with the rigs of the sharp schooners that preceded her. She had rather large square topsails on her foremast and a gaff main topsail. Overall, these features would make her a fast sailer in a fair wind. Such modifications did not reduce the beauty of the Chesapeake Bay schooner. As a matter of fact, it could be argued that

these postwar schooners were as handsome as the Baltimore schooners *Comet*, *Brutus*, and *Patapsco* that came before them.

A painting of the Baltimore-built schooner *H. H. Cole* by the artist Clement Drew is reproduced here. Drew painted her perfectly proportioned hull and sailplan in motion, carried by a brisk wind. Cleverly, he gives the schooner an

CLIPPER SCHOONER *H.H. COLE*. PAINTING BY CLEMENT DREW. *Peabody Essex Museum, Salem, MA.*

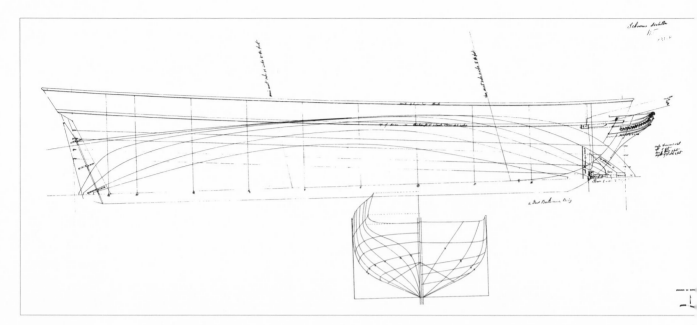

PLAN OF

ISABELLA, A PILOT

SCHOONER OF THE

1830s.

Independence

Seaport Museum,

Philadelphia.

illusion of greater than actual size. (She was really under 78' overall.) He effectively hypnotizes the viewer with the beauty of her form. Samuel Butler built *H. H. Cole* in 1843 for Gilbert Cassard who owned her for only a year. Sold to New England, her Salem owner was Robert Brookhouse. She sank after a collision in January 1846.[31]

The plan of *Isabella,* from the Lenthall Collection of the Franklin Institute in Philadelphia, shows the lines of a Chesapeake Bay schooner of–most likely–the 1830s. Howard Chapelle wrote that she was built in Baltimore in 1832. This is perhaps a guess.[32] At under 80', her size is similar to many of the small, sharp schooners built at Baltimore and elsewhere after 1820. Her hull, while having ample initial deadrise, was "full-built," as local shipwrights would describe the model. *Isabella* had a sharp entrance, the result of her slightly concave, flaring bow,

but she retained important characteristics of the Chesapeake Bay pilot schooner.

No register could be found for a schooner named *Isabella* built at Baltimore in 1832 with similar measurements, but Absalom Thompson of Talbot County built a schooner named *Isabella* in 1835 for Captain Matthew Kelly, a veteran privateer master of the War of 1812 and in 1835 a ship broker. Kelly resold that *Isabella* to Frederick W. Brune and James McAllister, two Baltimore merchants. This schooner's dimensions were 75'5" x 22'3" x 7', and she measured about 109 tons. She could easily have been the schooner whose lines are in the collection of the Franklin Institute. Brune and McAllister sold *Isabella* to foreign owners in 1836, just a few months after acquiring her.[33]

In the years between 1836, when records were first kept, and 1840, 631 schooners arrived at Baltimore from foreign ports, along with 819 brigs.

THIS DRAWING BY
FREDERIC ROUX
MAY REPRESENT
THE 1818 PILOT
SCHOONER
YOUNG BRUTUS.
Musée de la Marine,
Paris.

Baltimore's trade, handled for a century by schooners, was experiencing a change as a larger portion was handled by brigs after 1836. At the same time Baltimore's foreign trade continued to decrease in volume and value as New York became America's leading port.[34]

Treaties among most western nations as well as American laws in effect by 1820 outlawed the transportation of slaves from Africa to the Western Hemisphere under penalty of death. These punitive measures encouraged slave traders to employ a fast carrier in a trade that remained lucrative as demand for slaves in Cuba, Brazil and other Latin American nations and Spanish possessions remained strong. Cuba, for instance, had never developed a procreation program for its slaves, and depended almost entirely on replacements from Africa to keep the sugar plantations operating.

Although many Chesapeake Bay pilot schooners were sought by slave traders, there was need for a fast brig for this trade as well. George Gardner, who sold many of his schooners and brigs, all pilot-schooner types, to foreign buyers between 1820 and 1830, was, along with other Fells Point shipwrights, catering to the needs of these new customers. The vessel most wanted by a slave trader was usually a small brig or schooner to reduce investment, operating costs and draft, but with maximum capacity and enough speed to outsail most naval vessels. For the slave-ship owner, the brig was probably more reliable than the schooner for the voyage east to west with slaves on board. Because capacity was so important in view of their small dimensions, a new brig began to appear, and we may say that with it the Baltimore clipper was born.

Conjecture supported by some isolated facts to be presented suggests that the Baltimore clipper brig passed from slaver into legitimate commercial trade as shipbuilders, working with a new group of merchants and the survivors of Baltimore's financial shakeout of 1819, began to seek a new kind of vessel as a principal carrier during the years of economic recovery that followed.

Vessels with square rig were not new to Chesapeake Bay. Ships and brigs had been built by Virginia and Maryland country shipwrights before 1790 for Baltimore merchants. Fells Point shipwrights built an occasional square-rigged vessel prior to the War of 1812, and actually more ships than brigs. One of the early ones was the two-deck brig *Isabella*, built for Baltimore merchants in 1797.[35]

William Price built the flush-deck brig *Eutaw* in 1808 with a single deck, a vessel he typically described as pilot-boat-built. John Price, his son, built *Eclipse*, a single-deck brig, pilot-boat built, in 1811.[36] If there is a conclusion here, it is that Baltimore-built, larger two-deck brigs were similar in design to locally-built ships and that the early one-deck brig of pilot-boat design was the model for the postwar single-deck brigs with flush decks. These appeared in great numbers after 1830. In view of developments in shipbuilding on Chesapeake Bay after 1820, the fact that the Prices built brigs of pilot-boat design prior to the war serves as interesting background to the changes in progress as the senior Price entered the final decade of his career in 1822.

William Price was in his twenty-eighth year as a shipwright in Fells Point when he built the Baltimore clipper brig *Elizabeth*. This brig, built without a purchaser, was a speculation either because the old builder needed money, which is doubtful, or because he was reintroducing the single-deck brig to his customers. If the latter situation were true, history was being repeated. It was at the close of the eighteenth century that he built many of the first offshore pilot schooners on

PLAN OF HMS *ANDROMEDA,* BUILT AS THE BALTIMORE SHIPPED-RIGGED VESSEL *HANNIBAL,* BY WILLIAM PRICE IN 1811.
National Maritime Museum, London.

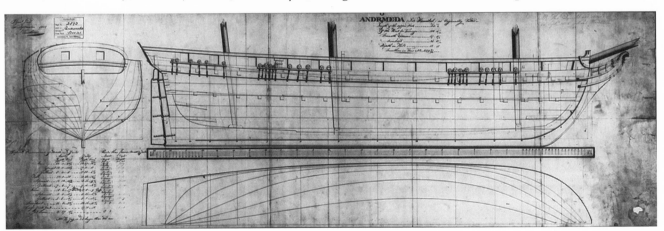

speculation, confident that the merchants of Baltimore would eventually accept the new model.

Price understood that change in ship design must parallel changes in the components of trade. Speed was desirable but related more to distance than to danger in 1822. Greater capacity was necessary after the war as cargo mixture, the size of shipments offered, and their weight-measure ratios became important considerations. These factors were closely related to the level of profits of a voyage. In the end, the carrier best designed for a commercial opportunity rewarded her owner with the highest return.

With *Elizabeth*, Price's objective may have been to move the design of the smaller, special-purpose, one-flush-deck brig to another level by building a 300-ton version which could carry profitable payloads under existing circumstances almost anywhere in the world. The builder's carpenter certificate has more limited information than normal as it fails to provide the brig's depth of hold even though she had but one deck. Her breadth was 28'7" moulded, and length on deck was 94'6". Later large single-deck brigs had less breadth, and on some of his Price added an extra set of beams, presumably for a false or temporary deck.[37]

William Price never gained the recognition he deserved as one of America's most innovative shipbuilders. It cannot be documented that William Price of Hampton, Virginia, is the same shipwright who after 1794 built so many flush-deck vessels at Fells Point, but the William Price

of Fells Point led the shipbuilding industry there for almost 38 years. Thomas Kemp gained fame for the Baltimore schooners that he built over a period of just ten years.

The first registered pilot schooners built by Price at Fells Point were *Infant Patriot* and *Atlas* in 1794. The latter, the first of a long list of beautiful large pilot schooners, was built for Robert Oliver. Between 1794 and 1799, Price built many of the first offshore pilot schooners later called Baltimore schooners. During that period it is believed that he also worked on USS *Constellation*. Price built the sloop of war USS *Maryland* and the Baltimore schooner USS *Experiment* in 1799, USS *Vixen* in 1803, and the brig USS *Hornet* in 1805. When Isaac Chauncey relinquished command of *Hornet* to John Dent, he wrote:

"The *Hornet* does not possess a single bad quality that I have discovered. She is strong and tight, sails remarkably fast by and large; steers and works well; is very stiff and an excellent sea boat. Her best sailing is on a wind, and her best trim fifteen inches by the stern—however I have never discovered that a few inches affected her sailing."[38]

Though most naval historians as well as official navy records credit Josiah Fox for the design of USS *Hornet*, the sharp-built sloop of war was probably designed after Price's USS *Maryland*. Certainly this theory is supported by a logical flow of documents and circumstances before and after *Hornet* was launched. The argument that Fox, after years of opposition to the ideas of the Humphreys, father and son, and to pilot-schooner design specifically, would suddenly design a Price-type hull for *Hornet*, then follow her a year later with *Wasp*, an almost identical sister, does not fit. The 1805-07 sloops of war represented Price's naval architectural ideas, and support for the pilot schooner design by William Doughty continued with the sloops of war USS *Erie* and *Ontario*, built by Thomas Kemp at Fells Point, and with the Wasp-class sloops built in northern shipyards during the war of 1812.

After the British instituted a blockade of Europe in 1807, Price built the blockade runners *Nonpareil*, *Herald*, *Inca*, *Luna* and *Dolphin*, all pilot-boat built schooners which predated his great Baltimore armed schooners of 1812, of which the following received letter-of-marque commissions: *Von Holden*, *Revenge*, *Price*, *Model*, *Daedalus*, *Maria*, *Hollins*, and *Mary*. Henry Didier, Jr., owner of *Maria*, wrote to his partner in Europe during the war to "return on *Maria*, 350 tons and considered to be one of the most handsome vessels that was built in this country."[39]

Price's ship-rigged vessels included *United States* (1805), *Philip* (1806), *Congress* (1809), *Melantho* (1810), *William and Ann* (1811) and *Hannibal* (1811).[40] He and other Fells Point shipwrights built many of these square-rigged vessels with modified pilot-schooner hull lines. They had fuller hulls which evolved into extreme Baltimore-model square-rigged ships such as *Ann McKim* in 1833 and *Venus* in 1838.[41] *Ann McKim* and

Venus differed from Price's earlier ships principally in the amount of fullness and deadrise in their hull forms. It should be noted that *Ann McKim* measured only about 100 tons more than the bigger schooners such as Kemp's *Chasseur* and *Mammoth* and Price's *Maria*.

William Price built *North Point*[42] in 1816 for John Donnell, continuing a series of sharp, flush-decked ships which he started with *Antelope*, built for Robert Oliver in 1794.[43] John Donnell placed *North Point* in the China trade. Price built the two-deck brig *Lady Monroe* for Jacob Adams and William H. Conkling in 1817. *North Point* and *Lady Monroe* were listed among the fastest vessels of this period by Carl Cutler in his book *Greyhounds of the Sea*.[44]

Following the death of Price's son John, who specialized in pilot-boat built vessels between 1808 and 1821, the elder Price built at least a dozen vessels that included the advanced *Elizabeth*. He never described his schooners or brigs as "pilot-boat built" again. His carpenter certificates referred to them as "flush-deck" or simply as full or sharp-built.

In the half-dozen years immediately preceding William Price's death in 1832, new patterns of trade evolved in the tidewater country. In tune with these new directions, Price's yard built four Baltimore clipper brigs between 1826 and 1831. A fifth brig was completed after his death.[45] He built *Louisa* in 1826 and *Mentor* in 1829, both hermaphrodite brigs.[46] Rigged with square sails on the foremast and a traditional fore-and aft-mainsail, they were a type finding favor at this time. Price built the brig *Argyle* in 1830 and delivered the last vessel of his lifetime, the brig *Erie*, to James Corner in 1831, 37 years after establishing his yard at Fells Point.[47]

Louisa's carpenter measure was 71'10-3/4" straight rabbet, 22'3" beam, 10'8" depth of hold, and 180 tons burden. The brig measured 92' length on deck and 200 tons burden. Neither Price nor her register provided additional information, but the above data suggests that she had a short raking bow combined with a long keel. Like *Elizabeth*, which preceded her by four years, *Louisa*, with less depth than two-deck brigs, had greater capacity proportionately due to shorter ends, a fuller hull and less deadrise, all of which were significant innova-

tions for the developing model.[48]

Owner preference determined the assignments of these new brigs, and it should be noted that some merchants continued to purchase the two-deck version. Shipping records (which start in 1833) show that many of the single-deck clippers were placed in South American trade on both coasts and in Baltimore's China trade with voyages originating from Fells Point and from the west coast of South America.

Lady Sarah was a small hermaphrodite brig that measured 69'6" x 21'6" x 8'4" and 106 tons burden. She was built in Mathews County, Virginia, in 1825, and her builder is unknown.[49] *Lady Sarah* had a fully-evolved clipper bow. She was handsome and efficient-looking and her

HERMAPHRODITE
BRIG *LADY SARAH,*
BUILT IN MATHEWS
COUNTY, VA, IN
1825, SHOWN IN A
PAINTING BY AN
UNIDENTIFIED
ARTIST.
*Peabody Essex
Museum, Salem, MA.*

145

model adds evidence to the theory that changes in pilot-schooner design, culminating in the Baltimore clipper brig model, may have, like the Chesapeake pilot schooner itself, appeared all over Chesapeake Bay during this period. While under 70' in length, increased breadth and short sharp ends gave *Lady Sarah* greater capacity in spite of her length. She is pre-clipper because she retains the deeper hold of earlier pilot schooners.

Price built *Mentor* in 1829 for John Hudson, the son of Captain Jonathan Hudson, a hero of the Revolution and a successful merchant. John and his partner, David A. Wilson, jumped into the South American trade, eventually becoming Brazilian coffee buyers. The partnership also bought Price's *Argyle* in 1831 and placed her in the coffee trade. She sailed from Rio to the Chesapeake in 38 days in July of 1833. John Donnell purchased her that year and on a voyage from Canton, China, in 1838 she arrived at the Capes in 90 days.[50] *Erie,* built for James Corner, formerly a sailmaker and now a shipowner, was also owned later by John Donnell, who sent her to the Mediterranean, to South America, and to the Far East.[51]

John Donnell was an early associate of Sam Smith, the patriarch of Baltimore's prewar trade. Unlike Smith, Donnell survived the difficulties of 1818-20 and entered the opium business to supply specie for his coffee trade in the Dutch East Indies. Samuel Kinnard, a new name in Fells Point shipbuilding in 1830, built *James Ramsay*, a single-deck brig for Donnell to carry opium between Smyrna

and Baltimore, where the cargo was then transhipped for Batavia. *James Ramsay*, 84' length on deck and carpenter measure of 76' straight rabbet, was a full Baltimore clipper and very fast.[52]

Richard Alsop of Philadelphia owned the Baltimore clipper brig *John Gilpin*, which was built in St. Michaels and fitted out by James Beacham, another new shipyard owner at Fells Point in 1831. She was one of the larger one-deck brigs at 94' length overall and 283 tons burden.[53] Alsop operated in the China trade from Valparaiso and from the east coast of the United States. *John Gilpin*'s schedule dovetailed with that of McKim's *Yellot* and *Ann McKim*, suggesting that opium, copper products and other items were transhipped between the two traders, particularly when Alsop turned *John Gilpin* around at Valparaiso.

James Corner purchased *Dido* from an unknown Fells Point builder in 1833. She was trading on the west coast of Africa in 1834 and arrived at Baltimore 28 days from the Cape Verde Islands with hides, salt, skins and ivory. *Dido* was a single-deck brig. These voyages, all taking place after 1833 and not isolated, provide a picture of Baltimore's changing trade and the carrier chosen for it.[54]

Andrew Flannigain, son of William Flannigain, one of the versatile builders of the Baltimore schooner period, built a Baltimore clipper brig, a plan of which is in the collection of the Mariners' Museum. This plan was discovered by Howard Chapelle, who presented it as an isolated model rather than an example of

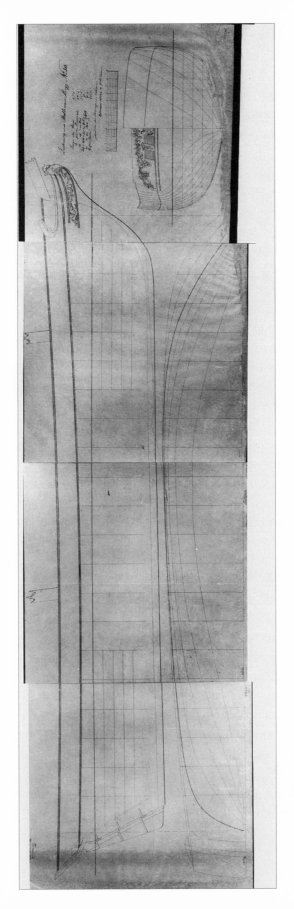

PLAN OF A ONE-DECK CLIPPER BRIG BUILT BY
ANDREW FLANNIGAIN.

The Mariners' Museum, Newport News, VA.

one of Baltimore's principal cargo carriers in the period between the War of 1812 and the Civil War. Since the name of the brig was not printed on the plan, it will be referred to as the Flannigain plan. It is reproduced on the previous page.[55] Chapelle dates the launching of this vessel between 1828 and 1832, but like her name this remains to be discovered. The brig's long keel, short ends, and full-built body all suggest that she was built later in this period of change.

The Flannigain brig's measurements, as shown on the drawing, were 87'5" x 22'7" x 9'2", and her keel was 73'6". A deeper bow with reduced rake, and a long straight keel with less drag, made cargo space more accessible for better stowage. Of all of the changes in design that occurred as the pilot-built model experienced a metamorphosis with these one-deck brigs, none were more important than the reduction in deadrise. This change gave Flannigain's brig a sharp turn to her bilges, further increasing capacity.

Although they may have lacked weatherliness, light-displacement brigs like this one had deep external keels and were sharp-ended at the post to increase maneuverability. Some aspects of the compromises of the new clipper hull hint of another famous Chesapeake Bay design, the log canoe.

The word clipper was used on occasion by Baltimoreans as early as the War of 1812, and frequently by Royal Navy captains as "clippers" left them disappearing wakes to ponder. Its local origin may have been a promotion of Baltimore's newspapers seeking a new image for Fells Point's shipbuilders. By the middle 1840s most of the launching notices printed by the *Baltimore Sun* used the prefix clipper in announcements: brig clipper *Ernami*, 1848; schooner clipper *Alexander Dyott*, 1848; schooner clipper *Jones*; clipper schooner *Skinner*; and schooner clipper *Union*, all in 1850.[56]

James Guy Evans, the artist who painted *Kite* as reproduced on page 124, created a highly stylized picture, sails set with perfection, a handsome painted hull and a gentle sea. Moses Navy of Dorchester County, Maryland, was listed as owner on her temporary Baltimore register. He was a ship broker for the northern buyer who commissioned the painting.

Kite was a Baltimore clipper, a single-deck brig with hermaphrodite rig, built in 1847 at the end of the long period of development which commenced with *Elizabeth* and other brigs immediately after 1820. Her builders were William Hunt and William Waggner of Fells Point. *Kite*'s length overall was 99'4" and her depth of hold was 9'2". With keel measuring 96'4", straight rabbet, and a full body extending from a sharp bow to short raked stern, she was the epitome of her model. Where once the Chesapeake Bay pilot schooner cut across waves at hull speed, the Bay's popular new contribution to naval architecture, the brig with a single flush deck, full or hermaphrodite rigged, surfed on one cheek or the other, lifted onto a plane by steady trade winds or a booming offshore breeze.[57]

IDENTIFIED ONLY
AS "GOELETTE
BALAOU
AMÉRICAIN" IS
THIS DRAWING
OF A TOPSAIL
SCHOONER AT
ANCHOR.
*Musée de la Marine,
Paris.*

ENDNOTES - CHAPTER SEVEN

1. James Weston Livengood, *The Philadelphia-Baltimore Trade Rivalry, 1780/1860* (Harrisburg: The Historical & Museum Commission, 1947), 26.

2. Jean Baptiste Marestier, *Memoire sur Bateaux a Vapeur des Etats Unis d'Amerique* (Paris: La Ministre de la Marine et des Colonies, 1824), Vol. I, Appendices, 241-51.

3. Ibid., Vol II, Plates XI, XII, and XIII.

4. *Mammoth*, Baltimore schooner, built by Thomas Kemp, 1813. Baltimore register #10, dated 7 March 1814. RG41, National Archives, hereafter cited as NA. Marestier, 242.

5. Marestier, Vol. I, App. 245; Vol. II, Plate XII, Figures 109 & 113.

6. Ibid.

7. Carl Cutler, *Queens of the Western Ocean* (Annapolis: U.S. Naval Institute, 1961), 130 & 363n, quoting the *Baltimore American*, 14 July 1817.

8. *Virginia Ross*, pilot schooner, Baltimore carpenter certificate signed by Robert Robinson, 30 June 1820; Baltimore register #83, 30 June 1820; Baltimore register #58, 1822; schooner lost on Tampico bar, 22 June 1824. RG41, NA.

9. Marestier, Vol. II, Plate XIII, Fig. 115.

10. Marestier, Vol I, 243 and Vol II, Plate XII, Figures 108 & 118

11. *Theban*, pilot schooner, 91' x 76' x 22'9" x 10'3", carpenter certificate signed by William Price, 29 November 1820. Baltimore register #140, 1820, *Clio*, pilot schooner, built 1820 by James Beacham, 90'6" x 65' x 22'3" x 9'9"; carpenter certificate dated December 1820. Baltimore register #142, 1820. *Rossie*, pilot schooner, built winter of 1820 by James Beacham; 9' x 65' x 22'4" x 9", carpenter certificate and Baltimore register #75, 6 June 1820. RG41, NA.

12. Marestier, Vol. I, 243.

13. *Rossie*, Baltimore pilot schooner; carpenter certificate signed Kemp & Gardner, 8 June 1815; privateer-built. RG41, NA.

14. Letter, Isaac McKim to Warren R. Davis, 15 August 1829; Maryland Historical Society, herafter cited as MHS MS 610; *Plattsburgh*, Baltimore schooner, reg. #306 1815. RG41 NA.

15. Letter, Isaac McKim to Warren R. Davis, 15 August 1829; MHS, MS 610.

16. *Niles' Register*, 16 November 1816.

17. MHS, MS 610.

18. *Yellot*, Baltimore pilot-boat schooner, Baltimore carpenter certificate signed George Gardner, 29 October 1823; Baltimore register #118, same date. RG41, NA.

19. Ibid.

20. Letter, Isaac McKim to Warren R. Davis, 15 August 1829; MHS, MS 610.

21. *Niles' Register*, 18 August 1827.

22. Carl C. Cutler, *Greyhounds of the Sea* (New York: Halcyon House, 1930), 89-93. Page 92, author quotes the *Baltimore Sun*, 7 November 1838, "A Baltimore Clipper." *Ann McKim*, the famous ship built by Kennard & Williamson of Fells Point, was designed not unlike a large pilot-boat schooner. Ships of her design had been developed over previous decades by Chesapeake Bay shipwrights. An early example with elements of the *Ann McKim* design was USS *Maryland*, designed and built in 1799 by William Price. *Maryland* had extremely low freeboard for a ship, her gun deck only 18" above her waterline. Price's square-rigged ships, like his pilot schooners, had rising floors, long runs and flush weather decks. William Doughty designed the five sloops of war built during the War of 1812, which included the very fast *Wasp* II, All were of a modified Baltimore schooner design. The beautiful *Ann McKim* followed naturally in line with her predecessors and represented a continuation of the Baltimore model rather than the beginning of a new era of clipper ships. There are no important design links between her and American clipper ships built after 1840 except in the minds of maritime writers who assume an idealized continuity through the name "clipper."

23. Cutler, *Greyhounds*, 92.

24. *Greyhound*, pilot schooner, built at Fells Point by James Beacham, Baltimore temporary register # 77, 1826, all owners listed on the register as shown in the text.

25. Basil Lubbock, *The Opium Clippers* (Glasgow: Brown, Son & Ferguson, Ltd., 1933), 61, 83, 87, 88, 127.

26. *Dart*, schooner, built by Gardner Bros. in 1844 at Fells Point; temporary register #77, 1844.

27. Letter-of-Marque Commissions, *Brutus* # 567, *High Flyer* #7, *Macedonian* #950 and *Spartan* # 942; State Department, War of 1812 Papers, NA.

28. *Mork*, pilot schooner, carpenter certificate signed by Levin and Standby Richardson, 14 June 1824. RG41, NA.

29. *Niles' Register*, 7 May 1825.

30. *Mary and Francis*, clipper schooner, built at Baltimore by Israel Riggin and Edward Tennant, 1832, for Henry Spearing of New Orleans. Carpenter's measure: 74' x 22' x 8.5'; Baltimore register #104, 1832; 92'9" x 22'5" x 8'2", 153 tons. RG41, NA.

31. *H.H. Cole*, Baltimore clipper schooner, built at Baltimore, carpenter certificate signed by Samuel Butler, 31 May 1843. RG41, NA. *Ship Registers of the District of Salem and Beverly, 1789-1900* (Salem, Massachusetts: The Essex Institute, no date). Register dated 1 March 1844; lost 1-11-1848.

32. Gail E. Farr and Brett F. Bostwick, *John Lenthall, Naval Architect, A Guide to Plans and Drawings of American Naval and Merchant Vessels, 1790-1874* (Philadelphia: Philadelphia Maritime Museum, 1991), 21.

33. *Isabella*, clipper schooner, built in Talbot County, carpenter certificate signed by Absalom Thompson; owner Captain Matthew Kelly, September, 1835. Bill of Sale, Kelly to Frederick W. Brune, 19 November, 1835, $3,000. New owners, Brune and James McAllister; sold to foreigners in 1836. Baltimore register #106, 1835. RG41, NA.

34. MHS, MS 610.

35. *Ranger*, brig, two decks, built by William Price at Fells Point in 1797; Baltimore register # 193, 1797.

36. *Eutaw*, brig, one deck, built by William Price for Richard Gittings at Fells Point, 1808: Baltimore carpenter certificates, Box 9, RG36, NA. *Eclipse*, one-flush deck, built by John Price for Robert Oliver, 1811. Baltimore carpenter certificates, RG36-41; Baltimore register #104, 1811.

37. *Elizabeth*, brig, one deck, built by William Price at Fells Point in 1822 and sold to Baptiste Mizick and others in 1823. Baltimore carpenter certificates, RG36-41; Baltimore register #29, 1823.

38. Letter, Isaac Chauncey to John H. Dent, 7 March 1806. Dudley W. Knox, USN, Ret., Editor, *Naval Documents Related to the United States Wars with the Barbary Powers,* Vol. VI, 1805-07 (Washington, D.C.: U.S. Government Printing Office, 1944), 382.

39. Henry Didier, Jr., Letter Book, MHS, MS 295.

40. Carpenter certificates signed by William Price: *United States,* 26 July 1805; *Philip,* 25 July 1806; *Congress,* 15 June 1809; *Melantho,* 9 September 1810; *William and Ann,* 4 September 1811; and *Hannibal,* 25 November 1811. RG41, NA.

41. *Ann McKim,* sharp flush-deck ship, built in 1833 by Kennard & Williamson, carpenter certificate signed 19 August 1833; *Venus ,* sharp flush-deck ship built by W. & G. Gardner, carpenter certificate signed 4 July 1838. RG41, NA. Also, Carl C. Cutler, *Greyhounds,* 89-93, 107, 391.

42. *North Point*, flush-deck ship, carpenter certificate signed by William Price, 22 May 1816. RG41, NA.

43. *Antelope,* flush-deck ship, William Price, builder, as per Baltimore register #131, 29 August 1794. RG41, NA.

44. *Lady Monroe,* brig, carpenter certificate signed by William Price, 21 August 1817. RG41, NA. Also Cutler, *Greyhounds,* 398.

45. *William Price,* brig; built at Fells Point, 1831-33, carpenter certificate dated 8 April 1833; Baltimore register #25, 1833. RG41, NA.

46. *Mentor*, hermaphrodite brig, built at Fells Point, 1829; carpenter certificate signed by William Price, 26 October 1829. RG41, NA.

47. *Erie*, brig, carpenter certificate signed by William Price, 17 August 1831. RG41, NA

48. *Louisa*, hermaphrodite brig, built in 1826 by William Price, carpenter certificate; RG36-41 and Baltimore register #137, 1826.

49. *Lady Sarah*, brigantine, built in Mathews County, Virginia, 1825; Baltimore register #21, February 1826, owner, H.H. Kuble. RG41, NA; *Marine Paintings and Drawings in the Peabody Museum,* Marion V. and Dorothy Brewington, Editors (Salem, Massachusetts:

The Peabody Museum of Salem, 1981), 392.

50. *Argyle,* brig, one deck, two sets of beams, built by William Price at Fells Point, 1830, carpenter certificate, RG36-41; Baltimore register #26, 1831, RG41, NA.

51. MHS, MS 610.

52. *James Ramsay*, brig, one deck, built by Samuel Kennard at Fells Point in 1830; carpenter certificate; RG36-41, NA; Baltimore register #92, 1830. RG41, NA.

53. *John Gilpin*, brig, one-deck hull built at St. Michaels, fitted out by James Beacham for Matthew Kelly at Fells Point, 1831. Baltimore register #47, 1831. Acquired by Richard Alsop of Philadelphia in 1832, owner until 1841; Baltimore register #39, 1832. RG41 NA.

54. *Dido*, brig, one deck, builder unknown, Baltimore register #94, 1833. RG41 NA.

55. Howard I. Chapelle, *The Search for Speed under Sail* (New York: W. W. Norton & Company, 1957, Bonanza Edition), 297 & facing 299.

56. *Baltimore Sun,* 5 May and 22 September 1848; 7 April 1849, 7 January 1850, 4 February 1850, 1 April 1850, 21 August 1850, 12 September 1850, 25 and 30 November, 1850 and 2 April 1851. Data compiled by Marion V. Brewington, MHS.

57. *Kite*, brig, one deck, built by William Hunt & William Waggner at Fells Point in 1847, carpenter certificate, Baltimore temporary register #115, 1847. RG41 NA.

THE SLAVER *L'ANTONIO* IS SHOWN ON THE BONNY

RIVER ON THE COAST OF WEST AFRICA IN THIS

ETCHING BY W. M. CONDY & J. D. DUNCAN.

National Maritime Museum, London.

CHAPTER EIGHT

Slave and Opium Clippers

Captain Richard Drake, a slave trader, writing in his memoirs, recalled his voyage as first mate and doctor on *Napoleon*, which he described as a 90-ton Baltimore clipper of symmetry and speed. It was the vessel's third voyage as a slaver, and her cargo consisted of 250 men and 100 children from Africa delivered to a consignee named Pedro Gomez in Havana. Drake estimated that each slave cost $16.00 and the average sale price was $360.00, resulting in profits in excess of $100,000 for the voyage. No record of a schooner named *Napoleon* exists in Baltimore registers. There was a brig named *Napoleon* built in 1832 in Baltimore and sold to Boston owners shortly thereafter.[1]

Chesapeake Bay pilot schooners and brigs were frequently purchased for the business of slave running. As yachts and aircraft are used in the cocaine trade in the twentieth century, fast vessels were used in the slaving and smuggling that flourished prior to 1860. It would be wrong to conclude that the Chesapeake flyers of the 1830s, or planes and yachts in our time, shared any of the disgrace of an illegal trade. It would be wrong to assign blame to the men who built them. Frederick Douglass worked at several shipyards in Fells Point, including Gardner Brothers and Walter Price's yard where Hugh Auld, his owner, was foreman. Auld was self-employed from time to time and on these occasions Douglass worked with his master. The last yard he worked in was that of Butler and Lambdin. Ironically, Frederick Douglass worked on schooners and brigs sold to slave traders.[2] If blame for immoral and illegal behavior is assigned, then most of it must go to the shipowners and captains who entered the slave trade for its considerable profit.

A Federal law was passed in 1820 that declared traffic in slaves an act of piracy. While the slave buyers were the obvious villains in this business, elite merchants, pious shipbuilders, and "honest" politicians and government officials reaped big profits, too. Walter Price and other Fells Point shipyard owners, and some of the merchants of Baltimore, retained ownership shares in slave ships. No direct evidence links Price, the businessman, to the slave trade, as no investigation of individuals in the trade was made for this study. There is strong circumstantial evidence, however, linking William Price's son to vessels in the slave trade.

The Baltimore American of 14

December, 1836, published a notice placed by a master "who can give satisfactory references" for a vessel about 100 tons, light draft, sharp built, "he to sail her, in a certain trade with which he is acquainted and which will ensure a profitable business. Address A.B., P.O. Box 60, Post Office." That a captain advertised to obtain a vessel for trafficking in slaves could be interpreted that no heavy demand existed for masters in the trade at Baltimore. It certainly indicated that laws were not enforced. That the captain desired a clipper schooner of 100 tons indicates that he expected to employ her between West Africa and the Southern Hemisphere or to buy slaves in Cuba or Brazil for resale in South America, the West Indies, or even the United States.

Captain Theophile Conneau in his memoirs of slave trading described some of his ships and voyages. One vessel, *Esperanza*, a clipper schooner, was captured by a Royal Navy cruiser with 375 slaves on board. Conneau did not say where she was built.[3] Later in Captain Conneau's account, he was aboard *Estrella*, which he described as a dashing clipper schooner of 120 tons, built in the United States. Her cargo was 480 slaves.[4] He also notes *Aquila de Oro* (Golden Eagle) which he describes as "a splendid clipper born of the famous waters of the Chesapeake."[5]

Walter Price reopened the family shipyard in Fells Point again after Hugh Auld joined him. Accompanying Auld was the young slave Frederick Douglass. One of the first vessels built under Auld's supervi-

sion was a schooner named *Guatemala Packet*.[6] Price, referring to himself as a shipwright, built the schooner *Esperanza* in 1836, and Hugh Auld countersigned the carpenter certificate.[7] This vessel measured less than 50' on her keel. Rumored to be a slave carrier, she was probably smaller than Captain Conneau's schooner of the same name. Another vessel rumored to be a slaver was *Delores*, built at the Price yard in 1836 and sold to James I. Fisher, Baltimore merchant and ship broker, whose name was frequently associated with ship sales to Cuba. Her captain was William Woodland[8] and she had measurements of 91' x 21'2" x 8'7".

Fisher was 31 when he took over the business of R.H. Douglass & Company, following the death of Richard Douglass in 1829. The firm bought prize goods in the West Indies, sold ships, and imported coffee and sugar. Douglass sold a number of schooners in Havana before he died. Little of the firm's activities can be traced today as the commercial papers of Fisher, once in the hands of the Maryland Historical Society, cannot be located. No direct evidence linking Fisher to the slave trade has come to light, although his record of ship sales in Havana during the period of heavy slaver activity between 1830 and 1840 is circumstantial evidence. Fisher and an associate, Peter Pascal, purchased *Emanuel*, a sharp schooner built by L.H. Dunkin in 1836,[9] and sold her to Cuban owners in 1837, for example.[10] This seems to have been a typical transaction for the firm in the 1830s. Although Fisher's primary business was selling flour and purchasing coffee and sugar, selling schooners in Cuba, and possible financial participation in slave trading, can be strongly suspected, the lure of great profits and small risk being all but irresistible.

It was a common practice for the American shipowner interested in entering the slave trade to charter a vessel and crew to a slave dealer for a voyage which would include fitting-out for the trade and delivering the vessel to Africa where ownership passed to the charterer. The American crew became passengers at this point and the American owner would cancel her registry. In the case of *Delores*, Fisher cancelled her American registry in 1837, a year after acquiring her, although he may have sold her months earlier.[11]

After 1820 most European nations were bound by treaty to stop the traffic in slaves, and Britain's Royal Navy took up the policing of the oceans. The British Admiralty commissioned a number of fast schooners and brigs, some built in Great Britain and others in the West Indies and Bermuda. Additionally, a number of captured slave-trade vessels were taken into the Royal Navy. It was a simple strategy of fighting back with ships as fast as slavers. Two of the most successful vessels in the squadron assigned by the Admiralty to Africa were a brig and a schooner-brig, both designed along the lines of the Chesapeake pilot schooner. They were *Black Joke*, ex-*Henriquetta*, a brig, and the hermaphrodite brig *Fair Rosamond*, ex-*Dos Amigos*. *Black Joke*, taken into the service in 1827, captured *Dos Amigos* in

1830.[12] No vessels with such names appear in Baltimore registers.[13]

Black Joke, a brig of about 260 tons burden, with dimensions of 90'10" x 26'7"was, according to Basil Lubbock in *Cruisers, Corsairs & Slavers*, flying the Brazilian flag when captured, having completed several voyages between Africa and Brazil from 1825 to 1827.[14] The only brig found close to this size in Baltimore registers and sold to Brazilians in this time period was *Griffin*, registered in 1824 and sold to the Emperor of Brazil in 1825.[15]

Black Joke stayed on the African station for several years and evidently was never sailed to the Portsmouth dockyard for repairs and to be measured. She was eventually broken up in Africa after her long record of captures made her the darling of the Royal Navy. *Black Joke* and *Fair Rosamond* worked together until *Black Joke* was decommissioned in 1832. *Fair Rosamond* continued to track down slavers until 1837.[16]

Fair Rosamond was drydocked and measured at Portsmouth after several years of successful anti-slaver action and her plan is reproduced here. She was a small Baltimore-type schooner-brig, measuring about 75' on deck. She had a clipper bow and her wide beam followed the design of similar Baltimore-built vessels of that era. Her plan, however, contains design elements that seem to indicate she was not built at Fells Point or on Chesapeake Bay. First, her deep hold (10'+) suggests origin in Great Britain, Bermuda, France, or somewhere in the

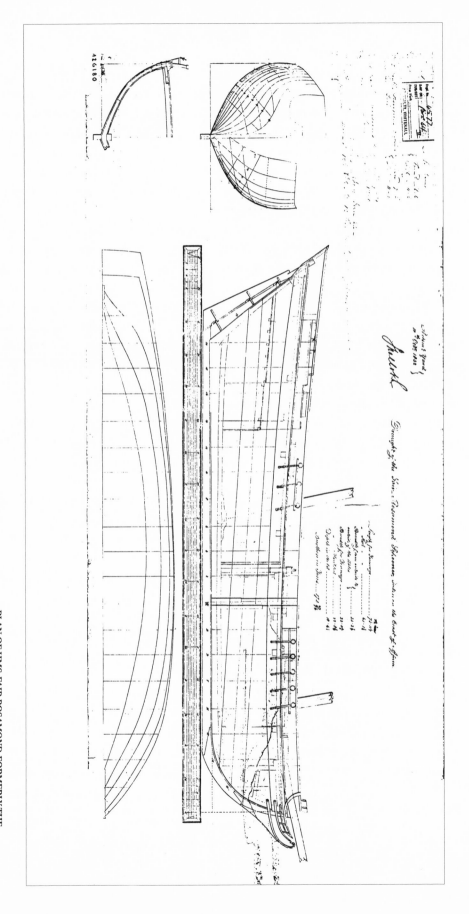

PLAN OF HMS *FAIR ROSAMOND*, FORMERLY THE
SLAVER *DOS AMIGOS* CAPTURED BY
THE ROYAL NAVY IN 1830.
National Maritime Museum, London.

Caribbean such as Jamaica. Her keel, with a decreasing amount of deadwood in the stern, is characteristic of Bermuda-built schooners. Finally, *Fair Rosamond*'s round bottom shape and unusually slack bilges were not at all typical of Chesapeake pilot schooners of the 1820s. While both *Black Joke* and *Fair Rosamond* have been attributed to Fells Point builders, no evidence of this has been found, and these characteristics suggest otherwise.

An intriguing trail left in Baltimore's Customs records is that of Andrew Patrullo of New York. Patrullo came to Fells Point to have at least six vessels built. Three, *Chesapeake, Susquehanna* and *Beacham*, list the builder as James Beacham.[17] Two, *Raritan* and *Delaware*, have no carpenter certificates on file at the National Archives.[18] The last and most interesting of Patrullo's vessels was named *Engineer* and built by Beacham in 1832.[19]

Engineer had three masts, the first identified three-masted schooner built at Fells Point since William Flannigain's pilot schooners of 1805. But even more startling are her measurements of 120' on deck; her extreme beam of more than 30', and her tonnage of only 310.[20] Her carpenter certificate states that she had a full-built hull with depth of hold of just 9'. With length-depth ratio of 13.33:1, she was unusually shallow-hulled and must have been crank and tender in a blow.

Beacham, delivered to Patrullo in April of 1832, was the smallest and sharpest of his six purchases. Her dimen-sions were 77'5" x 18'11" x 7', and only 92 tons burden.[21] Though builder's certificates for *Raritan* and *Delaware* are not in the National Archives, it may be assumed that they were sister schooners to *Chesapeake* and *Susquehanna*, as the four pilot schooners measured exactly the same: 73'6" x 20'6" x 7'9" and 102-28/95 tons burden.[22] Slightly shallower and of greater breadth than typical Baltimore schooners, they were probably very fast with reasonable stability. These little schooners could pack 300 or 400 slaves in false decks. Patrullo sold all six schooners in Havana in 1832, so it seems more than likely that they were built for the slave trade.

Henry A. Wise of Accomac, Virginia, became the United States minister to the court of the Emperor of Brazil in 1844. Although he had slaves back in Virginia, Wise proved to be an opponent to the African-Brazilian slave trade in which American vessels played a large role. The British government's treaties with a number of foreign maritime nations allowed the Royal Navy to board and search their vessels for slaves. The United States government, because of sensitivity to any policy of search on the high seas, was not a party to these agreements, and this independent position allowed American shipowners to hide behind the flag, and with complicated charter parties participate in the trade.

While most American participants resided north of the Mason-Dixon line, Maryland citizens and Chesapeake Bay schooners and brigs had active roles in the nasty business. Wise pointed out that of 22 vessels of the U.S. merchant marine engaged in the slave trade between Africa and Brazil from June, 1845, to March, 1846, only four hailed south of Philadelphia and they were from Baltimore.[23] Court cases and British Admiralty records, the only reliable sources, were not searched for this discussion, but ship registers show that at least three vessels owned by Baltimoreans were condemned during this period. Seized by the U.S. Navy were *Elizabeth*, a barque, in Rio, owned by Pierson Baldwin; *Sarah Linda*, owned by James Sullivan, Robert B. Walters, and her master, Stephen S.K. Durkee, off Turks Island south of the Bahamas; and *Nymph*, owned by Hugh Birckhead and Charles R. Pearce in 1836.[24]

Contrary to what many maritime scholars believe, the principal employment of Chesapeake Bay pilot schooners after 1820 was not the slave trade, although many vessels built to the design around the world were slavers. To suggest that most post-1820 pilot schooners were slavers is to ignore commercial schooners and Baltimore clippers built between 1823 and 1860. These decades of vast industrial and commercial innovation included significant changes in ships and trade routes. Chesapeake Bay shipwrights responded by building ships such as *Ann McKim* as well as pilot schooners, clipper schooners, clipper brigs, opium brigs, navy and revenue schooners, coastal schooners and brigs, coffee schooners, brigs and barques, packet schooners,

pilot boats, oyster schooners, and clipper-model yachts, all close to pilot-schooner design or derivatives of it. If the name was ever appropriate, this was the period of the Baltimore clipper.

Howard I. Chapelle, with some awareness of the conflicting directions his writing was taking, called the Chesapeake Bay schooners Baltimore clippers almost before the village on the Patapsco came into existence. He continued to call Chesapeake Bay pilot schooners Baltimore clippers down through the decades in spite of the fact that such a name was never applied to these craft by either their builders or owners. When vessels for the slave trade, usually brigs, appeared as derivatives of the pilot schooner design after 1820, and were widely referred to as Baltimore clippers, Chapelle extracted himself from the structure he had created by announcing the end of his Baltimore clipper with the appearance of the slave models. Chapelle's influence has been mountainous, particularly with unquestioning authors of theses, books and scholarly studies that touch on the period of the Chesapeake Bay pilot schooner.

Thomas C. Gillmer, a leading designer of pilot-schooner replicas (*Pride of Baltimore* I and II), echoes Chapelle's words 50 years later. He identifies the Baltimore armed schooner of the War of 1812 as a Baltimore clipper. Then, as the Chesapeake Bay pilot schooner is adapted to the slave trade and is called the Baltimore clipper all over the world, he writes from his naval architect's point of view that in 1830 the Baltimore clipper ceased to exist. This seems to have become dogma, creating a degree of denial when strong arguments for revision are presented.[25]

A set of pilot-schooner plans found in the French marine archives at Vincennes supports the contention that the pilot-schooner design was applied to all-purpose schooners built during the several decades after 1820 and not necessarily on Chesapeake Bay. This draft, dated 1841 and signed John A. Robb & Brother, is for a medium-sized schooner, usable for many purposes that could include opium smuggling and inter-island trading, such as the Cuban-built *Amistad* pursued, piloting or trading in slaves. Robb, a Nova Scotian, arrived at Fells Point 15 years prior to 1841 as Henry Eckford's foreman for the construction of the Brazilian frigate *Baltimore* under subcontract from Eckford to James Beacham at Fells Point.

The unnamed schooner's length was 75', and her beam was only 18', which makes her proportions comparable to schooners of 1812, although overall she was much smaller. There were a number of schooners built between 1836 and 1842 with comparable dimensions: *General Gates* (75'3" x 18'11" x 7'2") sold to Mobile pilot Andrew Dorgan in 1836; *Racer* by Robb (75' x 18'7" x 7'10") in 1838, sold in Havana; *Clara* by Robb (74'9" x 18'6" x 7'10"), sold to unidentified foreign owners; *Laura* sold to Andrew Dorgan of Mobile (78'8" x 19'3" x 7'6"); *Sea* (74' x 18'6" x 7'7") sold to J.I. Fisher who sold her foreign the same year; and a second

Clara (75'2" x 19'3" x 7'4") sold to Andrew Dorgan of Mobile.[26] The plan of the schooner found in France has bulwarks and gun ports. The plan can be said to represent Robb's version of a standard small schooner of the time.

Perhaps the most famous of these schooners of under 80' and 100 tons is *Amistad*, a Cuban schooner transporting captive Africans from one port to another. The Africans broke their bonds and began an uprising on board *Amistad* on 2 July 1839, her fourth night out of Havana, setting in motion a series of events that continued over two years, and changed the lives of the 54 illegally transported Africans and of many Americans involved in the incident, including a president, Martin van Buren, and an ex-president, John Quincy Adams.[27] The *Amistad* incident became a high-profile court case decided by the Supreme Court in the winter of 1841. *Amistad* was a coastal clipper schooner built on Chesapeake Bay or in Cuba about 1833. An American register at New London in 1841, made possible by an act of Congress, transferred her from Spanish to American ownership following an auction. This register includes her dimensions: 64' x 19'9" x 6'6", burden of 70-46/95 tons and her new American name, *Ion*.[28]

Published information that *Amistad-Ion* was built on the Chesapeake six years prior to her sale to Cuban owners, that she was named *Friendship*, and that she was of 120 tons burden, seems to be incorrect.[29] There was a schooner named *Friendship* of 120 tons burden built in

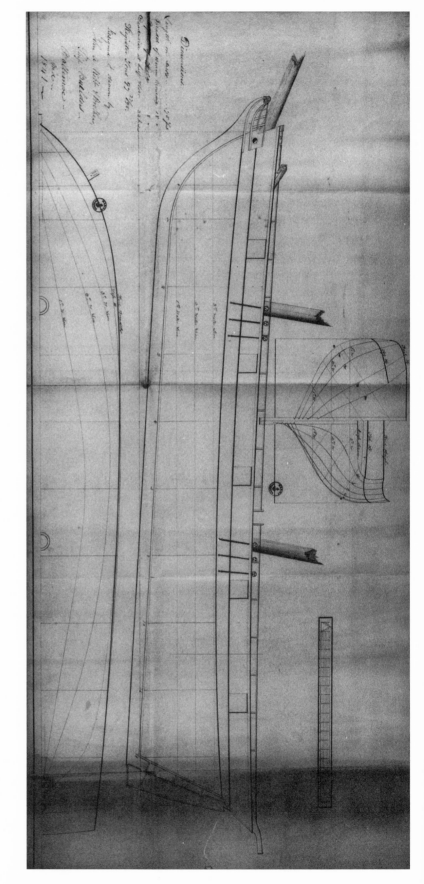

**PLAN OF BALTIMORE SCHOONER SIGNED
BY JOHN A. ROBB & BROTHER.**

Service Historique de la Marine, Vincennes.

Somerset County, Maryland, in 1811.[30] She was sold to Cubans in 1819, and it is possible that she was renamed *La Amistad de Rues*, a schooner that became involved in another Supreme Court case in 1820.[31]

Amistad, the schooner involved in the slave uprising, was detained off Long Island, New York, 26 August 1839, and placed in the custody of a U.S. Marshal at New London. The Federal court instructed him to have her appraised. Her cargo, not including her Cuban passengers and African captives, was valued at $6,626.84, a substantial amount of freight for so small a vessel. The appraiser valued the schooner at $600.00, which tells historians little.[32] What raises an important question is the ability of this small schooner to carry passengers, the captive Africans, and a rather large and bulky cargo. *Amistad*, no bigger than a large pungy, with a keel estimated at 47', with her cargo and 60 people would have been packed like a jar of rolled anchovies.[33]

The best information about the schooner, supplementing her register data, is the inventory of her spars and sails recorded by the Marshal for the court. Her spars and rigging included two masts, a main boom and a bowsprit with a jibboom. Also listed were a yard for a course sail and a topsail yard. The inventory listed one square topsail and two gaff topsails, in addition to her regular pilot-schooner rig— that is, a jib and two large sails for fore and main masts. It is possible that *Amistad* was rigged with double gaff topsails and a boomed course sail for a light following breeze. She also carried two flying jibs and was equipped with sweeps.[34]

The Africans were purchased by José Ruiz and Pedro Montes at an auction held at a barracoon somewhere outside Havana. They had recently arrived from Lomboko Island at the mouth of the Gallinas River on board a Spanish slaver. Their new owners claimed they were Ladinos, slaves brought up in Cuba. During the United States District Court hearings, testimony of witnesses and the Africans themselves proved that they were Bozals, free Africans recently captured in their homeland and transported to Cuba.[35] This was an important determination, as in 1839 Spanish treaties with other nations forbade the transport of new slaves from Africa to Cuba, even though shiploads were arriving there on a weekly basis.

The Africans worked out of their chains and killed *Amistad*'s master. Two or more crew members escaped in a small boat. The only surviving crew member on board was a slave, the property of the schooner's dead owner-master. The revolt's leader Sing-gbe and the other Africans, once free, kept their owners alive to help navigate *Amistad* to Africa. The vessel wandered up the East Coast and, short of food and water, anchored off Long Island after 63 days. Finally, the schooner, the Africans and their former owners were taken into custody by the USS *Washington*, a navy brig on survey duty. The *Washington* was formerly a revenue cutter built in Fells Point several years earlier.[36]

In a Federal lower court trial, convened to decide the fate of the Africans, their attorneys argued that the men were free and not property. On this legal thread dangled freedom or slavery, for if the court held that they were illegally captured Africans, they could not be considered property. Luckily, the Africans came ashore in New York where slavery was outlawed and then were tried in Federal court in Connecticut, where, free of Southern pressure, the decisions were based on law and treaties, not the political passions of the times.[37]

The *Amistad* incident exposed to public view the horrors of slavery in Cuba where agricultural slaves were worked to death and replaced with a continuing supply of illegal imports. Treated like machinery without maintenance, they lasted about seven years. The complete labor force of the island was caught in this grinding system, which could only be supported by replacements. Two Havana insurance companies underwrote the slavers as more than one ship a week entered Havana with cargoes. Sing-gbe and his mates were all males except for three female children, as women slaves were not in demand even for breeding under the replacement system.[38]

After a lower court trial and appeals, the fate of the Africans was finally decided by a Supreme Court decision based on constitutional law and international treaties. It held that the Africans were illegally transported and entered into Cuba, a Spanish colony, and Sing-gbe and the other survivors of the mutiny were captive freemen, not property. They could not be returned to Cuba by United States authorities. They would be returned to

Africa. It was a decision that widened the existing distrust between the North and the South.[39]

Ion, ex-*Amistad*, had many characteristics of a small Chesapeake Bay clipper schooner: her rig, the proportions of her measurements in her original New London register, and a traditional Chesapeake Bay square stern. She was smaller than *Virginia Ross* or the clipper schooner designed by John Robb which appears on page 160. To obtain a picture of her sail plan, see Marestier's Fig. #116, reproduced on page 128.

On the other side of the world another lucrative and controversial trade was in progress conducted by English and American traders and some from India. A number of American adventurers participated in the transport of opium to China during the first half of the nineteenth century, but as this book is limited to Chesapeake Bay pilot schooners, no detailed study of the opium trade was made. The sale of opium was first dominated by the East India Company, and after 1834 by British trading houses at Canton, Macao and Hong Kong, with some participation by Indians and Americans. The opium trade had great similarities to the cocaine trade of modern times. Opium, illegal in China, was grown and refined, mostly in India. British, American, and some Indian shipowners transported cargoes of the drug from Bombay to the coast of China, from whence it was smuggled ashore. Later, the Americans in the trade obtained opium in Turkey.

For many years British trade in the Far East and India was under the monopolistic control of the East India Company which endeavored to keep other nations and even other British traders out. One clever way around this was to obtain a consular appointment to China from some obscure state, and once there set up in an opium business. In 1831 there were 26 British and 21 American merchants other than the staff of the East India Company doing business in China. Thomas Dent of Dent and Company had gotten a foothold as Consul of Sardinia. James Matheson of Jardine, Matheson & Co. was Danish Consul, and the Magniac brothers were all attached to the Consulate of Prussia. Dent and the Jardine, Matheson partnership became large shipowners. Russell & Company of New England led the American contingent.[40] The British East India Company's monopoly was broken in 1834.

The British, American and other firms set up opium warehouses, in this instance floating warehouses, outside the reach of China's weak naval forces. Chinese distributors picked up the opium from these anchored ships for their networks of opium sellers inside the country.[41] Opium had extremely negative effects in China, not unlike the crisis in America's inner cities in the closing decades of the twentieth century.

One of the principal merchant adventurers in China before 1840 was Robert Bennet Forbes. Young Forbes made several voyages to China on ships owned by J. & T.H. Perkins of Boston, the firm owned by

his uncles. Conveniently, an employee of the Perkins brothers, John P. Cushing, was the American Consul at Whampoa. He converted a Perkins ship, *Levant*, into a stores or warehouse ship for opium in 1828.[42]

Forbes arrived in China in 1823 as a young shipmaster, and in a few years was deeply involved in the drug trade, including carrying opium from Turkey to China. His ship *Danube*, loaded with a cargo of Turkish opium, was escorted, in 1828, through Greek waters by the United States Navy schooner *Porpoise*. On that voyage he fell in with Joseph Peabody's brig *Leander* of Salem, also carrying a cargo of opium. Neither ship was supposed to know that the other was transporting the drug.[43] In a later sojourn in China, Forbes became managing partner of the Boston firm Russell & Company, successor to J. & T.H. Perkins.

Most of the vessels used for opium smuggling were Baltimore-type clipper schooners, brigs and barques. Only a small percentage were built in America, and of these just a handful were built on Chesapeake Bay. However, the strong influence of the Chesapeake Bay pilot schooner filtered into the opium trade from several directions. In addition to the Baltimore clippers actually employed, ex-slavers such as *Black Joke*, *Psyche* and *Nymph*, British fruit schooners like *Time* and *Hellas*, and American privateer types such as *Red Rover*, all heavily influenced by Chesapeake Bay design, made up the bulk of the drug fleet.[44]

The three Cowes-built schooners pic-

SHOWN IN THIS
DRAMATIC PAINT-
ING BY F. G. HENEY
IS THE SCHOONER
DENIA, BUILT IN
ENGLAND AND
SAILED TO CHINA
FOR THE OPIUM –
SMUGGLING
TRADE.
*National Maritime
Museum , London.*

tured are examples of British adaptations of Baltimore clippers. *Omega*'s builder is unknown but was possibly J. & R. White who built *Denia* and *Wild Dayrell*.[45] *Omega*, placed in service by Dent & Company in 1837, was 178 tons. *Denia*, a smaller schooner of 133 tons, was built by White in 1840 and placed in the opium trade by Dent in 1846. Her dimensions were 84'2" x 20'1" x 12'5". *Wild Dayrell* was built for Dent & Company by White in 1854. She measured substantially more than *Denia*, 103'3" x 23'7" x 13'3". These sharp-built schooners were probably built by White on designs of fast fruit

schooners that had been part of Britain's merchant fleet since before the War of 1812. The major differences from Chesapeake Bay pilot schooners were in depth of hull and, on occasion, their extreme deadrise.

The British fruit schooner was clearly designed for speed. *Emma* is an example of an early fruit schooner, built in the Salcombe region of Devon, England, according to the Science Museum in London, where the model shown on page 167 is exhibited. She was built prior to the War of 1812.[46] A rising standard of living in Great Britain after 1800 created demand

for fresh tropical fruit, imported from the West Indies, Central America, and from the ports of the Mediterranean. A sharp flush-deck schooner able to make fast passages was best suited for the trade.

Emma is described by the museum as a Sidmouth trading schooner employed in the West Indies fruit trade. But research produced no mention of anything identified as a Sidmouth schooner, and as that seaside town is not a port the assumption is made that the museum's reference to Salcombe's fruit trade later in its publication is more to the point.

The principal difference between *Emma* and *Nonpareil*, to which the museum compares her, is in her depth. *Emma*'s builder increased her cargo capacity with a deeper hold, producing a length-depth ratio of 7.4:1, and providing the pilot schooner with greater capacity and stability for the long voyage from the Caribbean to England. As with Royal Navy schooners, this change in design was not unusual in Great Britain. *Emma*'s dimensions as listed by the museum were 88' x 64.4' x 24.8' x 12'.

Pilot schooners were popular with fruit traders throughout the nineteenth century, and this did not change until steamships replaced fast sailing craft.

THIS F.G. HENEY PAINTING SHOWS *OMEGA*, ANOTHER OPIUM SCHOONER BUILT IN ENGLAND, ARRIVING IN CHINA. *National Maritime Museum, London.*

OPIUM SCHOONER
WILD DAYRELL
IS SHOWN HERE IN
A SERENE PAINTING
BY AN UNKNOWN
CHINESE ARTIST.
Mystic Seaport
Museum, Mystic, CT.

Salcombe's shipyards produced many such schooners, some of which survive on canvas. The earlier ones, *Lady Brougham*, *Candidate*, and especially *Beau Ideal*, built by John Ball, and *Phoenix*, built by a shipbuilder named Bonker, catch the design of Chesapeake schooners in hull and rig.[47] Pictured on next page is *Mary*, perhaps a Mediterranean fruit carrier.

By 1840, American shipwrights from Maine to Texas were producing brigs and schooners of the Chesapeake type. William H. Webb built his first so-called clipper brig, *Malek-Adhel*, on the model that year. His plan is reproduced at the end of this chapter, on which he states that she was built for the Pacific trades.

Perhaps this is a reference to the opium trade. She was arrested at Batavia in 1841 and sent to Baltimore. The Chesapeake's clipper schooners and brigs were also being built in the West Indies, Great Britain, and in the Far East by 1840.[48]

Augustine Heard & Co. of Boston placed an order for the Baltimore clipper brig *Frolic* in 1844. Under command of Captain Edward Faucon, she sailed from Baltimore for Bombay in December of 1844, arriving at the Indian port during the winter of 1845.[49] As will be seen from the sailing notice reproduced below, *Frolic*'s Bombay agent posted her to sail 5 May 1845, bound for China with a cargo of opium.[50] At her launching, the

Baltimore Sun called her a clipper brig, and when her sailing date was posted in Bombay she was called an opium clipper. This use of clipper as a word interchangeable with speed over the water was English usage, first spoken in America by Royal Navy officers referring to Baltimore's privateer schooners.

Frolic's carpenter certificate (which is dated three months after her first register-entry) gives her length as 97' without stating how she was measured. Her Baltimore register, which states her length overall at 99'2", does not provide enough additional information to reliably speculate on her design.

If the first measurement above is of

RIGGED MODEL OF
THE BRITISH FRUIT
SCHOONER *EMMA*.
Science Museum ,
London.

the brig's keel, she was of an extreme design as her combined rake, fore and aft, was something less than two feet, resulting in an almost vertical stem and stern post. Furthermore, her builders, William and George Gardner, described her as sharp built, which traditionally meant that the vessel had substantial deadrise. If

BRITISH CARGO
SCHOONER *MARY* AT
MALTA. PAINTING BY
W. G. HUGGINS, 1835.
The Mariners'
Museum, Newport
News, VA.

FOR CHINA,
TO SAIL ON 5TH MAY,
THE fine new Baltimore-built Clipper Brig FROLIC, 210 tons measurement, commanded by Captain EDWARD FAUCON. For Freight of Opium, having two-thirds of her Cargo engaged, apply to
MARTIN, MURRAY & Co.
Rampart Row, 29th April, 1845.   (456)*

SAILING NOTICE
FOR SCHOONER
FROLIC.
Bombay Times, *April
30th, 1845.
Given to Maryland
Historical Society by
Dr. Thomas N. Layton,
San Jose State
University.*

these interpretations are correct, she was unlike most other single-deck brigs built during the preceding 25 years. This conflicting information, accompanied by a register dated prior to the carpenter certificate, suggests that the latter is bogus.

Frolic's register-entry provides her other two dimensions. Her depth of hold at 9'11", although less than earlier two-deck brigs, was average for a single-deck model of her length. However, her width of 24', combined with high deadrise, could have made her crank or tender in a blow. Her master, Edward Faucon, wrote to her owners that she was too shallow to be a powerful vessel in a strong wind.[51] This New Englander's comments are not surprising, but his disappointment should have been accompanied by the realization that a heavier brig would not provide clipper speed. Files that contain the complete specifications and voyages of Heard's schooner are at Harvard's Baker Library and would need to be consulted to obtain a clear understanding of this brig's design and performance.

Frolic returned to the West Coast in 1850 with a rich cargo of Chinese goods for the booming San Francisco Gold Rush market. Due to an error in navigation, she was wrecked on the California coast above Mendocino, more than 100 miles north of her destination, San Francisco Bay. When *Frolic* sank in relatively shallow water her cargo, particularly that part stowed in the upper level of her hold, became accessible to salvagers over the next 150 years. Bringing bits of Scottish ale bottles, broken Chinese plates, newspaper stories and the owner's records of the brig together in a monumental project is Dr. Thomas Layton of San Jose State University. Dr. Layton led an archaeological team that has produced a unique record of this Fells Point-built brig, her voyages, and the impact of her wreck on the native population of northern California.[52]

As a model, design, or class of vessel, Chesapeake Bay schooners and brigs, fast and nimble as dolphins, were built anywhere a fast vessel was needed 20 years after the War of 1812. In addition to clandestine uses, mariners had an increasing need to acquire sailing craft with sufficient speed to remain competitive with steamships on short trade routes and to keep up with their competitors on longer voyages. Thousands of legitimate owners sailed their schooners and brigs unheralded in the 1820s and 1830s while opium traders and slavers captured the imaginations of the public and historians.

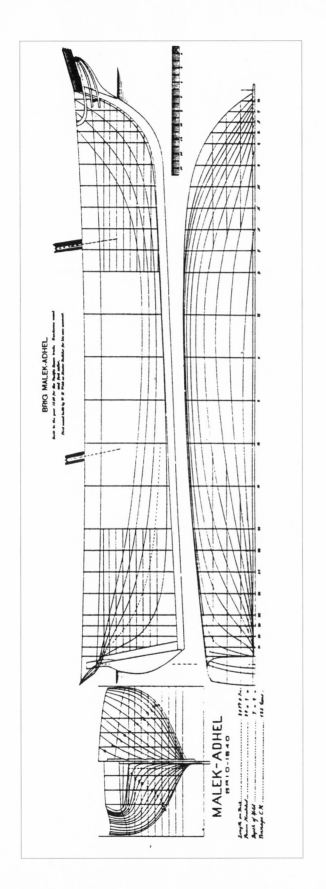

PLAN OF CLIPPER BRIG *MALEK-ADHEL*.

FROM THE PUBLISHED PLANS OF WOODEN

VESSELS BUILT BY WILLIAM H. WEBB.

Endnotes - Chapter Eight

1. *Napoleon*, Baltimore brig; Baltimore register #117, 24 December 1832; built at Baltimore, 1832, for Tildale Paul who sold her to Zachariah Jellison of Boston. RG41 National Archives, hereafter cited as NA. Also, *Revelations of a Slave Smuggler: being the Autobiography of Captain Richard Drake, an African Trader for Fifty Years*, excerpted in *Slave Ships and Slaving* by George Francis Dow (Salem, Massachusetts: Marine Research Society, 1927), 247-48.

2. Dickson J. Preston, *Young Frederick Douglass—The Maryland Years* (Baltimore and London: Johns Hopkins University Press, 1980), 146.

3. Théophile Conneau, *Adventures of an African Slaver*, edited by Malcolm Cowley (Garden City, New York: Garden City Publishing Company, 1928), 188-204.

4. Ibid. 254-70.

5. Ibid. 271.

6. *Guatemala Packet*, schooner, built at Fells Point in 1836; carpenter certificate signed by Walter Price, counter-signed by Hugh Auld. RG41, NA.

7. *Esperanza*, schooner, built at Fells Point in 1836; carpenter certificate signed by Walter Price, countersigned by Hugh Auld. RG41, NA.

8. *Delores*, schooner, built at Fells Point in 1836 for James I. Fisher; carpenter certificate signed by Walter Price; master, William Woodland, owner, James I. Fisher; Baltimore register #56, 1836. RG41, NA.

9. *Emanuel*, schooner, built at Baltimore by L.H. Dunkin for James I. Fisher; carpenter certificate signed by Dunkin, 1836; Baltimore register #54, 1836, RG41, NA.

10 *Emanuel*, owner James I. Fisher; master Peter Pascal; sold 1837; Baltimore register #54, 1836, RG41, NA.

11. *Delores*, Baltimore register #56: "sold 1837" noted on register. RG41, NA.

12. Basil Lubbock, *Cruisers, Corsairs & Slavers* (Glasgow: Brown, Son & Ferguson, 1993), 140-47; 211-12.

13. Baltimore registers, 1824-30; RG41, NA.

14. Lubbock, *Cruisers*, 141.

15. *Griffin* , brig, built at Baltimore 1824; Baltimore register abstracts, 1824-26; RG41, NA.

16. Lubbock, *Cruisers*, 143-47, 207-12, 225-27.

17. *Chesapeake*, *Susquehanna* , and *Beacham*, schooners built for Andrew Patrullo, 1832, by James Beacham. RG41, NA.

18. *Delaware*, schooner, no carpenter certificate found; Baltimore register #24, 1832. *Raritan*, schooner; Baltimore register #26, 1832. RG41, NA.

19. *Engineer*, three-masted schooner, built by James Beacham for Andrew Patrullo per carpenter certificate; RG41, NA.

20. *Engineer*, three-masted schooner, 120' x 30'10" x 9'5", 310 tons burden; owned by Andrew Patrullo, sold Havana; Baltimore register #35, 1832. RG41, NA.

21. *Beacham*, schooner, owner, Andrew Patrullo, built at Baltimore, 1832, sold Havana, 1832. Baltimore temporary register #36, 1833. RG41, NA.

22. *Delaware*, schooner, built at Baltimore 1832, sold Havana, 1832; Baltimore register #24, 1832; *Chesapeake*, schooner, built at Baltimore, 1832, sold Havana, 1832; Baltimore register #25, 1832; *Raritan*, schooner, built at Baltimore 1832, sold Havana 1832; Baltimore register #26, March 1832; *Susquehanna* , schooner, built at Baltimore 1832, sold Havana, 1832; Baltimore register #27, 1832. "Sold Havana" on registers. RG41, NA.

23. Letter from Henry A. Wise to an unnamed party, March, 1846. From: Barton H. Wise, *The Life of Henry A. Wise of Virginia* (New York, The MacMillan Company, 1899), 115.

24. *Sarah Linda*, schooner, built in Somerset County, 1825; owners: James Sullivan, Stephen S. K. Durkee, Robert B. Walters; master, John Durkee; condemned, Turks Island, 1832. Baltimore register #57, 1832. *Nymph*, schooner, built by L.H. Dunkin, 1834, at Baltimore; owners Hugh Birckhead and Charles R. Pearce; master Napoleon Robertson; vessel condemned, 1836; Carpenter certificate and Baltimore register #102, 1834. RG41, NA. *Elizabeth*, barque, built at Baltimore, 1826; Register Abstracts, MHS/MS 2306.

25. Howard I. Chapelle, *The Baltimore Clipper* (Salem, Massachusetts: The Marine Research Society, 1930), 108, 137-41. Thomas C. Gillmer, *Pride of Baltimore, The Story of the Baltimore Clippers* (Camden, Maine: International Marine Publishing Company, 1992). 88-

91. Both authors discount the importance of the "Baltimore clipper" schooner of 1835 because of its involvement in the slave trade; furthermore, they define the new slaver model rather differently. Chapelle states on page 108 that "the results of construction for this [slave] trade may be summarized as follows: increased deadrise and draft, sharper waterlines..." On page 90 of his book, Gillmer writes that the slavers were smaller schooners "with less deadrise." A superficial study of slavers reveals that there was no specific slaver design, except for a preference for Baltimore-schooner and -brig models, regardless of where they were built.

26. Baltimore registers; RG41, NA.

27. *Journals of John Quincy Adams*, edited by Charles Francis Adams (Philadelphia: J.B. Lippincott & Company, 1874-77); Vol X, 133-35, 196, 358-457, 450 and 470. Also, John W. Barber, *A History of the* Amistad *Captives, Being a Circumstantial Account of the Capture of the Spanish Schooner* Amistad *by the Africans on Board; their Voyage and Capture near Long Island, New York, with Biographical Sketches* (New Haven, Connecticut: E.L. & J.W. Barber, 1840; reprinted 1993 by the *Amistad* Committee, Inc., New Haven) and including the correspondence of John Forsyth, Secretary of State in the Administration of Martin van Buren, published by a resolution of Congress as Document No. 185, 23 March 1840. No page numbers.

28. *Ion*, ex-*Amistad*; New London register #5, 1841.

29. Barber, no page numbers.

30. *Friendship*, schooner, New York register #137, 1819, which includes the information that the schooner was built in Somerset County, Maryland, in 1811. RG41, NA.

31. Ibid; also, Supreme Court Case, 5, Wheaton 385 (1820) from John T. Newton, Jr., *The Antelope* (Berkeley, California: University of California Press, 1972), 95 & 181n.

32. Supreme Court: *Amistad* Case; Roll 47, National Archives., Washington; also Appraiser's Report, District Court: *Amistad* Case, Roll 48, National Archives, Washington.

33. Ibid; also, Abstracts of Registers and Enrollments, Newport, Rhode Island, register #988, 28 October 1841. RG41, NA. *Ion*'s tonnage is recalculated at 59 tons burden by reducing her depth of hold from 6'6"

to 5'4". *Amistad-Ion*'s hold becomes crawl space; her new measurements do not create the proportions normal for Chesapeake Bay craft.

34. Appraiser's Report; Roll 48; NA.

35. W.O. Blake, *The History of Slavery and the Slave Trade* (Columbus, Ohio: H. Miller Publishers, 1859), 290-95.

36. Supreme Court and District Court: *Amistad* Case, Rolls 47 & 48, National Archives, Washington.

37. Ibid.

38. Blake, 290-95.

39. Adams, Vol X, 441; Supreme Court: Roll 48, NA.

40. Basil Lubbock, *The Opium Clippers* (Glasgow: Brown, Son & Ferguson, 1992), 33-34.

41. Peter Ward Fay, *The Opium War, 1840-42* (Chapel Hill, North Carolina: University of North Carolina Press, 1975), 45.

42. Lubbock, *Opium Clippers*, 61, 83-84.

43. Ibid. 85-86. Thus, the names Perkins, Cushing and Peabody are confirmed additions to the list of American opium merchants.

44. Ibid. 17.

45. Ibid. 189, 339, 382-84.

46. Collection register #233, 89, The Science Museum, London.

47. Muriel and David Murch and Len Fairweather, *Sail and Steam in Salcombe Harbour* (Plymouth, England: Westway Publications, 1987), 3-4.

48. William H. Webb, *Plans of Wooden Vessels Built by William H. Webb* (New York, by author, 1897); Record Group 45, Box 622, NA.

49. *Frolic*, Baltimore brig, built at Fells Point by William and George Gardner; carpenter certificate signed 1 December 1844; Baltimore register #78, September 1844. RG41, NA. *Bombay Times, Shipping Intelligence*, March-April 1845.

50. *Bombay Times*, insert dated 29 April 1845. This research is the work of Thomas N. Layton, San Jose State University, given to the Maryland Historical Society.

51. Lubbock, *Opium Clippers*, 282, 287-88. Fay, 112, 129, 137, 176, 271, and 336-38;

52. Thomas N. Layton, *The Voyage of the Frolic* (Stanford, California: Stanford University Press, 1997), 19-20.

SAIL PLAN OF USS *LYNX,*

BUILT AT THE WASHINGTON NAVY YARD IN 1814.

National Archives.

CHAPTER NINE

NAVY, REVENUE, AND DISPATCH SCHOONERS

The influence of the Chesapeake pilot schooner on the world's naval and commercial schooner fleets was profound. Indeed, the sweeping conquest of owners, designers, and builders of schooners beyond the limits of Chesapeake Bay in the nineteenth century is the monumental legacy of the craft. It was, as the title of this book states very boldly, a triumph of ship design and ship building that came out of North America's tidewater colonies in the eighteenth century.

How the design originated is not important. The pilot schooner's uniquely shaped hull was the product of many hands, shaped indeed by the shores of the region. Attempts to trace who invented the "scooner" have failed. Where topsails originated, or who put raked masts in a vessel first, or lightened construction, or cleared out quarterdecks, is unknown. It was a combining of components through trial and error that produced a vessel called by William Price, its master builder, "a schooner, pilot-boat-built."

In the end, Chesapeake Bay shipwrights created a new craft, just as elements combined in different proportions produce new chemical substances. Builders were constantly reminded that

speed and maneuverability were the controlling factors in the successful careers of these vessels. As long as an owner wanted a fast sailing schooner to maneuver the curving shorelines of many rivers, escape a chasing enemy, deliver unspoiled a perishable cargo or, in later years, beat a racing competitor, the pilot schooner remained the choice—and it remained the choice for more than a century. Although fast craft developed in other parts of the world at other times, the pilot schooner flowered under a special mixture of conditions that existed around the world in the nineteenth century.

The United States Navy, never an enthusiastic patron of Baltimore schooners, used them for several missions following the War of 1812. Continuing problems with the Dey of Algiers made small, fast, maneuverable vessels handy in the Mediterranean, and there were hundreds of slavers and pirates to deal with in the South Atlantic and the Caribbean when the U.S. Navy joined with the Royal Navy in chasing them down. Although more active against pirates than slavers, the American navy played an active role with a small fleet of tidewater schooners.

Nonsuch, the successful Baltimore

letter-of-marque armed schooner, taken into the U.S. Navy in 1812, continued in service until 1825. Most other small vessels acquired during the war were sold out in the years between 1815 and 1820. USS *Lynx*, a Baltimore schooner built at the Washington Navy Yard in 1814 and spared the torch, was blockaded for the rest of the war. She vanished at sea in 1820.[1] Her sail plan is shown here.

In the fall of 1814 Captain David Porter and Captain Oliver Hazard Perry were appointed to buy or build two squadrons of schooners and brigs for action against Great Britain's merchant ships, supplementing the successful work of American privateers. Perry was in New England supervising the construction of two brigs for his group as the war ended. Porter purchased the Baltimore letter-of-marque schooner *Grampus*, renamed USS *Spitfire*, along with *Flambeau*, ex-*Leader*, and *Firefly*, ex-*Volant*, in early December in New York. He also purchased a Baltimore schooner called *Torche*, and a brig named *Warrington* which he renamed *Spark*. All of Porter's acquisitions were sold out in a year except for USS *Spark*.

While much remains to be learned about *Spark*, some details have been discovered. Included in the John Lenthall collection of plans formerly at the Franklin Institute, and now held by the Independence Seaport Museum in Philadelphia, is a drawing identified as the brig *Spark,* with no other information on it except a sheer, half breadth and body plan, and a separate design for a tran-som.[2] In the collection of ship plans at the National Archives in College Park, Maryland, there is a Ware drawing of the brig *Spark*'s navy sail plan with Ware's drawing of the profile view of the hull.[3]

No other contemporary draught of *Spark* was found, but in the National Archives there is a well-drawn and detailed plan of the U.S. brig *Spark*, drafted by Samuel Hartt Pook and dated 1834, eight years after the vessel was sold out of the service. The drawing shows a vessel of the design of a Baltimore schooner-brig.[4] This plan is quite different from the unsigned plan in the Lenthall Collection in which *Spark* is drawn with only a minor amount of rake to her stem and post, little deck sheer or drag to the keel.

A lack of information accompanying the Lenthall drawing suggests that it was a preliminary draft made by someone before the brig was commissioned, or perhaps a plan for a proposed brig to replace *Spark*. John Lenthall was born in 1807 and only 18 years old when *Spark* was decommissioned. Hence, the Pook plan is more logically a true copy of the plan of the U.S. brig *Spark*. It is signed by a reputable naval constructor. There was even a reason for Pook to have drawn it eight years after *Spark* was sold out, as he was preparing to use her as a model for a new design.[5]

Five Baltimore-type schooners were built in 1821 to answer the navy's need for small fast schooners to run down slavers and pirates off the African coast and in the Caribbean. Built were *Alligator, Porpoise, Shark* and *Dolphin* from a

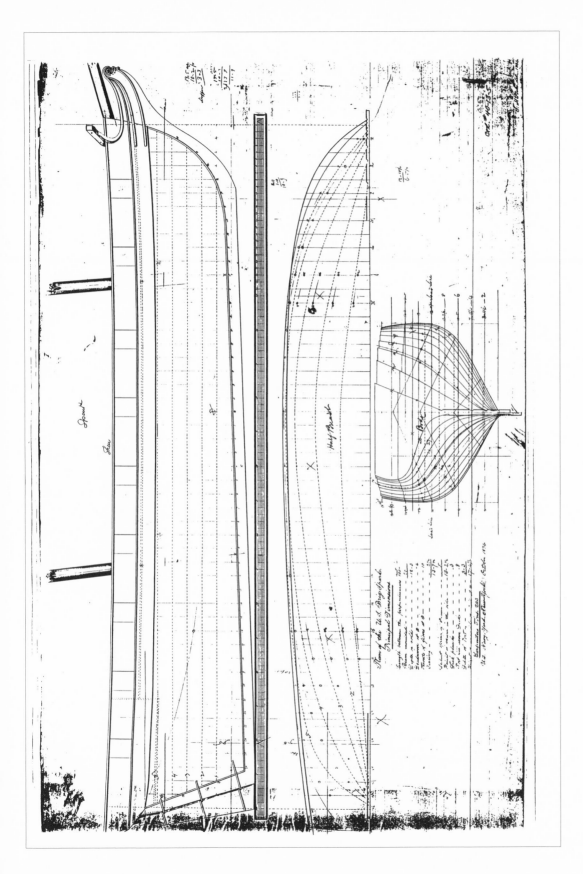

PLAN OF USS *SPARK* DRAWN BY
SAMUEL HARTT POOK IN 1834.

National Archives.

since the first one, *Experiment*, was built in 1799.[7] (See appendix A-2) *Alligator* was commissioned 3 April 1821, and dispatched immediately to Africa where slave ships were clustered in known locations along the coast in that booming trade. She took three slavers, *Mathilde*, *L'Eliza* and *Daphne*, but was lost in a storm in 1823. After many years of service, the sea also claimed *Porpoise* (1821-33) and *Grampus* (1821-43). The navy lost USS *Shark* on a sandbar in the Columbia River on the West Coast in 1846.[8]

A number of small schooners were taken into the service in 1822 when Commodore David Porter received authorization to purchase eight Chesapeake Bay pilot schooners. The little squadron was called Porter's mosquito fleet, and included *Greyhound*, *Jackal*, *Beagle*, *Wildcat*, *Terrier* and *Ferret*, all shallow-draft. Deployed in the waters off Cuba and Puerto Rico, their mission was to hunt down pirates. They were out of the service by 1825.[9] *Ariel*, a Chesapeake Bay pilot schooner built by Dorgan & Bailey of Baltimore, was purchased and took up guard duty over navy live oak supplies on the Florida coast in 1831 and 1832.[10] Also in 1831 and 1832, the U.S. Navy launched three schooners designed by Samuel Humphreys, who, like William Doughty, was a partisan of the Chesapeake Bay pilot schooner model. The new schooners were named *Boxer*, *Experiment* and *Enterprize*.[11]

For many years the U.S. Navy showed

design by William Doughty, naval constructor at the Washington Navy Yard, and *Grampus*, designed by Henry Eckford of New York and built under Doughty's supervision at Washington.[6]

Doughty's schooners closely followed pilot-schooner design. His models had sharply rising floors, deep drag to their keels, low profiles and pilot schooner sail plans with a gaff topsail on the main and square topsails on the foremast. They were considered fast but difficult to handle. Eckford's *Grampus*, with her double square-topsail rig, was very much a Baltimore schooner.

The estimate of the cost of a schooner of the Shark class, as presented to Congress, was $15,000. Live oak was probably supplied for the schooners from navy stocks. Nevertheless, the price of a naval schooner in 1820 had not changed much

no real enthusiasm for pilot schooners or Baltimore schooners. Naval politics and officer resistance to what was considered dangerous service made them a hard sell. The navy lost a number of schooners in bad weather, in some cases possibly as a result of crew inexperience. In the Royal Navy, command of these fast vessels was awarded rising officers for outstanding service, and these young officers often had little experience with such untamed horses.[12] By contrast, around Chesapeake Bay male children went to sea on tender schooners and the best were masters before they left their teens.

Samuel Humphreys' schooners of 1831-32 were the last built for the U.S. Navy and were aptly named. *Experiment's* namesake was the navy's first Baltimore schooner; *Enterprize* was the service's most famous schooner, and commanded by many of its best officers; and *Boxer* was the first *Enterprize's* last major victim when both were brigs at the time of their engagement. Only 88' overall, the new schooners did not differ greatly from the first navy schooners in size or model. This similarity is a characteristic of the pilot schooner design, for if the builder stayed with it he got predictable results; if he

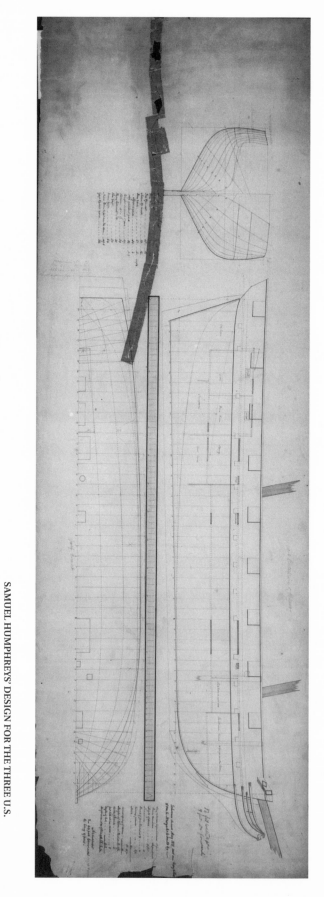

SAMUEL HUMPHREYS' DESIGN FOR THE THREE U.S.
NAVY SCHOONERS, EXPERIMENT, ENTERPRIZE
AND BOXER.
National Archives.

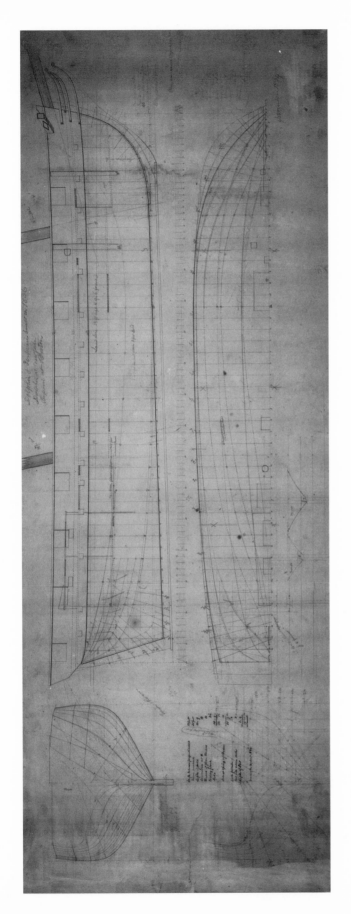

PLAN OF USS *DOLPHIN/PORPOISE*
DRAWN BY WILLIAM DOUGHTY.

National Archives.

strayed too far from the model, his vessel would have undesirable sailing qualities.

The United States Revenue Service, a division of the Treasury Department, and a part of the navy in time of war, embraced the Chesapeake Bay pilot schooner design from the first schooners ordered by Alexander Hamilton in 1790. The service's mission was to chase down smugglers and other maritime lawbreakers, and to generally guard the coastal waters of the United States. In the age of sail, revenue cutters attracted the best designs as naval constructors and shipyards competed to create the top performers. The fastest and most beautiful vessels, and thus the choice, were the pilot-schooner designs of the tidewater.

During the first half of the nineteenth century, revenue cutters, yachts and pilot boats were not just influenced by the Chesapeake pilot-schooner model. They were pilot-boat schooners. Hamilton's first cutters, *Active* and *Virginia,* were pilot-boat-built, and no other design was ever seriously considered or used until cutters powered by steam were introduced.

The Revenue Service, later absorbed into the Coast Guard, was usually subject to navy control during wartime. Naturally enough, naval constructors designed most sailing cutters (a name that in no way relates to their rig). Typical were the designs of William Doughty, naval constructor at the Washington Navy Yard, during the War of 1812. He designed three different classes of schooners for the Revenue Service in 1815, all of which had shallow bows and deeper keels that dragged radically. With sweeping sheer, he designed a fast, highly maneuverable and probably very wet craft. According to Jean-Baptiste Marestier's calculations, Doughty's medium-sized cutter had depth in the stern twice that of the bow.[13]

These William Doughty cutters had strongly raked stern posts and stems with long sweeping curves in their hull lines. More than normal beam, widest forward of amidships, and a full bow with relatively short entrance, provided them with a good clean run to a sharply contoured stern. Doughty's middle-sized cutters were not as deep as Bay pilot schooners. Extra breadth provided stability for these fast boats.

As time passed the Revenue Service operated larger vessels. An important group was called the Morris class, built to fulfill a need for offshore work. A number of cutters, including USRC *Louis McLane,* (usually called just *McLane*) were built in 1832 by Webb and Allen of New York. The schooner *Morris* was built at the Brooklyn Navy Yard, and the vessels that were given the name were about 75' in length and very similar to the smaller, fuller schooners then being built on Chesapeake Bay. This class was replaced by the Joe Lane class, a handsome pilot-schooner design named for the Pacific Coast revenue cutter that was named in turn for an Oregon politician. *Phillip Allen,* a Joe Lane cutter built in Portsmouth, Virginia, served on Chesapeake Bay for a number of years. During the War Between the States, she

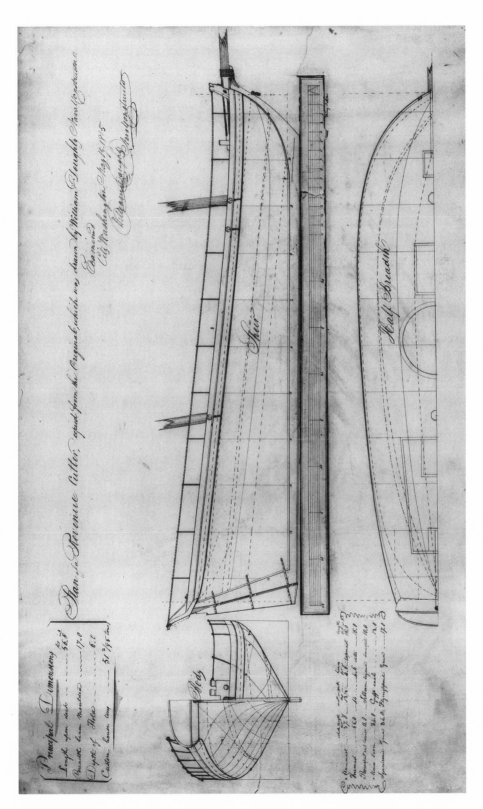

**PLAN OF THE MEDIUM-SIZED REVENUE CUTTER DRAWN BY
WILLIAM DOUGHTY FOR CONSTRUCTION IN 1815.**

National Archives.

took a station off Fort Monroe, blockading Confederate vessels inside Hampton Roads and the James River.[14] These were the last sailing vessels built for the Revenue Service. *Philip Allen*'s sail plan is in the sail-plan books of Loane Brothers,

which are part of the collection of the Maryland Historical Society.

The Chesapeake Bay's French connection existed from 1755 to about 1850. Beginning with the arrival of French refugees from Acadia (Nova Scotia) in 1755, Baltimore benefited from a number of emigrations of people of French background. The presence of French naval power on Chesapeake Bay set the stage for victory at Yorktown, creating a vast store of goodwill for America's ally. Marylanders' welcome to French colonial refugees and outcasts of France's revolutions and wars, during periods in which Baltimore grew rapidly in size and wealth, created bonds impervious to war. Even through France's aggression against America's merchant fleet during the Quasi War, deeply-rooted French bonds to Baltimore remained unbroken.

Baltimore's mercantile houses, many of them with partners living in France and France's colonies, maintained commercial and social relations with their merchant French colleagues, principally at Bordeaux, in war and peace. Along the wharves of Fells Point, refugee French merchants, agents and shipbuilders supplied the needs of French mariners after war with England flared up once again in 1793.

The French purchased pilot schooners, first baycraft and then the very first Baltimore schooners, to use in France's *guerre de course* against the British. These early purchases of Chesapeake pilot schooners cloud their origin, and have created the myth that Chesapeake Bay's great schooners owed their origin to France. If that fiction still runs through the minds of readers, consid-

er France's intense interest in the products of Fells Point's shipyards after 1792, an interest that remained strong through the first decades of the nineteenth century.

The fact is that schooners came late to France's naval, merchant and fishing fleets. Further, Marestier's investigative mission of 1820 was obviously one of industrial espionage. After peace returned to Europe and America, the French Navy looked to Fells Point once again for its designs, just as its mariners had two decades earlier. While no indepth study of the schooners of France

AN UNIDENTIFIED
U.S. REVENUE
CUTTER IS SHOWN
AT ANCHOR IN THIS
DRAWING BY
GEORGE F. MORSE.
*Peabody Essex
Museum, Salem, MA.*

was undertaken for this study, strong evidence exists that the French Navy appropriated Chesapeake Bay schooner designs for vessels built in 1822 and 1823.

The story of French pilot schooners begins at Yorktown in 1781. The Virginia Navy schooner *Patriot's* successful Revolutionary War service terminated when a British sloop carrying a contingent of 50 marines overwhelmed the pilot schooner in the James River the summer before the Battle of Yorktown. *Patriot* was attached to Lord Cornwallis' forces as a British dispatch boat.

With the victory of the combined French-American forces led by George Washington on land and Le Comte de Grasse at sea, *Patriot* was awarded to the French Navy. The younger Commodore James Barron, USN, an eyewitness to *Patriot's* last engagement on the James River, wrote in his journal that the French sent the pilot schooner to Cap François, San Domingo, where the government placed her in packet service.[15]

Perhaps *Patriot's* transfer from Chesapeake Bay to the French West Indies in 1781 provides partial explanation for the early appreciation of the pilot schooner by French colonial merchants, privateer owners and French navy commanders there. After 1793, with attacks by British forces on the French West Indies, the colonists were harassed by the Royal Navy just as the patriots of Maryland and Virginia had been in 1776. It was at this time that pilot schooners were acquired in numbers by French colonial interests. William Price's *Infant Patriot* with its

intriguing name, suggesting a play on the name of the earlier *Patriot*, was one of dozens of schooners built on the Bay for French owners after 1792. Chapter 4 tells this evolving story.

No nation's maritime community involved itself more completely with the Chesapeake Bay pilot schooner than that of France. Because of the continuing war with Britain during a long period of internal upheaval, a prelude to the Napoleonic era, France encouraged her great mercantile families to fight the Royal Navy with privateer vessels. In many instances they purchased Chesapeake Bay pilot schooners, and eventually the design reappeared as French-built naval schooners and privateers during the 20-year *guerre de course* with Great Britain.

The French Navy purchased the Baltimore schooner *Superior* in 1801, and no doubt there were other such purchases at this time. William Taylor purchased USS *Experiment* at auction in November 1801, and sold her to foreign buyers at the French port of New Orleans in August of 1802. Other U.S. Navy ships and merchant vessels, sold to foreigners at this time, merely disappeared and probably ended up under the French flag.

A drawing by Ange-Joseph Antoine Roux of Marseilles depicts a Baltimore-type schooner under construction in France.[16] This image of a Chesapeake Bay pilot schooner brings credence to the legend that Maryland builders crossed the Atlantic on different occasions to build schooners for French owners. This may have happened in 1796-97, prior to

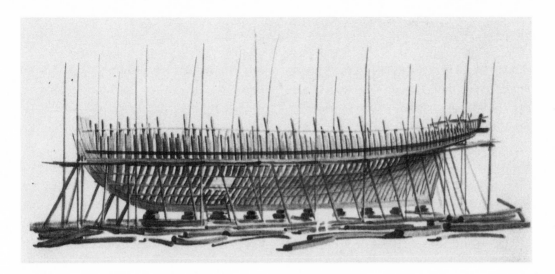

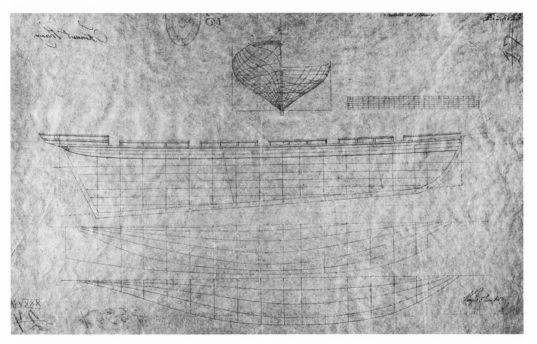

America's Quasi War with France, and perhaps again after the English and French blockades of 1807 were instituted. If it happened at all, these were the most likely periods that Chesapeake shipwrights would have sought work in France.

Roux's caption states that the schooner under construction in the print is called *Duguaitrouin.* Among the vessels named *Duguay Trouin* are an aviso (dispatch) vessel listed in 1797, and later renamed *La Dangereuse.* There was also a corsaire (privateer) of that name taken by HMS *Narcissus* in 1810.[17] At the time of her capture, the corsaire was owned in Brest. She measured 163 tons, comparable to *La Superieure, Experiment, les Quatre Freres, Adventure* and other early Baltimore schooners that were sold to the French or captured by them.[18] There were other French vessels, naval and privateer, given the name *Duguay Trouin* between 1793 and 1810. There is no evidence in French maritime history of the pilot schooner design appreraring in France or the West Indies prior to the time that French citizens and their government began to purchase Chesapeake Bay pilot schooners around 1792.

Jacques Conte of Bordeaux acquired and fitted out the goelette (schooner) *La Phenix* between 1807 and 1810. A draft of her found its way to a Copenhagen museum. This is a plan of a schooner of the Baltimore model with unusual deadrise. *La Phenix*'s entrance is slightly concave, and sharp, placing her greatest breadth closer to her actual midsection than most Bay-built pilot schooners. These small differences are not conclusive but suggest that she was built in France. Although the plan gives no dimensions, Conte's *La Phenix* measured 120 tons. She made at least two successful privateer cruises, one to Cayenne in the West Indies. The Royal Navy frigate HMS *Aigle* captured her in 1810.[19]

The French Navy goelette *L'Estaffette*, launched between 1810 and 1813, is remarkable in her resemblance to a Chesapeake-built pilot schooner. The lines of her bow, convex and with beautifully raked stem, give her an entrance similar to that of *Nonpareil* or just about any other small Baltimore schooner. Her hold as measured is a little deeper proportionately than Baltimore models built after 1807, and her midsection is farther aft. *L'Estaffette*'s deadrise and turn of bilge is subtle, and these details of her hull suggest the work of a Fells Point shipwright. Dimensions are given in feet in the drawing, presumably French measure, which are approximately seven percent longer than the British or American units. The dimensions, 74' x 19'8" x 8'10", convert into approximately 79.2' x 21' x 9.3' American measure. *L'Estaffette* was lost at sea in 1836.[20]

It appears that schooners of pilot-boat design were first built in France during the first decade of the nineteenth century. They do not resemble schooners built there during the previous decade.

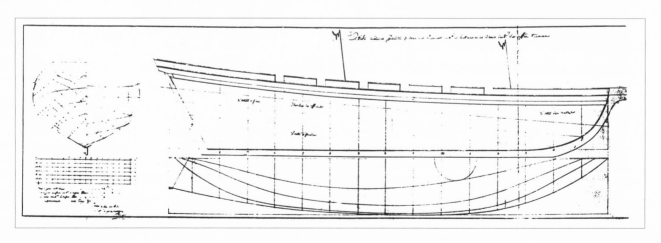

GOÉLETTE CORSAIR
JEAN BART,
A FRENCH
PRIVATEER, SHOWN
SAILING OUT OF
MARSEILLES.
PAINTING BY
CAMIELLIERI.
Musée de la Marine,
Paris.

GOÉLETTE NO. 10,
A SCHOONER OF
THE FRENCH NAVY,
PAINTED IN 1829 BY
FREDERIC ROUX.
Musée de la Marine,
Paris.

Without an evolutionary history of the pilot-schooner design, it is impossible to accept any theory other than that made fairly obvious by Marestier's book, that France copied Chesapeake Bay models from drawings or from captured or purchased schooners. The French artist Camillieri painted the corsaire schooner *Jean Bart* standing out of Marseilles in 1811.[21] She was built about the same time as *La Phenix* and *L'Estaffette.*

Two classes of French Navy schooners, both built in France after the War of 1812, and both modeled on the design of the Baltimore schooner, provide further evidence of the acceptance of Chesapeake pilot schooners by the French Navy. While other nineteenth-century schooners dropped specific features of the design, the French schooners of 1822 and 1823 could almost be defined as clones.

After his return from his investigative voyage to the United States in 1820, Jean Baptiste Marestier received instructions from the French Ministry of Maritime Affairs to design a class of schooners for France's navy. The result was a fleet of 21 schooner-brigs called the La Gazelle class after the first vessel launched in 1822.[22] The evidence suggests that Marestier copied the design of an actual pilot

PLAN OF
MARESTIER'S
SCHOONER NO. 3,
FROM HIS
PUBLISHED STUDY
OF AMERICAN
VESSELS.

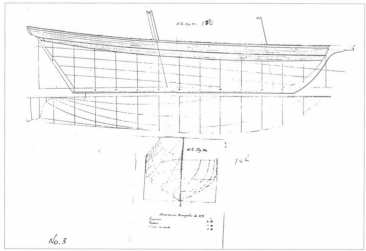

schooner he found docked or under construction at Fells Point. *La Gazelle* was modeled end to end on the Baltimore schooner, giving her and her navy sisters the more rakish look of a privateer than similar models built by the U.S. Navy and the Royal Navy during the same period.

In French archival records *La Gazelle* was not called a schooner, but rather a brick-goelette (brig-schooner) because of innovations to her sail plan. Marestier's sail plan reduced the size of her gaff foresail, and the large boomed course sail that Baltimore schooners carried for decades was replaced with the balanced square-sail rig of a brig.

Howard Chapelle wrote that Marestier obtained Samuel Humphreys' drawing dated 1819 of a proposed class of U.S. Navy schooners during his visit.[23] Although Marestier's schooner No. 4 and Humphreys' schooner design of 1819 are similar, it is the Frenchman's plan of schooner No. 3,[24] the lines of a Baltimore schooner, that Marestier probably chose as model for *La Gazelle*. Schooner No. 3 resembles a War of 1812 version of an

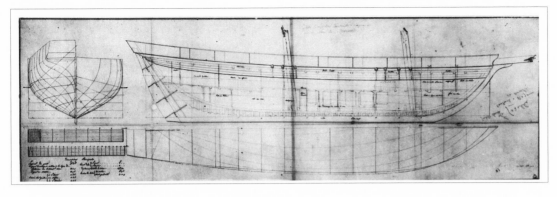

PLAN OF
LA GAZELLE,
DRAWING BY
MARESTIER.

armed schooner such as *Mammoth*—a vessel Marestier measured[25]— or one of the unnamed schooners he also measured in Baltimore. As Marestier fails to name the schooners he encountered except for *Mammoth*, it is not possible to be definitive.[26]

It seems quite remarkable that Marestier would design a navy schooner with such extreme lines. He not only did that, but France continued building vessels of pilot schooner design through to *Le Cerf* in 1833, and vessels of the class remained a part of the French Navy until mid-century.[27]

COMPARISON OF NO. 3 AND *LA GAZELLE*
(Dimensions in Meters)

Schooner No. 3	*La Gazelle*
Length 31.33	30.11
Beam 7.92	8.0
Depth 3.63	3.85

In comparing the two drawings, both from the hand of Marestier, one notes the extreme rake of the stern post. The drawings, executed two years apart, have similar deadrise, and the hull profiles have similar sheerlines. The schooners have bows that look to be interchange-

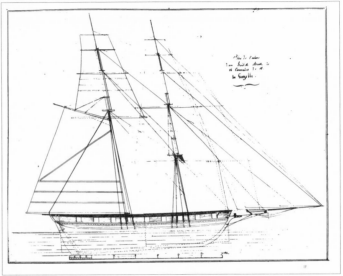

able. There are slight differences in the amount of tumblehome and bowspit steeve, as *La Gazelle* has slightly more of each than No.3. Similar to later Baltimore schooners of 1814-15, *La Gazelle*'s entrance is less convex.

A year after *La Gazelle* joined the French fleet, the Ministry of Maritime Affairs ordered construction of a second class of schooners. These were small schooners built to guard the offshore waters of France's colonies in Africa and the Western Hemisphere, duties roughly equivalent to those of the United States

SAIL PLAN OF
LA GAZELLE,
DRAWING BY
MARESTIER.
Musée de la Marine,
Paris.

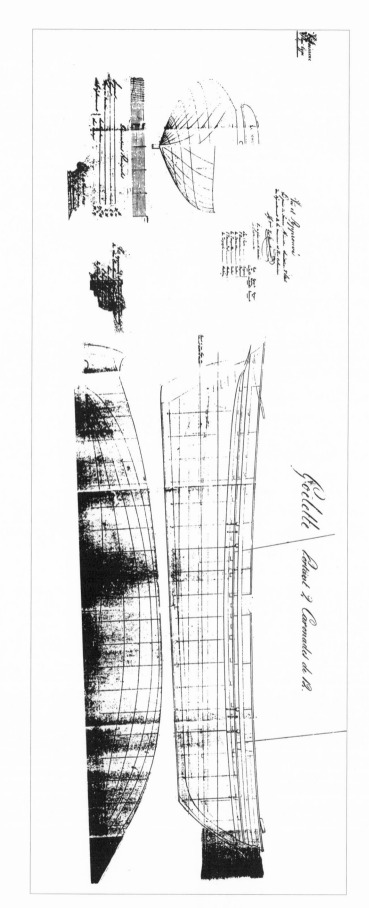

**PLAN OF FRENCH NAVY SCHOONER
L'ANÉMONE, OF 1823.
*Service Historique de la Marine, Vincennes.***

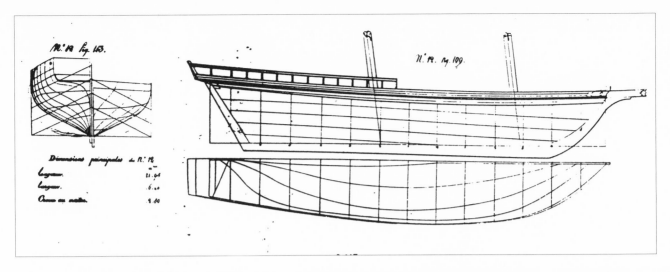

Revenue Service. With dimensions in American feet, *l'Anemone*, the first of her class, measured 68.86' x 19.02' x 7.7'.[28] Marestier's schooner No. 12's dimensions are 71.98' x 20.99' x 8.20'. As stated in Chapter 7, the designer of the l'Anemone class may have used Marestier's schooner No. 12 for his design. It is suggested that when Marestier drew No. 12 he may have taken off the lines of *Virginia Ross*, under construction at Fells Point at the time of his visit. *Virginia Ross*'s measurements are given in her register as 67'6" x 20'3" x 7'10", close to those of *l'Anemone*.

Conjecture is risky, and acceptance of circumstantial evidence that the three designs are one and the same is danger-ous. Marestier's calculations were esti-mates, and it is also possible that when the Frenchman originally made his con-versions from feet to meters he did not take into consideration the difference between an American foot and the nine-teenth-century French foot.[29] This would account for No. 12's greater size. This rea-soning is less important, however, than the fact that the drawing of schooner No. 12, known to be of a Chesapeake pilot schooner under construction at Fells Point when Marestier was there, is remarkably similar to the lines of *l'Anemone*.

Jean François Delamoriniére was selected by the General Inspectorate of

Shipbuilding to design the l'Anemone class.[30] Delamoriniére, a junior surveyor in the Ministry of Maritime Affairs, and only 30 years old, could hardly have avoided the guidance and advice of Engineer Marestier who, having returned from his successful investigative tour, received an appointment to the consulting commission and to the Board of Advisors of Marine Works. Along with Delamoriniére, he was assigned to the Ministry's office in Paris. Additionally, Marestier had recently completed work on *La Gazelle*'s plans. With access to Marestier's drafts, and in a junior position, Delamoriniére could not escape supervision by his senior, at that time the toast of France's maritime circles.[31]

Jean Boudriot, a French writer and draftsman, believes that by 1823 the transfer of technology [design] of pilot schooners was too diffuse for a comparison of Maryland and French schooners to be cogent. Boudriot plays down the importance of Marestier's report by suggesting that its principal subject was steam propulsion. He comments on the improbability that the designer of the schooners of the l'Anemone-La Jacinthe class was inspired by Marestier's work.[32]

Boudriot insists that the early schooners of Europe were inspired by Bermuda sloops, as were American vessels, and thus it might be more accurate to relate Chesapeake and European schooners to a parallel development from a common beginning.[33] Boudriot suggests that the principal influence of Baltimore schooners was one of rig rather than hull design.[34]

Though he may be in error, Monsieur Boudriot's thoughts are important. Almost all writers on the pilot-boat design perpetuate the myth that the design originated elsewhere than Chesapeake Bay. They see the model in more complicated terms—that is, as a variation of some earlier craft such as a Bermuda sloop, a Jamaican schooner, a Brittany lugger, a Turkish barge or a Mediterranean galley. Almost all maritime historians writing about Chesapeake pilot schooners, and particularly Baltimore schooners, follow a similar line of reasoning, varying only the original source of the model. None give credit for the design to Chesapeake Bay shipwrights.

The failure to credit Chesapeake Bay's shipwrights as the source of the pilot schooner design is due in large part to the lack of published material on the origins of the type. Inaccuracies and myths thrive like an unattended grapevine in the wild, the location of its roots lost in the underbrush. With so little information tracing the model from its source, the most famous, the most successful, the most beautiful of all sailing designs would naturally become universal.

The Royal Navy was impressed by Chesapeake Bay pilot schooners no less than the French Navy. In 1793 the Royal Navy captured the first French schooners built on Chesapeake Bay, and started taking them into the service. *Swift*, a Virginia pilot schooner, was in British hands in 1794. Between 1793 and the end of the War of 1812, hundreds of American vessels were captured. In just a two-year period, June 1812 to July 1814, the Royal

BALTIMORE SCHOONERS
IN THE SERVICE OF THE ROYAL NAVY
BETWEEN 1803 AND 1814

Year	Schooner	Original Name	Built	Remarks
1803	*SWIFT*	*SWIFT*	CIRCA 1794	Purchased in America; plan used for a class of dispatch schooner
1803	*SUPERIERE*	*SUPERIOR*	1801	Purchased by French; formerly *LA SUPÉRIEURE*, captured by RN, 1803, RN 1803-14
1803	*FIREFLY*	*FLYING FISH*	1801	Purchased by French; renamed *POISSON VOLANT*; captured by RN 1803
1807	*NETLEY*	*NIMROD*[37]	1803	RN 1808-1813
1808	*NONPAREIL*	*NONPAREIL*	1807	RN 1808-13
1811	*SEALARK*	*FLY*[38]	1807	RN 1811-20
1812	*EMULOUS*	USS *NAUTILUS*	1801	Brig 1812; RN1812-17
1812	*WHITING*	*ARROW*[39]	1811	RN 1812-16
1812	*COCKCHAFER*	*SPENCER*[40]	1811	RN 1812-15
1813	*ST. LAWRENCE*	*ATLAS*[41]	1808	RN 1813-15; Recaptured by *Chasseur*, Captain Boyle
1813	*HIGHFLYER*	*HIGHFLYER*[42]	1811	RN 1813-1815; Recaptured by USS *President*
1813	*SHELBURNE*	*RACER*	1811	RN 1813-17
1813	*MUSQUIDOBIT*	*LYNX*	1812	RN 1813-20
1813	*CANSO*	*LOTTERY*[43]	1812	RN 1813-16
1814	*GRECIAN*	*GRECIAN*	1812	RN 1814-22
1814	*ATALANTA*	*SIRO*[44]	1812	Recaptured the same year.

Navy sent 298 American merchant vessels to the naval prize court agent at Bermuda.[35] Many of the Baltimore schooners captured at this time were taken into the Royal Navy.[36] Here is a list of commissioned schooners built on Chesapeake Bay. This list is not complete.

The Royal Navy also captured the Baltimore ship *Hannibal* in 1812 and commissioned her HMS *Andromeda,* a sixth-rate frigate. The William Price-built ship served four years.[45]

It was written in an earlier chapter that the Baltimore schooner *Superior* was a pivotal vessel. Taken from the French, the Royal Navy commissioned her as

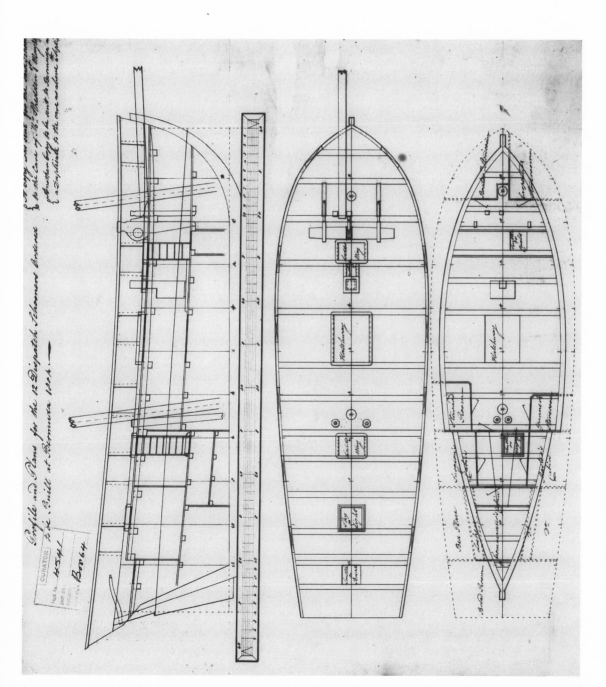

PLAN FOR THE TWELVE ROYAL NAVY DISPATCH
SCHOONERS TO BE BUILT IN BERMUDA
BEGINNING IN 1804.

National Maritime Museum, London.

HMS *Superiere* and thus she served under her third flag. Basil Lubbock, describing the British campaign against French privateers after 1793, wrote that *La Gracieuse* and *La Supérieure* were war schooners of French build, as was *Flying Fish (La Poisson Volant).*[46] *La Gracieuse* remains unidentified, but both *La Supérieure* and *Flying Fish* were built in Maryland. Lubbock's errors are typical misstatements of the place of origin of Chesapeake Bay pilot schooners. *La Gracieuse,* which served in the Royal Navy for several years, was likely a Baltimore schooner too.[47]

Prior to the commissioning of HMS *Superiere,* the Admiralty ordered its Portsmouth dockyard to take off the lines of the Chesapeake pilot schooner *Swift.* Though her date of construction on Chesapeake Bay is unknown, she originally arrived in Great Britain in 1794.[48] The Admiralty planned for this Chesapeake Bay packet boat to be the model for a squadron of dispatch schooners. The story goes that the Admiralty sent *Swift*'s plan, dated 12 March 1803, to its contractor in Bermuda, Edward Goodrich, with instructions to build several for the Royal Navy. Goodrich, the surviving brother of Bridger, was selected through the efforts of his brother-in-law, Robert Shedden of London.[49]

The Goodrich firm, as agents for the Admiralty, subcontracted the schooners to a number of Bermuda builders.[50] *Haddock,* which became the model for those built in England, was built by Isaac Skinner.[51] Then the story becomes confusing. Supposedly because of design and construction objections from Bermuda, the British Admiralty allowed changes to the Chesapeake Bay model. Somehow *Swift*'s plan was changed radically.

The dispatch schooners as built, whether the model was developed by the Admiralty or by the Goodrich firm, differed from *Swift* in all dimensions, but particularly in depth of hold, both actually and relative to other measurements. These differences may be studied by comparing the draft titled "Profile and Plans for the 12 Dispatch Schooners," said to be the plans used by the Bermuda shipwrights, to *Swift*'s draft in Chapter 4.

The bow of the Bermuda-built dispatch schooner was shorter and fuller. Depth added, just under three feet, with other changes, increased the dispatch schooners' measured tonnage from 46 tons to approximately 75 tons. As a result, the schooners, though perhaps inspired by the Virginia pilot schooner, were very different as built. There were seventeen of the class built between 1804 and 1807. They were *Ballahou, Barracouta, Bream, Capellin, Chubb, Cuttle, Grouper, Haddock, Mackerel, Flying Fish, Mullett, Pike, Porgey, Pilchard, Snapper, Tang* and *Whiting.* Of the total, seven were wrecked, six captured and just four completed service.[52]

The *Haddock* plan was sent to the Admiralty and served as a model for a second group named for birds and built in England between 1806 and 1808. As they were carbon copies of the Bermuda fish models, this throws doubt on the story that the Bermuda agent, Edward

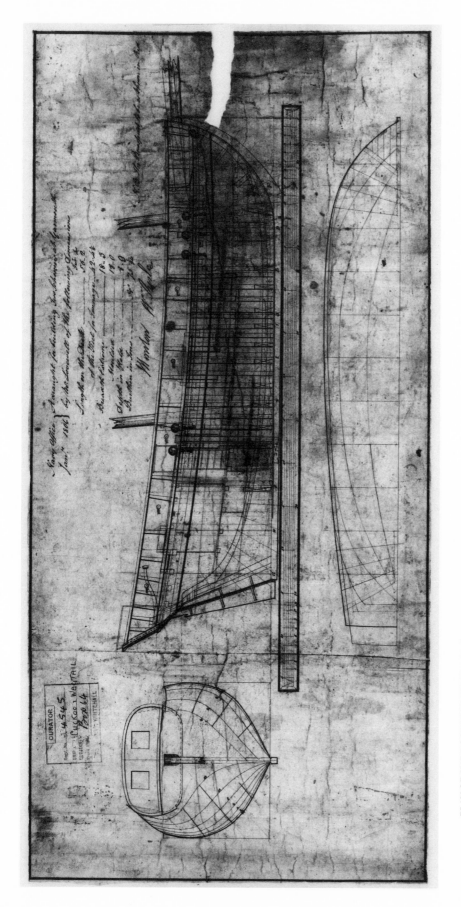

PLAN OF *HADDOCK*, THE MODEL FOR SUBSEQUENT SCHOONERS
*CUCKOO, WAGTAIL, LANDRAIL, JACKDAW, MAGPIE, PIGEON, QUAIL, ROOK,
SEALARK, CRANE* AND *WIDGEON* COMMISIONED BY THE ADMIRALITY.

National Maritime Museum, London.

Goodrich, changed the designs of the schooners built in Bermuda.

The French privateer *Diligent* captured *Whiting* in 1812.[53] *Ballahou* became a prize of the Baltimore armed schooner *Perry* on 20 June 1814.[54] The word ballahou eventually became the generic name for the West Indies and Bermuda versions of the Chesapeake Bay pilot schooner. There are contemporary French and British prints as well as surviving plans of ballahou schooners, sometimes merely described as American, as Europeans called all of the land area of the Western Hemisphere, including the islands of the West Indies.

The "Plan d'un Balaou Américain" below includes the information that the lines were taken off at Bayonne in 1811. Her measurements, converted to American feet, produce these approximate dimensions: 84.3' x 23.4' x 10.2'. A pilot schooner with extreme deadrise, and slack bilges carried almost to her deck, she had a fairly deep hold in proportion to her other dimensions. She was possibly a schooner built for the Royal Navy in Bermuda, a West Indies fruit schooner, or a French-built privateer. She was not built on Chesapeake Bay, although her roots are unmistakably there.

Among the pilot schooners built in England on the *Swift-Ballahou-Haddock* model were *Cuckoo*, *Wagtail*, *Landrail*, *Jackdaw*, *Magpie*, *Pigeon*, *Quail*, *Rook*, *Sealark*, *Crane* and *Widgeon*.[55] *Landrail* was captured in a spirited engagement with the Baltimore armed schooner *Syren*. Lieutenant R.D. Lancaster, master of *Landrail*, described her as a cutter, which referred to her duties or armament rather than to her rig.[56] These schooners or cutters, as described, were probably the first vessels of a Chesapeake Bay design built in Great Britain. Of the grand total of 28 schooners built in Bermuda and England from the altered *Swift* draft, 22 were lost at sea or captured and just six survived to be sold out of the service.

Frequent use of the name *Flying Fish* creates confusion for the historian. The drawings of a class of schooners referred to at the National Maritime Museum's Ship Plan Section as the Flying Fish class are a good example.[57] Six schooners were built from a plan of *Flying Fish*, a schooner evidently built from a plan of an unidentified three-masted Baltimore-built pilot schooner. A vessel that has attracted frequent comment by historians, *Flying Fish*, the schooner on which the class is modeled, remains obscure.[58]

Written on the plan of HMS *Flying Fish* is a statement that it is a "draught of His Magesty's Schooner *Flying Fish*, built at Baltimore and taken off September, 1806." William Flannigain, one of Fells Point's more creative shipwrights, built three of the three-masted schooners in 1805, *Revenge*,[59] *Luna*[60] and *Orestes*.[61]

The question is raised whether this *Flying Fish* is Flannigain's *Revenge*, *Luna*, *Orestes*, or another three-masted schooner? J.J. Colledge, in his directory of Royal Navy ships, overwhelmed by the confusion created by several vessels named *Flying Fish*, does not identify an American schooner of that period named

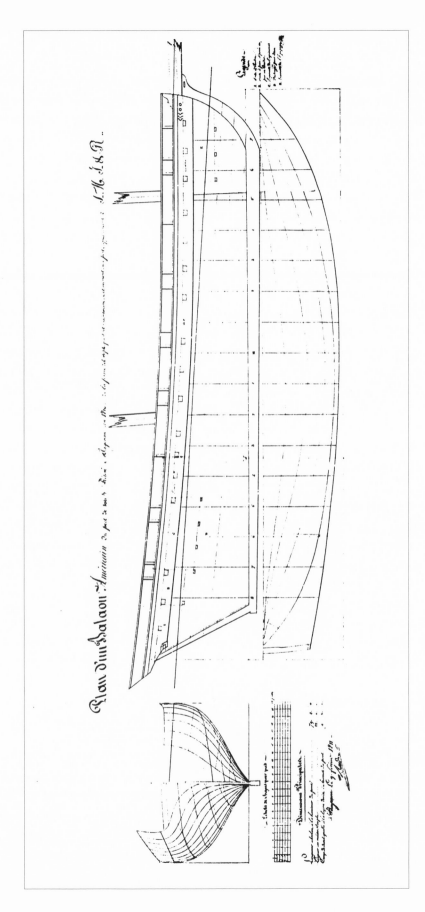

"PLAN D'UN BALAOU AMÉRICAIN" IS THE

IDENTIFICATION OF THIS DRAWING OF WHAT MAY

BE A WEST INDIES FRUIT SCHOONER,

A BERMUDA-BUILT ROYAL NAVY SCHOONER, OR A

FRENCH-BUILT PRIVATEER

Service Historique de la Marine, Vincennes.

or renamed HMS *Flying Fish*.[36] As a matter of fact, he lists no schooner of that name in the Royal Navy in 1806 of the size or of the type shown in the draft below. Furthermore, in Baltimore's registers for 1804, 1805, and 1806, no three-masted schooner named *Flying Fish* is listed.

Colledge's list and *Revenge's* Baltimore registers #114 and #216, 1805, supply evidence to raise doubts about the previously published material which states that *Revenge* and HMS *Flying Fish* are one and the same. On the face of *Revenge's* register #114, dated 10 June 1805, in pencil, is a notation: "left at St. Thomas, 6 November 1805." St. Thomas, Virgin Islands, at that time was a colonial outpost of Denmark, a country at war with Great Britain. Captain Nicolas W. Easton, owner of *Revenge*, re-registered her 2 November 1805, and on the back of register #216 is the notation: "Sold to foreigners; 27 January. 1806."[63] Although the time frame is correct, as the Admiralty Plan of HMS *Flying Fish* was drawn in September of 1806, it has never been demonstrated that *Revenge* and HMS *Flying Fish* are the same vessel. Furthermore, the dimensions of the two schooners are different, a fact that Howard I. Chapelle and those who copy his work ignore.[64]

Luna remained under the American flag until 1809.[65] *Orestes*, however, was sold in New York in 1805, and would have been available to the British in 1806.[66] The measurements of all three of Flannigain's schooners differ significantly from those of HMS *Flying Fish*.

In any case, it is known with certainty that the Admiralty had the lines of an unidentified Baltimore-built three-masted schooner taken off at Portsmouth in 1806. A set of three drawings that are titled HMS *Flying Fish* survives in the Admiralty collection at the National Maritime Museum at Greenwich. From these drafts six three-masted schooners, *Shamrock*, *Thistle*, *Mistletoe*, *Holly*, *Juniper* and *Bramble*, with dimensions of 79' length on deck and 22' breadth, were built in Bermuda in 1808 and 1809.[67] These measurements are close to those of *Flying Fish*, conforming to the Admiralty's instructions to build them according to plan.[68]

The Admiralty drawings of the hull plan of HMS *Flying Fish* certainly represent a Baltimore-built craft. This may be observed in her profile, her underbody, and her transom-rudder design in which the rudder post passes through the middle of the transom, a characteristic of Chesapeake pilot schooners. However, the sail plan of HMS *Flying Fish* is of British or Bermudian conception. The altered transom-rudder arrangement with the post abaft the transom, and the spars and sails, including the topsails, are also of British or Bermudian design.

The Admiralty placed the order for the six schooners with Bermuda's Edward Goodrich. The actual builders are not known. In this instance, a Royal Navy shipwright, William Bunce, was sent to Bermuda to supervise the project.[69] This action by the Admiralty suggests that variations in the *Swift* design originated in

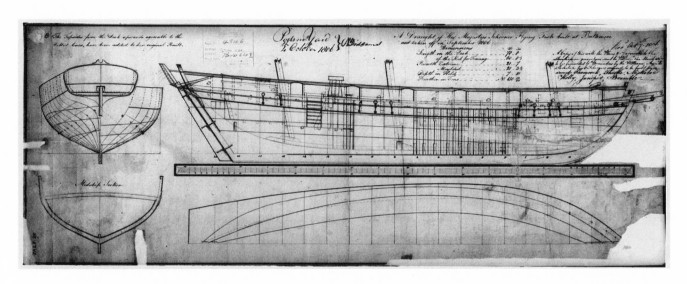

THE HULL PLAN OF HMS *FLYING FISH*. *National Maritime Museum, London.*

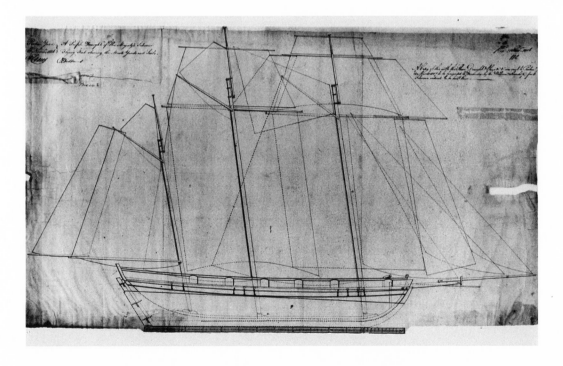

THE SAIL PLAN OF HMS *FLYING FISH*. *National Maritime Museum, London.*

H.M.S. "CADMUS"
GUNS   10
TONS   237
BUILT   1808

Bermuda and steps were being taken to avoid this in the construction of the Flying Fish class.

The three-masted schooners are an interesting variation of the pilot-schooner design. While the Bermuda design differs principally in rig, the Fells Point model and the Bermuda-built version had shallow hulls in proportion to their length. Three of the six-shallow draft schooners of the *Shamrock-Flying Fish* class, as listed in Colledge's directory, were lost at sea, which is not surprising since the plan suggests they would have had less stability than the two-masted Baltimore schooner model.

The navies of European nations were aware of ship developments among themselves and in America in the nine-teenth century. Advances in design by one were quickly copied by another if a need was filled. The successes of USS *Experiment* and USS *Enterprize* against French privateers was of some influence in bringing a realization to the British Admiralty that the Royal Navy was heavy with big ships. In 1808, the Admiralty created a new class of brigs which came to be known as the Cadmus-Cherokee class. The Science Museum in London has two hull models, one positively identified as HMS *Cadmus* and the other identified only as "A Naval Schooner, C. 1850." They illustrate the longevity of this class and the continuing need for small ships of sharp design. *Cadmus* is listed in Royal Navy directories as commissioned in 1808 and sold out in 1864.

Schooners and brigs were the principal Royal Navy vessels deployed to hunt pirates, privateers, and illegal slavers on the coast of Africa, in the South Atlantic, and in the Caribbean between 1820 and 1850. Matching speed with speed, the British took captured slavers into the service and also, in 1828, returned to Bermuda again to build additional pilot schooners. These were given the odd names *Pickle*, *Pincher*, and *Skipjack*. They were small, under 69' overall, and like previous Bermuda-built schooners had relatively great depth of hold–9'9". HMS *Pickle* was frequently cited in dispatches, sailing with *Black Joke, Fair Rosamond* and other ex-slavers in the Royal Navy's antislavery patrols.

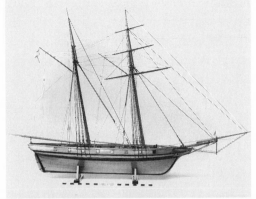

A RIGGED MODEL OF WHAT MAY BE THE ROYAL NAVY HORNET CLASS, CIRCA 1830. *Science Museum, London.*

A handsome fully-rigged model at London's Science Museum is labeled "Royal Navy Schooner, C. 1830" and otherwise unidentified. Her raked stem and stern post, her beautifully modeled underbody, her tall raked masts and schooner rig, create a strong image of a

UNIDENTIFIED ROYAL NAVY SCHOONER, PAINTING BY THOMAS BUTTERSWORTH. *The Mariners' Museum, Newport News, VA.*

postwar Chesapeake Bay schooner.[70] With the model pictured here is a photograph of a Thomas Buttersworth painting of an armed British schooner of the same period. As with the model, the schooner in the painting is unidentified.

The Hornet class of Royal Navy schooners was designed in 1829, and a review of Admiralty records suggests that the Science Museum schooner model is of that class. It is more risky to try to identify the schooner in the painting, except to say that she is Royal Navy and has strong Chesapeake-Bay roots. This model and the Buttersworth painting, added to what is known about the Royal Navy's antislavery fleet, restate the obvious: that vessels of pilot-schooner and clipper design were most effective against slave-trade vessels, hundreds of which were taken by the Royal Navy. *Hornet*, one of four Sepping-designed schooners, joined *Pickle* in Africa.

Just prior to ordering the Pickle-class schooners, the Royal Navy dispatched an officer to America on a mission of espionage to the navy yards, and he eventually arrived at Fells Point to study the secret of the speed of Baltimore schooners. Lieutenant Frederick Fitzgerald de Roos wrote that he observed a schooner under construction and that "she was the most lovely vessel I ever saw." He wrote that he tried to bribe the foreman of an unidentified yard who had "a book of drafts of all the fastest-sailing schooners built in Baltimore."[71]

Several other European navies placed pilot schooners in service. One example is *Experiment*, a Baltimore schooner built in Virginia for blockade running that became a Swedish Navy dispatch schooner and coastal patrol vessel. She served the Royal Swedish Navy for 46 years.[72] Her long service can be attributed to the cold water surrounding that Baltic nation, a condition of water and weather which limits rot and worms. This schooner would also have received excellent care over her long service. Subsequently, the Swedes built four exact duplicates of *Experiment*.

Armistead Davis built *Experiment* at his yard on the East River in Mathews County, Virginia, in 1808.[73] East River, a tributary of Mobjack Bay, is in the heart of tidewater Virginia. With the increase in demand for large pilot schooners after 1793, this region prospered as one of the principal shipbuilding areas of the Chesapeake. More than two dozen shipwrights, including members of the Davis family, the Gayles, the Hunleys, and the Smith family, built schooners and ships here for the merchants of Baltimore between 1790 and the War of 1812.[74]

Baltimore merchants depended on Virginia shipwrights for vessels prior to the time that Fells Point became a major shipbuilding center. Between 1798 and 1801, which included the period of the Quasi War with France, and a period of expansion of the Baltimore fleet, 15 of that port's letter-of-marque schooners were built in Virginia. During the same period only seven schooners commissioned were built at Fells Point. With the Royal Navy blockade in 1807, Baltimore ship owners pur-

BALTIMORE
CARPENTER
CERTIFICATE FOR
EXPERIMENT, BUILT
IN MATHEWS
COUNTY, VA, BY
ARMISTEAD DAVIS
AND SOLD TO THE
ROYAL SWEDISH
NAVY IN 1812.
National Archives.

chased several Baltimore schooners in Mathews County, including *Experiment* and *Globe*. Orders for Virginia-built Baltimore schooners came from Marylanders and seldom from Virginians.[75]

The buyer of Davis's *Experiment*, identified only as Robert Smith of Baltimore, appears on Davis's carpenter certificate. Dated 18 October 1808, this certificate is reproduced above and will correct data published previously in Sweden stating that the vessel was built in New York. Also reproduced here is *Experiment's* first permanent register at Baltimore. This document corrects her tonnage, mistakenly changed at the time of transfer, and it gives her length overall, not shown on the drawings prepared in Sweden. (Appendix B)

Almost immediately after registering *Experiment*, Smith sold her to Benjamin G. Minturn and John F. Champlin, merchants of New York City.[76] They owned her until her sale was arranged to the Royal Swedish Navy in 1812. Just prior to her voyage to northern Europe, *Experiment's* owners re-registered her in New York to reflect a change in masters. Captain William Vibbert replaced her previous master.[77] The King of Sweden approved the purchase 3 November 1812 for $12,000.[78] The King was assured that the schooner's bottom was coppered and that she was fastened with copper.[79]

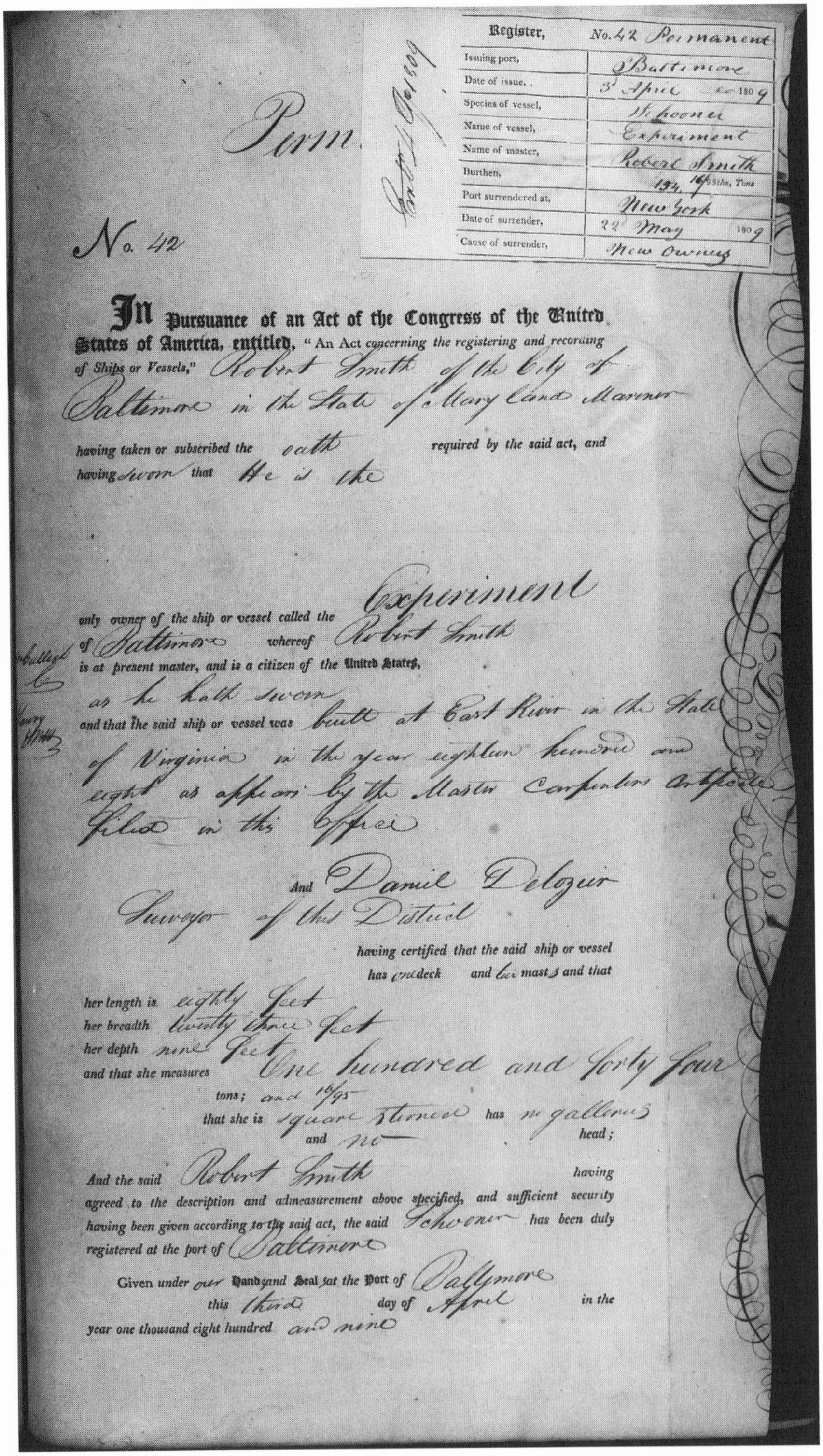

**BALTIMORE
REGISTER FOR
EXPERIMENT, 1809.**
National Archives.

Register,	No. 42	Permanent
Issuing port,		Baltimore
Date of issue,		3 April 1809
Species of vessel,		Schooner
Name of vessel,		Experiment
Name of master,		Robert Smith
Burthen,		144 16/95ths, Tons
Port surrendered at,		New York
Date of surrender,		22 May 1809
Cause of surrender,		New Owners

No. 42

In Pursuance of an Act of the Congress of the United States of America, entitled, "An Act concerning the registering and recording of Ships or Vessels," Robert Smith of the City of Baltimore in the State of Mary Land Mariner

having taken or subscribed the oath required by the said act, and having sworn that He is the

only owner of the ship or vessel called the Experiment of Baltimore whereof Robert Smith is at present master, and is a citizen of the United States, as he hath sworn

and that the said ship or vessel was built at East River in the State of Virginia in the year eighteen hundred and eight as appears by the Master Carpenters Certificate filed in this office

And Daniel Delozier Surveyor of this District

having certified that the said ship or vessel has one deck and two masts and that

her length is eighty feet
her breadth twenty three feet
her depth nine feet

and that she measures One hundred and forty four tons; and 16/95

that she is square sterned has no galleries and no head;

And the said Robert Smith having agreed to the description and admeasurement above specified, and sufficient security having been given according to the said act, the said Schooner has been duly registered at the port of Baltimore

Given under our Hands and Seal at the Port of Baltimore this third day of April in the year one thousand eight hundred and nine

The Royal Swedish Navy commissioned *Experiment* in early 1813 just in time for a short period of naval war. Norway, ceded to Sweden under terms of the Treaty of Kiel in January of 1814, refused to comply with the terms and the Swedes reacted. *Experiment*, tender to the frigate *Galatea*, was part of the fleet that attacked the Norwegian port of Fredrikstad. The Swedes with a fleet of four ships of the line, five frigates, and more than a hundred small vessels and transports, overwhelmed the meager forces of Norway. The victorious Swedes then formed a new alliance with Norway, and since that battle Sweden has avoided all wars. The Swedes soon reduced their naval forces, retaining only schooners such as *Experiment* and other small vessels, a fleet designed to guard the Swedish coast.[80]

Swedish surveyors took off *Experiment*'s lines in 1830. This plan and her sail plan, dated 1815, is included in Appendix B, along with a translation and explanation of the measurements provided by the Swedish Military Archives.

That Armistead Davis had built a blockade runner is reflected in her full flanks and the sweeping curve of her bilge, characteristics that would increase her cargo capacity. Her hold had slightly greater depth than the usual Baltimore schooner.

Experiment's sail plan was conservative. She did not have the double square topsail rig of the wartime schooners. Instead, she carried an unusually large gaff topsail on her mainmast along with pole extensions on her main gaff and boom for a ringsail. The foresail had no boom and overlapped the mainmast,

SRN Experiment - Mathews County, Virginia 1808

Measurements: American Feet and Inches; Swedish Fot and Tum; Meter = .297 Swedish Fot or .308 American Feet

Dimension	From 1st Permanent Baltimore Registration (1)	Carpenter's Certificate (2)	From Swedish Naval Take Offs (3)	To Meters
Keel	-	60'	-	18.48
Length Overall	80'	-	83 Fot (4)	24.64
Length Between Rabbets at Water Line	-	-	73 Fot 4 Tum	21.73
Breadth, Carpenter	-	22'6"	-	6.69
Breadth, Extreme	23'	-	23 Fot	7.08
Breadth, Waterline	-	-	20 Fot 4-3/4 Tum	6.06
Depth of Hold	9'	9'	-	2.77
Draft, Aft	-	-	10 Fot 3 Tum	3.05
Draft, Forward	-	-	6 Fot 9 Tum	2.04
Tons	144-16/95 Tons	120 Tons	85 Tons (6)	-
Sail Area	-	-	5931 Sq. Fot (5)	-

1. Permanent Register #42, Baltimore, April 3, 1809; RG41, National Archives (American Foot and Inches)
2. Carpenter Certificate, signed Armistead Davis, October, 1808; RG41, National Archives (American Foot and Inches)
3. Krigsarkivet (Military Archives) Stockholm, Sweden. (Swedish Fot and Tum)
4. 10 Tum = 1 Fot
5. Tackel-Forteckning-Experiment; Marinmuseum, Karlskona, Sweden
6. Displacement

which was normal even though her foremast raked less than her mainmast. Although not shown in the drawing, *Experiment*'s foremast was rigged for a giant course sail which had a boom and she carried two other square topsails on the foretopmast.

As a result of the data made available by the Maritime Museum in Karlskrona, the Swedish Military Archives (Krigsarkivit) in Stockholm, and the United States National Archives, integrated into a chart here, *Experiment* may be the most completely documented of all the Baltimore schooners. As the American measured foot differs from the Swedish fot, calculations provided in original documents were converted to meters.

Experiment remained at the Karlskrona navy base until 1830,[81] then she was transferred to the navy base at Stockholm. The Swedes decommissioned her in 1858.[82] A model, built when she was on station at Karlskrona, was photographed for this book.

Three of the four additional schooners

built in Sweden to *Experiment*'s specifications were *Falk* and *l'Aigle*, built in 1832 and 1833, and *Activ,* which was commissioned in 1847.[83] Information concerning *Admiral af Puke*, the fourth schooner, is not so clear. According to Krigsarkivet, *Puke*'s keel was laid in 1834, but she was not launched until 1863. She served as a coastal patrol vessel until 1876, at which time she became a training or stores ship at Karlskrona. The navy decommissioned her in 1887.[84] *Falk* and *l'Aigle* did foreign duty, convoying Swedish merchant ships in the Mediterranean in 1840.[85] The navy decommissioned *Falk* in 1871, and *l'Aigle* and *Activ* 1863.[86] *Falk*'s sail plan, complete in areas where *Experiment*'s is not, is illustrated in Appendix B.

The foreign naval schooners selected for this chapter have a traceable link to Chesapeake Bay. These are not vessels influenced by pilot-schooner designs, but rather clear examples of foreign-built Chesapeake Bay pilot schooners. This avoids the mistake of connecting the Chesapeake Bay pilot schooner to every flush-deck schooner built in the nineteenth century. Naval schooners of Chesapeake Bay design were beautiful and effective in the missions they were assigned. They were wonderfully conceived and near-perfect vessels for dispatch, patrol, and police duty–often chasing outlaws who were also sailing Chesapeake Bay pilot schooners. Admirals of several navies, some sooner, some later, understood this, and in the end many countries adopted the model.

ENDNOTES - CHAPTER NINE

1. *Nonsuch*, Baltimore schooner, temporary New York register #258, 28 July 1825. Other published information states that *Nonsuch* was broken up; however, her 1825 register suggests that she had a life after naval service. Her purchaser was Henry Pratt of Philadelphia. See Quentin Snediker and Ann Jensen, *Chesapeake Bay Schooners* (Cambridge, Maryland: Tidewater Publishers, 1992), 24; Thomas C. Gillmer, *Pride of Baltimore, The Story of the Baltimore Clippers* (Camden, Maine: International Marine Publishing, 1992), 91-95. USS *Lynx*, built at Washington Navy Yard. "*History of the Washington Navy Yard*," unsigned and unpublished, Latrobe Papers, Maryland Historical Society, hereafter cited as MHS, MS 526. This typed manuscript states that *Lynx*, built almost completely with live oak, was ready for sea when Captain Thomas Tinguey put a torch to the yard. She was spared. Also, *Dictionary of American Naval Fighting Ships* (Washington, D.C., U.S. Government Printing Office, 1959), Vol. 4, 172.

2. Plan of the brig *Spark*. John Lenthall Collection, No. F1 L90. 43. 29; Independence Seaport Museum, Philadelphia.

3. Ware sail plan of *Spark*. No. 14. RG45, National Archives, hereafter cited as NA.

4. Pook plan of U.S. brig *Spark*. No. 40.13.5. RG19, NA.

5. Samuel Hartt Pook plan for a proposed schooner, dated 1834, No. 109-4-9. RG41, NA.

6. William Doughty plan for *Alligator, Porpoise, Shark* and *Dolphin*, No. 79-11-8, 8A, 8B, 8C. *Grampus*, by Henry Eckford, No. 40-11-2F or 78-1-19A, 1821. RG19 NA.

7. *Documents Accompanying the Bill to Authorize the Building of a Certain Number of Small Vessels*, 27 March 1820. Printed by the Order of Congress by Gales and Seaton, Washington, 1820. Live oak (*Quercus virginiana*) is an evergreen native of the southeastern United States. It is a heavy fine-grained wood free of gallic acid, resistant to rot and of great strength. It was widely used on sailing vessels until forests were completely cut.

8. USS *Shark, Dolphin, Porpoise, Alligator* and *Grampus*; *Dictionary:* Vol. 1, 208, Vol. 2, 284; Vol. 3, 130; Vol. 5, 353; Vol. 6, 466.

9. *Greyhound, Jackal, Beagle, Wild Cat, Terrier, Ferret:* six of eight pilot schooners purchased in Baltimore. *Dictionary:* Vol. 1, 107; Vol. 2, 403; Vol 3, 158 & 482; Vol. 7, 105; Vol. 8, 301. No registers located.

10. *Ariel*, pilot schooner, built at Baltimore by Dorgan and Bailey; originally named *Fourth of July*. *Dictionary:* Vol. 1, 59 & 60.

11. *Boxer, Enterprize* and *Experiment*, Samuel Humphreys, designer; Plan No. 40-9-1A, part 1 and 2. RG19, NA.

12. Two examples: Oliver Hazard Perry lost USS *Revenge*, ex-Baltimore schooner *Ranger*, off Newport in 1811. USS *Somers* capsized off Vera Cruz, Mexico, in 1846; Lieutenant Raphael Semmes, commander.

13. Jean Baptiste Marestier, *Memoire sur Bateaux a Vapeur des Etats Unis d'Amerique* (Paris: La Ministre de la Marine et des Colonies, 1824). Vol 1, 247-48, Vol. 2, Fig. 110, et 114, pl. XII.

14. *Philip Allen*, US Revenue cutter, built at Portsmouth, Virginia, by Page & Allen; also, Official Records of the Union and Confederate Navies in the War of Rebellion, Series 1; Operations of the North Atlantic Blockading Squadron, Vol. 7, 635; Vol. 8, 465.

15. Robert Armistead Stewart, *The History of Virginia's Navy of the Revolution* (Richmond, Virginia: By the author, 1933), 108-11; a quote from the journal of Commodore James Barron, the younger; Virginia Historical Register, July 1849.

16. Jean Meissonnier, *Sailing Ships of the Romantic Era, A 9th Century Album of Watercolors by Antoine Roux* (Lausanne, Switzerland: Edita Lausanne, 1968), 24.

17. Jacques Vichot, *Repertoire des Navies de Guerre Français* (Paris: Edite par L'Association des amis des Museés de la Marine, 1967), 48.

18. Patrick Crowhurst, *The French War on Trade, Privateering, 1793-1815*. (Aldershot, England: Gower Publishing Co., Ltd., 1989), 69, 81, note 81: Admiralty Case HCA 32/914, 1005.

19. Howard I. Chapelle, *The Search for Speed Under Sail, 1700-1855* (New York: W.W. Norton & Company, 1957,

Bonanza Edition), 247; Crowhurst, 111, 116; Vichot, 107; J.J. Colledge, *Ships of the Royal Navy* (Annapolis: Naval Institute Press, 1987), 25.

20. *l'Estaffette*, French Navy schooner; Vichot, 53; Jean Boudriot, *La Jacinthe* (Paris: Published by the author, 1990), 19 top, 20 top and 22-23.

21. Vichot, 77. There are more than a score of French naval and privateer vessels listed in Vichot by that name. One, a *goelette corsaire* (privateer schooner) 1811-12, was captured by HMS *Blossom*, date not given.

22. Vichot, 62. Also Jean Boudriot, "Le Brick-Goelette *La Gazelle*," *Neptunia* No. 116, 1974, Association des Amis des Musées de la Marine, Paris. 13-20.

23. Howard I. Chapelle, *History of American Sailing Ships* (New York: W.W. Norton & Co., Inc., 1935), 240.

24. Marestier, Vol 1, 242; Vol. 2, Plate XI, Fig. 100 et 104.

25. Marestier, 242.

26. *Mammoth*, Baltimore armed schooner, built at Fells Point, 1813, measuring 112'. Baltimore register #10, dated 7 March 1814. RG41, NA.

27. *Neptunia*, a publication of Les Amis du Musée de la Marine, No. 116, 20.

28. Boudriot, *La Jacinthe*, 26.

29. Didier's notebook, Maryland Historical Society, MS-295.

30. Boudriot, *La-Jacinthe*, 26.

31. Marestier, VII & 68-70; also *Neptunia*, No. 116, 14.

32. Letter from David H. Roberts, translator for Jean Boudriot, to the author, dated 3 March 1992.

33. Ibid.

34. Ibid.

35. List of vessels (American) taken into Bermuda to July 1814, from the commencement of the American war. Papers of George Hulbert, Royal Navy Agent-Bermuda; National Maritime Museum, Greenwich: Ms 56-040:HUL-18.

36. Colledge lists ships of the Royal Navy, and their former flag if captured, and when known.

37. *Nimrod*, Baltimore schooner; Baltimore register #170, 1806; RG41, NA.

38. *Fly*, Baltimore schooner; Baltimore register #132, 1807; RG41, NA.

39. *Arrow*, Baltimore schooner; Baltimore register #202. 1811; RG41, NA.

40. *Spencer*, pilot schooner; Baltimore register #196,1811; RG41, NA.

41. *Atlas*, Baltimore schooner; Baltimore register #138, 1810; RG41, NA.

42. *Highflyer*, Baltimore schooner; Baltimore register #188, 1811; RG41, NA.

43. *Lottery*, Baltimore schooner; Baltimore register #51, 1811; RG41, NA.

44. *Siro*, Baltimore schooner; Baltimore register #159, 1812; RG41, NA.

45. *Hannibal*, ship, built by William Price; Baltimore register #186, 1811; RG41, NA.

46. Basil Lubbock, *Cruisers, Corsairs, & Slavers* (Glasgow: Brown, Son & Ferguson Ltd., 1993), 52.

47. Colledge, 153, 333; Vichot, 66.

48. Colledge, 336.

49. Henry C. Wilkinson, *Bermuda in the Old Empire* (London: Oxford University Press, 1950), 167.

50. Ibid., 167.

51. Ibid., 168.

52. Colledge, 160, 45, 47, 61, 72, 82, 98, 138, 157, 214, 235, 265, 269, 320, 341 and 380. Also, Frederick P. Schmitt, "List of Royal Navy Vessels Built in Bermuda," *Bermuda Historical Quarterly*, Vol. XVIII, No. 2, 55-56.

53. Colledge, 380.

54. *Perry*, Baltimore schooner; carpenter certificate signed by Thomas Kemp, 15 November 1813; Baltimore register #77, 1813; RG41, NA; John Philips Cranwell and William Bowers, *Men of Marque* (New York: W.W. Norton & Company, 1940), 305.

55. Colledge, 94, 96, 183, 196, 215, 265, 278, 294, 311, 374 and 360.

56. Court proceedings from the trial of Lieutenant R. D. Lancaster, Commander of the *Landrail*, Portsmouth, 20 May 1815; Admiralty 1-549, 242-45. Copy in MHS MS-2317. Also, Colledge, 196.

57. Admiralty Sheer Draught Collection: Associations Index, 1538; Ship Plans Section, National Maritime Museum, Greenwich, England.

58. Chapelle, *The Baltimore Clipper*, 46-53.
    "   *The Search for Speed under Sail*, 165, 171.
    "   *The History of American Sailing Ships*, 259.
    Chapelle, after stating his case on page 167 of *Search*, contradicts himself with a rare footnote on page 167

which he says is from *Revenge*'s register, which it is not. David R. MacGregor, *Merchant Sailing Ships, 1775-1815* (London: Argus Books, 1980), 156-57. Thomas C. Gillmer, *Pride of Baltimore, The Story of the Baltimore Clippers, 1800-1990* (Camden, Maine: International Marine Publishing Co., 1992), 63-66.

59. *Revenge,* three-masted Baltimore schooner; Baltimore register #114, 10 June 1805, RG41, NA.

60. *Luna,* three-masted Baltimore schooner; Baltimore register #228, 25 November 1805, RG41, NA.

61. *Orestes,* three-masted Baltimore schooner; Baltimore register #141, 2 July 1805. RG41, NA.

62. Colledge, 138.

63. Pencil notations on *Revenge*'s register #116, 10 June 1805, and register #216, 2 November 1805.

64. British measurements of HMS *Flying Fish* from Admiralty draft: 78'8" x 60'8-1/8" x 21'7" x 7'10" ; 150-32/94 tons.
    Federal Register measurements of:
    Revenge - 82' x * x 22'2" x 8' ; 128-31/95 tons
    Luna - 88'2;"x 67' x 22'7" x 8'2"; 144-58/95 tons
    Orestes - 85'2" x 62'7" x 23'3" x 7'11"; 138-3/95 tons
    *no carpenter certificate found.

65. *Luna*'s register #228, 1805, in pencil: sold to foreigners, 1809.

66. *Orestes*' register #141, pencil notation: sold at New York, 20 August, 1805. Dimensions, note 64.

67. Colledge, 314, 347, 187, 60, 230 and 171.

68. Wilkinson, *Bermuda*, 280.

69. Ibid., 280, 281.

70. Collection register #1660, Science Museum, London.

71. Frederick Fitzgerald de Roos, *Personal Narrative of Travels in the United States in 1826, with Remarks on the Present State of the American Navy* (London: 1827). Excerpted by Raphael Semmes, *Baltimore as Seen by Visitors, 1783-1860* (Baltimore: Maryland Historical Society, 1953), 72-73. Also Colledge, 173. To the author's knowledge no original plans of Baltimore schooners exist in Maryland collections.

72. Letter Krigsarkivet (Swedish Military Archives) to author, dated 2 August 1991, quoting Archives, Volume F.Ia, 44, No. 2494 and 2496 and BIa, 52, No. 1914, Stockholm, Sweden.

73. *Experiment,* Baltimore schooner, carpenter certificate signed by Armistead Davis, 18 October 1808; RG41, NA.

74. Baltimore carpenter certificates, 1790-1840; RG41, NA.

75. Ibid.

76. *Experiment,* Baltimore schooner, New York register #270, dated 22 May 1809; RG41, NA.

77. Ibid. New York register #56, dated 21 February 1812; RG41, NA.

78. Power of Attorney, Captain Vibbert to Lindegrin & Co., 30 November 1812, Krigsarkivet.

79. Purchase agreement, Forvaltningen av sjoarendena, Plenum 1803-14, B.1:1812, Vol. 2., Stockholm, 10 December 1812. Krigsarkivet.

80. Kleen, *Detaljer ur falttaget i Norge, 1814* (The War with Norway, 1814). Translated and summarized for the author by Lena Animmer.

81. Lars O. Berg, Svenska, flottans farty, 1808-1849. Forum Navale No. 24, Stockholm, 1968. Translated by Krigsarkivet for the author.

82. Ibid.

83. *Falk, l'Aigle, Activ* and *Admiral af Puke,* Baltimore schooners, Swedish Royal Navy skonerters, built on *Experiment*'s lines; Forum Navale ur 18, Krigsarkivet (Swedish Military Archives), Stockholm, Sweden.

84. Ibid., note 8.

85. Svante Holmberg, *The Schooner Falk,* Aktuellt Vanner i, Karlskona, 1973; Translated by Lena Animmer for the author.

86. Forum Navale ur 18, Krigsarkivet.

**PUNGY *ANDREW JOHNSON*, THOUGHT TO HAVE BEEN
BUILT ON THE BAY BETWEEN 1860 AND 1870.**

The Smithsonian Institution.

CHAPTER TEN

PILOT SCHOONERS OF THE OYSTER INDUSTRY

Anew invasion of Chesapeake Bay occurred in the nineteenth century when northern oyster buyers entered the Bay in significant numbers as beds in New York and New England became unproductive. Eventually the invading fleets of oyster schooners produced major alterations in the seafood industry of Maryland and Virginia, changed Baltimore's industrial base, and influenced transportation systems in the Middle Atlantic region.

When the first colonists arrived, they found that oysters were an important item in the diet of Native Americans. These early settlers and their gentlemen leaders did not consider the sea an important source of food. They had little fishing experience and they learned boatbuilding and fishing skills from the natives. Later, oysters became one of many courses on the tables of the plantation owners and their society. For slaves and freemen, seafood became a staple as the supply proved to be enormous and the cost low. When villages became ports and commerce began to bring people together, watermen commenced delivering oysters and other seafood to market. With Baltimore's population exploding after the Revolution, oysters became one of the many seafood items delivered to the city by a growing fleet of pilot schooners.[1]

Casually, during the period that included the two wars with Britain, the oyster industry developed. British ships and their Tory allies, disrupting the commerce of the Bay during the War of 1812, reported capturing baycraft filled with oysters. After bottling up the frigate USS *Constellation* behind Craney Island, a British squadron under Admiral George Cockburn captured several baycraft; one, the pilot boat *Flowing Cann*, was carrying oysters from Hampton to Norfolk.[2] Farther north, off Dorchester and Somerset Counties, the British and their loyalist allies captured hundreds of baycraft, including oyster boats, during the course of this war. In one such incident, the enemy took 15 baycraft that included the schooner *Madison* of Oxford with a cargo of oysters, turkeys, and geese.[3]

Around the time that watermen began to deliver oysters to Baltimore and other Chesapeake Bay towns, northern oyster production went into serious decline and oyster buyboats from northern states sailed into Chesapeake Bay in great numbers. Watermen living in the isolated communities along the shores of Tangier Sound and on the Bay's islands became the principal source of supply for these Yankee boats. Tonging oysters, a casual occupation in these remote Eastern Shore communities, kept production low and caused lengthy waiting periods for the New York and New England vessels before a full load was acquired. This set the scene for the introduction of dredge boats into Chesapeake Bay.

Communities of Chesapeake Bay watermen, situated on land only inches above the tidal marshlands that surrounded them, consisted of small family groupings, almost tribal in nature, sharing common backgrounds as refugees and outcasts. During decades of isolation these communities developed log-bottom boats and casual lifestyles not unlike those of the Native Americans from whom they acquired much of their knowledge of hunting and fishing. The principal resolve of these nearly amphibious people was to keep their unique communities intact. With no established religion or schools, and producing their own food and clothing, they built invisible walls between themselves and the rest of Maryland and Virginia. Many had opposed Maryland and Virginia's fight for independence and then proceeded to aid the British in the War of 1812. This caused them to be regarded as renegades and outlaws in the nineteenth century.

The area that borders Tangier Sound was more a lawless frontier than part of the nation in 1820. The War of 1812 left deep wounds. Many watermen were Tories or the sons of two generations of Tories who, for obscure reasons, support-ed the British through two wars–or so it was perceived. While the treasonous crimes of Joe Wheland, Jr., Marmaduke Mister and other "picaroons" were isolated acts of piracy, this poor region of uncomplicated people became ostracized by the victors. When earnings began to flow into the Eastern Shore communities from Yankee oyster buyboats, it was the first source of income enjoyed by the watermen of Devil's Quarters, Tangier Sound, Smith Island and the settlements along the Annamessix River since before the Revolution. To tame their sinful passions and to prepare them for rebirth, the floating preachers of the Methodist Church offered quick redemption under their terms. Not surprisingly, watermen accepted the oyster as the Almighty's reward for their conversion.[4]

Watermen tonged oysters when they felt like it. Frustrated northern buyer-captains, desperate to quicken the pace, introduced the dredge boat to the Bay. Boats equipped with mesh dredges, never seen here before, created immediate outrage, and in 1811 Virginia's legislature passed the nation's first conservation law, outlawing the dredge in Virginia-controlled waters.[5] As a result, Yankee dredge boats sailed further up the Bay into Maryland. Eighty years later, the oldest dredge boat operating on Chesapeake Bay was *Intrepid*, built at Brookhaven, New York, in 1810.[6]

The oyster dredge was an invention of the Romans, used in Britain to harvest Colchester and Whitstable oysters. New England watermen had been using dredges for decades. When dredge boats began to work Maryland waters, the tongers of rural Maryland objected strongly and the General Assembly passed the state's first law protecting its oyster industry. The law, passed in 1820, while designed to eliminate out-of-state watermen, became the first of many Maryland laws granting legal sanction to the waterman's philosophy that the Bay's seafood belonged to them to exploit.

The new law, "An Act to Prevent the Destruction of Oysters in this State," restricted oystering in Maryland in three principal ways.[7] The act eliminated dredging and scraping for oysters in county waters. (There is some doubt that it was written to include state-controlled areas of Chesapeake Bay, and it seemed to allow dredging on Pocomoke Sound, on the Potomac River and along the Western Shore. Later revisions banned all dredging.) No oysters could be taken by owners of vessels who had not resided in Maryland for a minimum of one year, and oysters could be transported out of Maryland only by a vessel owned by a resident of one year.

Over the years, state and county authorities made only faint efforts to control illegal dredging, but there was general compliance with the residency requirement of the law, as it suited the oystermen to be so protected. There was no effort to limit the transportation of oysters to Maryland vessels when the destination lay outside the limits of the Bay. As enforced, the law promoted the interests of the Chesapeake watermen.

Maryland's oyster fleet began to increase following the War of 1812. The total tonnage of baycraft enrolled and licensed at Baltimore, Oxford, Vienna on the Nanticoke River, and Snow Hill on the Pocomoke River, the four principal Customs stations in rural Maryland, totaled 38,582 tons in 1805. By 1820, this figure had mushroomed to 59,428 tons.[8]

Somerset County, the center of the expanding oyster industry, was where most oystering pilot schooners, called pungies, were owned in the nineteenth century. Fragments of Customs records that have survived for Hampton, Virginia, and other parts of the lower Bay suggest that construction of schooners of pilot-boat design also remained strong there prior to the Civil War.

Following the enactment of the first conservation laws in Virginia and Maryland, the production of the Bay's pilot schooners increased sharply. Demand for wood products and produce in urban centers increased during the same period, and it is not possible to separate the portion of baycraft production related to the higher oyster catch. However, since about 60 percent of Bay pilot schooners built between 1831 and 1860 listed owners in Somerset County, the center of the oyster industry, it is safe to conclude that their principal employment was in that expanding fishery.[9]

The production of Bay schooners, both keel and centerboard types, in the upper and central portion of the Eastern Shore and in southern Maryland was more directly related to the growth of gen-

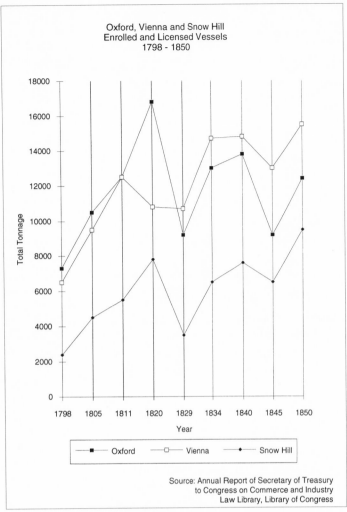

Oxford, Vienna and Snow Hill
Enrolled and Licensed Vessels
1798 - 1850

Source: Annual Report of Secretary of Treasury
to Congress on Commerce and Industry
Law Library, Library of Congress

The second graph shows the place of construction of 590 pungies (pilot schooners). Although it is not possible to determine the number of centerboard schooners or keel schooners built in the period covered by these charts, positive identification of almost 600 baycraft pilot schooners was made from carpenter certificates, journals, shipyard records and marine police records.

Several developments took place around 1829 to fuel the already rising demand for oysters. Baltimore's immigrants eagerly added this delicacy that had long been scarce in Europe to their table fare. Escalation of demand from Yankee buyboats continued. And finally expansion of America's inland transportation systems placed oysters on the dinner tables of families in new towns west of the mountains. There are no reliable statistics for the oyster catch prior to the Civil War, but the volume of oysters shipped to northern states is thought to have increased each decade, and Baltimore's oyster packing and canning industry is known to have expanded rapidly after 1835.

Another important factor in extending the area served by Chesapeake Bay's pilot schooners was the opening of the Chesapeake and Delaware Canal. After years of planning and failed starts, a narrow canal opened connecting the Elk River with Delaware Bay on 17 October 1829. The canal management's first broadside contained the information that the locks would accommodate vessels up to 100' in length and 22' in width, but the canal's shallow channel limited passage to vessels

eral Bay traffic in farm produce and building materials. Increased schooner construction further down the lower Bay, particularly in Somerset County, resulted in the main from increasing demand for oysters in Baltimore, Philadelphia, for seeding Delaware Bay, and for the markets and beds of New York and New England.

Two graphs will illustrate these developments. The first graph charts the growth in enrolled tonnage at Oxford, Snow Hill and Vienna, Maryland, after 1798. The jurisdiction of Customs stations included Pocomoke Sound and Tangier Sound in the center of the oyster fishery.

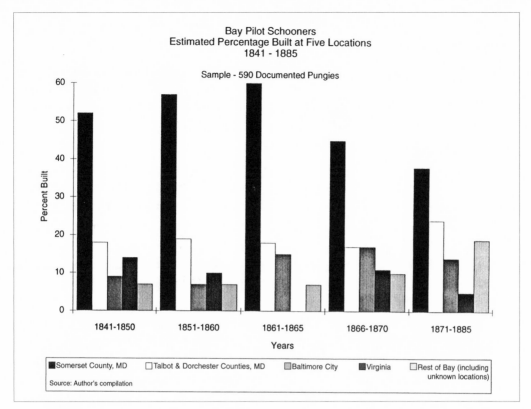

Bay Pilot Schooners
Estimated Percentage Built at Five Locations
1841 - 1885

Sample - 590 Documented Pungies

Legend:
- Somerset County, MD
- Talbot & Dorchester Counties, MD
- Baltimore City
- Virginia
- Rest of Bay (including unknown locations)

Source: Author's compilation

of 7' draft.[10] The Chesapeake and Delaware Canal was only 13-3/8 miles long, and not a major undertaking, but its economic impact on the Bay and its hinterlands proved to be immediate and significant.

The annual report of the canal management for 1833 recorded 2,975 baycraft carrying various commodities, including cotton, iron, oysters, fish, coal and whiskey, through the canal eastbound to Delaware Bay.[11] The canal's 1835 report stated that the number of oyster schooners from Chesapeake Bay passing through the canal was 418.[12] These oyster pungies were en route to Philadelphia, to Wilmington, to Delaware Bay for oyster re-seeding, and to northern states. The canal's tariff for oysters levied a charge on vessel tonnage rather than on the number of bushels carried, so that a figure for volume of oysters is impossible to calculate.

Oysters were commonly carried in bulk on deck or in the cargo hold.

The principal commodities transiting the canal each year from Chesapeake Bay eastward, in addition to thousands of tons of oysters, were cordwood, lumber, vegetables, grain, flour, building materials and eggs.[13] The canal put new life into the Eastern Shore's lagging economy and revived Talbot County's shipbuilding industry, which experienced a deep depression after the War of 1812. Ship-wrights from St. Michaels who built about a third of Baltimore's letter-of-marque fleet, received orders for pungies and other baycraft after the canal began operation.

About ten percent of the total number of pilot schooners built for the Bay trade in the period between 1820 and 1885 were built in Talbot County.

Caleb Maltby is a name not widely

known by Marylanders, yet the activities of this Connecticut entrepreneur and his colleagues changed the face of Baltimore's waterfront as he turned the casual oyster trade into a vast industry. The product of his great energy was a distribution system he organized to deliver fresh oysters to inland America. Maltby's Western Oyster Line of horse-drawn wagons operated from Baltimore west as an adjunct to his original distribution system at Fair Haven, Connecticut. Prior to the building of the eastern railroads, these wagon lines were a transportation link from the East Coast to junctions on America's inland river system. Wagons with general cargo including oysters and other perishables met steamboats which connected inland ports with the new cities and towns beyond the mountains. A Baltimore newspaper, copying a Cincinnati paper, reported "the receipt of fresh oysters in five days from Baltimore, carried overland to Wheeling by the new line of oyster wagons, and thence down the Ohio by steamboat."[14]

Holt & Maltby Packing Company of Baltimore bought oysters in the shell from runners. Oyster runners, mostly pungy schooners, purchased the catch of tongers working Tangier and Pocomoke Sounds. The packing house cleaned and graded these oysters, still in their shells, then repacked them into small wooden kegs. An alternate method of shipment consisted of shucked oysters packed with water in cans or wooden tubs packed in ice. Wagon trains transported these perishables west on the National Road to the Ohio River or to one of its tributaries.

Thus the market for Chesapeake Bay oysters grew.

When Maltby opened his packing plant in Baltimore in 1836, the tracks of the Baltimore and Ohio Railroad reached Point of Rocks, just west of Frederick, Maryland. A five-year halt in railroad construction forced Maltby to continue to use coaches and wagons west from this point. As the railroad extended its tracks mile by mile, Maltby, now joined by many other northern packers, expanded the volume of shipments as the route improved. While the growth of the B & O Railroad had multiple and complex effects on foreign trade, distribution, manufacturing activity, and finance in Baltimore and Maryland, what is emphasized is the special relationship between the new iron horse and the old wind-powered pilot schooner. Before Maltby and the B & O, oystering was a casual industry. After their alliance it was a major industry.

An estimate in 1840 placed Maryland's oyster harvest at 710,000 bushels.[15] By that date a new industry had started up along Baltimore's waterfront. Cooked oysters in airtight tin cans made it possible to ship the product west without special handling. Foul-tasting but cheap compared to the fresh, the canned oysters became the food of the working man, with the Chesapeake the principal source for the whole country. In 1842 the B & O reached Cumberland and a freight rate for oysters was set at 50 cents per 100 pounds in shell and $1.00 a box for canned oysters. From the railhead at Cumberland, cargo was transshipped by wagon to

Pittsburgh, Wheeling, Louisville and Nashville.[16]

The tracks of the Baltimore and Ohio Railroad reached the Monongahela River on 22 June 1852, making possible the transport of oysters by a rail-steamboat route into Pittsburgh. Shipments via the railroad soon reached a million pounds.[17] Deliveries of oysters by baycraft to Baltimore's Basin increased just as dramatically. With San Francisco and St. Louis now markets for several hundred thousand bushels in hermetically sealed cans, annual receipts at Baltimore reached 1,350,000 bushels.[18] Packers and canners along Baltimore's waterfront employed thousands of Marylanders, mostly free blacks, for shucking. Women and children were given unskilled work.

Holt & Maltby contracted with shipwright Henry Brewster for the schooner *Swan* in 1852.[19] The packer used the new schooner to haul oysters from Chesapeake Bay to Fair Haven in Connecticut. Bedded there, the oysters were harvested the following season, thus extending the productivity of the Long Island Sound oyster industry. Each year Chesapeake Bay oysters were shipped north to restock oyster beds from New Jersey to Rhode Island, the movement totalling hundreds of thousands of bushels.

The fleet in this annual spring movement consisted of a mixture of northern boats and Chesapeake Bay schooners, some owned by northerners, others chartered from locals. The Chesapeake schooners built for this annual run were larger than Bay pungies. *Swan*, a typical vessel, measured 89' x 24'6" x 7.6".[20] Large shallow-draft clipper schooners like *Swan* were a new variation on the pilot-boat schooner. Brewster built an unnamed schooner for Maltby in 1856 that measured 74' in length but had depth of hold of just six feet.[21] Many Chesapeake-built schooners now had less drag to reduce their draft further still. The question is whether these new large shoal-draft schooners were properly pilot schooners, a question that cannot be answered exactly. After 1840, as full-bodied centerboard schooners became popular on the Bay, similarly shaped keel vessels called clump schooners were built and joined the fishing and oyster fleets. As a class or model of schooner, these were never clearly defined.

Schooners like *Swan* may well have influenced the development of the northern model that Massachusetts fishermen called "clippers." Small schooner design by the 1850s along the U.S. Atlantic coast had become somewhat homogenous, blurring the origins of designs. The fast, unstable clipper schooner model built with a tall rig for New England's fisheries in the 1860s and 1870s seems to fit this category.

The Baltimore and Ohio Railroad opened its service to Wheeling, West Virginia, in January of 1853, and the Parkersburg division reached the Ohio River in 1857. Thirty or more carloads of oysters moved west on the railroad daily. Receipts of oysters at Baltimore were estimated to total 1,660,000 bushels for

1857.[22] Many years later the United States Fish Commission issued revised figures which placed receipts in 1857 at 2,610,000 bushels.[23] These estimates are guesses as no government agency was charged with inspection of the catch. One thing is certain, however: the pace of exploitation of Chesapeake Bay beds by Maryland and Virginia watermen was linked to the westward advance of the tracks of the Baltimore and Ohio Railroad.

The Delaware, New Castle & Frenchtown and the New Castle & Wilmington Railroad reached Seaford, Delaware, in December 1856, connecting the small Eastern Shore town at the head of the Nanticoke River with Wilmington and Philadelphia.[24] Trains departing Seaford in mid-afternoon arrived at Wilmington and Philadelphia the same day. This railroad, the first on the Eastern Shore peninsula, placed the oyster beds of Tangier Sound only a day away from the oyster houses of Philadelphia, improving on the all-water route which made slow progress through the C & D Canal. A long line of Somerset County pungies filled with oysters commenced the northeasterly run up the Nanticoke River to Seaford. Eventually, this railroad's tracks passed through Salisbury, Maryland, on the Wicomico River, with off-line services to Cambridge and Oxford. The railroad reached Crisfield, a port built on the shells of the bivalve, in 1866, only a few years before the industry reached its peak level of production in 1870.

Seaford, as a transfer point, became an overnight success. Although there are no statistics and little other information about an oyster industry there before the Civil War, when the war began several northern canners opened facilities at Seaford, more politically stable than Baltimore, to supply the Union Army with canned oysters.

The Nanticoke River, running dark and deep, penetrates into Delaware. Probably better known in the nineteenth century than in the twentieth, its muddy shores and endless miles of marshes are unsuitable for vacationers. The river's deep channel continues far into the interior, which made it an important link in commerce and shipbuilding. Vienna, Maryland, 20 miles upriver from Tangier Sound, was an important Customs station in the nineteenth century as thousands of Bay pilot schooners and other vessels were enrolled.

Forests that lined the Nanticoke's shores beyond the marshes became the source of timber for the region's ship production in the last century of sail. Vienna, Sharptown and Galestown in Maryland, and Bethel in Delaware, produced many of the Bay's last great schooners and barks. Even in the area of Federalsburg, about 60 miles from the Bay, on the Northwest Branch of the Nanticoke, now called Marshyhope Creek, shipwrights built schooners. The oldest pilot-boat schooner on the Bay at the beginning of the twentieth century was *Juvenile*, built in 1827 at an unknown location in Sussex County, Delaware. She became the oldest schooner licensed for dredging in the 1892 season.[25] Measuring 60.2' x 21' x 5.1',

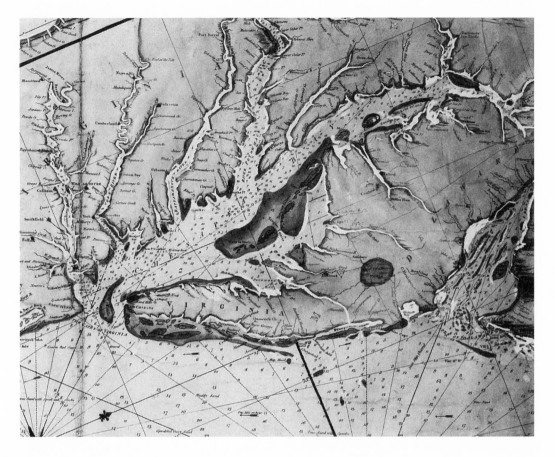

DETAIL OF "A NEW
CHART OF COAST
OF AMERICA FROM
PHILADELPHIA TO
GULF OF FLORIDA,
1815" BY JOHN
WILLIAM NORIE.
*Maryland Hall of
Records, Huntingfield
Map Collection,
Annapolis.*

she was beamy and shallow-hulled like
Maltby's schooners. *Juvenile*'s original
owners may have built her to haul seed
oysters through the C & D Canal's 22'-
wide locks to their oyster beds in
Delaware Bay.[26]

The western shore of Tangier Sound
was a peninsula with Tangier Island its
southern tip. Long ago solid land, in the
nineteenth century it was covered by
flood tides, leaving only a line of disappearing islands: Bloodworth, Holland,
South Marsh, Smith, Goose, and its
anchor, Tangier Island. When the first settlers reached Tangier Sound they found a
body of water rich in sea life. In 30 years

between 1820 and 1850 watermen
stripped the bottom of about two thirds of
its oysters. Those that survived lived in
deep water beyond the reach of tongs.

After the shallower waters were
depleted, Eastern Shore legislators, a
powerful voting bloc in the State House at
Annapolis, pressed to repeal laws against
dredging and to allow the use of small
dredges called scrapes. A court at Princess
Anne, the county seat of Somerset
County, was jammed by illegal dredging
cases. Daniel Jones was arrested in March
1852, for example, for dredging from the
pungy *Fair American*; the sheriff arrested
George Gladden on board *Emiline* at the

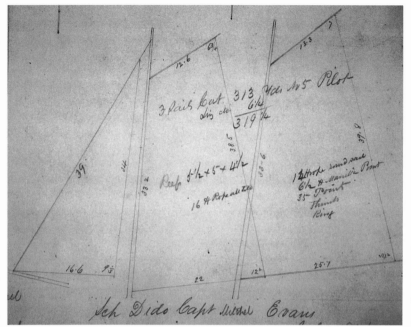

same time.[27] The list of court cases length-ened as the sheriff increased the number of arrests. Joel T. Webster, John Walker, George Guy, John Earen and William D. Howeth had trials during the spring court session of 1852. The fall term included the cases of Bradshaw, Evans, Webster, Parks, Shores, Bosman and Wilson, all making court appearances for illegal dredging.[28]

Watermen, particularly those from Somerset County, pressured their repre-sentatives to vote to approve a law allow-ing scrapes. Dorchester County's citizens, already fighting an invasion of Somerset oystermen on their portion of Tangier Sound, decided on an independent course they hoped would provide greater protection for their oysters in the north-ern part of the Sound. Voters instructed their delegates to vote no to a dredge law. An act passed in 1854 which allowed scrapes in the Sound but excluded the

Dorchester portion.[29] This legislation set the scene for the first oyster war fought among Marylanders. Somerset dredge boats invaded upper Tangier Sound and the Dorchester County sheriff put together a small navy to repel the invasion.[30]

Dorchester oystermen of Hooper Island, Fishing Creek and the area called "the neck" at the southern end of the county acquired or built a small fleet of pilot schooners at this time. *Express*, a pungy built in Somerset County in 1852, listed Dorchester County as home waters.[31] Her owners were James Tylor and George Wallace. Other pungies owned in Dorchester County in 1852 included *Mary Wesley*,[32] *Druzilla*, built in 1847,[33] *California*,[34] *Kite*,[35] *Mary Francis*,[36] and *Three Brothers*.[37] It is unlikely that Dorchester residents acquired these pilot schooners solely in anticipation of the passage of a scrape law in 1854. Some would have been oyster runners hauling oysters harvested by tongers to Baltimore.

The victory of Somerset County watermen in Annapolis represented a major but not unexpected acquiescence of the Maryland legislature to pressure from special interests. Dredging had already wiped out the world's best oyster beds over previous centuries; wiser Maryland and Virginia leaders of earlier times knew this and declared all dredging illegal. Somerset watermen, with their history of violence, led the pro-dredging pack. An ugly coalition of Somerset oys-termen and relocated Connecticut packers and canners in Baltimore persuaded Maryland legislators to pass the law. Dorchester County's more reasonable viewpoint, compared to the unabashed aggression of the Somerset watermen, had roots in the historical differences of Dorchester County on one hand and Somerset County on the other. It did not represent a difference in attitudes towards natural resources.

Marylanders and Virginians fired many guns in anger over the rich oyster beds of Chesapeake Bay. The first aggression resulted from the dredge boats that invaded the Bay just after the nation became free of British rule. There was a long border dispute between Maryland and Virginia, and it was in reality a war over the Bay's resources. Then came Pennsylvanians through the C & D Canal and into the upper Bay. The longest war of all, which continued to the middle of the twentieth century, would involve continual battles between tongers and dredgers and dredgers and the police. These commenced after the passage of the act of 1854, then escalated in 1865 with passage of a Maryland law to allow dredging in state waters. This will be discussed in chapter Eleven.

While most naval architects and historians agree that the pungy of the nineteenth century is a true pilot schooner, almost no one links the origin of these last pilot schooners to baycraft that hauled grain to the Basin at Baltimore in the middle of the eighteenth century. Through 150 years the proportions of the Bay model remained basically unchanged,

although the size generally was greater in 1854 than in 1754. The rig changed little; the only important alteration was the elimination of the overlapping foresail in about 1850, to be replaced by a boomed foresail. Cotton sails replaced hemp and linen in the years immediately following the War of 1812. Pungies continued to be framed and planked with white oak.

John Goldsborough Earle collected information and studied Chesapeake Bay craft for 50 years prior to his death in 1992. He walked the decks of the last pungies, collected lists of them, talked to old watermen, recorded schooner measurements, and gathered photographs of the last of them and of their skeletons. His records are probably the most complete in existence. Earle wrote in 1936 that he had found his first half model of a pungy. This was *Ida*, built in Talbot County in 1873 by Thomas H. Kirby.

Built a dozen years prior to the last pilot schooner of 1885, *Ida*'s model is a good example of the later schooners. She was 58' x 20.5' x 6.0', with length/width ratio 2.83:1, and therefore of greater breadth, proportionately, than earlier pilot schooners. Her length/depth ratio, 9.96:1, resulted in less depth compared to the pre-Civil War model.[38]

Earle took off *Ida*'s lines from her half model and his drafts appear on the next page along with a photograph of the pungy builder's half model. With carefully placed lighting, Earle was able to highlight the shape of the baycraft hull. He wrote that this model illustrated the typical characteristics of the pungy,

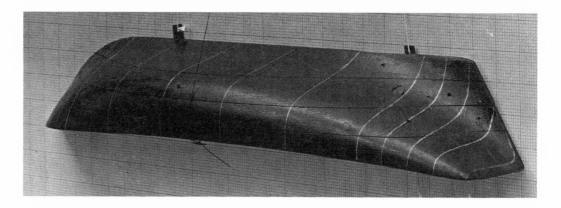

which he summarized here.[39]

1. Full convex bow; clean, slightly hollow run, with displacement well forward.

2. Sharply raking stem, curving into the keel to form a gently rounded forefoot.

3. Sharply raking sternpost leading directly to transom (no counter). Later pungies, such as *Ida*, had the transom set at a sharper rake than the post, with the rudder stock [post] piercing the lower edge of the transom.[40]

4. Relatively sharp sections. Deadrise of midship section of *Ida* is 1'9" in six feet, or about 16.25 degrees.

5. Forward sections are all convex, and flare boldly, consistent with the strongly raking stem, to form a full, beautifully-rounded deck line forward.

6. The after sections within six feet of the stern become nearly horizontal for the greater part of their lengths, fairing into the sternpost rabbet in a concave curve and on the outboard ends, rounding into the stern in a quick convex curve. High, flat after sections with shallow quarters, are typical of the pungy. *Ida* had no tumblehome.

From observation of the half model, it is apparent that Kirby gave *Ida's* keel only a slight amount of drag. This raises the question of why Earle failed to mention this, as pilot schooners down through the years had significant drag which produced greater draft at the stern.[41]

Ida was one of a group of pilot schooners that were the last built on Chesapeake Bay. The adjustments in design are attributed to a desire to reduce the draft of the big pungies on the silting rivers of the Chesapeake estuary. This must have been a contributing factor, but more importantly these last pilot schooners were competing with fuller-bodied centerboard schooners that had greater capacity and less draft. As these big pungies were built with full hulls, the question arises whether they were still true pilot schooners. This a matter of degree as the line where a pungy becomes the bulky keel schooner of the Bay, called a clump schooner by watermen, is conjecture without drawings or half models to guide the historian.

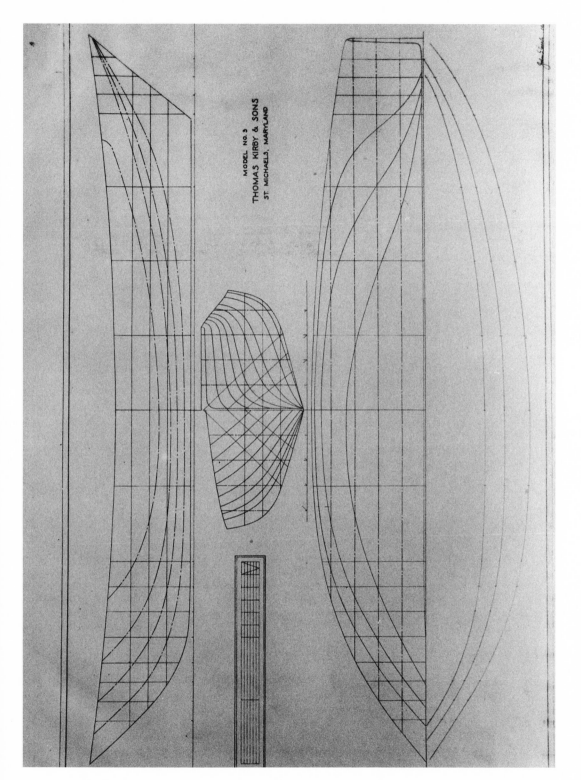

MODEL NO. 3
THOMAS KIRBY & SONS
ST. MICHAELS, MARYLAND

LINES OF THE PUNGY *IDA*, DRAWN BY
JOHN GOLDSBOROUGH EARLE AND
GIVEN TO THE AUTHOR.

Chesapeake Bay Maritime Museum, St. Michaels, MD.

ENDNOTES - CHAPTER TEN

1. *The Maryland Journal*, 16 November 1784: "Pickled Oysters for Gentlemen Going to Sea from George Willis;" also, *The Maryland Journal*, 7 April 1778.

2. C.S. Forester, *The Age of Fighting Ships* (Garden City, New York: Doubleday & Co., Inc., 1956), 140-41.

3. *The Baltimore American*, 19 November 1814.

4. Adam Wallace, *Parson of the Islands* (Cambridge, Maryland: Tidewater Publishers, 1961); "The Battle of Chester River," *Frank Leslie's Illustrated Newspaper*, 19 April 1891; "The Battle of the Choptank," *The Baltimore Sun*, 14 June 1889; Hulbert Footner, *Rivers of the Eastern Shore* (New York: Farrar & Rinehart, 1944). 40-134; John R. Winnersten, *The Oyster Wars of Chesapeake Bay* (Centreville, Maryland: Tidewater Publishers, 1981), 17-54.

5. Virginia Laws, 1810-11, Chapter XVII.

6. *Intrepid*, schooner, USCG Documentation No. 12161; built 1810 at Brookhaven, New York. *List of merchant Vessels of the United States*, hereafter cited as LMV, 1893.

7. Maryland Laws, 1820-21, Chapter 24.

8. *Commerce and Navigation*, Annual letters of the Secretary of the Treasury, 1815-50. (U.S. Government Printing Office, Washington, D.C.)

9. Identified pungies, 1831-60; list compiled by the author from contemporary documents.

10. 1829 broadside (advertisement) announcing C & D Canal opening. Historical Society of Delaware, here after cited as HSD.

11. Thirteenth Annual Report, C&D Canal, HSD.

12. Fifteenth Annual Report, C&D Canal, HSD.

13. C & D Canal Reports, 1829-1919, HSD.

14. *The Baltimore American*, 17 November 1835. From the research of James Dilts.

15. Charles H. Stevenson, *"The Oyster Industry in Maryland,"* Bulletin of the U.S. Commission of Fish and Fisheries, Washington D.C., November 1893, 210.

16. Minute Books of the Board of Director's meetings, Baltimore & Ohio Railroad, B&O Railroad Museum. Research by James Dilts.

17. B&O Annual Reports, 1850-55: Shipments westward from a chart. A.J. Nichol, *"The Oyster Packing Industry of Baltimore,"* Bulletin of the Chesapeake Biological Laboratory, Solomons, Maryland, August 1937, 5.

18. Stevenson, 265. An estimate, not an official statistic.

19. *Swan*, pilot schooner, *The Baltimore Sun*, 1 September 1852. Data compiled by M.V. Brewington and deposited in the Maritime Reference Files of the Maryland Historical Society, hereafter cited as MHS.

20. Ibid.

21. *The Baltimore Sun*, 15 September 1856. Brewington files, MHS.

22. Report of Baltimore Board of Trade, 1857. MHS, MS-177.

23. Stevenson, 265.

24. John C. Hayman, *Rails along the Chesapeake* (Marvadel Publishers, 1979), 23; also, timetables of the Delaware, Frenchtown and New Castle and Wilmington Railroads. Delaware State Achives, Dover, Delaware.

25. Stevenson, 241.

26. *Juvenile*, schooner,13983, built in Sussex County, Delaware, 1827. LMV 1893. Renamed *Mary O'Brien*, 1896; USCG Individual Vessel File, RG41, NA. Also Stevenson, 241.

27. Somerset County Circuit Court Records, Maryland Hall of Records, hereafter cited as MdHR 7266, 1851-52. *Fair American*, pungy, 9721, built in Somerset County, date unknown, LMV 87; Vessel *Emiline*, no record.

28. Ibid.

29. Maryland Laws, 1854, Chapter 4.

30. Elias Jones, *New Revised History of Dorchester County, Maryland* (Cambridge, Maryland: Tidewater Publishers, 1966), 251.

31. *Express*, pungy, 8398, built in Somerset County, date unknown, LMV 87; Dorchester County Assessor's book, Maryland Hall of Records, 11597-8.

32. *Mary Wesley*, pungy, 17896, built in 1850, LMV 70. Assessor's book. Maryland Hall of Records, 11597-8.

33. *Druzilla*, pungy, 6009, built in Somerset County,

1847, LMV 1887. Assessor's book, Maryland Hall of Records 11597-8; Hazen & Co. Daybook, MHS Ms 1532.

34. *California*, pungy, 4015, built in Somerset County, 1850, LMV 1870; also, Admeasurement book A, Folio 209, RG41, NA; also, Loane Bros. Sail Book, Radcliffe Museum, Maryland Historical Society; Assessor's book, Maryland Hall of Records, 11597-8.

35. *Kite*, pungy, 14010, built 1850, Dorchester County. Baltimore Enrollment #158, 1860 and LMV 87; Dorchester County Assessor's book.

36. *Mary Francis*, pungy, 17874, LMV 1870. Assessor's book, Maryland Hall of Records 11597-8; Hazen & Co. daybook, MHS MS-1532.

37. *Three Brothers*, pungy, 24016, LMV 1887. Also Admeasurement book B, Folio 213, RG 41, NA; Assessor's book, *Maryland Hall of Records*, 11597-8; Commander Maryland S.O.P. Report, December 1869. *MHR, Maryland Hall of Records*, 7887-9.

38. *Ida*, pungy, built by Thomas Kirby & Sons, St. Michaels, Talbot County, 1873. USCG Doc. No. 100095, LMV 1887. Also, John Goldsborough Earle's unpublished notebooks, Chesapeake Bay Maritime Museum.

39. Earle's notebooks, no page numbers. Earle photographed the half model upside-down and got the highlights and shadows of *Ida*'s contours.

40. Earle notes that later pungies had rudder posts piercing the transom. He evidently had not seen other drawings, particularly of earlier pilot schooners such as *Wave*, as rudder posts of pilot schooners almost always passed through the middle transom.

41. Earle recorded this information in 1936 when his studies were in their initial stages. Later he would have noted that pilot schooners had substantial drag to their keels. Kirby's *Ida*, like many of the last pungies, had less drag than their predecessors. *Wave*'s lines, taken off by C. Lowndes Johnson in 1940, show greater drag because she was built earlier. The drawings of *Mary and Ellen* were taken off her half model by Eric Steinlein. Like *Ida*, *Mary and Ellen*, built in 1881, had less depth at the bow than at the keel, though drag had decreased noticeably during the nineteenth century.

MARYLAND PILOT BOAT *COQUETTE,* BUILT AT
BALTIMORE IN 1845 BY WILLIAM F. SMITH FOR JOSEPH
AND JOSHUA SHAW, OWNED BY THE MARYLAND
PILOTS ASSOCIATION IN 1847. PAINTING BY AN
UNIDENTIFIED ARTIST
Maryland Historical Society, Baltimore.

CHAPTER ELEVEN

PILOT BOATS AND PILOT-SCHOONER YACHTS

Competition among Maryland pilots ended in 1852, and in Virginia it ceased with the start of the Civil War.[1] Organization of the Maryland Pilots Association that year and the Virginia Pilot Association after the war in 1866 eliminated the need for speedy craft as pilot boats no longer raced to be the first to meet inbound ships. Previously, the piloting trade, conducted by families or teams, was a serious competition among crews intent on outmaneuvering and outsailing one another. The trade began with the arrival of the first tobacco ships at the capes of the Chesapeake and remained competitive for generations. It was this spirited rivalry that produced the incomparable Chesapeake pilot boats more than a century before 1852.

Off Cape Henry, pilots of the two states worked the incoming ships according to their destinations inside the Bay. Both colonies, then states, had boards of commissioners to set fees. Gilbert Middleton served on Maryland's board in 1803, along with Thomas Tenant and other shipowners.[2] Maryland pilots guided vessels from Baltimore to Cape Henry, and were taken on board their pilot boat to await northbound ships sailing into

Maryland waters. One of the earliest communities of mariners resident at Fells Point were pilots who guided tobacco ships in and out of the Patapsco. Generations of members of the Middleton family and other pilot families boarded ships off Annapolis Roads and guided them into the Severn River, up to the northern Bay and to Fells Point's harbor. Maryland pilots also handled ships from the Virginia Capes to Georgetown.

Hampton, Virginia's oldest port, and homeport of the pilot schooners *Liberty* and *Patriot* of Revolutionary War fame, produced its popular Hampton pilot boats until the Civil War. Enrollments for the years between 1815 and 1845 contain records of many pilot boats as well as hundreds of baycraft pilot schooners. These Hampton schooners sometimes migrated out of the Bay. William H. Somers, a New Orleans pilot, registered *John Hope*, built in Hampton in 1815, at the Louisiana port in 1817. Her measurements were 57' x 17' x 6'.[3] Early Hampton pilot schooners fall into two categories. Using a sample of 20 Hampton-built boats of this period from federal records, the average size of the commercial type was 48' x 15.65' x 5.0'.[4] Boats built for pilots, such as *John Hope*, consistently exceeded the size of pilot schooners that sailed in freight service.

Further evidence that boats for pilots in the early nineteenth century were larger than the cargo version is the schooner *Esther*, built by Matthew Caleb Clarke for the pilots of St. Marys County on the Potomac River in Maryland. Built in 1824, she measured 63' x 18' x 7' and 69 tons burden, carpenter measure, substantially larger than most Bay pilot schooners built then for freight.[5] Clarke described her as a pilot boat.

It is possible to recognize pilot boats in old records by owner occupation, and by their unique design and size. Marestier, upon his arrival on the Bay in 1820, made notes or drew a plan of three schooners which he described as used by the pilots of Norfolk. He designated these as schooners 14, 15 and 17.[6] Marestier's Norfolk pilot boats 14 and 15 were approximately the same size as *John Hope*. Marestier noted that the measurements he recorded for pilot boats 14 and 15 were similar, but that these two schooners differed from schooner 17, a vessel he called a pilot boat. He wrote: "La différence de tirent d'eau est beaucoup moindre que dans les goelettes nos. 14 et 15."[7] Roughly translated, he wrote that the difference in draft at the bow compared with the draft at the stern of vessel 17 is much less than the differences in the fore and aft drafts of the pilot boats 14 and 15. He continued that this difference was in the elevation of the keel at the bow; or, in more normal usage, the keels of pilot boats 14 and 15 had more drag at their

sterns than did pilot schooner 17.

The deeper forefoot of schooner 17, with resulting reduction in drag, was designed to increase cargo space. Observed also between schooner 17's masts is a fuller hull for cargo. Schooner 17's greater beam is just under three times her length overall, a greater proportionate width of hull characteristic of commercial baycraft.

PRINCIPAL DIMENSIONS OF PILOT BOAT 14

Length = 18.95 meters - 62.17 feet

Width = 5.49 meters - 18.01 feet

Depth at midsection = 1.83 meters - 6.0 feet

Draft at bow = 1.22 meters - 4.0 feet

Draft at stern = 2.13 meters - 6.99 feet

DIMENSIONS OF MARESTIER'S SCHOONER 17

Length = 17.45 meters - 57.25 feet

Width = 5.55 meters - 18.21 feet

Depth at bow = 2.13 meters - 6.99 feet

Depth at midsection = 1.83 meters - 6.00 feet

Depth at stern = 2.36 meters - 7.44 feet

Overhang of bow = 3.05 meters - 10.01 feet

Rake of sternpost = 1.84 meters - 6.04 feet

Distance midsection
    forward of center = 1.68 meters - 5.51 feet

Length of mainmast = 18.3 meters - 60.04 feet

Length of foremast = 17.7 meters - 58.07 feet

Marestier wrote that schooner 17 was a pilot boat. Here the probability exists that the term "pilot boat," as used contemporarily, had the broader generic meaning, thus confusing the French visitor, as it has confused generations of writers and naval architects since Marestier's time.

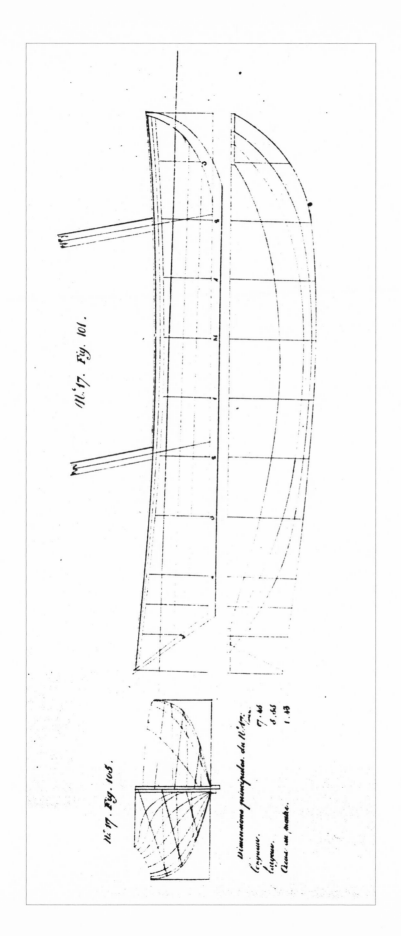

MARESTIER'S SCHOONER NO. 17, FROM HIS STUDY
OF AMERICAN VESSELS, PUBLISHED IN 1824.

Dart, York, Eclipse and *Coquette* were among the last generation of Chesapeake Bay pilot boats that competed for pilotage prior to the organization of the Maryland Pilots Association. *Coquette* measured almost 67' on deck, several feet longer than Marestier's pilot boats of 1820, but her proportions were close to those of the traditional pilot-schooner model. When the Maryland legislature created the pilot's association in 1852, some of the older boats, including *Coquette*, became part of the group's fleet. She was still in service in 1860. As the Maryland Pilots Association replaced this last generation of fast pilot boats, the new vessels were more burdensome and equipped with more home comforts to accommodate association pilots as they waited for incoming vessels. When *Coquette, Eclipse* and their sisters retired from pilot service, the Maryland version of the Chesapeake Bay pilot boat ceased to exist. Virginia's fast pilot boats disap-

peared with the opening of the Civil War.[8]

Pilots from New England to Louisiana bought Chesapeake pilot boats. While there is little doubt that Samuel Horatio Middleton's Annapolis pilot boats of 1744, and the fast Hampton boats working the Virginia Capes in the middle of the eighteenth century, were among the first vessels of pilot-schooner design, New England mariners sailed similar craft out of Portsmouth during the Revolutionary War. Hampton pilot boats could be found off the entrance to New York harbor around 1800. Pilots up and down the coasts of America, wherever the business was competitive, placed Chesapeake Bay pilot schooners into service as the nation extended its seacoast.

Chesapeake Bay craft were a familiar sight at New Orleans when the United States annexed Louisiana. Previously, Fells Point shipwrights and shipowners sold many vessels to the French at that port. After the Louisiana Purchase of

1803, the first Department of the Treasury revenue cutter assigned to New Orleans was the pilot schooner *Louisiana*, built at Fells Point by order of Albert Gallatin, Secretary of the Treasury. William Parsons was the builder and she took her station at New Orleans in 1804.[9]

An early pilot boat stationed at New Orleans was *Nonpareil*, built in St. Mary's County, Maryland, in 1794, and registered at New Orleans in 1804.[10] James Doyle, her owner from southern Maryland, sailed her to New Orleans. *Regulator*, a Hampton pilot boat built in 1802, was registered in New Orleans in 1806.[11] Lewis Mitchell Robert of New Orleans purchased the pilot boat *Thomas Jefferson* at Baltimore in 1811.[12] *Eliza*, a schooner built at Hampton in 1817, was registered in New Orleans in 1818. Her master for three years was James R. Sterett, of a family associated with Baltimore shipping since before the Revolution.[13]

New Orleans pilots continued to purchase Hampton pilot boats for several decades. Included were *John Hope* and *Virginia*, both built in Hampton in 1815.[14] The Pilots Benevolent Association of Plaquemines, Louisiana, purchased *Argus*, built in Hampton in 1837.[15] Previously, the association owned *Lafayette*, built by William Shores of Hampton in 1831.[16] Thomas Dobbins of Hampton built *James Connick* in 1832 and John Shores built a second *Lafayette*, which the Louisiana pilots purchased in 1838.[17]

The preference for Chesapeake Bay pilot boats spread to Mobile and Galveston. One of the first Mobile pilot boats built at Fells Point was *William Tell*, registered to Andrew Dorgan at Baltimore in 1837 and re-registered by him at Mobile on 31 October 1837.[18] *William Tell*, almost 52' in length, had depth of hold of only 5'4". The Dorgan family were shipbuilders at Fells Point, and a yard bearing their name closed there in 1838.[19] John Dorgan traveled to New York and purchased a pilot boat named *Mary Ann* and sailed her to Mobile. She was built at Hampton in 1823 and enrolled in New York in 1834. She measured 52' 9" x 16' 2" x 6' 2", dimensions fairly standard for the earlier pilot boats of both coasts.[20] Andrew Dorgan purchased *Clara* in Baltimore in 1841, as Mobile pilot boats reached the size of offshore pilot schooners and coastal schooners of the period.[21] The Fells Point builder of *Clara* was John A. Robb, and like the pilot schooners sold to Gloucester fishermen during this period or the slavers being built locally, her shallow draft enabled her to pass over the sandbars at the entrance to Mobile Bay.

Mobile pilots bought *Relief* at Baltimore in 1843. William Thomas Norville signed on as a member of the crew of *Relief* at Baltimore for her maiden voyage.[22] The Dorgan and the Norville families of Fells Point provided Mobile with several generations of pilots. *Alabama* (1858),[23] *Florida* (1860),[24] and *Baltic* (1860), all built in

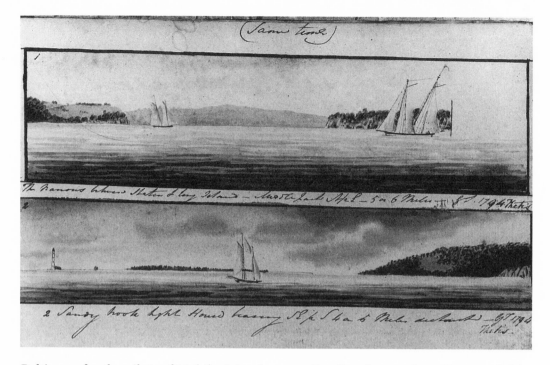

Baltimore for the pilots of Mobile, joined that port's fleet just prior to the Civil War. The builder or builders of the first two pilot schooners are unknown, but John A. Robb built *Baltic*.[25] During the same period Baltimore shipwrights built the schooners *Two Sisters* and *Sam Houston* for the pilots of Galveston. In the shipping news at the time of their launching, the *Baltimore Sun* described both as pilot boats.[26]

Although most New York pilot boats were built locally after the War of 1812, pilots purchased boats constructed on Chesapeake Bay in earlier years. *Ranger*, a pilot boat built at Hampton in 1800, appears among New York enrollments in 1807; she had been purchased by an association of New York pilots earlier that year. They kept her in service there for only a few months.[27] There were others, and the

small pilot boats that George Tobin sketched at the entrance to New York harbor in 1795 are very similar in design to Hampton pilot boats. As previously noted, John Dorgan purchased the Hampton pilot boat *Mary Ann* in New York.

In the years between 1812 and 1820, the New York shipbuilding community made great progress in design and construction following the strong work of its shipwrights on the Great Lakes in the crash program of building the fleet that held back the British invasion from Canada during the War of 1812. The New York group included Henry Eckford, Christian Bergh and Adam and Noah Brown, fine shipbuilders who, along with that city's merchants and bankers, led the port of New York into a dominant position in world trade, banking and shipping in the nineteenth and twentieth centuries.

Eckford and Bergh trained the next generation, which included Isaac Webb and Stephen Smith (by Eckford); Jacob A. Westervelt (by Bergh); and David Brown, who served an apprenticeship with Adam and Noah Brown. This group, with others, built America's great deepwater vessels in the mid-century zenith of commercial sail. Their ships crisscrossed the nearly limitless seas of nineteenth-century commerce, leaving to Baltimore's shipowners their specialty, the short sea routes of Chesapeake Bay schooners and brigs, supplemented by an occasional full-rigged ship equal in size and speed to the leviathans of the New York shipyards.

Marestier's "Schooner No. 16," a New York pilot boat of 1820, had the familiar design of the Chesapeake model with variations to compensate for heavier weather in the North Atlantic.[28] She had length overall of approximately 59', similar to Chesapeake Bay pilot vessels. Hampton or Norfolk pilot boats had more drag to the keel and somewhat greater rake to the stern post, but New York pilot boats had bows of greater depth and more pronounced deck sheer. These changes made the New York model more seaworthy, or at least less likely to ship green water when sailing into a high sea. Additionally, the floors of pilot boats built in the Chesapeake rose sharply, but seemed to have less deadrise than New York models illustrated by Marestier's schooner 16 and William Webb's plan for *John McKeon*. The New York model had continuously rising bilges to the water-line, where they uniformly took a turn, beyond the vertical, giving the topsides slight tumblehome for the full length of the hull. Marestier's schooner 16 had bulwarks and a low quarterdeck.[29]

Isaac Webb's New York pilot boat *John McKeon*, a drawing of which is dated 1838, had dimensions of 78' x 20' 7" x 7' 6", a substantially larger craft than other pilot boats examined.[30] Her overall design is similar to Marestier's schooner 16. *John McKeon* had bulwarks (as did schooner 16) at the quarters, a break in an otherwise flush deck, and the steeve of her bowsprit was more pronounced than the Chesapeake version. The basic design of the hull, her standing rigging and her sail plan, were similar to Hampton pilot boats.

New York pilot boats continued to evolve under the drawing pencil of George Steers, who gave his pilot boats sharper concave bows and more tapered hulls that put their greatest breadth farther aft. The hull of Steers' schooner yacht *America* illustrates the changes. These have been hailed as substantial innovations, although Thomas Kemp's design of *Grecian* in 1812 was somewhat similar in this respect. Steers took much of the rake out of *America*'s sternpost, but in most other aspects of her design and rig she is a typical Chesapeake pilot schooner, as were most other schooner yachts and pilot boats in the United States for several decades.

A yacht is normally designed for speed. She pleases her owner when he outsails his yachting rivals–a simple

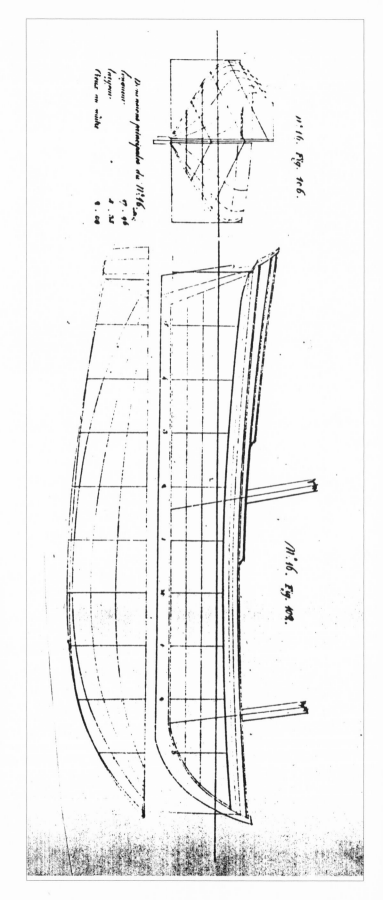

MARESTIER'S SCHOONER NO. 16, FROM HIS STUDY
OF AMERICAN VESSELS, PUBLISHED IN 1824.

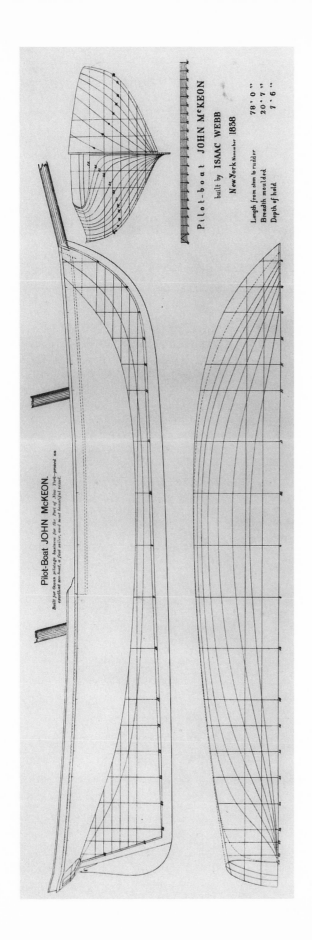

Pilot-Boat JOHN McKEON.

Built for Ocean pilotage business for the Port of New-York—proved an excellent sea-boat, a fast sailer, and most beautiful vessel.

Pilot-boat JOHN McKEON

built by ISAAC WEBB

New York November 1838

Length from stem to rudder	78' 0 "	
Breadth moulded	20' 7 "	
Depth of hold	7' 6 "	

LINES OF NEW YORK PILOT BOAT *JOHN McKEON.*
BUILT IN 1838 BY ISAAC WEBB, FROM *PLANS OF
WOODEN VESSELS BUILT BY WILLIAM WEBB.*
Peabody Library, Baltimore.

**LINES AND SAIL
PLAN OF THE
SCHOONER YACHT**
AMERICA, 1851.
Musée de la Marine,
Paris.

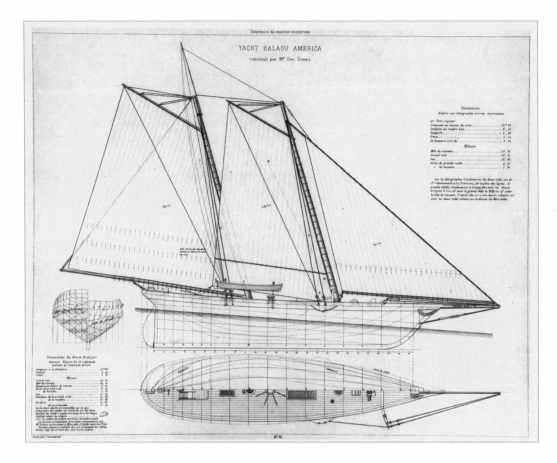

enough mission on which millions have been spent then and now. Isaac Webb designed and built a very early schooner yacht for "a club of young men of New York," a yacht described as "the first built at that port." Named *Dream,* this significant yacht is shown in the plan that appears on page 240.[31]

Webb's *Dream* was closely modeled after a Chesapeake baycraft. Her hull had a straight keel with considerable drag, and raking stem and stern post. She had shallow depth at the bow and substantially greater draft at the stern. Webb gave *Dream* a rounded transom and a rudder different in shape from that of the con-

temporary Chesapeake pungy boat. It should not be surprising that a New York builder would design the city's allegedly first schooner yacht after the nation's best-performing oyster schooner or pilot boat. A Boston group that included Captain Robert Bennet Forbes purchased *Dream* in 1834, and at the same time established the first yacht club east of Cape Cod, a group that called itself the Dream Club after the yacht.[32] Isaac Webb's yacht *Dream* has real significance in yachting history as she had the distinction of being one of the first schooner yachts at New York and then took her place in the early yachting history of New England.[33]

Other famous yachts after *Dream* were *Northern Light*, built in 1839, and *Coquette*, built in 1846, both for owners in the Boston area.[34] These early yachts were designed as pilot boats and used interchangeably. Louis Winde built *Northern Light* in 1839. The drag of her keel and her sharp rise of floor made her a fast and maneuverable sailer. William B. Winchester, her original owner, sold her after a few years of racing. Following a failed venture as a packet boat, her owners began a voyage to Gold Rush California, only to lose her in the Straits of Magellan.[35] This happened in 1850, just one year before *America*'s famous victory at Cowes.

Winde's shipyard, Winde & Clinkard in Chelsea, Massachusetts, built *Coquette* for a Boston owner in 1846. She had a relatively beamy hull, 66' x 19', and she was a pilot-schooner type modeled closely on pungies and coastal schooners built on Chesapeake Bay. *Coquette* was first a yacht, then a Boston pilot boat.[36] Similarities in design of Boston yachts, pilot boats and some New England fishing schooners have suggested to some writers that the builders of early Gloucester fresh-fish sharpshooter schooners took their design from Boston yachts and pilot boats. This is possible, but it does not alter the fact that New England schooner yachts, early pilot boats, and sharpshoot-

SCHOONER YACHT *AMERICA*, SHOWN IN A LITHOGRAPH BY DEANE AND SON.

National Maritime Museum, London..

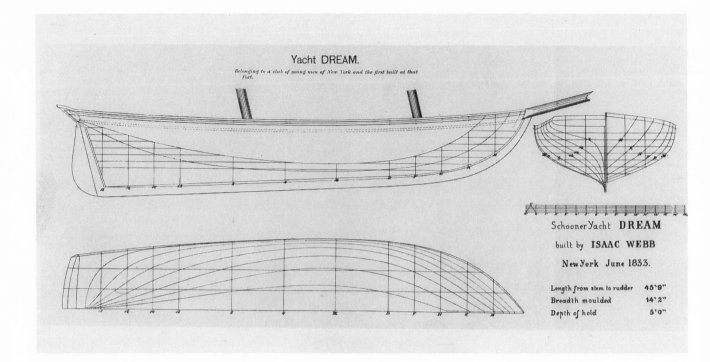

Yacht DREAM.

Belonging to a club of young men of New York and the first built at that Port.

Schooner Yacht **DREAM**

built by **ISAAC WEBB**

New York June 1833.

Length from stem to rudder   45'9"

Breadth moulded   14'2"

Depth of hold   5'0"

ers were all heavily influenced by the Chesapeake Bay pilot-schooner model.

Northern schooner yachts and pilot boats retained the basic pilot-boat sail plan of large jib, lug foresail and main with various other sails, including flying jibs and bonnets. *America*, enroute to France in 1851, used the pungy boat's fore-and-aft sail plan, and a large course [square] sail that the crew called Big Ben. James Steers noted in her log the use of a gaff topsail, two different sizes of jibs, a topmast staysail and bonnets on *America*'s foresail and jib.[37]

It is not difficult to follow the Chesapeake pilot schooner model through the West Indies, over to Western Europe and in the ports of the American South. However, New England maritime traditions make it more difficult to find agreement on the Chesapeake Bay pilot schooner's influence on northern schooners. Certainly in the cargo trades Chesapeake influence was minor prior to the time that canal and rail transportation opened wide areas of interior America to fresh fish. At that time, 1847, New England fishermen asked their shipwrights for faster vessels–quick-to-market vessels– and they responded with a schooner they called a sharpshooter.

Throughout his writings, Howard I. Chapelle expressed the conviction that the Chesapeake Bay pilot schooner, specifically the pungy boat, had a major influence on the design of the fresh-fish schooners of Essex and Gloucester. In his *History of American Sailing Ships*, he wrote: "It has been a popular idea that the Baltimore clipper [schooner], as exemplified by the slaver, disappeared with the coming of the [Yankee] clipper ships; the fact is, however, that the old model merely changed names becoming the pilot-boat type of early American yachts, the sharpshooter type of Gloucester fishermen and the basic model of every fast keel schooner for another fifty years."[38] Then, in his last major work, *The American Fishing Schooners, 1825-1935,* he wrote: "It has not yet been established that any of the southern [Chesapeake] schooners were in Gloucester prior to 1847, when *Romp,* [an early sharpshooter], was launched at Essex, so it is doubtful that these schooners could have had any influence on the sharpshooter model."[39] This remarkable reversal becomes more confused as Chapelle proceeds then to describe *Romp's* design almost exactly as he had described the Bay's pungy boats in previous writings.[40]

Naval architects and maritime historians write as if northern owners and their builders worked in isolation from outside influence. Samuel Eliot Morison made reference to the influence of Chesapeake Bay craft on New England mariners in his discussion of the ketch *Eliza.* He pointed out her debt to the "Baltimore clipper" schooner and footnoted it by quoting a newspaper notice concerning "the fast sailing Virginia built schooner *Fox,* 30 tons, 58 feet," for sale in the *Salem Gazette* on 15 July 1796.[41] There were many other Chesapeake schooners in New England during the first half of the nineteenth century. William Corey of Providence purchased the Hampton pilot boat *I.J.,* in

May, 1831.[42] Built in 1816, she was owned in Boston in 1830. *John Randolph,* a pilot schooner built in 1830 at Hampton by Thomas Dobbins, was owned in Barnstable and Yarmouth in 1844.[43] These examples only touch the surface.

A close working relationship between Chesapeake and New England mariners existed after oysters began to move from Chesapeake Bay to Cape Cod, Rhode Island, and destinations on Long Island Sound prior to the War of 1812. After the war, the Chesapeake Bay pilot-schooner design was familiar to New England mariners as adaptations of the model were employed as cargo schooners, revenue cutters for the Navy, packet boats, pilot boats, fruit carriers and, of course, carriers in the oyster trade with New England.

New England vessels picked up and delivered cargo at Chesapeake ports and landings for a hundred years prior to the

THE BOSTON
YACHT
NORTHERN LIGHT
IS SHOWN IN A
PAINTING BY AN
UNIDENTIFIED
ARTIST.
*Peabody Essex
Museum, Salem, MA.*

time that Maryland and Virginia began to build merchant fleets around 1730. Yet, as Maryland began to build its own cargo schooners, there is no evidence that local owners or shipwrights continued to look to New England craft, a common sight on Chesapeake Bay, for their designs. Likewise, Chesapeake Bay models never had much influence on New England builders until there developed a need for speed. Then the development of the fresh-fish market produced the sharp-shooter model to replace older New

1847, the need for a new fishing-schooner model was apparent. The new fresh-fish markets forced fishing fleet owners, and therefore the builders of New England's Atlantic Ocean fishing schooners, to move quickly to build a new Gloucester fleet. The older, slower vessels, designed to catch and salt fish at sea, had become obsolete almost overnight.

It was thought that the new-vessel problem could be solved by adapting the design of Chesapeake Bay pungies and oyster boats that had sailed into New

A GLOUCESTER SHARPSHOOTER IS SHOWN TO THE RIGHT OF CENTER IN THIS PAINTING BY FITZ HUGH LANE. *Cape Ann Historical Association, Gloucester.*

England schooner designs that featured capacity rather than speed.

There seems to have been ample reason for Chesapeake Bay influence on the New England fishing schooner after about 1847. With the destruction of the Marblehead fishing fleet by a North Atlantic storm in 1846 and then the extension of a railroad spur to Gloucester in

England ports for 50 years. This was not a simple task as the pungy was a baycraft and the fishing schooners were expected to sail in the North Atlantic. With the sharpshooters, Essex shipwrights built a hull with a more pronounced turn of the bilge and deeper holds for greater capacity and stability. The new schooners had keels with pronounced drag, but with more powerful bows than the pungy boat to withstand pounding into big seas. The rake of the stern post was reduced, too, for the purpose of strengthening that portion of the sharpshooter's hull. In spite of these changes, the sharpshooter and the pungy had many similarities, although without question the sharpshooter was a better vessel at sea.

Above the waterline, New-England-built sharpshooters closely resembled Chesapeake baycraft. The rig of the sharpshooter had raking spars and the traditional tall rig of the pilot schooner. Like the pungy, sharpshooters had little steeve to their bowsprits, and they adopted the flush deck of the Chesapeake model and the simple transom, rudder and tiller arrangement. The Essex sharpshooters captured the beauty of the fast Chesapeake Bay craft, as can be observed in the paintings of Fitz Hugh Lane.

While the original sharpshooters had hulls and rigs similar to Chesapeake pilot schooners, the model evolved into the Gloucester clipper schooner, which left a legacy of failure engraved on stone memorials devoted to the thousands of fishermen lost in the 1870s and 1880s. A number of these shallow-draft schooners were built on Chesapeake Bay for Gloucester owners and for New England oyster packers operating between the Bay and New England beds. Evidence indicates that these shoal-draft schooners, satisfactory for running loads of oysters coastwise, were literally out of their depth on the North Atlantic fishing grounds.

One of the Chesapeake Bay shoal-draft schooners owned in Massachusetts, *Iowa*, is mentioned by Chapelle in *The American Fishing Schooners*. He established her year of construction in Dorchester County, Maryland, as 1854, although a prior bulletin of the Smithsonian Institution, where Chapelle was curator, gave her construction date as 1844,[44] which is the year Levin Fooks built her in Dorchester County.[45] Probably too small for coastwise packet service (100 tons), *Iowa* left the Merchant Line after a short period. She had Massachusetts owners at that time, and in 1860 she is listed as a Newburyport-to-Boston packet.[46] By giving her date of construction as 1854, Chapelle seems to be forcing his conclusion that Chesapeake Bay craft were unknown in Massachusetts at mid-century.

The *Baltimore Sun* noted in its shipping news the launching of an 80-ton schooner for Riggs Brothers of Gloucester on 15 May 1851.[47] Her builders were Fardy & Auld. This shipyard built the schooner *Garland* for Timothy MacIntire of Gloucester in 1850. Her dimensions were 80' x 21' 3" x 7' 6". These are examples of shallow-draft Chesapeake Bay schooners built to accommodate Gloucester's harbor.[48] In 1852, *S.E. Sawyer* was built for Gloucester owners and a Baltimore shipwright built *Lancet* for Harwich owners.[49] The facts seem clear: that Gloucester as well as other New England fishing ports had access to these designs and their builders and were familiar with Chesapeake Bay schooners such as pungies, centerboard and clump schooners long before 1854.

While boating for pleasure caught on in the north before the Civil War, yachts were not widely owned on Chesapeake Bay until the twentieth century. Even then, because of the continuing Oyster Wars, pleasure boats were not numerous. There were exceptions, particularly around Baltimore. Members of the original Baltimore Yacht Club had the schooner yacht *Rena* built in 1880 and the painting below was possibly commissioned to celebrate the occasion.[50] Seen are two schooners and a sloop. Based on records of sailing yachts owned in Baltimore in 1880, these may be [from left to right], the sloop *Blue Wing*, built in Baltimore in 1870, *Rena*, and *Clytie*, a centerboard schooner yacht built in Baltimore in 1878.[51] Whatever their identities, the yachts that James E. Buttersworth painted into the picture are not unlike northern yachts that preceded them.

About twenty years later, photographer John Dubas recorded the three principal sailing workboats of the Bay at the entrance to Baltimore harbor. In the fore-

YACHTS UNDER FULL SAIL ARE SHOWN IN BALTIMORE HARBOR, CIRCA 1876 IN THIS PAINTING BY J. E. BUTTERSWORTH. *Courtesy of Oliphant & Co., New York.*

ground is a sloop; in the background, a large centerboard schooner, and in between a pilot schooner similar to *Rena*.

Launchings of pilot boats, pilot schooners, clipper and clump schooners, and pungies by Chesapeake Bay shipwrights diminished quickly in the 1880s. Sloops, bugeyes, skipjacks and centerboard schooners took over the Bay's trades and fisheries although many of the pungies, built from mid-century into the 1880s, were very long-lived. The last working pungies disappeared during the decade preceding World War II. Only in the West Indies did island shipwrights continue to build keel workboat schooners well into the twentieth century.[52]

In 1976, the city of Baltimore financed the building of a replica of a Baltimore schooner of 1812. Thomas C. Gillmer designed *Pride of Baltimore*, using as his model various Baltimore schooners built between 1807 and 1815. Among those he mentions as contributors to the first *Pride*'s lines is the Swedish Royal Navy schooner *Experiment*.[54] Melbourne Smith signed on as builder, and the launching took place in February of 1977. After several goodwill tours to European and other world ports, *Pride* fell victim to a sudden squall and capsized in the Caribbean on 14 May 1986. Her captain and three crew members were lost.

Howard I. Chapelle re-drew the hull lines and sail plan of the Swedish Royal Navy schooner *Experiment* when he included information about her in *The Search for Speed Under Sail, 1700-1855*.[54] He called *Experiment* sharp, and calculat-ed her prismatic coefficient at 0.62.[55] Thomas Gillmer described *Experiment* as an extreme "Baltimore Clipper."[56] Aside from the fact that both Chapelle and Gillmer consistently misname these schooners, it is possible by using their figures to understand Gillmer's problems with the design of *Pride of Baltimore*, for which he calculated a prismatic coefficient at 0.58. He described her as conservatively sharp.[57]

Pride's admeasurement certificate states her length overall at 79.6'. Her extreme beam as provided by designer Gillmer was 23 feet. Her depth of hold, evidently incorrectly recorded [as 9.2 feet] by a Coast Guard admeasurer and by Melbourne Smith on her carpenter certificate, was actually 7.67 feet according to Thomas Gillmer. *Pride of Baltimore*'s measurements, then, were 79.6' x 23' x 7.67'.[58] These dimensions, presumably correct, were calculated in a manner sim-

WORK BOATS IN BALTIMORE HARBOR WERE PHOTOGRAPHED CIRCA 1900 BY JOHN DUBAS. *Peale Museum, Baltimore.*

PRIDE OF

BALTIMORE,

SKETCHED BY JOHN

C. RITTER SAILING

BY BALTIMORE'S

1980s WATERFRONT.

Courtesy of the artist.

ilar to the procedure prescribed for a customs surveyor measuring for ship registration in 1812.[59] They produce the following ratios:

Ratio, length-width – 3.46 : 1
Ratio, length-depth – 10.38 : 1

It is important to note that *Pride of Baltimore*, as built, had less than normal depth of hold, and as a result her centers of buoyancy and gravity were higher than normally found in the original Baltimore schooners from which she was copied.

Gillmer designed a schooner with a length-width ratio almost exactly matching the Swedish schooner *Experiment*'s

3.48 : 1. However, *Pride*'s hull differs in her length-depth ratio from most of the original Baltimore schooners, (9.03 : 1, in the case of *Experiment*). With the first *Pride*'s shallow depth of hold producing a length-depth ratio of 10.38 : 1, Gillmer and Smith altered the Baltimore schooner's traditional proportions, her hull shape and center of buoyancy. Therefore, *Pride of Baltimore*, carrying the tall spars and sail plan of a Baltimore schooner, and with her reduced stability, would be a crank sailer except in light air or when heavily ballasted.

Armed Baltimore schooners of 1812 had sharp hulls and large sail areas. They enjoyed great success with skilled cap-

tains at the helm and experienced profes-
sional crews on deck. This combination
enabled them to evade pursuers in a fair
wind, but made them dangerous in a gale.
Pride of Baltimore II replaced Maryland's
lost schooner in 1988. She is a sturdier,
deeper vessel with watertight bulkheads

and increased ballast.

Other replicas have been built in
addition to the two city of Baltimore
schooners. *Lady Maryland*, a pungy
schooner designed by Gillmer and built
by Peter Boudreau, is owned by the Living
Classroom Foundation, an educational

institution. She is one of many topsail schooners operated by private and public bodies–recently-built replicas, restorations of older topsail-schooner yachts, schooners of various provenance given square topsails and other Chesapeake-schooner details. The closer they resemble the Chesapeake Bay pilot schooner, the more beautiful they are.

Developed as a pilot boat sometime after 1730, the model became the tidewater's commercial carrier–the schooner pilot-boat built. It disappeared, finally, in the twentieth century, its work assumed by other forms of transportation. The Chesapeake Bay pilot schooner shares the necessary quality of other great human creations, a unique form that faithfully follows function. These striking vessels were on the American scene for more than two centuries as part of an equation for survival, a formula for success and riches, and with perfect proportions the essence of beauty.

STERN ORNAMENT
FROM PUNGY
AMANDA F. LEWIS.
THIS CARVING,
ATTRIBUTED TO
HAMMOND SKINNER,
IS IN THE COLLECTION
OF THE SMITHSONIAN
INSTITUTION, ON LOAN
TO THE MARYLAND
HISTORICAL SOCIETY.
Courtesy of the author.

ENDNOTES - CHAPTER ELEVEN

1. The Maryland Pilots Association was created by an act of the Maryland legislature, June, 1852. Virginia pilots were under military control during the Civil War. The Virginia Pilot Association was created by an act of the Virginia legislature in 1866.

2. Maryland Statutes, Act of 1803: To Establish Pilots and Regulate Fees.

3. Hampton, Virginia, enrolment #11, 4 July 1815. RG41, National Archives (hereafter cited as NA). Enrollments researched and compiled by Charles Shoemaker of Hampton, Virginia.

4. Hampton, Virginia enrollments, New Orleans enrollments and registers, RG41, NA, (Charles Shoemaker).

5. *Esther*, pilot boat, Hampton carpenter certificate signed by Matthew Caleb Clarke, 20 May 1824. RG41, NA, (Charles Shoemaker).

6. Jean Baptiste Marestier, *Memoire sur Bateaux a Vapeur des Etats Unis d'Amerique* (Paris: La Ministre de la Marine et des Colonies, 1824), 246-47.

7. Ibid, 247

8. *Coquette*, pilot boat, built by William F. Smith, 1845; enrollment #185, 1845, register #176, 1860, Maryland Board of Pilots. RG41, NA. *Eclipse*, pilot boat, built in 1845 at Baltimore by William Hunt and William

Wiggins. Baltimore enrolment #135, 1845. RG41, NA. This pilot boat was sold in 1849 and new owners sailed her to California. A second pilot boat, *Eclipse*, was built in 1849 by John Robb at Fells Point; *Baltimore Sun*, 3 July 1849 and RG41 NA. *Canton*, pilot boat, built by Foster & Booz, *Baltimore Sun*, 8 December 1848. *Dart*, pilot boat, built by Hugh Auld for William Griggs, pilot, *Baltimore Sun*, 5 November 1850. *York*, pilot boat, was a Confederate privateer in the Civil War.

9. Correspondence, Albert Gallatin-Robert Purviance, June, 1807; Department of Treasury papers: Revenue Cutters: RG56, NA. Also: registers and enrollments of New Orleans, compiled by the WPA, Vol. 1, 1804-20. University of Louisiana, Hill Memorial Library, 1941. *Louisiana*, schooner, No. 527, register #33, 2 October 1813.

10. *Nonpareil*, pilot schooner, New Orleans register #21, 2 June 1804; WPA New Orleans registers, (hereafter cited as WPA NO).

11. *Regulator*, pilot boat, built at Hampton, 1802; New Orleans register #10, 1806, WPA NO #740.

12. *Thomas Jefferson*, pilot boat, built in St. Marys County, Maryland, in 1811 by Bennett Jones. Baltimore carpenter certificate. Also, Baltimore register #195, 1811:

owner, Lewis Mitchell Robert, New Orleans. RG41, NA.

13. *Eliza*, pilot boat, built at Hampton, 1817; register #137, NO, 1819. RG41, NA, (Charles Shoemaker). Also, New Orleans registers WPA NO, #250.

14. *John Hope*, pilot boat, built at Hampton, 1815. Enrollment #11, Hampton, 1815; (Charles Shoemaker), register #72, WPA NO, October, 1815. *Virginia*, pilot boat, built at Hampton, 1815, enrollment #15, 1815, Hampton, (Charles Shoemaker), register #11, NO, 1818. RG41, NA.

15. *Argus*, pilot boat, built at Hampton in 1828; register #100, WPA NO. Owner: Pilots Benevolent Association of Plaquemines, Louisiana. RG41, NA, (Charles Shoemaker).

16. *Lafayette*, pilot boat built at Hampton, 1831, carpenter certificate signed by William Shores, enrolment #14, 1831, Norfolk, register #101, 1837, WPA NO, Pilots Benevolent Association, (Charles Shoemaker).

17. *James Connick*, pilot boat, built at Hampton, 1832, by Thomas Dobbins; enrollment #42, Norfolk; register #69, WPA NO, 1837. *Lafayette*, pilot boat, built at Hampton, 1833, by John Shores; enrolment #60, 1833; register #99, 1833, WPA NO, Pilots Benevolent Association, RG41, NA, (Charles Shoemaker).

18. *William Tell*, pilot boat, built at Baltimore, 1837; Baltimore register #98, 4 October 1837; written notation on register: surrendered at Mobile, 31 October 1837. RG41, NA.

19. William J. Kelly, unpublished manuscript on Baltimore shipyards; MHS MS-2264; also see note 62: John Dorgan was associated with a Fells Point shipyard, 1831-38.

20. *Mary Ann*, pilot boat, built at Hampton, 1823; enrolment #34, 1825, Norfolk; register #342, 1839, New York: property change, owner, John D. Dorgan of Mobile. RG41, NA, (Charles Shoemaker).

21. *Clara*, pilot boat, built at Baltimore, 1841; Baltimore temporary register #81, 1841; owner Andrew Dorgan, Mobile. W.M.P. Dunne, unpublished manuscript, "Mobile Bar Pilotage, 1702-1965."

22. *Relief*, pilot boat, built at Baltimore, 1843; Baltimore temporary register #64, 1843; RG41, NA.; W.M.P. Dunne manuscript.

23. *Alabama*, pilot boat, built at Baltimore, 1858; Baltimore temporary register #122, 1858: owners: William T. Norville, Charles Wallace, Frederick Smith and William Johnson. W.M.P. Dunne manuscript.

24. *Florida*, pilot boat, built at Baltimore 1860; Baltimore temporary register #95, 1860, same owners. W.M.P. Dunne manuscript.

25. *Baltic*, pilot boat, built at Baltimore, 1860. Baltimore temporary register #101. 1860. W.M.P. Dunne manuscript. Vessel built by John A. Robb. Information supplied by Hazel Robb Cizek, great-great-granddaughter, Baltimore, 1992.

26. *Two Sisters*, pilot boat, built at Baltimore by Muller for Galveston pilots; *Baltimore Sun*, 5 May 1858. *Sam Houston*, pilot boat built at Baltimore by T. Rutter for Galveston pilots. *Baltimore Sun*, 17 January 1860. Data compiled by Marion V. Brewington. Also Baltimore register #13, January, 1860. RG41, NA.

27. *Ranger*, pilot boat, built at Hampton, 1800; enrollment #165, NYC, 18 August 1807. RG41, NA, (Charles Shoemaker).

28. Marestier, Vol. 1, 247; Vol. 2, Plate XI, Fig. 102 and 106.

29. Ibid.

30. William H. Webb, *Plans of Wooden Vessels Built by William H. Webb* (New York: Published by author, 1897).

31. Ibid.

32. *Dream*, schooner yacht, built in New York in 1832, enrolled 5 July 1833, owner: Henry Bohler. Enroled in Boston, 29 August 1834, owner: Thomas H. Perkins, Jr.; sold 1841 to George L. Schuyler of New York. RG41, NA. Compiled by William P. Stephens, *Traditions and Memories of American Yachting* (Camden, Maine: International Marine Publishing, 1981), 160, 164, 274.

33. Ibid., 111, 269, 316.

34. *Northern Light*, schooner yacht, designed and built by Louis Winde, 1837, *The Rudder*, July, 1904. Stephens, 162-64, 270. *Coquette*, schooner yacht-pilot boat, built by Winde & Clinkard, 1846. Stephens, 165 and 168.

35. Stephens, 165.

36. Ibid., 165.

37. Log of *America*, schooner yacht, 1851; kept by James R. Steers enroute to France and England. Frank Gray Griswold, *Clipper Ships and Yachts* (New York: E.P. Dutton, 1927).

38. Howard I. Chapelle, *The History of American Sailing*

Ships (New York: W.W. Norton, 1935), 175, 253.

_____, *The Baltimore Clipper* (Salem, Massachusetts: Marine Research Society, 1930), 147-49.

_____, *The Search for Speed under Sail* (New York: W.W. Norton, 1957), 152-53.

_____, *The Watercraft Collection*, Bulletin No. 219 (Washington, D.C.: Smithsonian Institution, 1960), 167-68, 194.

_____, "The Gloucester Fishing Schooner," Part 1, *Yachting*, November, 1933, 43.

39. Howard I. Chapelle, *The American Fishing Schooners*, 1825-1935 (New York: W.W. Norton & Co., 1973), 66.

40. Ibid., 65.

41. Samuel Eliot Morison, *The Maritime History of Massachusetts*, 1783-1860 (New York: Houghton Mifflin Company, 1921), 100; 8n.

42. *I.J.*, pilot boat, built at Hampton, 1816; New York register #357, 1830, owner: John Scott of Boston. Enrolled 1831, Providence, Rhode Island, owner-master: William Corey. RG41, NA, (Charles Shoemaker).

43. *John Randolph*, pilot boat, built at Hampton by Thomas Dobbins, 1830. Norfolk enrollment #22, 1830. New York enrollment #230, 1844; owners David T. Glover of New York, William Howes of West Yarmouth and Harston Hallett, Jr. of Barnstable. RG41. NA, (Charles Shoemaker).

44. Howard I. Chapelle, *Fishing Schooners*, 66. Also, Bulletin 127, United States National Museum, Smithsonian Institution, 98.

45. *Iowa*, schooner, built in Dorchester County, Maryland, 1844, carpenter certificate signed by Levin Fooks, 7 September 1844. Baltimore enrollment #112, 16 September 1844: New Vessel. RG41, NA.

46. Bulletin 127, Smithsonian, 98.

47. Unnamed schooner built for the Riggs brothers in 1851 by Fardy & Auld of Fells Point. *Hunts Magazine*, xii #190; Brewington, Maryland Historical Society.

48. *Garland*, schooner, built at Baltimore and carpenter certificate signed 15 April 1850 by Fardy and Auld. RG41, NA.

49. *Samuel E. Sawyer*, schooner, built at Baltimore, 1852. Baltimore register #93, 1852, surrendered at Gloucester, 8 September 1852. RG41, NA. *Lancet*, built at Baltimore, 1852; Baltimore register #100, 1852; surrendered at

Harwich, Massachusetts, RG41, NA.

50. *Rena*, schooner yacht, built at Baltimore in 1880 for the Baltimore Yacht Club. *Field and Stream*, Vol. 14, No. 11, 379; Vol. 14, No. 19. also, *List of Merchant Vessels of the United States*, 1887, 220, USCR No. 110430; owned in New York.

51. *Blue Wing*, sloop yacht, built at Baltimore in 1870 for Ben Jenkins, carpenter certificate, bundle 6754, RG41, NA. *Clytie*, centerboard schooner yacht, built at Baltimore, 1878; USCR No. 125675; *List of Merchant Vessels of the United States*, 1887, 89.

52. Douglas C. Pyle, *Clear Sweet Wind, Sailing Craft of the Lesser Antilles* (Preston, Maryland: Easy Reach Press, 1981).

53. Thomas C. Gillmer, *Pride of Baltimore, The Story of the Baltimore Clippers* (Camden, Maine: International Marine Publishing, 1992), 76-78.

54. Chapelle, *The Search*, 201, 203 and 204; Plate 1.

55. Ibid., 201.

56. Gillmer, *Pride*, 78.

57. Ibid., 123.

58. Ibid., figure 4-2, 119 and 122.

59. Act of Congress, 4 August 1790, Section 44; also, W.M.P. Dunne, "An Essay Pertaining to the Tonnage Measurement of the United States Navy, 1794-1815," unpublished manuscript, 5-6.

ON SHORE AT RIGHT ARE PUNGIES UNDER
CONSTRUCTION AT ALEXANDRIA, VIRGINIA, DURING
THE CIVIL WAR.

National Archives, Washington.

CHAPTER TWELVE

THE LAST PILOT SCHOONERS

Pungy, the name that Chesapeake watermen gave to their beloved pilot schooners, seems to have created confusion and, more importantly, historical revision. Enigmatic colloquialisms evade explanation. Words such as pungy have no roots in the English language. Historians have taken more interest in the name of this craft than in the origins of its prototype. Many associate the name pungy with the small Eastern Shore town of Pungoteague. This village, which consists of a few houses at a crossroads above the headwaters of Pungoteague Creek, is in a region that remained isolated from the outside world until a railroad passed through it to connect Cape Charles and Norfolk to Wilmington, Delaware, in 1884. Land deeds, complete to the beginning of settlement, contain no records of significant shipbuilding activity in the vicinity of Pungoteague Bay. No information has come to light linking the town or creek with the name of the pilot schooner.

Historians and naval architects writing about these schooners have failed to note that the pungy's design is the same as the Bay's pilot-boat schooner of the eighteenth century. The pungy is not a cut-down version of the larger Baltimore schooner. The belief that the pungy is a nineteenth-century creation was perpetuated by the introduction of its name into common use at mid-century. Just by casual examination of pre-Federal and Federal enrollments, it becomes clear that the design of the pungy remained basically the same as that of the pilot-boat schooners *Dolphin, Plater, Liberty* and *Patriot*, all built at the beginning of the Revolutionary War.

Small pilot schooners were generally called baycraft when they started to haul grain to Baltimore, and mariners often referred to their vessels as schooner boats in the eighteenth century. During the Revolution, the commercial models were called pilot boats, pilot-boat schooners, or pilot schooners. As the use of the name pungy spread during the nineteenth century, baycraft such as *Hotspur*, up for sale in 1831, were still described as pilot-boat built schooners.[1]

Lavina Ann, listed for sale at the shipyard of Z. Skinner & Son of Baltimore in 1847, was described as a pungy.[2] The following year a notice in a city journal listed a pungy of 48 tons for sale.[3] Captain Lauchlan B. Mackinnon of Great Britain visited Baltimore at mid-century and published a book about his travels in

1852. He wrote, "the pongees or oyster boats, and the Chesapeake Bay coast vessels, are the most elegant and yacht-like merchant craft in the world." Comparing them with a British sailing ship lying in Baltimore's harbor, he called his country's vessel a hog amid a herd of antelopes.[4] Robert Burgess, author of several books on Chesapeake Bay watercraft, wrote of discovering a letter written in 1850 by Ben Somers to a shipwright named Boggs in Accomac, Virginia. Somers ordered what he called a pungy boat from Boggs with "about 42 ft. keel, 7 ft. hole, 21 ft. wide, and built of the best materials."[5]

The Dorchester County Assessor's book for 1852 is lodged with county archival records at the Maryland Hall of Records.[6] In it the employees of the county government laboriously noted the taxable property of all county residents. Benjamin Hart owned one half of the "punga" *Mary Francis,*[7] and Robert Insley owned the "punga" *Black Hawk.*[8] James Montgomery owned two "pungas" named *Jerome Richardson*[9] and *Mary Wesley.*[10] Doctor Joseph Weatherly owned one-third interest in the "punga" *George B. Foxwell.*[11]

The Baltimore Board of Trade's 1859 report mentioned that pungies delivered the largest portion of the oyster catch to Baltimore, and that the beds *dredged* one year became more productive the following season.[12] The report must have been alluding to scrapes, legal on the lower portion of Tangier Sound after 1854. The note about dredging making an oyster bar more prolific the following year was waterman propaganda, and it served them well through the nineteenth and twentieth centuries.

Pungy building continued during the Civil War, but the numbers produced decreased.[13] Hazen & Company, a Baltimore shipyard, built the pungies *Mary L. McGee*[14] and *Robert H. Griffith.*[15] Both of these, launched in 1864, were ordered by watermen who paid approximately double the prewar price for their large pungies. *Mary L. McGee* measured 61' on deck and cost $4,650.00, which included $90.00 government tax and $19.00 for a gilded eagle.[16] W. H. Bradshaw paid $4,500 for *Robert H. Griffith.*[17]

Just as pilot schooners had in prior wars, pungies played active roles in the Civil War. Following the occupation of Maryland by federal troops and a naval blockade of Chesapeake Bay and the Potomac River, southern sympathizers pressed pilot schooners into service as blockade runners. As in the War of 1812, during which Baltimore's letter-of-marque schooners completed successful voyages between Baltimore and France and the West Indies, pungies breached the Union blockade to land contraband in Virginia. Official dispatches mention only the schooners that did not escape. While the U.S. Navy's Potomac flotilla made some captures, gaps in the blockade, and the ease of slipping through at night, allowed much contraband to reach Virginia by running into the Rappahannock and York Rivers, and from southern Maryland across the Potomac River into one of the many creeks on the south shore.

To control vessel movements, the Union Navy placed guard vessels at several points on the Potomac. The fleet consisted of small steam vessels supplemented by several schooners, a force that captured *Ocean Wave*, described as a fine little pungy. The U.S. Navy refitted her as a dispatch vessel.[18] Renamed *Scout,* this pilot schooner made a number of captures for the northern forces.[19] Those pungies caught went to auction in prize courts. Successful Maryland buyers returned them to blockade-running. Most survived the conflict to become oyster dredgers or runners. This group included *Artist,*[20] *Coquette,*[21] *Mt. Vernon,*[22] *Pocahontas,*[23] *Four Brothers,*[24] *Exchange*[25] and *Hampton.*[26]

The U.S. Treasury Department, its Customs Service and Revenue Marine, working with the Union Army and Navy, endeavored to contain the movement of Maryland craft into Virginia. Pungy captains and crews were made to sign oaths of allegiance to obtain voyage permits.[27] Boards of Trade issued passes to identify the buyers of goods on board, in hope of eliminating diversions to Virginia.[28] According to contemporary journals, none of the permit and licensing systems did much to block the flow of goods through a porous blockade.

Several Maryland Customs officials risked their positions and freedom to support the southern cause. An agent on Deal Island issued voyage permits to Virginia vessels, sometimes going so far as to enrol Confederate-owned schooners.[29] Calling at Baltimore for cargo, these pungies then sailed quietly at night to Virginia. Customs officials at Snow Hill hid the true ownership of pilot schooners enrolled at that port.[30] Southern owners of the pungies *Artist,*[31] *Chesapeake*[32] and *John McCabe*[33] remained undetected in this manner.

After the war, pilot schooners found employment in the oyster industry on a large scale. Grain production in the United States moved to the great agricultural regions of the Midwest during the nineteenth century, and railroads in post-Civil War America ran trainloads of wheat and corn from Ohio and Indiana to the east coast. The low yield of tidewater farms, and a transport system that relied on small pilot schooners and other sailing craft, could not match the economies of large farms and efficient rail haulage. But with the legalization of oyster dredging in 1865, pungies, centerboard and clump schooners, and other baycraft, swarmed over the Bay to exploit this bonanza.

The Maryland legislature in 1865 passed a law opening Chesapeake Bay's state-controlled oyster bars in waters deeper than 15' to dredging.[34] The new law, called a licensing act, was the politicians' capitulation to the packers and canners of Baltimore and to the watermen of the lower Eastern Shore. Chaos and wars over territory would follow and the predictable end would be the destruction of Chesapeake Bay's oyster beds. Richard H. Edwards, writing in a U.S. Government publication in the 1880s, pointed out that the famous beds of Tangier and Pocomoke Sounds had been rendered almost barren by scrapes before the Civil War. He predicted that an oyster famine on the Bay would come "unless there is a radical change."[35] Change never came.

The principal duty of the Maryland Marine Police was enforcement of the 1865 oyster licensing act. After the 1868-69 oyster season, there existed a clearer picture of the enormous number of pilot schooners and other baycraft participating in the massive dredging that began in 1865. The number of dredge boats licensed for the 1868-69 season was 563 and the total catch by dredgers and scrapes in state waters was 6,305,600 bushels.[36] Of the total dredger licenses issued that season, 238 dredge-boat owners resided in Somerset County and 240 listed Baltimore City as their homeport. Eighty-five percent of all dredge boats, therefore, sailed out of these two locations, with 15 percent located in all other counties in Maryland. In Calvert County, where Isaac Solomon had located his cannery, only one local dredge boat held a state license in 1868.[37]

The number of licensed dredge boats continued to increase, the commander of the Maryland Marine Police reporting 600 working the Bay in January of 1870. He arrested nine pungies and two sloops that month.[38] Statistics accumulated on pungies for the period between 1840 and 1885 show that more than a thousand of these pilot schooners were built in that interval. During the 1870-71 oyster season, it is estimated that over 75 percent of all dredge or runner licenses were issued to owners of pungy schooners.[39]

Baltimore's packing and canning industry continued to expand and became a major component of the city's industrial base after the Civil War. The nation's appetite for oysters, even the canned variety, was insatiable. The Baltimore market received 5,000,000 bushels in 1870 and remained above that figure for the next 20 years.[40] While the canning industry continued to expand along the city's waterfront, growth of the raw-shucked oyster trade leveled off at Baltimore after 1874 at approximately 1,875,000 bushels as packing houses opened at principal waterfront towns in tidewater Maryland. Eastern Shore towns that developed major wholesale markets included St. Michaels, Oxford, Cambridge and Crisfield, as well as Annapolis and Solomons Island on the Western Shore. Numerous packing houses for fresh oysters, raw or in the shell, sprang up along these and other village waterfronts.[41]

Dredge-boat captains in rural areas drew crew members from large Eastern Shore families and their communities. Often, African Americans handled hand winches, the work brutally hard and dangerous. Hiring agents delivered crews to Baltimore boats. These boats, many owned by speculators, had crews scooped up along the waterfront and handed over for the season. The plight of these men resembled the fate of the impressed American sailors shanghaied into the Royal Navy in the years preceding the War of 1812. The seasonal nature of the employment allowed captains to abuse and overwork their crews, not unlike the treatment of some of the less-fortunate indentured servants of the colonial era. To keep their vessels operative, captains locked their men in the dark wet holds at night. Crew members, most having consumed their earnings through advances, left their dredge boats at the end of the season sick, bruised, broken and with no funds. If a captain owed his crew money at the end of the season, they could be swindled out of it—or worse, propelled overboard by a sudden jibe of a boom.

Across the Bay from Crisfield and Tangier Sound is a region that spreads across Maryland's southern counties to the Potomac River and Virginia. These are Mayland's southern tidewater counties: Ann Arundel, Charles, St. Mary's and Calvert in a region that depended on a one-crop economy, tobacco, into the twentieth century. Even after World War I, tobacco continued to dominate life in this agricultural hinterland. Tobacco farmers supplemented their meager earnings by harvesting the rich seafood of Maryland's Potomac and Patuxent Rivers, and boat-building had been an industry here since Cecil Calvert set up his colony at St. Mary's City in 1634. In isolated Calvert County, population reached a peak in early years and for generations a few families dominated life and politics.

Sandy Island, located in the southern end of the county, in the curve of Drum Point's long arm at the great harbor of the mouth of Patuxent River, had one old house on it when Isaac Solomon, a Baltimore oyster packer, purchased it in

1865.[42] There he built a cannery close to the central Bay's richest oyster beds. He constructed a shipyard and a marine railway to launch and repair his fleet and to tend to the upkeep of the dredge boats upon which his cannery depended. Solomon opened his facility in 1867, and in short order runners and dredge boats, most of them pilot schooners, delivered their catch to Solomons, his island now taking the name of its owner.[43]

Isaac Solomon took a partner in his marine facilities, Isaac Davis, a member of Dorchester County's famed shipbuilding family who legend says had returned to Chesapeake Bay from Webb's yard in New York City. Davis settled on Solomons Island, and soon the shipyard, Solomon & Sons and Davis, would become a leader among vessel builders in the central Chesapeake. Solomons Island became a center for fine baycraft and yachts over the next 75 years.

Isaac Solomon & Sons, the canning company, operated a fleet of baycraft which included two schooners, eight pungies, several barges, and two yachts. The yachts were used to ferry Isaac Solomon between his office and his estate across the river in St. Mary's County.[44] Solomon's schooners and barges hauled supplies and his canned product between the plant and Baltimore. The pilot schooners *Isaac Solomon,*[45] *Daniel and Augustus,*[46] *Exchange,*[47] *Carpenter,*[48] *Dove,*[49] and *Mary,*[50] were equipped with dredging equipment.[51] As there are no records of catches by vessels in this fleet named *American Eagle*[52] and *Father and Sons,*[53] it is assumed that Solomon used these pungies as runners or buyboats.

Records of the oyster receipts at Solomon's cannery for a short period—March, April and May 1869—are in company journals at the Calvert Marine Museum at Solomons. These records show that prices paid over the three-month period remained constant. However, Isaac Solomon paid independent dredge captains bonuses for delivering their catch on an exclusive basis.[54] It was one of these independent contractors who took over Solomon's pungy *Carpenter* in the Spring of 1869.

Carpenter dredged 22 days in the month of March 1869. Her poorest day produced 36 bushels and her best day 189 bushels. Her catch for 22 days was 1,783 bushels. Solomon paid 37-1/2 cents per bushel.[55] *Exchange* recorded 13 days dredging in May 1869. Her total for the month was 586 bushels.[56]

The photographer who captured the image of the pungy *Isaac Solomon*, (shown on the next page) Percy Budlong, mentions in his scrapbook that when he took this photograph in 1906, she had an African-American crew.[57] By then black oystermen frequently owned pungies, although the numbers are unknown because federal licenses issued to watercraft owners did not specify race.

African Americans had found employment on the water since colonial times. Black Chesapeake Bay pilots, oystermen, mariners, both free and slaves, merchant seamen and Navy enlistees, sailed on and out of Chesapeake Bay. Free African Americans looked to the sea for a livelihood as life on the water isolated them from harassment and produced a living without great investment. Farming, vending, cooking and a few other occupations were open to black people, but the water offered a greater degree of freedom. Standby Batton, a black man, purchased the baycraft *Resolution* in 1799. The schooner, built in 1786 on the Choptank River, measured 43' x 13'9" x 5' and 25 tons, and was, no doubt, a pilot-boat schooner.[58] It is difficult to assess how common it may have been on the Bay for a black man to own a schooner—or, for that matter, how many African Americans made their living harvesting the Chesapeake. Maryland records in the pre-licensing period before the Civil War have no breakdown of watermen by race.

African Americans, including free men, began to face restrictive laws as tension grew in the years preceding the Civil War. The Maryland legislature passed an act in 1836 that made all vessels subject to forfeiture unless the owner placed a white captain older than 18 at the helm.[59] Virginia law required an inspection of all vessels entering state waters for "the better protection of slave property."[60]

Prior to the Civil War, Virginia's oyster industry consisted largely of slaves trained as tongers. Naturally enough, black watermen dominated tonging in that state after four years of inactivity during the war. In 1865, Virginia adopted a policy of leasing oyster grounds to private citizens, which placed the river bottoms in control of the white establish-

THE PUNGY
ISAAC SOLOMON
PHOTOGRAPHED AT
ANCHOR BY PERCY
BUDLONG ABOUT
1906. AT THAT TIME,
THIS ORIGINAL
SOLOMONS ISLAND
SCHOONER WAS
OWNED BY
AFRICAN-AMERICAN
WATERMEN.
The Mariners'
Museum, Newport
News, VA.

259

ment, changing radically the direction of Virginia's oyster industry and access to productive beds for African-American watermen. Dredging remained legal on these private beds after a general ban on dredging Virginia's public oyster beds was instituted.

Commander Hunter Davidson of the Maryland Marine Police stated in 1869 that 3,560 men made up dredger crews, and of this total 1,453 were African American. A total of 3,325 men received tonging licenses that year and approximately 50 percent were black, according to Davidson.[61] Black oystermen were even better represented in the lower Bay. An estimated 9,000 tongers worked Virginia's oyster beds following the war, of which almost 6,000 were African American.[62]

Many white owners of dredge boats sold their pilot schooners to buy less expensive craft after 1880. Bugeyes, which gained popularity for a short period, replaced pungies as owners struggled to reduce vessel and crew costs as the catch

Chesapeake Bay oyster production continued to fall through the twentieth century, causing many African-American watermen to migrate to New Jersey. Sailing their pungies north into Delaware Bay, they established new communities along that bay's northern shoreline and continued to dredge for oysters. Thirty-five Chesapeake Bay pilot schooners listed their hailing ports in New Jersey, Delaware, and Pennsylvania as early as 1893.[63]

Hunter Davidson's licensing reports provide no breakdown of types of vessels dredging. Continuous references to bugeyes and skipjacks in twentieth-century documents have caused many to believe that these later craft were the principal dredge boats of Chesapeake Bay during the oyster bonanza. Nothing could be wider of the truth. Somerset County watermen and the Baltimore owners preferred pungy boats. These strong schooners had the power and speed that dredgers preferred.

BELOW IS A HALF MODEL OF *MARY AND ELLEN*, A PUNGY BUILT IN 1881 BY HENRY BRUSSTAR & BROTHERS. SHE WAS PERHAPS THE LAST PILOT SCHOONER BUILT AT FELLS POINT, AND HER LINES MAY BE COMPARED WITH THOSE OF *NONPAREIL* AND STEEL'S "VIRGINIA" PILOT BOAT OF 1805. *Calvert Marine Museum, Solomons MD.*

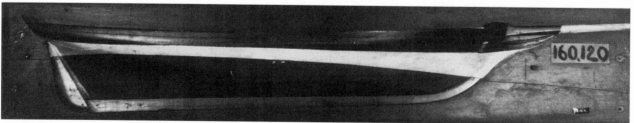

fell. Later the skipjack, sometimes called a two-sail bateau, replaced the bugeye as the oyster bars became increasingly unproductive. As the hardy old pungies were sold off, blacks purchased them at favorable prices in a last-ditch attempt to eke out a living oystering.

For a two-year period starting in 1876, shipbuilder Isaac Davis's day book lists 475 repair orders at his Solomons yard. Only 32 bugeyes (canoes) were repaired in that interval while 279 pungies passed through the yard.[64] These figures refute the claim that bugeyes and skipjacks dominated the dredging industry in the nineteenth century. The Davis log is particularly convincing in this instance as Solomons Island existed solely as a port for oyster boats.

Hazen & Co. operated a repair facility in the Federal Hill section of Baltimore, and their marine railway logbook for the period between January 1864 and November 1866 recorded 71 schooners other than pungies, eight sloops and 83 pungies entering the yard for repairs.[65] From November 1866 to August 1867, the yard then operated by Thomas H. Hooper & Co. recorded 61 pungies, 12 sloops and 30 other schooners repaired.[66] Between 1884 and 1902, Booz Brothers operated a repair facility at Baltimore for Bay and other craft. Their haulage book shows that schooners dominated their work with 635 work orders, followed by pungies with 269.[67] None of these figures for Baltimore yards, showing strong schooner presence, are surprising. At that time a significant number of larger schooners were employed in coastal trade, most without involvement in the oyster industry.

Mary and Ellen, built at Fells Point in 1881 by Henry Brusstar & Brothers, was perhaps the last pilot schooner built there. She was also one of the few new pungies ordered by a Virginian in these final years for these famous vessels. *Mary and Ellen* was built for Thomas I. Woodland and William Shackeford of Gloucester County, Virginia, who enrolled her at Yorktown on 29 August 1881. Her measurements—64.4' x 20.8' x 6.3'—are close to those of a pungy half model in the National Watercraft Collection that has been incorrectly identified as built in 1858. The error was perpetuated when lines were taken off the half model for the publication of the *Historic American Merchant Marine Survey*. There is no record of a pungy of this name or size built in 1858.[68]

A significant portion of Virginia's oyster harvest went to Maryland packing houses. Northern buyers shipped large quantities of Virginia's oysters to New York and New England. In later years, as bugeyes replaced pilot schooners dredging in Maryland, Virginia watermen purchased many of the old Maryland pungies. By 1893, it is estimated that approximately 27 percent of all pungies enrolled listed home ports in Virginia. To give meaning to this figure, the estimated number, 138 owned in Virginia, exceeded the number owned then in Somerset County, Maryland, approximately 125 pungies.[69]

The Chesapeake Bay pilot schooner's last war was a dirty one. The oyster industry, in a boom fed by an expanding transportation system, praised as a gift of God by missionaries, and coddled by politicians, proceeded to split itself between tongers and dredgers. Their fight continued as long as oysters remained plentiful enough to make the battle worthwhile. The inevitable result of the fighting came after World War II, when the oyster catch dropped so low that only a few do-or-die watermen, caught in the pleasant light of a community's love for tragedy, continued

THE PUNGY
JAMES A. WHITING
PHOTOGRAPHED BY
PERCY BUDLONG
CIRCA 1906. THIS
SCHOONER WAS
BUILT IN
POCOMOKE CITY IN
1880.
*The Mariners'
Museum, Newport
News, VA.*

to dredge the almost clean bottom of Chesapeake Bay.

When the law allowed the dredging of Maryland's Chesapeake Bay bottom in 1865, the 500 or so licensed dredgers (and hundreds of pirates) cleaned it so quickly that the dredgers could no longer operate profitably within the legal boundaries. Very quickly the dredge boats crossed these invisible marks on the water and commenced filling their decks as they made licks (i.e. dredging runs) across bars reserved for tongers. A law officer wrote the Commander of the Maryland Marine police that "...dredgers have, for the time, taken possession of the St. Mary's [River], driving the licensed tong men from its waters and threatening destruction to property and death to the citizen who dares interfere." He said that at Benedict on the Patuxent River the tongers worked in daylight and the dredgers worked at night.[70]

Dredge-boat captains moved aggressively soon after Hunter Davidson quit his

command of Maryland's Marine Police. No one questioned his bravery, so a failed attempt to murder him by Gustavus T. Rice, master of the pungy *J. C. Mahoney*[71] had less effect on him than the rising influence of the packer-dredger alliance in Maryland politics. Through the decade starting in 1871, the dredging armada of pungy boats sailed almost at will on the Bay and its oyster-producing estuaries.

The occupation of Chesapeake Bay by dredge-boat fleets out of Baltimore and Somerset County in the 1870s eventually produced outrage in the 1880s. *Harper's Weekly* reported in January 1886 that the poachers' strategy called for actual attacks on the Bay's law enforcement, a supreme effort to break the will of the police-boat crews. In one attack dredge boats in Fishing Bay, Dorchester County, opened fire on the police steamer *Kent*. This attack failed, according to the journal, and the incident was one in a series of escalations by the pirates to rout the forces of the law.[72]

TRANSFERRING GRAIN FROM OXCART TO SKIFF TO PUNGY, CIRCA 1911. THE SCHOONER BEING LOADED MAY BE *FRANCIS J. RUTH*. *Maryland State Archives, Annapolis.*

IN THE FOREGROUND *MARY AND ELLEN*, IN THE REAR
ELLEN AND ALICE, BOTH PUNGY SCHOONERS BUILT
FOR DREDGING AND HAULING OYSTERS, AND OWNED
BY VIRGINIA WATERMEN STRUGGLING TO REBUILD
THEIR FISHERY AFTER THE CIVIL WAR.

Photograph courtesy of the author.

THE LAST
PILOT
SCHOONERS

The law was not powerless or timid. Captain Thomas C.B. Howard, as aggressive in 1888 as Commander Davidson was in 1868, took the police steamer *Governor McLane* into the Chester River looking for the *J.C. Mahoney* after her master, Gustavus T. Rice, fired on the Chesapeake Bay passenger steamer *Corsico*. *J.C. Mahoney* was another postwar pungy with a length on deck exceeding 63'. After the Civil War, schooner owners wanted more versatile craft, usable for multiple purposes, and able to sail outside the Bay.[73] Captain Howard found the *J.C. Mahoney* and rammed and sank her. Rice escaped but his crew, locked in the hold, drowned. Howard also managed to corner the pungy *Julia A. Jones*, and she too was sent to the bottom.[74]

While the Oyster Wars did not end until after World War II, firmer resolve by politicians, stronger police forces in Maryland and Virginia, and most of all a disappearing resource to fight over, reduced violence in the twentieth century. Nevertheless, there was violence. Raymond Spears, a Northern adventurer, writing in *Forest and Stream* in 1906, described what he found on Choptank River. "Capturing the violators is sometimes a matter of a wild midnight race along the river, firing the .45 till the pirate comes to, or vanishes in the murk. Sometimes there is shooting back, and the flash of the guns darts out from two craft in mimic warfare. Some men like that sort of thing and ride the waves of the bay regardless of consequences, so long as they can get huge catches of oysters."[75]

In addition to serving the oyster industry, many other pungies were used to carry cargo, within the Bay and up and down the coast, sometimes on the old pilot-schooner trade routes to and from the Caribbean. A typical vessel was *Francis J. Ruth*, built to carry freight to Jamaica and other West Indian islands and to return with cargoes of fruit. She entered this trade in the 1870s, completing the loop begun by pilot schooners pressed into West Indian service during the Revolution. In the fruit fleet of the 1870s, *Francis J. Ruth* sailed with *Ruth A. Price*, a pungy about 73' in overall length.[76] Both of these later nineteenth-century schooners, close to the measurements of *Virginia Ross* of 1820, were larger than *La Jacinthe* and *l'Anemone*, schooners of pilot-boat design built for the French Navy in 1823.[77]

The *Ruth A. Price* log records several voyages to Jamaica from Chesapeake Bay and back to Baltimore or Philadelphia. A rather spectacular voyage commenced at the Wicomico River at six in the morning on 18 April 1876, with her reaching the northeast end of Jamaica at midnight May 1— 13 days elapsed time including seven hours anchored off Fortune Island in the Bahamas riding out a storm. On the return voyage with a cargo of bananas, the pilot schooner took 14 days from Port Antonio to Brandywine River in Delaware Bay. Three days out of Jamaica her topmast was carried away.[78]

The log of the next voyage notes that she set a flying jib. For this trip, the big pungy loaded her cargo in eight hours and

THE PUNGY
FRANCIS J. RUTH,
BUILT TO CARRY
FREIGHT TO THE
WEST INDIES AND
BRING BACK
CARGOS OF FRUIT.
Photograph by
John G. Earle.

proceeded to sea 6 a.m., July 11. Eight days later she came abeam of Fortune Island. Three days later the mate, J.H. Baker, reported that fruit was ripening and some had begun to rot. The vessel made Fenwick Island light off the Maryland-Delaware coast July 28.[79] On a voyage from Philadelphia to Green Turtle Cay in the Bahamas, in 1877, the *Price*'s mate wrote

in the log on June 14th and 15th that the master took in all light sails, but unfortunately he does not identify these sails. From previous voyages it is known that she carried a flying jib and a topsail. She made 200 miles June 14th.[80] The last entries in the log concern a voyage from Port Antonio, Jamaica, to Baltimore in 1878. The mate, Charles Taylor, noted that

THE SURVIVING 5 PUNGIES. LEFT TO RIGHT ~
GENEVA A. KIRWIN ~ JAS.A.WHITING ~ WAVE ~ AMANDA F. LEWIS ~ MILDRED ADDISON

Ruth A. Price's cargo consisted of 1,863 bunches of bananas. Departing at 9:30 p.m., April 28, the *Price* had Cape Henry at the entrance of Chesapeake Bay bearing NW 8 miles at 8 a.m., May 9. The passage was made in 11 days.[81]

There exist no logs of any comparable voyages by Baltimore schooners, the largest and fastest pilot schooners, sailing between Jamaica and Chesapeake Bay. *Ruth A. Price*'s voyages must be compared to colonial Maryland craft. The Maryland-built sloop *Hopewell*, on a passage between Jamaica and Annapolis, took 33 days in 1753. An early Maryland-built schooner, *Sophia and Ann*, departed Jamaica 9 July 1756 and entered Annapolis August 25, 47 days enroute. In 1761, the schooner *Peggy* arrived at Oxford August 15, 33 days out of Jamaica. In 1769, *Molly and Sally* sailed into Baltimore June 15th, 27 days out of Jamaica.[82] Time passed, and shipwrights built faster schooners. The 69-ton-burden pilot schooner *Ruth A. Price* completed passages from Jamaica in less than half

THE LAST FIVE PILOT SCHOONERS, FROM A DRAWING BY LOUIS FEUCHTER. *Courtesy of the author.*

CHAPTER
TWELVE

that time, the best recorded being 11 days, as noted above.

In the twentieth century, the Bay's pungy schooners were used increasingly to carry freight. Pilot schooners and other baycraft remained in use on the Potomac River long after their numbers had waned on the rest of the Bay, and dozens of old pilot schooners played out the last act of their long history sailing between St. Mary's River in Maryland and from the Virginia creeks on the Potomac's south shore to Baltimore or Washington. Among the last pungies on the Potomac, and therefore the last pilot-boat schooners, were *Thomas Henry Bailey Brown*, in her last years called *Mildred Addison*[83] and *Patterson and Bash*,[84] built in Mathews County where shipwrights had built pilot schooners since the eighteenth century. The Chesser family of St. George Island[85] at the mouth of St. Mary's River owned several pungies, including *E.R.S. Daugherty*[86] and *J. S. Smith*.[87]

Not the last pungy, but supposedly the last one in freight service, *Amanda F. Lewis*, was built by Joseph W. Brooks in 1884 and owned by Gus Rice of Coan River, Virginia, a tributary of the Potomac. Rice was written about frequently as one of the last of the breed, and no one disturbed his folk-hero status to determine his relationship to the infamous Gustavus T. Rice. Rice and the pungy *Amanda F. Lewis* became symbols of bygone days that attracted painters, historians and photographers during the 1930s.[88]

Working out of his row house in east Baltimore, Louis Feuchter documented these last pilot schooners with some of the most beautiful paintings ever created of regional craft. Pungies were painted green and pink, so Feuchter approached Captain Rice to determine the mixture of colors normally used by pungy owners. Rice told him, first off, that it was not green and pink, but rather pungy bronze and flesh. The mixture for the bronze was made from dark blue, raw sienna and vermilion; the flesh was made from a mix of white, vermilion and a small amount of raw sienna.[89]

One reason for the continued use of pilot schooners to haul freight into the twentieth century was the stability of charges against the cargo. Sailing his pungy *Julia and Annie* from farms on the Potomac to the B&O grain elevator at Locust Point in Baltimore harbor in the early 1920s, Captain Clarence Biscoe charged 6 to 8 cents per bushel for transport. In 1828, almost 100 years earlier, the rate for hauling grain to Baltimore from the lower Bay (East River, Virginia), was 6-1/4 cents per bushel.[90] This price stability was made possible as costs to the pungy owners remained constant. The cost of new baycraft including pungies remained fairly level at approximately $2,500.00 throughout the nineteenth century except for the Civil War period.[91] Repairs done at Ewell's Marine Railway in the 1920s, according to twentieth-century schooner captain Clarence Biscoe, cost $3.00 per day for carpenters. The charge to haul the Biscoe family's *Julia and Annie* or *Francis J. Ruth* on the marine railway was $12.00. Thomas H. Hooper & Co.'s charge for haul-

SCHOONER
AMANDA F. LEWIS,
ALMOST THE LAST
OF THE PUNGIES.
Courtesy of the
author.

ing out at their Federal Hill yard in 1866 averaged $10.00. The labor charge was $3.00 a day.[92] In 1877, Isaac Davis's labor charge for repairs at Solomon & Sons and Davis was 30 cents an hour for a carpenter or $3.00 for a ten-hour day.[93] A Maryland ship carpenters' rate of pay in 1884 was $3.00 for a day's work.[94]

Even after World War I, M.M. Davis and Son, Inc., of Solomons paid top craftsmen only 65 cents per hour.[95] Staggering inflation came only after World War II, a result of influences that included America's involvement in massive international inflationary politics, the costs of hot and cold wars, a successful labor union movement, slower growth, and an explosion of the amount of paper money and credit. These brought to a close a century of price stability.

The pungy era on the Bay reveals not only price stability but an equally remarkable design stability. The pungy schooner *Mary and Ellen*, previously noted, was built just four years before Joseph W. Brooks of Dorchester County built the last pilot schooner. A baycraft, but large enough to run oysters north, she shows

striking similarities with the pilot schooners in Marestier's drafts. *Mary and Ellen* has sweeping sheer, a hogged bow and pronounced steeve to her bowsprit. In the photograph on page 264 she is pictured with *Ellen and Alice*, a schooner with a more traditional bow.[96] *Mary and Ellen*'s stern, described as elliptic, differed from the square sterns of earlier pilot schooners. These are details. More remarkable is how little the design changed over a century. *Mary and Ellen*'s under-deck capacity was 33.75 tons burden. She spent her last years in New Jersey and was abandoned in 1935.

Joseph Brooks built the last Chesapeake Bay pilot schooner, a pungy boat, in 1885. Brooks had built *Amanda F. Lewis* the year before. She hauled freight out of Coan River, a tributary of the Potomac, and was the last of her model in commercial service on the Bay. Her owner converted her to power in 1940.[97] *Wave*, a pungy converted to a yacht after decades of service as an oyster boat and Bay freighter, sank in 1957, five years short of her one hundredth year.[98]

ENDNOTES - CHAPTER TWELVE

1. *The Baltimore American,* 1 September 1831.

2. *The Baltimore Sun,* 5 July 1847.

3 Ibid., 29 November 1848.

4. Raphael Semmes, *Baltimore as Seen By Visitors, 1783-1860* (Baltimore: Maryland Historical Society, 1953). Quoting Captain Lauchlan B. Mackinnon, *Atlantic and Trans-Atlantic Sketches, Afloat and Ashore* (New York: 1852).

5. Robert G. Burgess, *Chesapeake Bay Craft, Part I* (Cambridge, Maryland: Tidewater Publishing Company, 1975), 59.

6. Assessor's Book of 1852. Maryland Hall of Records, hereafter cited as MdHR, 11597-8.

7. *Mary Francis,* pungy, Official No. 17874, built at Crisfield, 1842. MdHR 11597-8 and Hazen & Co. daybook, Maryland Historical Society, hereafter cited as MHS MS-1532.

8. *Black Hawk,* pungy, Assessor's book, MdHR 11597-8. Not listed elsewhere.

9. *Jerome Richardson,* pungy, 75003. *List of Merchant Vessels of the United States,* hereafter cited as LMV, 70. Assessor's book, MdHR 11597-8.

10. *Mary Wesley,* pungy, see Chapter VIII.

11. *George B. Foxwell,* pungy, built in Somerset County, 1852. Admeasurement book ., Folio 117, RG41, National Archives, hereafter cited as NA. Assessor's book, MdHR 11597-8.

12. Baltimore Board of Trade Report, 1859. MHS, MS-177.

13. Seventy-five pungies estimated built, 1861-65. Statistics compiled from lists of documented pungies in author's possession.

14. *Mary L. McGee,* pungy, 17875. LMV 87. Built at Baltimore 1864, Hazen & Co. daybook, MHS MS-1532; also Charles W. Booz and Sons account book, MHS MS-1267 & 1671.

15. *Robert H. Griffith,* pungy, 21025. LMV 93. Built at Baltimore 1864, Hazen, MHS, MS-1532.

16. Hazen, MHS, MS-1532.

17. Ibid.

18. *Ocean Wave,* pungy; *Official Records of the Union and Confederate Navies of the War of the Rebellion* (Washington, D.C.: U.S. Government Office, 1896), Series 1, Vol. 4, 591-93. U.S. Coast Guard Register Number 19251, built 1848, Somerset County or U.S. Coast Guard register Number 19528, year and date of building unknown, RG41, NA.

19. Ibid.

20. *Artist,* pungy, 874. Yorktown Enrollment 1866, RG41, NA. Built at Baltimore, 1850, William Skinner. Admeasurement Books, Folio 78, RG41, NA. Captured 25 July 1861, *Official Records,* V4, 586-87.

21. *Coquette,* pilot schooner, 4020, built at Baltimore 1855. LMV 1887. Sold in Prize Court, *Official Records,* V5, 344-490.

22. *Mount Vernon,* pungy, 16089, Built in Accomac, Virginia, LMV 93, Baltimore Enrollments, RG41, NA; also, Hazen, MHS, MS-1532.

23. *Pocohantas,* pungy, 20236, built in Mathews County, Virginia, 1848. LMV 93, Edwin W. Beitzell, *Life on the Potomac River* (Abell, Maryland: Author, 1968); Official Records, V4, 588, 603.

24. *Four Brothers,* possible pungy, 9803, LMV 93, built in Somerset County, Baltimore Enrollment #119, July 1861, RG41, NA. *Official Records,* V4, 409-774.

25. *Exchange,* pungy, 8381, built in Accomac County, Virginia, 1849. Solomons Account Book, Calvert Marine Museum, Booz Railway Book, MHS, MS-1267-1671; *Official Records,* V5, 209.

26. *Hampton,* pungy, 11908, built in Somerset County. LMV 93; Baltimore Enrollment #137, 1860, Official Records, V5, 209-13.

27. Treasury Department Correspondence, Georgetown Letters, E-1227, RG41, NA.

28. Board of Trade Permits, Harrison Collection, V8, 6-7. MHS, MS-432.

29. *Official Records,* V4, 586.

30. *Official Records,* V4, 586.

31. *Artist,* Note 20; *Official Records,* V4, 587.

32. *Chesapeake,* schooner, 5318, built in Somerset County, 1857. LMV 87. Probably not a pungy. *Official Records,* V4, 587.

33. *John McCabe.* No record. *Official Records,* V4, 587.

34. Maryland Laws, 1865, Chapter 181.

35. Richard H. Edwards, *The Oyster Interests of Maryland,*

Part C, Review of the Oyster Industry, *The Fisheries and Fishing Industries of the United States,* Edited by George Brown Goode. (Washington, D.C.: U.S. Government Printing Office, 1887), Section 11-C-159:429-39.

36. Hunter Davidson, *"Report Upon the Oyster Resources of Maryland to the Secretary of Labor and Agriculture, 1869",* MdHR, 19.

37. Charles H. Stevenson, *"The Oyster Industry in Maryland,"* Bulletin of the U.S. Commission of Fish and Fisheries, Washington, D.C., November 1893, 215. Stevenson, 265.

38. MdHR, 7887-13.

39. Statistics compiled from the author's pungy lists.

40. Stevenson, 265.

41. Ibid., 266.

42. Geoffrey M. Footner, *The Last Generation—A History of a Chesapeake Shipbuilding Family* (Solomons, Maryland: Calvert Marine Museum, 1991).

43. Ibid.

44. Isaac Solomon & Sons account book. Davis Archives, Calvert Marine Museum, hereafter cited as CMM.

45. *Isaac Solomon,* pungy, U.S. Coast Guard Number 100077; built at Solomons, 1872. LMV 93, Individual Vessel File RG41, NA; Isaac Davis daybook, CMM, Beitzell, 148.

46. *Daniel and Augustus,* pungy, USCR No. 6563, built at James Island, 1867 by Moses Geoghegan. Marion V. Brewington research files, CMM, LMV 93, Davis Daybook, CMM.

47. *Exchange,* pungy, see note #37; there existed at least two pungies by this name, (*Exchange,* U.S. Coast Guard Number 7341, LMV 93), Brewington Files, CMM.

48. *Carpenter,* pungy, U.S.Coast Guard Number 4396; LMV 87: built in Philadelphia, date unknown, Davis daybook, CMM.

49. *Dove,* pungy, U.S. Coast Guard Number 6387; LMV 93, and *Dove,* pungy, U.S. Coast Guard Number 6592, date and place of building unknown. LMV 93. Davis daybook, CMM, Beitzell, 142.

50. *Mary,* pungy, U.S. Coast Guard Number 16390, built 1848, Accomac County. LMV 93; Town Creek bond book, MdHR 13536/SSA 300; Loane Bros. sail plan books, Radcliffe Maritime Museum, MHS; Admeasurement Book B, Folio 208, RG41,NA.; Solomons account book, CMM. *Mary,* possible pungy, U.S. Coast Guard Number 16096, LMV 70. Also Admeasurement Book D, Folio 189, RG41, NA.

51. Solomons account book, CMM.

52. *American Eagle,* pungy, U.S. Coast Guard Number 1674. LMV 93 lists her as built at Solomons, 1869. Baltimore Enrollment #121, 28 September 1858, built in Somerset County, RG41, NA., Also Davis daybook, CMM.

53. *Father and Sons,* pungy, U.S. Coast Guard Number 9942, built at Newtown (Pocomoke City), 1870, LMV 93. Solomons account book, CMM; Beitzell, 144.

54. Solomons account book, CMM.

55. Ibid.

56. Ibid.

57. Percy Budlong's scrapbook, Vol. 3, after p. 103, Mariners' Museum, Newport News, Virginia.

58. Schooner *Resolution,* bill of sale. Copy in author's pos session.

59. Jeffery R. Bracket, "The Negro in Maryland," *Johns Hopkins University Studies in Historical and Political Science,* Herbert B. Adams, Editor. Vol. 4, 206. Also, Maryland Laws, 1836, Chapter 150.

60. Virginia Laws, 17 March 1856. Inspection certificate in collection of Howard and Louise Adkins, Salisbury, Maryland.

61. "Hunter Davidson, Report upon the Oyster Resources of Maryland to the Secretary of Labor and Agriculture, 1869", MdHR PAM 1393.

62. Edwards-Goode, *The Oyster Interests in Virginia,* 11-C-160:440.

63. From List of Merchant Vessels of the United States and the author's pungy records.

64. Davis daybook, CMM.

65. Hazen, MHS, MS-1532.

66. Thomas H. Hooper & Co., daybook, MHS, MS-1532.

67. Booz, MHS, MS 1267 & 1671.

68. *Mary and Ellen,* pungy, built Baltimore, 1881, Yorktown carpenter certificate signed by Henry Brusstar & Bro., and Yorktown enrollment #8, 29 August 1881, RG41, NA. Also see *Mary and Ellen,* pungy, 91357, LMV 1887 and 1930. A half model in the

collection of the Museum of American History, Smithsonian Institution, on loan to Calvert Marine Museum. Reference USNM 160120. See also, *The National Watercraft Collection,* U.S. National Museum Bulletin 219, Howard I. Chapelle, Curator, Museum of History and Technology (Washington, D.C., U.S. Government Printing Office, 1976) 199; and *Historic American Merchant Marine Survey,* Eric Steinlein, Delegate, Survey 5-56, 1 & 2, Works Progress Administration, Washington, D.C.: U.S. Government Printing Office, 1983. Written on the underside of the *Mary and Ellen* half-model is the following in script: U.S.N.M. 160,120, Oyster schooner *Mary Ellen,* built Baltimore, Maryland, 1859. Scale 7/16 inch to 1 ft. Gift of William Skinner & Son. Collected by J.W. Collins. Then the notation, upside-down, *Mary & Ellen.* Chapelle's *The National Watercraft Collection* states that William Skinner and Son built *Mary and Ellen* in 1858, a statement that disagrees with the information on the back of the model and with Custom House enrollments of 1858 and 1859, RG41, NA. There are no Baltimore enrollments or registrations in 1857 through 1862 of a Baltimore-built schooner named *Mary and Ellen.* An alternate conclusion is that the half model is not a builder's model of 1858-59, but is a half-hull model of the pungy *Mary and Ellen,* built at Baltimore in 1881 by Henry Brusstar & Brothers. This pungy measured 64.4' x 20.8' x 6.3', according to her carpenter's certificate, dimensions similar to the measurements (64' 10" X 20') taken off the half model. Both agree with the information contained in *Mary and Ellen'*s first enrollment at Yorktown.

69. Author's statistics: Home ports, 1893: Delaware Bay-33; Virginia-138, Baltimore-181; Crisfield-125; and Miscellaneous-38. Source: LMV 93.

70. S.O.P. Reports, MdHR 7887-26.

71. *J.C. Mahoney,* pungy, U.S. Coast Guard Number 12491, built at Somerset County, 1870. LMV 93; Davis daybook, CMM.

72. "The Oyster War," *Harpers Weekly,* New York, 9 January 1886.

73. Analysis of a sample of 72 documented pungies built after 1871 produces an average length overall of 59.5' and depth of 5.7'. Source: Author's lists.

74. *Julia A. Jones,* pungy, U.S. Coast Guard Number 75173, built at Baltimore, 1869. LMV 93; Admeasurement Book 11, Folio 204. RG41, NA. John R. Wennersten, *The Oyster Wars of Chesapeake Bay* (Centreville, Maryland: Tidewater Publishers, 1981), 78-81.

75. Raymond S. Spears, "A Cruise in a Converted Canoe," *Forest and Stream,* 24 November 1906, 808.

76. *Francis J. Ruth,* pungy, U.S. Coast Guard Number 120011, built at Dorchester County, 1871, by Joseph W. Brooks, LMV 93. Marion V. Brewington, *Chesapeake Bay, A Pictorial Maritime History* (New York: Bonanza Books, 1953), 89; Robert H. Burgess, *Chesapeake Circle,* (Cambridge, Maryland: Cornell Maritime Press, Inc. 1965), 9; Beitzell, 59, 60, 146 and 279.

77. *Ruth A. Price,* pungy, U.S. Coast Guard Number 110082, built in Somerset County, 1873. LMV 93. Though called a pungy, she was a pilot schooner similar in size to coastal schooners such as *Iowa* of 1844 and *Virginia Ross,* 1820. *Price* measured 73.3' x 23.8' x 7.9'; *Ross* measured 67'6" x 20'6" x 7'10". *Price's* wide and shallow hull is comparable to post-War, of-1812 pilot schooners.

78. Log of the *Ruth A. Price,* Wicomico Historical Society, Salisbury, Maryland.

79. Ibid.

80. Ibid.

81. Ibid.

82. Annapolis and Baltimore pre-federal Naval Officer Reports, entrances and clearances. MdHR 1372-1-2.

83. *Mildred Addison* ex. *Thomas Henry Bailey Brown,* pungy. U.S. Coast Guard Number 24858, built at Somerset County, 1870. LMV 93; Beitzell, 256; Charles G. Davis, *Ships of the Past* (New York: Bonanza Books, 1939), 40, 42.

84. *Patterson and Bush,* pungy, U.S. Coast Guard Number 150095, built in Mathews County, Virginia, 1876. LMV 1893; Beitzell, 276; Norfolk Enrollments, 1865-76, RG41, NA.

85. Philip J. Chesser, "Home for Christmas," *Chesapeake Bay Magazine,* January 1986, 45; Wendell J. Chesser, "From Boyhood to Manhood Aboard a Pungy," *Chesapeake Bay Magazine,* November 1988, 33.

86. *E. R. S. Daugherty*, pungy, U.S. Coast Guard 135161, built in Somerset County, 1875. LMV 93; Beitzell, 266,

272, 286. Beitzell writes that the *Daugherty* had a centerboard. If this is correct, watermen would refer to
her as a she-pungy.

87. *J. S. Smith*, pungy, U.S. Coast Guard Number 75415,
built in Somerset County, 1872. LMV 93; Beitzell, 291;
Chesser articles.

88. Eric J. Steinlein, "Amanda Lewis Is Last of Bay's True
Clippers, "*The Baltimore Sun*, 6 March 1938; *"In
Pursuit of the Pungy,"* *The Skipper*, April 1965; "Pungy
Boats of the Chesapeake," *WoodenBoat*, Vol. 45, April,
1984, 57. Howard I. Chapelle, *The American Fishing
Schooners, 1825-1935* (New York: W.W. Norton & Co.,
1973), 66, 83, 86, 89 and 90. On page 90, Chapelle
drew lines of Half Model USNM 76101, from the collection of The Smithsonian Institution. He calls her a
pungy. She is not. See also *The National Watercraft
Collection*, by Chapelle; pages 15, 25, 40, 43, 67, 167-
68, and 194-206. See Brewington, *Chesapeake Bay, A
Pictorial Maritime History*, Burgess, *Chesapeake Circle*,
and Frederick Tilp, *This Was the Potomac River*
(Alexandria, Virginia: Author, 1978).

89. Undated postcard from Robert H. Burgess to Mr.
Geoghegan of The Smithsonian Institution, with a
note added by Louis Feuchter, artist. Museum of
American History, Transportation Division, The
Smithsonian Institution.

90. Christopher Tompkins Account Book, Virginia
Historical Society: MSS 1-T 599 6c, 161.

91. Ibid.,Tompkins paid $2,450 for a schooner, fitted-out,
in 1831; Dorchester Assessor Book, 1852, new pungy
assessment, $2,000, MdHR 11597-98

92. Hooper account book, MHS, MS-1532.

93. Davis daybook, 120.

94. First Biennial Report, Bureau of Industrial Statistics
(Maryland), 181.

95. Geoffrey Footner, *The Last Generation*, 108.

96. *Ellen and Alice*, pungy, USCR No. 135268, built at
Gloucester, Virginia, 1877, John Earle's vessel list.
MHS, MS-2306; LMV 1887 and 1930.

97. *Amanda F. Lewis*, pungy boat, carpenter certificate
signed by Joseph W. Brooks, 1884. Record Group 41,
National Archives, Washington, D.C.; Robert H.
Burgess,

Chesapeake Circle (Cambridge, Maryland: Cornell
Maritime Press, Inc., 1965), 197; M.V. Brewington,
Chesapeake Bay, A Pictorial Maritime History
(Cambridge, Maryland: Cornell Maritime Press, Inc.,
1953), 89, 164; U.S. Coast Guard Documentation
Number 106304, LMV, 25th List (Washington, D.C.:
U.S. Government Printing Office, 1893).

98. *Wave*, pungy boat, built Accomac County, 1863; sank,
Zug Island Canal, Detroit, Michigan, 24 June 1957:
U.S. Coast Guard official No. 26694; RG41, NA.

EPILOGUE

During the second half of the nineteenth century, the fleets of Chesapeake Bay schooners diminished as gains by steamship lines, with increasingly reliable service and greater capacity, forecast the end of commercial sail. Owners of fast schooners observed the scales tip against them as capacity replaced speed on most trade routes where sail was still economical. Large bulky schooners, brigs, barks, and ships able to carry more freight more economically were built to haul specific cargoes such as ice, fertilizer, coal, coffee and other bulk commodities. The time of the fast sailing vessel on most trade routes was passing. An arguable exception was the great American and British clipper period of mid-century, which arrived suddenly and departed just as quickly a few decades later.

On Chesapeake Bay, full-built clump and centerboard schooners with greater capacity than pilot schooners took over a large portion of the intra-Bay and coastwise trade. But surviving pilot schooners stayed busy on the Bay after the Civil War, mostly because of their usefulness in the oyster trade. The pungies were quick and strong, taking their licks on the Bay's oyster bars. And when they were replaced by bugeyes and skipjacks after 1880, they found employment for a while as oyster runners. Speed was still an attraction as watermen delivered loads of oysters in one day to Baltimore and two days to Philadelphia.

The building of pilot schooners ended in 1885, the launchings of bugeyes about two decades later. Production of skipjacks continued as a result of a political decision to make dredging legal for sailing vessels only. Had it not been for this conservation law, the small gasoline engine which came to the waterfront at the turn of the century would have eliminated the old two-sail bateau, too.

The principal subject of this book is a schooner model that remained useful in its home waters from the 1730s to 1935. Although various versions differed in size, its hull and rig remained essentially the same. Schooner boats of 1750, Baltimore schooners of 1812, Baltimore clippers of 1840, and the pungies of the last half of the nineteenth century were of the same distinctive pilot-boat design.

That there existed a single design for roughly 150 years is important, even remarkable. Beginning with the pilot boat of Hampton and Annapolis, and then finding trade as a grain carrier to Baltimore in 1750, across centuries to Captain Biscoe's grain-hauling pungies of the 1920s, the baycraft version worked. The Chesapeake Bay pilot schooner's role in America's first six wars: the Revolution, the Quasi War with France, the Barbary Wars, the War of 1812, the Mexican War and the Civil War, was significant. As a slaver, as the celebrated Baltimore clipper, as carrier of Baltimore's fine flour, opium clipper, packet boat, coffee schooner, blockade-runner, fruit schooner, naval schooner for several navies, and most importantly, and through many decades, as cargo carrier out of Baltimore and other world ports, these vessels served their owners profitably. As pilot boats, as revenue cutters, and in yachting, their success is legendary.

Virginia, long credited with the development of pilot schooners, was dominated by planter-merchants who, for the most part, owned sloops. Marylanders, particularly Baltimore merchants, were the driving force behind the development of fast schooners. Ironically, the pilot schooner may have originated in the Hampton Roads area of Virginia, and some of the finest builders of pilot boats, commercial pilot schooners and the offshore Baltimore schooners were Virginians. Nevertheless, most of Chesapeake Bay's pilot-schooner fleet operated out of Maryland. Only one or two of the Baltimore armed schooners of 1812 are known to have had Virginia owners.

Although the Baltimore armed schooner of the War of 1812 gained fame during that conflict, the model originally developed in response to France's *guerre de course* against Great Britain's merchant service in 1793. Its renown grew during America's Quasi War with France in 1798, and particularly after the successes of the United States Navy's two Baltimore schooners, USS *Experiment* and USS *Enterprize*. Offshore pilot schooners reached full glory as blockade runners in 1807. Called "pilot-boat built" by builders that included William Price and Thomas Kemp, these large pilot schooners replaced traditional topsail schooners. It was an act of self-preservation for Baltimore merchants to desert their conventional fleet for Baltimore schooners, pilot-boat built, after their success in the French West Indies and during the Quasi War.

And although William Price and his colleagues at Fells Point were in the forefront of the development of the Baltimore schooner, the offshore model did not originate at Fells Point. When offshore versions of typical baycraft appeared after 1792, they were built at locations all over the Bay, and particularly at St. Michaels on the Eastern Shore and in Mathews County in Virginia.

The Chesapeake pilot schooner, a design which changed only in details over this long period, spread around the world. Care must accompany any conclusions concerning the spread of the design of the Chesapeake Bay pilot schooner to other countries, or even in America after 1830. There exists the danger of crediting the design, after a century of existence, with a patent on its components, routinely incorporated into new schooners by shipwrights and naval architects everywhere. If claims on behalf of the Chesapeake Bay pilot schooner are made they relate to the original model, and then very carefully to clones. Schooners of the pilot-boat model from other regions and countries are presented here to establish the importance of the Chesapeake Bay model throughout the maritime world. Secondly, by discussing foreign versions of the Chesapeake Bay pilot schooner, claims to the origin of the model, common around the world, will subside as information about these influential schooners' origins in Virginia and Maryland spreads.

APPENDIX A

1. COST OF THE BALTIMORE SCHOONER *PATAPSCO*

A. To Thomas Kemp's account, ($5556.48):

Kemp's invoice included the charge for sheathing *Patapsco*'s hull, but not the cost of the copper sheets ($1642.20). Furthermore, owner Andrew Clopper supplied Kemp with copper bolts and spikes ($952.77) and with patent nails ($231.50). All other costs for labor and materials for the schooner's hull and spars were included in the shipwright's charge of $26 per ton. Kemp opened a yard in Fells Point in 1804 as a maker of masts and spars. He built his initial reputation in this speciality. Kemp received the contract to make the frigate USS *Java*'s masts and spars in 1814, for which he was paid $3728.00.[1]

B. For hemp rope ($2092.54):

As the vessel's husbanding agent, Clopper was an astute purchaser. Instead of buying thousands of feet of rope to rig *Patapsco*, he purchased raw hemp and then contracted with John Gordon's ropewalk ($342.54) to have it made into rope. Hemp fiber can be any one of several fibers when the word is used in a generic sense for rope. Cannabis sativa was widely used for cordage. Gordon's firm spun the hemp into threads, called yarns, then twisted the threads into strands. On a ropewalk, the strands were wound together into rope. A tar coat to the finished rope made it waterproof.

C. For sailcloth and a sailmaker ($1802.20):

Clopper once again pinched his supplier by purchasing sailcloth in bolts and then awarding a contract to the sailmaker, B. Hardister & Co., to cut and sew *Patapsco*'s sails. He paid only $457.70 to the sailmaker and $1344.50 for sailcloth, no doubt less than the cost would have been if Hardister had made the outlay for cloth.

Clopper purchased a total of 72 pieces of sailcloth. If the assumption is made that one piece equals a bolt of 100 yards, his purchase totaled 7200 yards. One third of the cloth consisted of regular Russian duck, a flax or linen cloth. He purchased 1300 yards of lightweight Russian duck and five bolts of Russian sheeting, an even lighter linen cloth, and nineteen bolts of Raven's duck, a fine quality hemp cloth. Of special note, Hardister cut sails from 300 yards of No. 4 cotton duck and 700 yards of No. 3 cotton duck, a cloth only just beginning to be used for sails.

Isaac McKim wrote in 1829[2] that to his knowledge the Baltimore schooner *Tuckahoe* used cotton sails first in 1813, and that she had a reputation for outsailing all other Baltimore schooners. McKim said that in 1815 he had the sails of two schooners, *Tropic* and *Plattsburg*, made of cotton, and both were "uncommon fast sailing vessels." He wrote that in the year 1823 he built the fast-sailing schooner Yellot, "and this vessel's sails are entirely made of cotton, both light and heavy sails; her reputation for fast sailing is not exceeded, if equalled, by any vessel in her class." George Gardner built *Yellot* and he described her as "pilot-boat built" on his carpenter certificate.[3]

McKim, in his letter, gave three reasons why cotton was superior to linen: it costs less, it outlasts linen, and a vessel with a suit of cotton sails will sail nearly a mile an hour faster. He closed by saying that "all the fast sailing boats in the Chesapeake Bay have no other sails than cotton duck."

D. To Thomas Morrell, blacksmith ($827.77):

Hardware for a Baltimore schooner consisted of a multitude of iron fittings, much of it crafted by independent blacksmiths: iron spikes, bolts, plates, straps, hooks, pins, shackles, sheaves, hinges, nails and all sorts of iron manufactures made for the hull and standing rigging.

E. To the plumber ($420.05):

Davis McCaughan, a highly specialized craftsman, was hired to fair the transverse frames, a skill sometimes called "horning the frames."

F. To John Share, brass founder ($119.21):

Brass for early nineteenth-century shipbuilding consisted of copper and tin. It had various applications for fittings, hardware and equipment aboard sailing vessels. Polished brass used with fine woods for joiner work made the interior finish of vessels beautiful.

G. To John Illard, rigger ($183.00):

A rigger's work had the same importance to a sailing vessel as a mechanic's work has today for an engine. There are two types of rigging, standing and running. Standing rigging consists of the blocks, lines, ropes, eyebolts, deadeyes, lanyards, shrouds, stays, all utilized primarily to support the masts and other spars. Running rigging consists of lines and tackle used to hoist and lower sails and to adjust the sails underway.

H. For ballast ($214.00):

While Thomas Kemp called *Patapsco* "privateer-built," Clopper and his consortium planned to send her out as a letter-of-marque trader. With cargo in her hold she required less ballast. Only thirteen tons–8 tons of stones, 2 tons of iron, and 3 tons of kentledge–were placed in her bilges. The purpose of ballast was to increase stability by lowering the center of gravity.

I. For ship's anchors (235.87):

Patapsco's anchors consisted of light and heavy types. For mooring the crew set heavy anchors. She carried a kedge anchor aboard to assist in floating the schooner if she ran aground or as a second anchor for holding the schooner fast in a fixed position. Blacksmiths made and sold anchors as stock items.

J. For arms, guns and powder ($1299.05):

Patapsco's first letter-of-marque commission, dated 15 September 1812, and numbered 460,[4] stated that the schooner mounted six carriage guns for her first voyage. Clopper's account includes only four guns purchased from Thomas Tenant. In addition to the ammunition for the carronades, *Patapsco*'s arms locker contained small arms and cutlasses. She was lightly armed; *Patapsco*'s owners did not expect that she would engage an enemy warship. If a Royal Navy ship did overtake her, this would probably be a consequence of being caught in a calm or on a lee shore, and her guns would then be of no use in her defense.

K. To William Jackson, block maker ($440.28):

The block maker's work could be compared in importance to a modern gear maker. A crew's seamanship, sail changes, reefing, in fact all sailhandling, depended on the quality of the rigging blocks. A Baltimore schooner was fitted with hundreds of blocks and spares.

L. For rigging leathers ($91.76):

Riggers employed leather to protect rope from chafing against a spar, a stay, or at the clew of a sail.

M. For boats, sweeps and oars ($199.50):

Baltimore schooners carried rowing boats as tenders and for towing in calm weather. Schooners, equipped with long oars called sweeps, could gain mobility and maneuverability for offense or defense, or to attempt an escape in a calm. Sweeps were used to maneuver during an engagement, to overhaul a prize or to flee if an enemy gained an upper hand.

N. To the cooper ($199.51):

John Fitz, the cooper working on *Patapsco* during construction, made the casks and barrels for the storage of water and spirits as well as for the storage of the crew's food supply. He built them on deck and in the ship's hold.

O. For ship's chandlery ($293.40):

A chandler is a supplier of miscellaneous equipment including candles, oil, galley utensils, food products, and fittings. Chandleries also provided slopchest items for a vessel's crew.

P. For a caboose $66.19):

The patent caboose, a stove or more properly an oven, was usually attached to the deck and used by cooks, principally to bake bread. The cook and his helpers baked and prepared meals for up to 120 men on privateers and for smaller crews on trading vessels. The captain considered the quality of meals critical to the maintenance of discipline. The master of the privateer *Harpy* awarded his ship's cook a dozen lashes for failure to cook the peas fully in the crew's soup.[5]

Q. For crew expenses and advances ($1683.68):

According to her commission, *Patapsco*'s complement of men, including officers and prizemasters, totaled forty on her maiden voyage. This number was more than she would carry in peaceful times on a cargo run, but a number far less than signed on for a privateer cruise. Captain James M. Mortimer, *Patapsco*'s master, received voyage instructions from her owners and a policy on the division of prize money. Owners reserved one half of the prize money, and under *Patapsco*'s plan the other half, divided in twentieths, included the following distribution:

Captain ---------3/20
Officers & clerks-1/20, each, total six
Crew-----------11/20

The crew expenses for the vessel's account included advances and fees for recruiting paid to Farrel and James, crew agents.

R. For stores ($617.97):

Due to space limitations and spoilage, the crew's grub was simple and limited: salt meat, bread, beans and peas, along with potatoes and onions. The men got daily rations of spirits: beer, cider or hard liquor. *Patapsco* carried three half barrels of flour for bread. Cooperage companies made special half barrels for "owners of sharp pilot built vessels."[6]

S. For a medicine chest ($38.50):

General practice required the vessel to have on board a man trained in medicine, particularly in bone-setting and dressing wounds.

T. To Thomas Galloway, painter ($128.63):

The topsides of Baltimore schooners were normally painted black, but occasionally two or more colors.

U. To William Denny, joiner ($310.99):

A joiner is a craftsman with wood, and was a vessel's cabinetmaker for paneling, doors, skylights, interior stairs, ladders and cabin furniture.

V. For port charges and voyage expenses ($164.20):

A vessel sailing to a foreign port will pay certain government fees and taxes.

There were clearance charges at the Baltimore Custom House, and consular fees paid to the resident representative of the overseas country of destination. The French fees for *Patapsco*'s first voyage included a charge for a visa and for the certification that the cargo's origin was the United States of America. Thomas Tenant received wharfage fees while Clopper berthed *Patapsco* at his George Street (now Thames St.) wharf in Fells Point to be outfitted and loaded. Voyage costs included pilotage to the Chesapeake capes, and were based on *Patapsco*'s draft of fifteen feet. There was also a three-day detention charge, due to bad weather or the British blockade.

W. For miscellaneous expenses ($285.97-1/2):

Mostly self-explanatory except for "punk," which is dried wood used to kindle the cook's stove.

The grand total for building, outfitting, obtaining a crew, port and voyage charges and miscellany, was $19,815.56.

Endnotes

1. Kemp Papers: Maryland Historical Society, MHS-MS2335.

2. Remarks and Correspondence on the use of Cotton Canvas: (Washington, DC: Jonathan Elliott, 1829), quotes a letter from Isaac McKim to Warren R. Davis, dated Baltimore, 15 August 1829, 13-14.

3. *Yellot*, pilot-built schooner, carpenter certificate signed by George Gardner, 29 October 1823. RG41, National Archives.

4. Jerome R. Garitee, *The Republic's Private Navy* (Middletown, Connecticut: Wesleyan University Press for Mystic Seaport, Inc.), Appendix A, 251-56.

5. Maryland Historical Society, MS 2321.

6. The *Baltimore American*, 21 January 1813.

2. ESTIMATE OF EXPENSE OF BUILDING AND EQUIPPING AS A VESSEL OF WAR, A SCHOONER OF 150 TONS, 1820

Hull, including ship carpenter's bill, live oak	@ $30./Ton -	$ 4500.00
Sheating, Copper, Etc.	@ $10./TON -	1500.00
Iron and smith bill	@ $ 8./TON -	1200.00
Cables, rigging & Cordage	@ $15./TON -	2250.00
Sails, masting & Rigging	@ $12./TON -	1800.00
Joiners & Carvers	@ $ 3./TON -	450.00
Coopers, Painters & Tanners	@ $ 3./TON -	450.00
Blockmakers, boatbuilders, plumbers and turners	@ $ 4./TON -	600.00
Armament, guns & cutlasses, bording pikes and battle axes	@ $12./TON -	1800.00
Contingencies		1000.00
Total estimated Cost		$15500.00

From documents accompanying the Bill to Authorize the Building of a Certain Number of Small Vessels, 27 March 1820. (Printed by order of Congress by Gales and Seaton, Washington, DC.)

Appendix B

**P-50. HULL PLANS, *EXPERIMENT*,
DATED 1825**

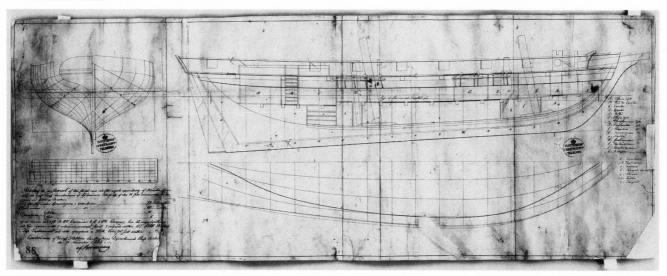

1. Translation Of The Text In The Drawing

One Swedish fot equals .2969 meter; ten tum equal one fot: drawing for a schooner of the same size as, and after measurements taken carefully of, the schooner *Experiment*, with which the schooners *Falk* and *Activ* are being built.

She is armed with six 12-pound cannon and two 4-pound cannon; has a crew of 24 men; can hold supplies for three months, water for one month. Displacement at above draft is 3204 cubic fot, salt water. Signed: Royal Navy Construction Department, Karlskrona, 6 September, 1830.

HULL PLANS FOR SWEDISH ROYAL NAVY SCHOONER *EXPERIMENT*, 1825.

Krigsarkivet, Stockholm.

Length from stem to stern between rabbets at waterline-	73 fot, 4 tum
Breadth moulded at waterline-	20 fot, 4-3/4 tum
Draft aft-	10 fot, 3 tum
Draft forward-	6 fot, 9 tum

P-51. SAIL PLAN, *Experiment,* **1815**

2. Translation of text and conversion of measurements from Swedish square fot to square meters. [one Swedish square fot equals 0.088 square meter]

Main Sail	1548 sq. fot	136.22 sq. meters
Gaff Topsail	240 " "	21.12 " "
Foresail	1258 " "	110.7 " "
Staysail [Jib]	780 " "	68.64 " "
Lower Fore Topgallant	819 " "	72.07 " "
Fore Topgallant	226 " "	19.89 " "
Jib	611 " "	53.77 " "
Flying Jib (middle)	449 " "	39.51 " "
Boomed square foresail		
(course sail)	no measurements provided	
Ringtail	" " "	
Outermost jib	" " "	

3. Inventory of *Experiment*'s tackle (standing & running rigging) located at Karlskrona's Maritime Museum. From this list, which encompasses 44 pages, the dimensions of *Experiment*'s spars were abstracted: (Swedish fot = .2969 meter).

Mainmast, length, deck to crosstree -	53 fot	15.74 meters
Mainmast, length to masthead -	8 "	2.38 "
Foremast, length, deck to crosstree -	51.5 "	15.29 "
Foremast, length to masthead -	7.5 "	2.23 "
Bowsprit, length, stem to forestay -	16 "	4.75 "
Jib-boom, extreme length -	22 "	6.53 "
Maintopmast, extreme length -	24 "	7.13 "
Maintopmast to crosstree -	23.5 "	6.98 "
Maintopmast head, length -	9 "	2.67 "
Foretopmast, extreme length -	25 "	7.42 "
Foretopmast to crosstree -	20.3 "	6.03 "
Mainboom, length -	32 "	9.50 "
Ringtail yard -	11 "	3.27 "

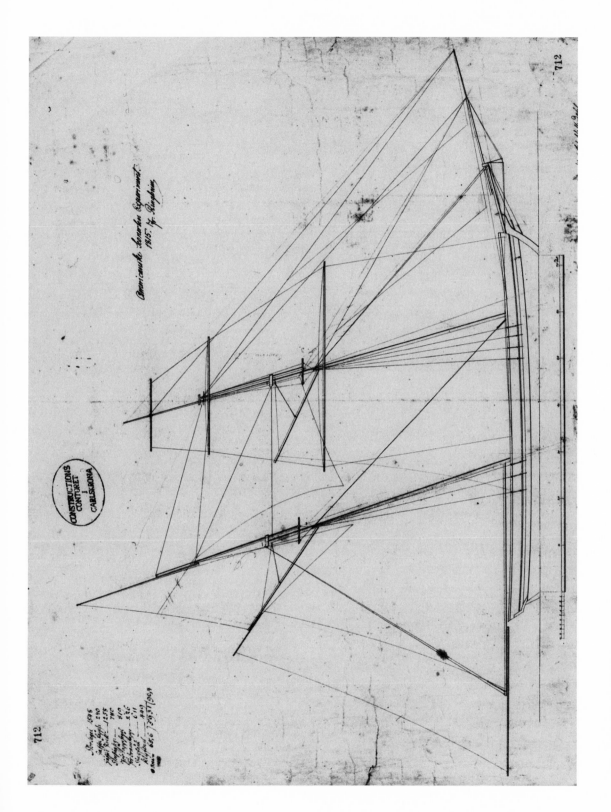

SAIL PLAN FOR EXPERIMENT.

Krigsarkivet, Stockholm.

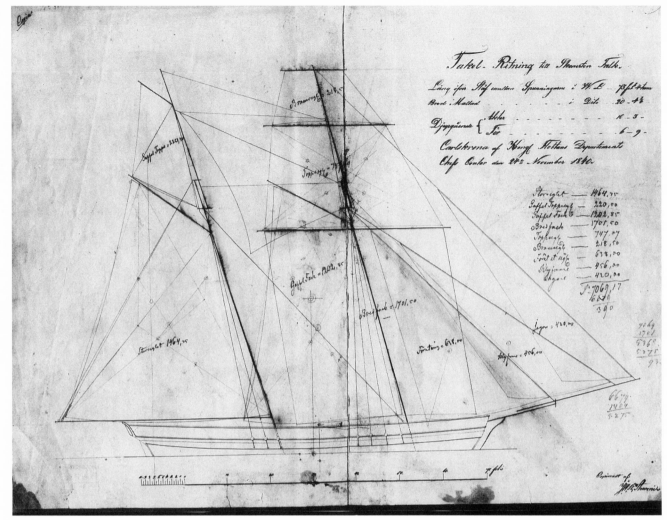

SAIL PLAN FOR
SWEDISH ROYAL
NAVY SCHOONER
FALK.
Krigsarkivet,
Stockholm

P-52. *FALK'S* SAIL PLAN

4. *Falk*'s Sail Dimensions (Conversion Of Sail Sizes From Swedish Square Fot and Tum To Square Meters)

Sail	Swedish Square Fot	Square Meters
Main Sail	1464.0	128.83
Main Gaff Topsail	220.5	19.40
Foresail	1202.85	105.85
Fore Square Sail	1701.5	149.73
Fore Gallant	747.07	65.74
Fore Top Gallant	218.5	19.23
Fore Staysail	638.0	56.14
Jib	456.0	40.13
Flying Jib	420.0	36.96

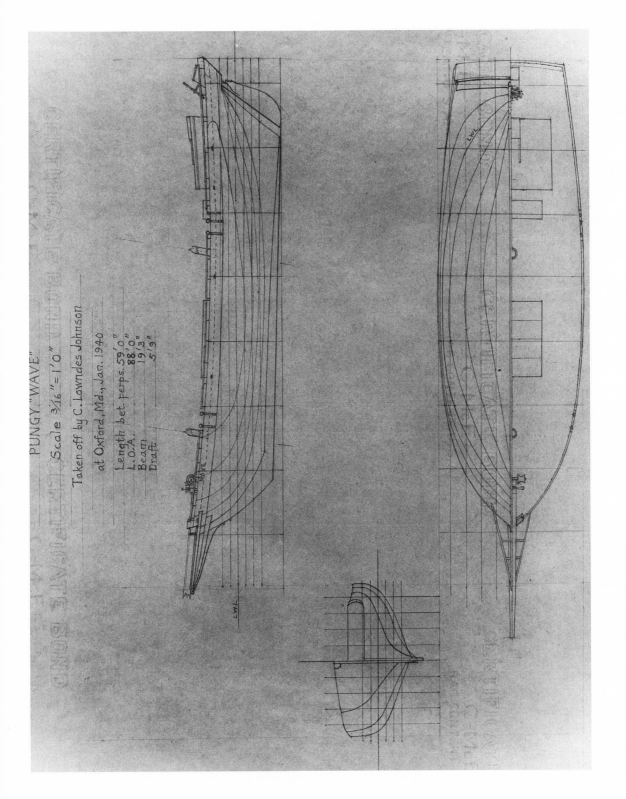

PUNGY "WAVE"

Scale 3/16" = 1' 0"

Taken off by C. Lowndes Johnson

at Oxford, Md., Jan. 1940

Length bet. perps.	59' 0"
L.O.A.	88' 0"
Beam	19' 3"
Draft	5' 9"

LINES OF PUNGY WAVE, TAKEN OFF AND DRAWN

BY C. LOWNDES JOHNSON

Maryland Historical Society. Baltimore.

289

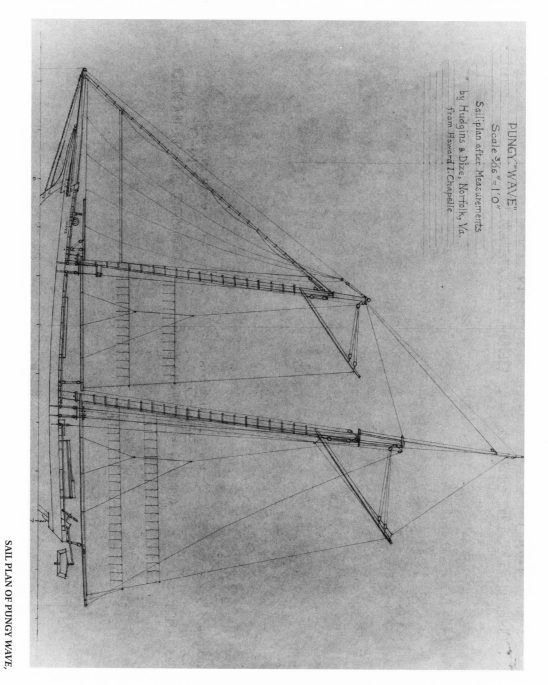

PUNGY "WAVE"
Scale 3/16" = 1'0"
Sail plan after Measurements
by Hudgins & Dize, Norfolk, Va.
from Howard I. Chapelle

SAIL PLAN OF PUNGY WAVE,
REDRAWN BY HOWARD CHAPELLE.
Maryland Historical Society, Baltimore.

GLOSSARY

AMIDSHIPS–a location near the middle of the vessel or the middle portion of the vessel's hull volume.

BADGES–carved ornaments on a vessel around its quarter or stern windows.

BAYCRAFT–a generic term applied to craft built to sail within the confines of Chesapeake Bay.

BILGE–the bottom of a vessel from the keel outward to the point where it turns to form the topsides.

BRIG–a square-rigged vessel of two masts with foremast and mainmast rigged with yards and square sails.

BULWARK–a raised, fully planked rail around the edge of the main deck.

BUOYANCY–the property of rising or floating in the sea. The center of buoyancy is the point that marks the center of the weight of the displaced water.

BUTTOCKS–the concave or convex part of the vessel's stern forward of the post and above the waterline.

CEILING–the inner planking of a vessel.

CUTWATER–a carved timber covering the stem and the keel at the point of their scarfed intersection.

DEADRISE–the angle that a vessel's bottom, floor and frame rise above the horizontal.

DEPTH OF HOLD–a measurement taken at the center of the mid-section from the top of the keelson to the underside of the main deck.

DRAG OF THE KEEL–the difference between the depth of the bow and that of the deeper stern.

DRAFT–the depth that a vessel sinks when afloat, measured from the waterline to the lowest point of the immersed part of the hull.

EXTREME BREADTH–the width of a vessel at its mid-section measured from the outside of its planks above the wales.

FLOOR(or FRAME FLOOR)–the first set of timbers fitted to the keel to which the futtock timbers are attached that form the vessel's frame.

FLUSH DECK–a deck that extends from end to end and from rail to rail with only hatch coamings and cabin tops protruding above it.

FULL-BUILT HULL–one with a conservative amount of deadrise from the keel outward to the point where it turns sharply upward, producing a full body to the rail.

FUTTOCKS–the shaped timbers that, when scarfed and bolted together and to the vessel's floor timbers, form the hull's frame.

GALLERY–a balcony or platform projecting from each quarter or around the stern of a vessel.

HERMAPHRODITE BRIG–a two-masted vessel, square-rigged on her foremast and schooner rigged on her main mast, (sometimes called a schooner-brig on Chesapeake Bay). A vessel thus rigged is called a brigantine in Great Britain and a brick-goélette in France.

LENGTH OF KEEL, STRAIGHT RABBET– a measurement from the sternpost to the point of intersection of the keel with the curve of the stem.

LENGTH ON DECK (LENGTH OVERALL)–the straight-line distance measured just above the main deck between the fore part of the stem and the after part of the sternpost.

MIDSECTION–the line along which is measured a vessel's extreme and moulded breadth.

MOULDED BREADTH–the widest part of a vessel measured from the outside of the mid-section frames.

PILOT BOAT–as originally defined on Chesapeake Bay, these were small schooners used to deliver and retrieve pilots to and from offshore vessels on the Bay. When these vessels were adapted to carry grain to Baltimore or as navy craft during the Revolutionary War, they were still called pilot boats, the name used generically thereafter for baycraft schooners.

PILOT SCHOONER, PILOT-BOAT SCHOONER, AND SCHOONER, PILOT-BOAT BUILT–names given to sharp-built keel schooners designed on the pilot-boat model from before the middle of the eighteenth century to the last one built in 1885 on Chesapeake Bay.

PINNACE–an open boat usually rigged with lug sails.

PLANKS–sawed lumber covering frames to form the outside skin of the hull as well as for ceiling the inside of the frames; also used for decks.

PUNGY–the name that Chesapeake watermen gave their pilot boats or pilot schooners sometime prior to the Civil War; origin of the word unknown.

QUARTERDECK–an area near the stern of a vessel, usually reserved for officers; this could be a cockpit, the top of a cabin or the roof of a raised deck.

RAKE OF THE MASTS–the inclination of a vessel's mast or masts (usually aft) from an upright position perpendicular to the keel.

RAKE OF THE STEM AND STERNPOST–their angle off an upright position perpendicular to the keel; the sternpost normally rakes in a reverse direction to the rake of the bow's stem.

RUN OF THE HULL–the narrowing of the vessel's sections abaft its midsection. A fine run continuously tapers from mid-section to a sharp stern, allowing the sea to move along the ship's bottom with the least resistance.

SCARF–an overlapping connection of two pieces of timber such as keel pieces or fut-tocks that when bolted together form the keel or a frame.

SHALLOP–an open boat propelled by sails or oars similar in looks to a large lifeboat.

SHARP-BUILT HULL–the bottom of a hull that rises significantly from the keel to the point where the bilge or bottom turns upward to form the vessel's top-sides. That rise in the hull's bottom is called deadrise, and the greater the angle above the horizontal the sharper the vessel's hull.

SHEER OF THE DECK–the curvature of the main deck from end to end.

SCHOONER–normally a vessel under three hundred tons rigged with fore-and-aft-sails on two masts. During the nineteenth century the number of masts increased as schooners grew in size.

SLOOP–a vessel with a single mast with fore-and-aft mainsail and one or more jibs.

STEEVE–the angle of the bowsprit above the horizontal.

STERNPOST–the upright timber at the stern which terminates the after end of a hull and to which the rudder is attached.

TRANSOM–the part of the hull extending above, below and beyond the after end of the main deck. In the pilot-schooner design, a transom normally consisted of three sections - upper, middle and lower. The transom when secured to the vessel's structural members formed the counter to strengthen the aft section of the hull.

TIMBER–a piece of shaped wood such as floor pieces and futtocks which, when scarfed to one another, form the frame of a wooden vessel.

TURN OF THE BILGE–the area at the outboard edge of the bottom of a vessel where the bottom turns upward. The turn can be slack when the deadrise is great or sharp when the deadrise is slight.

WAIST–the amidship portion of the main deck.

WALES–planks running along the length of the hull between the waterline and the main (gun) deck, usually attached to beam knees and futtocks to strengthen the hull.

INDEX

Page numbers in italics indicate illustrations. Page numbers followed by "n" indicate endnotes.

two-masted, 17
types, 15n2
Virginia-built, 26
schooners, pilot-boat built, 9, 14, 15n2, 173, 277, 280
Baltimore, 63-81
clippers, 133, 144
definition of, 292 1807-1815, 103, 112
prototypes, 26-27
Revolutionary War, 58
Schuyler, George L., 250n32
Scott, John, 251n42
Scout, 255
scrapes, 221-222, 254, 256
S.E. Sawyer, 243
Sea, 159
Seaford, Delaware, 220
Semmes, Raphael, 209n12
Seven Years War, 25, 39
Shackeford, William, 261
shallop, 292
shallow-draft schooners, 243
Share, John, 280
Shark class, 176
sharp schooners, 137
sharp-built hull, 292
sharp-built schooners, 10, 135, 144, 245
opium traders, 164
sharpshooters, 243
Gloucester, 240-241, *242*
Sharptown, Maryland, 220
Shaw, John, 86, 93
Shaw, Joseph, *228*
Shaw, Joshua, *228*
Shedden, Robert, 196
sheer of the deck, 292
she-pungy, 274n86
ship's bread, 23
ship's chandlery, 281
shipwrights, 84
Shoemaker, Charles, 250n14, 250n16, 250n27
Shores, John, 233
Shores, William, 233
Shores case, 222
Sidney, 42
Sinclair, John, 50Sing-gbe, 161-162
Siro, 119-120, 194
Skinner, 148
Skinner, Hammond, *249*
Skinner, Isaac, 196
skipjacks, 245, 260, 276
slave trade, 153, 155, 157, 203
slavers, 14, 127, 141, 203, 276
clippers, 158-159, 171n25
schooners, 173
slavery, 32, 38, 70, 141, 162, 258
slaves, 258-260
sloops, 20-21, 39-40, 245, 261
Bermuda-model, 38-39

Bermuda-type, 10
definition of, 293
Wasp class, 144
Smith, Frederick, 250nn23-24
Smith, John, 23, 96
Smith, John, Jr., 67, 79
Smith, Melbourne, 245-246
Smith, Robert, 86, 93-94, 96, 205
Smith, Sam, 146
Smith, Samuel, 67-69, 108
Smith, Stephen, 235
Smith, William, 84
Smith, William F., *228*
Smith Island, 214, 221
Smyth and Sudler, 25
snow, *20-21*, 39
Snow Hill, Maryland
baycraft 1798-1850, 215-216
Customs, 255
Solomon, Isaac, 256-258
Solomon & Sons and Davis, 257, 270
Solomons Island, Maryland, 256-257, 261
Somers, Ben, 253-254
Somers, Richard, 94-96
Somers, William H., 229
Somerset, 40
Somerset County, Maryland, 33, 36-37, 42, 215
oyster industry, 221-223, 256, 260-261, 263
shipbuilding, 121, 215, 217, 220
trade, 18, 37, 63
Sophia and Ann, 267
South American trade, 132, 145-146
South Marsh Island, 221
Spain, 25, 64
Spartan, 136
Spear, William, 23
Spearing, Henry, 150n30
Spears, Raymond, 265
speed, 134, 137-138
Spencer, 194
Spencer, Henry, 84-85
Spencer, Hugh, 85
Spencer, Perry, 54, 84
Spencer, Richard, 54, 74, 84-85
Spencer Shipyard (Gray's Inn Creek), *20-21*, 36, 39-40
Spy, 78
square rigs, 142
SRNS *Activ*, 208, 285
SRNS *Experiment* (ex-*Experiment*), 204-205, 207-208, *208*, 245
hull plans, 285, *285*
sail plan, 207-208, 286, *287*
tackle and spar dimensions, 286
SRNS *Falk*, 208, 285, 288, *288*
SRNS *l'Aigle*, 208
St. Eustatius, 40, 46-47, 49
St. George Island, 268

St. Mary's County, Maryland, 28, 257
shipbuilding, 121, 233
St. Michaels, Maryland, 116, 277
oyster industry, 256
shipbuilding, 217
St. Patrick, 75
St. Thomas, Virgin Islands, 200
Stafford, William J., 123n61
State Shipwright, 84
Statia. *See* St. Eustatias
Steel, David, *44*, 59, *59*
Steele, John, 79
Steers, George, 235
Steers, James, 240
steeve, 293
stem, 292
Sterett, Andrew, 93
Sterett, James R., 233
Sterett, John, 40, 63
Sterett family, 23
stern ornaments, *249*
sternpost
definition of, 293
rake of the stem and sternpost, 292
Stevenson, George P., 120
Stewart, Charles, 76, 92
Stewart, David, 74
Stiles, George, 119-120
Stodder, David, 55-56, 73, 76, 78, 97
Stoddert, Benjamin, 83-84, 86
stores, 282
Storey, Mr., 69
Stricker, John, 86, 94, 96, 108
Stump, John, 53
Sullivan, James, 158
Superior, 90, 92, 184, 194-196. *See also* HMS *Superior*; *La Supérieure*
Surveyor, 120
Susannah (pilot schooner, 1741), 28
Susannah (pilot schooner, 1791), 55
Susquehanna, 157
Susquehanna River, 54
Sussex County, Delaware, 220
Sutton, Asbury, 28
Swallow (pilot schooner, ~1742), 19
Swallow (schooner, 1734), 37
Swan, 219
Swedish Royal Navy, 14, 204-205, *205*, 207, *208*
Swedish trade, 9, 64
Swift, 194. *See also* HMS *Swift*
Syren, 198

T
Talbot County, Maryland, 79, 121, 136, 217
Tangier Island, 49, 221
Tangier Sound, 214-215, 218, 220-222, 254-256
Tasker, Benjamin, 19